AFTER-SCHOOL CENTERS AND YOUTH DEVELOPMENT

This book examines after-school programs in light of their explosive growth in recent years. In the rush to mount programs, there is a danger of promoting weak ones of little value and failing to implement strong ones adequately. But what is quality and how can it be achieved?

This book presents findings from an intensive study of three after-school centers that differed dramatically in quality. Drawing from 233 site visits, the authors examine how – and why – young people thrive in good programs and suffer in weak ones.

The book features engaging in-depth case studies of each of the three centers and of six youths, two from each center. Written in a highly accessible style for academics, youth workers, after-school program leaders, and policy makers, the study breaks new ground in highlighting the importance of factors such as collective mentoring, synergies among different programs and activities, and organizational culture and practices. Guidelines are included for program improvement.

Barton J. Hirsch is Professor of Human Development and Social Policy at Northwestern University. An internationally recognized authority on after-school programs and positive youth development, his earlier book, *A Place to Call Home: After-School Programs for Urban Youth*, won the Social Policy Award for Best Authored Book from the Society for Research on Adolescence.

Nancy L. Deutsch is Associate Professor of Educational Leadership and Foundations at the University of Virginia's Curry School of Education and Associate Director for Methodology at Youth-NEX, University of Virginia's Center for Effective Youth Development. A scholar of the social ecological contexts of development, she is the author of *Pride in the Projects: Teens Building Identities in Urban Contexts*.

David L. DuBois is Professor in the Division of Community Health Sciences within the School of Public Health at the University of Illinois at Chicago. His research focuses on youth mentoring relationships and programs for positive youth development. He is the co-editor of the *Handbook of Youth Mentoring*, which received the Social Policy Award for Best Edited Book from the Society for Research on Adolescence.

After-School Centers and Youth Development

CASE STUDIES OF SUCCESS AND FAILURE

Barton J. Hirsch
Northwestern University

Nancy L. Deutsch
University of Virginia

David L. DuBois
University of Illinois at Chicago

CAMBRIDGE
UNIVERSITY PRESS

CAMBRIDGE UNIVERSITY PRESS
Cambridge, New York, Melbourne, Madrid, Cape Town,
Singapore, São Paulo, Delhi, Tokyo, Mexico City

Cambridge University Press
32 Avenue of the Americas, New York, NY 10013–2473, USA

www.cambridge.org
Information on this title: www.cambridge.org/9780521138512

First published 2011

Printed in the United States of America

A catalog record for this publication is available from the British Library.

Library of Congress Cataloging in Publication Data
Hirsch, Barton Jay 1950–
After-school centers and youth development : case studies of success and failure /
Barton J. Hirsch, Nancy L. Deutsch, David L. DuBois.
p.   cm.
ISBN 978–0-521–13851–2 (pbk.) – ISBN 978-0-521-19119-7 (hbk.)
1. After-school programs – United States – Case studies.   2. Youth development –
United States – Case studies.   3. Student activities – United States – Case studies.
I. Deutsch, Nancy L.   II. DuBois, David L.   III. Title.
LC34.4.H57   2011
371.8–dc22   2011000636

ISBN 978-0-521-19119-7 Hardback
ISBN 978-0-521-13851-2 Paperback

CONTENTS

PREFACE

This research project has gone through some interesting transformations. Our original grant application to the William T. Grant Foundation proposed a year of qualitative research followed by a year of quantitative research. We were very grateful when the foundation's then senior vice president, Robert Granger, encouraged us to focus on the qualitative portion only.

We hadn't expected to be taken by surprise by the nature of the three after-school centers that we were going to study, but we were. A few years earlier, we had studied six Boys and Girls Clubs and had written two books based on that experience: Hirsch's *A Place to Call Home: After–School Programs for Urban Youth*, and Deutsch's *Pride in the Projects: Teens Building Identities in Urban Contexts*. We had thought that the clubs in the current research would be reasonably similar to the six we had studied earlier, but that was not the case. With one of the clubs (referred to as North River), it was clear from the very beginning that it was a lot worse than any of the clubs we had come to know previously. Nothing during the rest of our year of data collection served to change our mind about this. Indeed, as time went on, we became more sharply aware of differences across all three of the clubs. We became convinced that to do justice to this situation, we needed to expand our research focus. Our initial objective was to conduct an intensive study of youth-staff relationships, as such relationships had emerged as an important factor in our prior studies. We have done that. But we also added an organizational level of analysis to capture the different cultures and operations at the three sites. The varying perspectives are reported via case studies of each club and of two youth at each club. The book that grew out of this more comprehensive effort is richer, and it is both more theoretical and more applied as a result.

As with our earlier publications, we made an agreement with the clubs to keep their identities confidential. Accordingly, the locations of the clubs are not specified and their names have been changed, as have the names and potentially identifying characteristics of both the clubs and individuals. Each youth chose his or her own pseudonym, and we assigned pseudonyms to the various staff members and administrators.

We owe a debt of great appreciation to the youth, staff, and administrators at the clubs for their cooperation and support. We are pleased to acknowledge the contributions of Leah Doane, Carrie Luo, and Kim Star who served as research assistants. Thanks also go to James G. Kelly, Dan Lewis, Megan Mekinda, and James Spillane, who generously commented on earlier drafts of some of our chapters. We are very grateful to the William T. Grant Foundation, and especially Robert Granger (now president of the Foundation), for its support over the years. Thanks go as well to our editor at Cambridge, Simina Calin.

We cannot end without acknowledging our wonderful families, including Margherita Andreotti, Rachel Hirsch, and David Hirsch; Jon Rice; and Natalie and Lily, Gwyneth, and Rebecca DuBois.

INTRODUCTION

1

The Quality of After-School Centers

Youth programs can be found in abundance throughout our communities. Nowhere, however, are they more prevalent than in the after-school arena. The past decade has witnessed explosive growth in after-school programs. The federal government launched a billion-dollar initiative, the 21st Century Community Learning Centers. California's Proposition 49 channeled more than 400 million additional dollars to after-school programs.[1] Several major foundations have put after-school programs at the core of their concerns. And city after city is scaling up its after-school programs.[2] Much of this growth has involved after-school centers that typically are home to a wide array of programs and services. These include the Boys & Girls Clubs of America, which more than doubled the number of its clubs, from 1,800 in 1997 to 4,000 in 2008. Clearly there is a push to make after-school programs part of the educational and youth services infrastructure. We believe in the promise of after-school programs but also are concerned about the pitfalls. We have seen both good programs and bad programs, strong centers and weak centers. It is critical to understand the factors that lead to quality and to positive youth outcomes if the after-school movement is to be built on a solid foundation.

It is easy to appreciate the push for more after-school programming. This is especially true for the school-age adolescents in low-income urban communities who we studied in this research. These young people need to cope with violence and poor schools on

[1] The expansion is discussed by Ames (2007).
[2] Holleman, Sundius, & Bruns (2010); Noam and Miller (2002)

a daily basis.[3] Job opportunities are often few and far between. Adult role models can be in short supply as the middle class has largely abandoned these neighborhoods, many men are in prison, and parents often have work shifts that leave little time for guidance and support. After-school programs hope to step into these gaps and supplement what youth receive from family and school.[4]

Becoming an adolescent involves entering a period of increased susceptibility to emotional and behavioral problems as well as disconnection from school.[5] But adolescence is not just a time of increased risk. Other hallmarks of adolescence – experimentation with possible identities, exploration of new roles, intimacy in relationships, and concern with the future – bring with them important opportunities for growth. Increasingly, researchers and practitioners who work with teens are doing so within the frame of "positive youth development." This lens emphasizes the strengths that youth bring with them to the table, examining how contexts can support the development of characteristics such as character, confidence, connections, and competence.[6]

Good after-school programs and the centers that are home to them can provide the nurturance and challenge that young people crave. The adult staff, often of the same race and ethnic background, can appreciate the youth's life circumstances and provide mentoring, with plentiful amounts of warmth, encouragement, and

---

[3] Juvenile arrests are heavily concentrated during the after-school time period of 3–6 PM (Snyder & Sickmund, 1999), suggesting that during this time youth are most vulnerable to being victims as well as most likely to be perpetrators.

[4] For an excellent discussion of how after-school programs can link to school goals and curricula, see Noam, Biancarosa, & Dechausay (2003). Low-income, minority youth are less involved in after-school activities than their wealthier, suburban counterparts (Pedersen & Seidman, 2005).

[5] See, e.g., Costello, Mustillo, Erkanli, Keeler, and Angold (2003); Laird, DeBell, Kienzl, and Chapman (2007); Rumberger (1987); Seidman, Allen, Aber, Mitchell, and Feinman (1994). The effects of poverty are especially evident in the educational domain. Rates of proficiency in reading and mathematics among 8th-graders from low-income families (13% in each subject) are well below half that among those from more economically advantaged families (35% and 39%, respectively; Perie, Grigg, & Dion, 2005; Perie, Grigg, & Donahue, 2005); similarly, students from low-income families are six times more likely to drop out of school (Laird et al., 2007). These figures do not capture the effects of being a student in an urban school, which data suggest compound the effects of family income level (Lutkus, Weiner, Daane, & Jin, 2003).

[6] Important work on positive youth development approaches include Hamilton & Hamilton (2004b); Lerner (2004); Villarruel, Perkins, Borden, & Keith (2003).

guidance. Staff can demonstrate positive values in action, showing by example how acting responsibly elicits respect.[7] Centers can offer challenging programs and activities that promote learning and developmental growth as well as teach young people how to navigate dangerous situations. The safe environment of a high-quality center can shelter youth from violence, keep them out of trouble, and give them a chance to develop the knowledge, skills, and attitudes that they need as a foundation for adult life.

Most after-school programs have focused on younger, elementary-school age youth. So, too, has much of the research. By focusing on older youth in this study, our aim was to learn more about how after-school programs and centers can effectively engage adolescents and help prepare them for a successful transition to adulthood.

On balance, initial findings from evaluations of the effects of after-school programs are promising. In a recent meta-analysis, which involves a statistical synthesis of quantitative research studies, Joseph Durlak, Roger Weissberg, and Molly Pachan found evidence that after-school programs had positive effects on a range of psychosocial and academic outcomes, such as youths' self-esteem and self-confidence, school bonding, grades, and problem behavior.[8] A National Research Council report also emphasized an array of positive evaluation findings.[9] Although these reviews are encouraging, they cannot be regarded as definitive. Only a few studies met the highest standard of evaluation research: a true experimental study in which youth are randomly assigned to either an after-school program or a control group. Many of the studies that were reviewed did not examine traditional after-school programs, but rather highly structured prevention programs. Moreover, some high-profile studies of after-school programs did not find effects;[10] even though those studies may have flaws, one should not ignore the warning flags that they raise.

[7] Deutsch (2008); Hirsch (2005).

[8] Durlak, Weissberg, & Pachen (2010).

[9] National Research Council (2002).

[10] See, e.g., the evaluation of the 21st Center Community Learning Centers Program (Dynarski et al., 2003; James-Burdumy, Dynarski, & Deke, 2007, 2008). See also Gottfredson, Cross, Wilson, Rorie, & Connell (2010) for an experimental evaluation of an after-school program for middle-school students that did not find significant results.

We also are cautioned by how little is known about why some after-school programs are effective and others are not. This is known as the "black box" problem and it arises regarding lots of different kinds of interventions, not just after-school programs. In essence, we may know the basics of what goes into the box – the kinds and numbers of youth, the general type of program to which they are presumably exposed – and what comes out of the box – youth outcomes – but have little detailed knowledge of what happens inside the program. Clearly, not all after-school programs or centers are created equal. Some programs may be inherently superior to others by virtue of how they are designed, such as providing just the right level of developmental challenge combined with optimal approaches to instruction.[11] In the meta-analysis referred to earlier, for example, those after-school programs that included sequential, active forms of learning and an explicit focus on developing personal or social skills had notably larger effects on outcomes.[12]

Of equal if not greater importance is the quality of program implementation. Implementation research is essential to uncovering what goes on inside the black box.[13] When implementation is studied at all, the focus is typically on dosage, or the frequency of attendance in prescribed activities. Being exposed to more program activities – a higher dosage – is typically associated with improved outcomes.[14] It is more time consuming and difficult to study how skillfully activities are implemented on the ground. As a result, fewer of these studies have been conducted. It is hard to imagine, however, that this would not be a critical factor in program effectiveness. In our earlier research with after-school programs, we documented widespread problems in how carefully and competently program elements were implemented by Boys & Girls Club staff.[15] Accordingly, we devote considerable attention to the quality of program implementation in the new research reported here.

Careful examination of program design and implementation is essential for determining how, when, and for whom intervention

---

[11] Vygotsky (1978) would refer to the need to be in the zone of proximal development.

[12] Durlak et al. (2010).

[13] See Durlak and DuPre (2008) for a good discussion of implementation research.

[14] Gottfredson (2001).

[15] Hirsch (2005).

processes lead to outcomes.[16] Without deep understandings of these sorts, in our rush to mount more and more after-school programs, there is a danger that we will promote weak programs of little value and fail to implement strong programs adequately. There are leaders in the after-school community who share this concern. Jane Quinn, for example, concluded that program quality is "the number one opportunity and challenge in today's after-school landscape."[17] Similarly, most of the articles in a 2010 special issue of the *American Journal of Community Psychology* on after-school programs are concerned with program quality.[18] But, frankly, there are others whose focus on increasing community access to programs does not appear to leave much room to be troubled about the quality issue.[19]

Identifying and making sense of what goes on in the black box of after-school programs and centers is the focus of this book. We study how particular processes are linked to youth outcomes over the course of a year within comprehensive after-school centers. Throughout this book we make a distinction between after-school programs and centers. Boys & Girls Clubs and similar organizations (e.g., Y's, Beacons) are best thought of as comprehensive after-school centers rather than as programs in the traditional sense of this term. The typical center offers numerous programs, and youth frequently end up participating in more than one of these, if not at the same time, then at different points in the same school year. The importance of understanding the totality of a youth's experience in comprehensive after-school centers, across

---

[16] As is apparent from our discussion, we view program quality as encompassing features of both a program's design and its implementation. In many instances, however, we found that these two dimensions could not be neatly separated. Many programs, for example, lacked the type of detailed blueprint or manual that would have allowed us to reliably discriminate the core intended components of the program and those that were attributable to variation in implementation.

[17] Quinn (2005, p. 481). See also, for example, Granger, Durlak, Yohalem, & Reisner (2007); Grossman, Campbell, & Raley (2007); Pittman, Tolman, & Yohalem (2005); Wilson-Ahlstrom (2007).

[18] Cross, Gottfredson, Wilson, Rorie, & Connell (2010); Durlak, Mahoney, Bohnert, & Parente (2010); Durlak, Weissberg, & Pachan (2010). Granger (2010); Hirsch, Mekinda, & Stawicki (2010); Larson & Walker (2010); Pierce, Bolt, & Yandell (2010); Sheldon, Arbreton, Hopkins, & Grossman (2010); Shernoff (2010), Smith, Peck, Denault, Blazaevski, & Akiva (2010); Yohalem & Wilson-Ahlstrom (2010).

[19] Hirsch et al., (2010).

multiple programs, activities, and relationships in the same center, is a major theme of this book.

Our focus on quality arose not only because this is important to the development of the field, but because our data gave us no choice but to do so. In studying many programs at three comprehensive after-school centers, it was clear that the programs differed enormously in quality: Some were excellent, with challenging activities led by dynamic staff; others appeared to be of modest value in themselves, but when combined with other programs contributed in important ways to youth gains; and still other programs and activities, it must be said, were led by unenthusiastic staff who implemented procedures poorly, in ways that hindered and perhaps even hurt their youthful charges.

There was one other aspect of our experience that forced us to prioritize the need to understand implementation quality: It was impossible not to notice that the three after-school centers differed dramatically in quality. One of the centers had several fine programs and a number of staff with good relationships with youth. What enabled it to achieve such excellence? At the other end was a center where the quality of programs and activities was uniformly poor and youth-staff relationships were often fraught with tension; nonetheless, the young people still came. What kept attendance up and why could staff not capitalize better on the youth's evident motivation? In the middle was a center where only pockets of excellence existed. Why weren't they able to learn from what they did well to do a better job across the board?

In this book we analyze what worked so that we know better how to help young people. And we dissect what went wrong so that current and future after-school providers will be less likely to repeat the errors of their predecessors. As noted previously, there is a bandwagon that has developed for after-school programs. We share the underlying enthusiasm and will present evidence that supports it. But the field needs more than advocacy. There is also a need for sympathetic souls to stand outside of it, to be objective and critical in a tough-minded way, because that is needed to build a strong foundation as much as advocacy. We will not be critical as an end in itself. When we discuss what went wrong, we suggest how the situation could have been handled better. We intend this to be research that joins together understanding and prescription for action.

Our approach to accomplishing these complementary objectives is to present a series of intensive case studies. This is a well-trod path in the early stages of research for most fields of intervention. Focusing on three comprehensive after-school centers – all Boys & Girls Clubs – enables us to sort out relevant similarities and differences as we seek to understand contributors to the quality of individual programs and after-school centers more broadly.

Each of the three clubs provided a wide array of programs and activities. There were sports and other recreational activities, academic assistance, arts, field trips, computer work, community service, skill clubs, youth leadership opportunities, and psychoeducational groups. Each club had about half a dozen core adult staff members, supplemented by part-timers and volunteers. As sites for after-school programs, there was some level of organizational complexity, and an organizational lens is needed to appreciate the full dynamics behind program quality. So we include a case study of each club as an organization.

We then present in-depth studies of two youth at each club. We visited each club approximately twice a week and ultimately made a total of 233 site visits over the course of an academic year. This exceptional longitudinal database provides us with a unique vantage point from which to understand the course of a youth's involvement in different components of an after-school center and the various factors that helped or hindered that young person's development. This mix of organizational- and individual-level analyses enables us to provide a more comprehensive account of what quality means at after-school centers and what it takes to achieve it than would be possible using either of these lenses alone.

A THEORETICAL FRAMEWORK

Figure 1.1 provides a guide to how we understand the centers and their potential effects on youth. It presents our thinking about how various individual, group, and organizational factors combine to lead the centers to influence, positively or negatively, the lives of the young people who participate in their activities. This framework emerged from our data. Once we identified the main features of the framework, we used it as a lens for structuring our analysis. There are three distinct features of our theoretical framework that we should note at the outset.

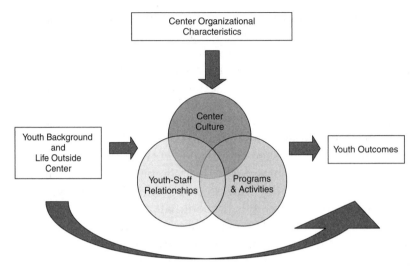

FIGURE 1.1. Conceptual framework for understanding the role of comprehensive after-school centers in youth development.

- The after-school center is by no means the sole force that impacts youth lives. That is why we have a long arrow that bypasses the center entirely. This book does not focus on those other factors – such as family and school – but they need to be accounted for in a more complete explanation of adolescent well-being and development.
- We are concerned with the effect of the center considered as an organization. Here our focus is on the adults who run and staff the center, and on how factors such as human resource practices, organizational learning, and staff cohesiveness affect the quality of young people's experience at the center. There is little prior research that considers how organizational dynamics can impact program quality and the experiences of program participants.
- Perhaps the most distinctive visual feature of the model is the set of overlapping circles in the middle that refer to programs and activities, youth-staff relationships, and the culture of the center. We shall distinguish elements within each circle, but they are intertwined with each other to a great extent.

Let us now turn to consider each part of the model.

Youth Background and Life Outside the Center

None of the young persons who enter an after-school program does so with a blank slate. At birth, each of these youth entered the world with a host of genetically influenced dispositions. In the years since, they have had a multitude of experiences that shape who they are when they arrive at a center. They enter with many inherent competencies, but also significant challenges as they navigate environments that do not always provide optimal support. Their family lives, financial resources, friends and neighbors, exposure to crime, access to quality schools, physical attractiveness, athletic ability, access to health care and proper nutrition, as well as personality and social skills will have a substantial impact on how they do years down the road, regardless of whether they participate in an after-school center.[20] After-school centers and programs can have an impact as well, and in some instances it will have a substantial impact, but it is never the sole influence.

There is another way in which what youth bring to the center is important and, in this instance, it is an important focus of our analysis. Center programs and staff respond differently to teenagers with different characteristics, so that their backgrounds and lives outside the center can influence their experiences in the center. We are especially alert to this possibility and examine how each young person's personality and outside experiences influence his or her life in the center.

YOUTH OUTCOMES

In after-school programs that are not comprehensive, there is often a single outcome (or set of outcomes) that is of interest. It may be developing a certain skill (such as acting) or preventing a particular behavior (such as drug use). In comprehensive after-school centers, a wider array of potential outcomes comes into play. In broad terms, these encompass academic and psychosocial outcomes.

With respect to the academic domain, there are some major markers that are of concern, especially keeping kids in school (retention).

---

[20] Durlak, Mahoney, Bohnert, & Parente (2010) present after-school programs in an ecological framework that addresses some of these factors (see also Mahoney, Vandell, Simpkins, & Zarrett, 2009).

In these communities, youth begin to drop out well prior to high school.[21] There is also a focus on promotion into high school (which is not automatic in this school system) and getting into a high school with a stronger academic reputation. Naturally, course grades, attendance, and behavior in school (e.g., fighting) are also of concern.

For the most part, the three centers we studied were most concerned with psychosocial outcomes. Although what is most important varied according to each youth as an individual, there were three domains of particular interest.

The first involved taking on responsible roles within the various settings in which the youth participates. Most of our data concerned youth roles at the center. This might involve attending events regularly and on time and performing tasks (such as selling food at the snack stand) that the young person had either volunteered for or had been assigned. Older youth, and youth who had participated in the center for some time, were expected to take on an increased load of tasks and responsibilities, and assume leadership positions. This emphasis is consistent with the views of developmental psychologists, such as Barbara Rogoff, who think of youth development in terms of increased ability to participate in the activities of relevant cultural communities.[22]

The second domain involved the development and maintenance of satisfactory relationships with other young people and with staff. This involved the closeness of ties, being able to find mutual satisfaction in shared activities, conflict resolution, emotional support, being part of a peer group, and serving as a role model to younger kids. Relationships are of special importance during adolescence, and close ties can help young people feel that they matter and belong.

Finally, overall psychological well-being and adjustment was important. In general, this involved attention to helping youth maintain a positive mood, develop skills in emotional regulation, and avoid involvement in problem behavior (e.g., joining a gang).

All in all, these outcomes correspond to what we generally think of as increased maturity or as "growing up."[23] They represent the kind

---

[21] Hirsch (2005).

[22] Rogoff (2003).

[23] Some youth development researchers suggest that we consider the extent to which youth are "thriving" as an overall conceptualization of well-being (e.g., Benson & Scales, 2009; Lerner, 2004).

of outcomes that parents would think of in terms of their children. At the same time, they have longer-term and broader societal significance. Certainly, high school graduation is an important milestone in our society and one that has life-long financial implications.[24] In the work world, being able to show up on time, accept assigned responsibilities, perform tasks satisfactorily, get along with the boss and co-workers, and show initiative and leadership are all highly valued. Many of these represent the kinds of "soft skills" that economists argue are increasingly important in the global economy.[25]

Although all of these outcomes are relevant to the young people we studied, the prominence of any particular outcome or domain varied by the individual and his or her developmental stage. We highlight the particular outcomes most relevant to each case study and analyze how the youth's experiences at the center (the three overlapping circles) may have contributed to those outcomes. It is always difficult to "prove" that some circumstances resulted in some outcome for a specific individual. Even large-scale experimental evaluation studies cannot do this; they can show that there was a causal effect on an outcome for the intervention group on average, but it is not possible to isolate any one specific individual in that group and say that the intervention had an effect on him or her. So we do our best, tracing linkages, evaluating their potential for being impactful, and being mindful of alternative explanations. In each case, we believe that we have compelling reasons for our conclusions, leading us to have confidence in our assertions if not definitive knowledge.

The Three Circles

This part of our framework focuses on three important parts of a comprehensive after-school center that are experienced by a young person: programs and activities, youth-staff relationships, and the culture of the center. Each of these center components responds to what the youth brings to the center and to higher-level organizational features of the center. In turn, the three components can influence youth outcomes.

---

[24] Among African Americans, there is a 25 percent gain in lifetime earnings for high school graduation (Day & Newburger, 2002).
[25] Murnane & Levy (1996)

Programs and Activities

Each center we studied had a substantial number of programs and activities available.[26] Not all centers had all programs or activities, and the presence or absence of a specific type of opportunity could make a meaningful difference in the impact of the center. Moreover, even when a particular program was available at each center, the program quality could differ dramatically by site. Some programs offered challenging activities, meaningful youth roles, and supportive relationships with staff, but others fell short, and some may even have set back those who attended.

Youth-Staff Relationships

In previous research, we identified the quality of relationships that early adolescent youth formed with adult staff as the heart and soul of the comprehensive after-school centers we studied.[27] Many youth formed emotionally close ties to multiple staff who in differing and often complementary ways provided guidance and support for navigating the tumult of adolescence in often unforgiving environments. These centers were often sites for the development of what has been termed "natural mentors" – adults with whom youth organically develop relationships. Such natural mentoring relationships have important benefits for youth.[28]

To understand these relationships better, in this new study we focus on how such ties developed and changed over time and look more carefully at how they can influence a youth's overall experience of the center and developmental growth. In doing so, we were struck by the importance of a phenomenon that has previously drawn little attention: collective mentoring by staff of individual youth. This type of mentoring occurs when a group of staff in a youth-serving program or organization assume shared responsibility

---

[26] For purposes of this book, we define a program broadly as an organized, sequenced set of activities that youth participate in over time with one or more adult staff as leaders. We define activities as more circumscribed social, recreational, and educational experiences that are made available to youth in after-school centers both within and outside of particular programs.

[27] Hirsch (2005); other studies have similarly found more positive outcomes for those youth who form close relationships with adult leaders in extracurricular activities (Mahoney, Schweder, & Stattin, 2002; Rutten et al., 2007).

[28] See, for example, DuBois & Silverthorn (2005b); for a review, see Zimmerman, Bigenheimer, & Behrendt (2005).

for a young person's development and collaborate to cultivate the youth's agency and competence, provide sponsorship for assuming important roles in the program or organization, and validate emerging positive identities.

Center Culture

Every organization – be it a school or workplace – has its own culture. After-school centers, too, have their own culture(s). In many cases, the culture may be precisely what attracts youth to the center – the opportunity for greater freedom of expression and spontaneity than at school, being able to have fun with friends in a safe environment, being able to pursue a host of different interests rather than being typecast or restricted, the warmth and caring reflected in interactions with adults, and conditions of respect and responsibility. However, as will be evident, each club had a distinct culture, and some features of the culture of the setting – especially rules and routines, and responsiveness to youth agency – differed dramatically across sites.

Social scientists have noted that an organization can contain several cultures that are experienced differently depending on factors such as gender, status in the hierarchy, or subunit.[29] Similarly, we found that there could be differences in the culture of particular programs and activities within the same center. In considering culture, we need to be alert to the culture of particular programs and activities as well as the overall culture of the center.

An Integrative Perspective

The three circles are interrelated in several ways. Each program or activity in an after-school center involves relationships and is characterized by a distinctive culture. To help concretize this notion and be able to refer to such involvements in an efficient manner, we will employ an acronym, PARC (program, activity, relationship, culture). The "C" here refers to the culture of the particular program/activity/relationship; as noted, this may differ from the overall culture of the center. Each PARC unit describes a particular involvement in these multiple facets. The profile of PARCs for a given young person captures the array of his or her center involvements at any one point

---

[29] Martin (1992, 2002).

in time. The PARC profile over time depicts patterns of constancy and change in a youth's involvements at a center. In this way, the PARC profile provides a potent means of depicting the implicit "curriculum" to which a young person is exposed over the course of a year.

The centers seemed most powerful when the different PARCs were working harmoniously and complemented each other. We refer to these as synergies. At such times, the different dyadic youth-staff relationships were in synch and benefits from participation in a program or activity run by one staff enhanced participation in other programs/activities run by that staff person or by other staff; moreover, this process was nourished by, and in turn contributed to, the culture of the center overall. Not all synergies were positive. In some instances, different PARCs interacted with each other to influence youth in ways that appeared to be detrimental. These instances can help us understand how things can go from bad to worse in weak centers.

As we became attuned to the potential for synergies, we focused our attention on identifying relevant instances of this phenomenon. These are highlighted in each youth case study. In brief, the question we set for ourselves was this: Would X (a particular PARC or center characteristic) have an impact, or have as much of an impact, if Y (another PARC or center characteristic) was not there? Likewise, we were equally diligent in looking for instances of potential synergies that were not realized (i.e., combinations of X and Y that might have made an impact had they been present). These questions focused our attention on issues of alignment and linkage and how elements of a setting can reinforce or enhance each other.

We appreciate that "synergy" is a bit of a buzz word, so we need to be careful to use it analytically. When we present an instance of synergy, we will specify the phenomenon, consider the context in which it occurs, and evaluate the benefit or harm that ensued. We note as well when synergies were available but not realized. Social scientists, whatever their discipline, often have trouble coming to grips with systems phenomena, and we hope that by addressing these issues we can facilitate the development of appropriate analytic frameworks. On a practical level, skilled administrators are always looking for positive synergies, for making the most of their resources, for being able to create additional value working with what they already have.

Center Organizational Characteristics

Every after-school center can be understood and analyzed in organizational terms. Our research over the years has convinced us that doing so is important not only for understanding the impact of the setting on youth, but for pointing toward how to improve the quality of its operations. In the present work, our focus is on organizational characteristics that do not directly involve youth, but that impact PARCs, which in turn impact youth.[30] Thus, we posit an indirect effect of organizational variables on youth.

Because after-school centers are filled with young people who are full – sometimes too full – of energy, each center needs to be concerned with maintaining order and control so that things do not get out of hand and cause harm. At the same time, after-school centers have a concern with teaching and developmental growth. Both goals are important. An important organizational feature is the extent to which a center is able to maintain a focus on both as fundamental priorities. Not all centers were able to do this.

Staff are of fundamental importance to running quality programs and establishing supportive, mentoring relationships with youth. Basic human resource practices, involving staff hiring, training, and supervision, may accordingly go a long way in determining how well a center achieves its goals. Each of the three centers had a very different human resource policy.

Every organization should strive to improve. Whether or not it does so often depends on the organizational learning that takes place. Key to any such effort will be reflective dialogue among staff (including center leadership).[31] In turn, a shared sense of purpose, trust, and collaboration is important if reflective and effective dialogue is to take place.[32] There were considerable differences among

---

[30] In terms of Bronfenbrenner's (1979) ecological model of development, we are treating organizational characteristics as exosystem variables. In a kindred spirit, Tseng and Seidman (2007) present a theoretical framework for understanding social settings for youth, which considers the impact of the organization of resources on social processes.

[31] The work of Karen Seashore Louis and colleagues on what they refer to as professional communities has been especially influential on our thinking (e.g., Louis, Kruse, & Marks, 1996). Their research is in reference to school reform. In chapters 2 and 14 we consider adaptations to their framework with regard to youth development outcomes and its implications for improving quality in after-school programs and centers.

[32] See Bryk and Schneider (2002) on the importance of trust.

the centers in staff cohesiveness and leadership and many missed opportunities, at every site, for organizational learning about effective practices for working with youth.

Understanding Quality

Let us now summarize the implications of our theoretical framework for understanding quality in after-school centers. Our analysis includes a consideration of the quality of a specific PARC in terms of its effect on youth outcomes. This is the traditional approach to examining program quality. In this book, examination of quality indicators for particular PARCs in relation to youth outcomes is foundational, the beginning rather than the end of our analysis. What is most distinctive about our findings on the quality of after-school centers is the importance of looking beyond any one specific program or activity. We focus in particular on two components of quality.

The first involves an integrative evaluation of each youth's PARC profile over time. These case studies suggest that analysis and interpretation of this profile provides the deepest explanation of developmental change and outcomes. Furthermore, we believe that when the centers have their greatest effect, there is a synergy among PARCs that most fully actualizes the potential of a comprehensive center as a rich developmental setting. Prior related work, such as that by Elizabeth Reisner, Deborah Vandell, and colleagues, has recognized the importance of studying how profiles of after-school activities are related to youth outcomes, but they were able to assess the quality of only one primary activity.[33] We add to this line of research by focusing on the quality of multiple PARCs and on how linkages among PARCs enhance or undermine developmental gains.

The second component of quality emphasizes organizational features of centers that influence the availability of PARCs and enhance or diminish PARC quality. There is little prior research in this field – or others – that looks intensively at the interplay of organizational dynamics with program quality and the experiences of program participants. What research there is has focused on a relatively

---

[33] Reisner, Vandell, Pechman, Pierce, Brown, & Bolt, 2007; Vandell et al., 2006. See Balsano, Phelps, & Theokas (2009) for other research on youth engagement in multiple after-school activities.

limited range of objective characteristics, such as a Public/Private Ventures study of youth-staff ratios and levels of staff training as predictors of quality.[34] Our analysis builds on this work by taking a broader perspective that incorporates more experiential and process-oriented features of comprehensive after-school centers, such as leadership, relationship dynamics among staff, organizational learning, and support for innovation.

By considering PARC profiles over time in relation to youth outcomes, and the centers as organizations that impact PARC quality, we are able to identify new standards of excellence and make recommendations that could have a very wide-ranging impact on program development and implementation. And these recommendations can be applied not only to comprehensive after-school centers but also to more targeted youth programs that exist within or outside of such centers.

GETTING TO KNOW THE YOUTH AND AFTER-SCHOOL CENTERS

The goals of our research necessitated that we get to know as much as we could about each of the youth and after-school centers that are the focus of our investigation. The assessments that we carried out were very intensive and used a variety of methods. These methods complemented one another and gave both depth and rigor to our analysis.

As noted earlier, our focus was on three comprehensive after-school centers. Each center was a Boys & Girls Club located within the same large city. There were approximately three gangs in the neighborhood of each club. The crime rate for the area surrounding each club was in the top third of all city neighborhoods; for two of the clubs (Midwest and North River), the crime rate was in the highest 10 percent.[35]

Initially, we made an effort to survey all youth in the centers who were ten years of age or older. We hoped in doing so to obtain information that, when aggregated, would aid in our understanding of the culture and environment of each center. To this end, the survey

---

[34] Grossman et al., (2007).

[35] Figures are based on Index crimes for 2002. Index crimes encompass eight categories of crime monitored by the Federal Bureau of Investigations (FBI) because of their seriousness and frequency of occurrence. They include both violent crimes (e.g., murder) and property crimes (e.g., burglary).

asked youth for basic demographic information as well as about their levels and history of participation in the club. We also asked how safe youth felt in their neighborhoods and whether they experienced the club setting as a "second home," both of which were highlighted as important in our prior research. Most often these data reinforced and thus helped validate themes that were evident elsewhere in our findings. In one notable instance, however, this was not case. At the North River Center, we found that youth came to the club regularly, even though the quality of the center culture, as well as much programming and some relationships, appeared poor. These anomalous findings were surprising, and we subsequently devoted some effort to understand how they could be reconciled. Each youth also was asked on the survey to identify the staff person at the center with whom he or she had the closest relationship.[36] These nominations were later used to direct our individual interviews with youth and staff to gather more in-depth information about these particular ties.

In total, we surveyed 265 youth at the 3 centers. The youth ranged in age from 10 to 17 years (Median = 12), were 60 percent female, and, in terms of race and ethnicity, were almost exclusively either Black (79%) or Hispanic (20%), with the remainder identifying as White or Asian-American. The vast majority (87%) were from low-income families, as indicated by receipt of subsidized lunches at school. Approximately three quarters (76%) of the youth reported coming to the club at least three days a week and a similar percentage had attended the same center in previous school years. Most youth (80%) reported staying at the center at least two to four hours each day they attended. These relatively high and sustained levels of involvement are similar to those found in our earlier research, but higher than those found in studies of a number of other after-school programs.[37]

---

[36] The survey item that asked youth to nominate the staff person to whom they felt closest at the after-school center listed all staff at the center so that the youth simply needed to circle the name of the relevant staff person. To ensure that youth nominated staff with whom they had the most significant ties, the item included the following explanation: "By 'closest', we mean the staff who you can count on the most, who cares the most about you and how you are doing, who inspires you to do your best, and who has the most influence on the choices you make" (adapted from DuBois, Neville, Parra, & Pugh-Lilly, 2002).

[37] Figures from our prior research are reported in Hirsch (2005); for figures from other after-school programs, see Dynarski et al. (2003); Grossman et al. (2002); Walker & Arbreton (2001).

The next step was to draw from our larger sample a smaller group of thirty youth distributed across the three centers for more in-depth study.[38] Our goal was to follow a limited number of youth over time as they participated in varying arrays of programs and activities within the distinctive cultures of each center and, consequently, also interacted with a range of different staff members in those settings. This approach seemed ideally suited to increasing our appreciation of the different elements of after-school centers reflected in the PARC acronym described previously and their potentially complex and synergistic interactions with one another.

To help ensure that we selected youth with differing interactional styles, we had club staff rate all youth in our larger sample in terms of their degree of extraversion. This personality characteristic was of particular interest because sociability is a protective factor that seems to enhance resilience among at-risk youth.[39] Young people who are more introverted or shy may be more challenging for adults to engage in positive relationships, thus reducing their opportunities for mentoring in settings such as after-school centers.[40] Because the typical youth was rated as more extroverted than introverted, we ended up selecting youth that reflected this distribution rather than attempting to have equal numbers within each category.[41] We also took into account gender so as to ensure approximately equal numbers of girls and boys. Pragmatics, furthermore, dictated a focus on youth who attended the club on a regular basis. Otherwise, our prior experience suggested that we would have found it difficult to collect the necessary data from each youth. The resulting sample was very similar demographically to the larger group of youth surveyed.[42]

---

[38] One youth subsequently dropped out of the research.

[39] Werner (1995).

[40] Spencer (2006).

[41] Staff rated youth on a seven-point scale with descriptors ranging from "extremely shy" to "extremely outgoing". The youth selected for more intensive study were rated, on average, as "moderately outgoing" (M = 5.2; SD = 1.3).

[42] The youth who we selected for more in-depth assessment were 52 percent female, ranged in age from 10 to 17 years old (Median = 12), in nearly all instances received free or reduced lunch (93%), and were predominantly Black (69%) or Hispanic (28%). All but one of the youth reported attending their after-school center at least three days a week, and the overwhelming majority (86%) had also attended the same center previous to the current school year. Approximately three-quarters (76%) indicated that they stayed at least two to four hours each time they came to the center.

As in our prior work, the foundation of our investigative approach was to function as ethnographers who were participant-observers. The team of observers consisted of two doctoral students in the Human Development and Social Policy program at Northwestern University, one doctoral student from the university's Department of Sociology, and one research assistant who had a master's degree in counseling psychology. All four observers were female and two were persons of color. Each brought distinctive life experiences and competencies to the project.

Two observers were assigned to the Midwest Center and North River Center, respectively, and the remaining two shared responsibility for observation at the West River Center. Beginning in September, each club for the most part was visited two times a week. Most visits lasted approximately three to four hours, spanning the late afternoon and early evening. This schedule was maintained through the end of the school year in June. In some instances, we visited a club more often if there was a special event or activity that we wanted to make sure to observe. Likewise, holidays and other circumstances sometimes resulted in less frequent visits. As noted, we made a total of 233 site visits to these clubs.

Our prior research in the clubs had underscored for us that a certain level of involvement was essential for ensuring that youth and staff became comfortable with us and our presence in the centers. This meant that observers joined in the occasional game of volleyball, helped staff with setup for an activity, or simply made sure to cheer for the home team.[43] The rapport we established with youth and staff facilitated our ability to explore issues or developments with them on an informal basis, which we did frequently.

The four ethnographers, along with the primary investigators (Hirsch and DuBois), met weekly throughout the year. These meetings served as a valuable vehicle for constantly comparing our observations across youth and clubs and over time. Our discussions tended to be quite lively and encompassed a wide range of theoretical perspectives. As such, they provided an effective venue for sharpening our observations and understandings and capitalizing on the diverse backgrounds of the research team. It is within these

---

[43] For a more detailed description of our participant-observer approach to working within the after-school centers, see chapter 1 in Hirsch (2005).

meetings, for example, that the concept of collective mentoring by staff first emerged and was subsequently refined.

Ethnographers recorded detailed field notes after each visit to one of the centers. Each field note included the ethnographer's observations and reflections as well as an account of any conversations with youth or staff. The principal investigator (Hirsch) reviewed these notes on an ongoing basis. Developments or issues that might benefit from additional investigation were highlighted for follow-up during subsequent visits to the club. Illustratively, at the North River Center, when it became apparent that club leadership had ignored or thwarted several efforts to improve programming for girls, we spent time talking with both staff and youth to deepen our understanding of this situation and its effects on them.

Along with our ethnographic observations, we conducted a series of semi-structured interviews with each of the youth at the three centers who had been selected for more intensive study. We also interviewed the primary staff members at each center. A total of four interviews were conducted with each youth and three with each staff. The interviews included both open-ended and more structured questions and thus allowed us to gather a complementary mix of qualitative and quantitative data.[44]

The initial youth interview focused on gathering information about the youth's background and life outside of the after-school center, thus ensuring that his or her experiences at the center could be interpreted and understood in a broader context. A subsequent interview honed in on the youth's relationships with different staff members at the club. Many of the questions asked specifically about the youth's tie with the staff person to whom they felt the closest according to his or her report on the initial survey described earlier.[45]

---

[44] Prior to initiating our research, we conducted a focus group at each club with the youth whom we had selected for intensive study to elicit their suggestions for how to make our planned assessment activities both enjoyable and engaging. To maintain their interest, youth suggested that interviews should include varied types of questions and be interspersed with other types of activities. We thus took care to avoid undue amounts of repetition in the format or content of our interview questions and scheduled the interviews to alternate with other forms of assessment as much as possible.

[45] Prior to conducting interviews, we asked youth whether they continued to feel closest to the staff persons who they had identified feeling closest to on the initial survey. Six youth changed their preferences and thus were asked questions about a different staff person.

In a third interview, we administered several scales taken from standardized survey measures. These scales were used to increase our understanding of youth in areas such as their self-esteem and self-efficacy beliefs, quality of relationships with peers and adults, and aspirations and expectations for the future. At the end of the year (June), we conducted a brief concluding interview with each youth. We asked them to reflect on what they had gained from coming to the after-school center over the past year and in what ways their involvement in the center had made a difference in their life.

Several innovative assessments were interwoven into our interviews to ensure that youth had other, more creative opportunities to express themselves. In these activities we had youth draw maps of their social networks and create visual timelines of significant events in their lives both in and out of the club.[46] We also had them take pictures of significant people and places in their lives with disposable cameras and then discuss the pictures with us.

In our interviews with staff, we gathered relevant information about their personal backgrounds such as whether they grew up in a neighborhood similar to the ones served by the center, as well as their education and history of employment at the club and in other youth organizations. To enhance our understanding of the overall environment of each club, we asked staff for their perspectives on different aspects of the club's organizational characteristics, such as administrative leadership and levels of staff cooperation and conflict. We also asked about the relationships that staff persons had with those youth who had identified them as the staff person they felt closest to at the after-school center. The combination of youth and staff vantage points enriched our understanding of these relationships.

From the pool of thirty youth whom we studied intensively, we selected two youth at each center to be the focus of case studies for this book. The demographic and background characteristics of these youth are summarized in Table 1.1. We purposively selected youth whose most salient experiences at the centers revolved around participation in differing types of programs and activities and whose relationships with staff ranged in both intensity and types

---

[46] See Loder and Hirsch (2003) for how we used social network maps to understand peer ties among girls in comprehensive after-school centers. See Deutsch (2008) for how photo projects were used as a lens into youths' lives inside and outside after-school centers.

TABLE 1.1. *Overview of case study participants*

Pseudonym[a]	Center	Age	Gender	Ethnicity	Low-income family[b]	Age started at center	Number of days attending center each week	Number of hours at center each visit
Pocahontas	Midwest	14	Female	Hispanic	Yes	7	4–5	4+
Bill	Midwest	14	Male	Hispanic	Yes	9	4–5	2–4
Beyonce	North River	10	Female	African American	Yes	9	1–2	2–4
Tweetie	North River	14	Female	African American	Yes	9	3–4	1–2
Midnight	West River	17	Male	African American	Yes	15	3–4	2–4
Tommiana	West River	12	Female	African American	Yes	5	4–5	4+

Note: All information was reported by youth on the survey they completed at the start of the school year.

[a] Each young person chose his or her own pseudonym to protect anonymity.

[b] Low-income status was indicated by receipt of free or reduced-price lunches at school.

of support.[47] We similarly made it a point as well to include youth whose experiences illustrated the potential for both positive and negative synergies across different areas of the club environment. As this suggests, we did not restrict ourselves to youth who seemed to benefit the most from their involvement in the centers. Rather, our aim was to select youth whose experiences would illuminate the "black box" of comprehensive after-school centers as brightly as possible, with an eye in particular toward how young people can be affected for better and for worse by their time spent in these settings.

The extensive and varied types of data that were available concerning each after-school center and the youth who were the focus of our case studies made it desirable to synthesize this information in ways that could facilitate the writing of this book. In the case of the after-school centers, we prepared reports that provided integrative accounts of all the available data on the organizational practices and culture of each club. We similarly gathered together all the material for each youth and then used it as the basis for a two-hour case conference for that youth. All three authors of this book and two of the research assistants participated in these conferences. The findings of each conference were summarized in a memorandum. For both the after-school centers and youth, we found it helpful to organize our efforts at synthesis according to the different areas of our theoretical framework. In doing so, we consistently devoted attention to what the clubs could have done better (even when they did a generally excellent job) so as to highlight promising future directions for practice. We paid attention to the dynamics of our group discussion and considered how they might resemble the processes that after-school centers would go through in attempting to put our recommendations into practice.

BOYS & GIRLS CLUBS AND OTHER AFTER-SCHOOL ORGANIZATIONS

All three of the centers we studied were Boys & Girls Clubs. Here we provide some background on the Boys & Girls Clubs of America

---

[47] Purposive sampling involves selecting participants based on some characteristic or set of characteristics of interest and is popular in qualitative research (Patton, 1990). The type of purposive sampling that we employed for our case studies most closely resembles a theory-based approach in which the emphasis is on finding manifestations of theoretical constructs of interest so as to elaborate and examine these constructs (Patton, 1990).

(BGCA) and compare it to two other prominent after-school organizations so that readers can judge the relevance of our research to other sites.

BGCA began around the turn of the twentieth century.[48] Currently, there are approximately 4,000 clubs nationwide, with about 4.2 million youth participants. There is a large urban and minority presence (65% minorities nationwide). Many clubs, such as the three in this book, have their own buildings, but BGCA is increasingly managing clubs in public schools (approximately one-third of all clubs as of 2008).[49] Activities are offered in many areas, including recreation, academic support, psychoeducational programs, arts, computers, and entrepreneurship (including fund-raising).[50]

BGCA brings in large sums of public and private financing. Many of the club programs discussed in this book are nationally sponsored (e.g., Keystone, Torch, Smart Girls). Yet the influence of the national organization at the ground level should not be overstated. Yes, we have seen nationally developed assessment instruments on the bookshelves of club administrators and occasionally observed a youth completing such an assessment on the computer for national headquarters, but we never heard of such data discussed at the club level. And although national headquarters has produced manuals for their programs, we shall see in this study (as we did in earlier research) that the manuals are often not consulted by club staff, little or no training is provided, and program implementation often leaves much to be desired.[51] The best programs and activities we found in this study were developed on-site by talented and committed staff. BGCA does fund club requests for specific projects, but the sums quoted to us by club administrators were modest ($5,000). Each club does substantial fund-raising on its own.

The Beacons are a much more recent undertaking that have attracted considerable interest. Beacon Community Centers were first developed in New York City in the early 1990s. They are

---

[48] See Mahoney, Parente, & Zigler (2009) for a historical account of after-school programs in America.

[49] Figures were downloaded on August 2, 2010 from http://bgca.org/whoweare/facts.asp and taken from Boys & Girls Clubs of America (2009).

[50] See Arbreton, Sheldon, & Herrera (2005) for an overview of research on the clubs; for more recent studies, see, for example, Arbreton (2009) and Fredricks, Hackett, & Bregman (2010).

[51] For a detailed account of the implementation of Smart Girls, see Hirsch (2005).

located in public schools, operated by community-based organizations, and serve both youth and adults. There are currently eighty
NYC Beacons. There are also Beacons in Philadelphia, Savannah,
Palm Beach County (Florida), Minneapolis, Denver, San Francisco,
and Oakland.

In 2007, the NYC Beacons launched a new initiative to direct
resources to the needs of middle-grades youth, who would be
similar in age to most of the youth we studied for this book. An
evaluation of the middle-school initiative revealed that the overwhelming majority of youth were minorities (84%).[52] Youth were predominantly low-income (68%). Average attendance was 1.5 days/
week. The typical Beacons had fifteen staff members assigned to the
middle-school initiative, which included college students, program
specialists (e.g., dance and sports coaches), and certified teachers.
Youth spent most of their time in academic enrichment or recreation during programs offered over the school year, though activities
were also offered in cultural enrichment, life skills, civic engagement, and career awareness.

Another major national youth program, 4-H clubs, also began
around the turn of the twentieth century. Today, 4-H clubs reach
6 million youth, more than any other program (BGCA comes in
second). 4-H is historically based predominantly in rural areas and
even today, 70 percent of participating youth live on farms or in
towns under 50,000. There are considerably fewer minorities participating in them: 77 percent are white or Caucasian.[53]

4-H clubs are very much project-based, either planning events
or completing projects for entry at competitions (e.g., state fairs).
The majority of clubs meet once per month, although youth may

---

[52] Russell, LaFleur, Scott, Low, Palmiter, & Reisner (2010). We are grateful to Jennifer
LaFleur and Elizabeth Reisner of Policy Studies Associates for discussions about
some of those data. See also New York City, Department of Youth & Community
Development (2010) for figures on free or reduced-price lunch, which appears
to be based on all youth at the Beacon centers and not just the middle-school
sample.

[53] Demographic information was taken from the national 4-H Web site (downloaded
August 2, 2010 from http://4-h.org/b/Assets/MediaCenter/Fact%20Sheet-
Youth%20Statistics.pdf). There can be differences across states, and within
counties, on the nature of 4-H activities. The report that follows is based on
the experience of Wisconsin, on which we have the most information. We are
grateful to JulieAnn Stawicki of the University of Wisconsin-Extension for her
assistance (see also University of Wisconsin-Extension, 2009).

occasionally have project meetings that are in addition to the club meeting. Meetings can be held at the offices of local country officials (the extension service) that support 4-H, though they also can meet at schools, libraries, or church halls.

Clubs are led by volunteers rather than paid staff; there needs to be at least one adult leader, and the number varies from club to club. Parents are encouraged to participate, and many club meetings consist of 25–33 percent adults. Every county (within a state) has a leaders' council that is the governing board for the clubs in that county. The leaders' council includes both adults and youth and typically meets once per month.

What are the implications of these similarities and differences to the Boys & Girls Clubs in this book? Both BGCA clubs and Beacons are comprehensive after-school centers with a wide range of activities and approximately a dozen staff members. The Beacons, like the Boys & Girls Clubs in this study, primarily serve minority youth, as do other comprehensive urban centers such as those operated by the Y's. Our sample had a slightly greater proportion of minority youth and low-income youth, but we do not believe this difference to be important for our analysis. A difference that is likely to be more important concerns youth attendance; youth in our sample attended their center much more than did Beacons youth. This means that there was more contact between center staff and youth; however, many programs and activities were offered on a weekly basis at the clubs, so that would be similar to the Beacons. Overall, we think that our model and findings are likely to be quite relevant to other comprehensive centers in urban communities, or those whose demographics parallel that of urban communities, even in those centers that have fewer staff.

The differences are greater with 4-H clubs and other sites that do not offer a comprehensive range of programs and activities. For those programs, our analysis of the quality of particular programs and activities, and experiences in youth-staff relationships, should still be of considerable interest. The PARC as a unit of analysis is just as applicable. As single-focus programs often have fewer staff, there will be less organizational complexity. Nonetheless, our attention to whether the site had a consistent focus on positive youth development, the extent of staff learning, and the varied ways in which adults can mentor youth remain highly relevant.

OUTLINE OF THE BOOK

We devote four chapters to each of the three after-school centers that we studied. In each set, the first chapter presents an organizational study of the center. This chapter is followed by chapters devoted to the two adolescents who were selected for case studies at the center. A fourth, briefer chapter brings together the themes and implications of material presented in the prior chapters. The book's concluding chapter emphasizes priorities for improving quality.

MIDWEST CENTER

2

Pockets of Excellence

The Midwest after-school center occupies a building that housed a bank for many years. It is the smallest of the three clubs, particularly in the size of the gym. The former bank lobby, which has been converted to a gym, has less space and lower ceilings than gyms in the other clubs. The center is located in a community that used to be predominantly Latino, but has recently witnessed the arrival of increasing numbers of African American families. As is true of the neighborhoods near all of the centers we studied, there are a number of gangs in the area. Violence and drugs are major concerns. The crime rate in the area surrounding Midwest is higher than that found in 90 percent of neighborhoods in the city.[1]

Our initial survey questionnaire provides a good sense of those youth who came to the center who were at least ten years old. The survey was completed by 62 youth ages 10–16, with a mean (average) age of 12.16 (of the clubs we studied, Midwest has the fewest youth). The sample was 66 percent Hispanic, 34 percent African American, 8 percent white, and 2 percent Asian American (figures sum to more than 100%, as some youth checked more than one box). It was a high-poverty sample, as 83 percent reported receiving free or reduced-price lunch. It was also a high-attendance sample, as most of the young people had been coming to Midwest for several years and came almost every weekday for at least two to four hours

---

[1] Crime rate was based on FBI Index Crimes, which combines violent crimes (e.g., murder, criminal sexual assault) and property crimes (e.g., burglary, theft). To maintain the anonymity of the city in which the clubs are located, we are not able to provide the specific references for this figure.

daily.[2] At the beginning of the year, there were five full-time and two part-time staff (which includes a full-time administrator); by the end of the year, two additional full-time staff had joined the center.

This chapter focuses on the Midwest center as an organization, on its capacity to provide high-quality mentoring relationships, activities, and programs. In a sense, we are providing an in-depth site report. Most site visits occur over one or two days; our visits took place twice weekly over the course of an entire academic year. So we have an extensive database to draw from and can meaningfully analyze trends over time. We systematically review the center's efforts in each domain, pointing out strengths as well as weaknesses.

What is most striking about Midwest is that it has pockets of excellence, most of which revolve around the efforts of one staff member, Manuel. Ultimately, we need to understand why Midwest was not able to achieve a more uniform level of excellence.

Our analytical framework for understanding Midwest and the other centers has three parts: organizational goals, range and quality of program development and implementation, and human resource development. As we utilize this framework in all three organizational case studies, let us spend a bit of time elaborating it now.

ANALYTICAL FRAMEWORK

Goals

Any organization needs to be considered in relation to its goals. In the business world, it is often easy to specify and measure goals. Yearly profit, sales, market share, and so on are specifiable in

---

[2] Only 21% had just started coming to the club the year of our research; on average, youth had starting coming to the club at age eight. The great majority of these young people came to the club at least three-to-four days per week (76%), with 59% reporting that they came four-to-five days per week. Similar high attendance rates are reported for the NYC Beacons (Warren, Brown, & Freudenberg, 1999). These figures contrast markedly with participation rates at the 21st Century Community Learning Centers and at the San Francisco Beacons, where middle school students attended on average only one day per week, and at the Extended-Service Schools initiative, where average attendance for this age group was less than twice per week (Dynarski, et al., 2003; Grossman, et al., 2002;. Walker & Arbreton, 2001). It should be clear, therefore, that our sites represent high-attendance settings, the kind of participation that is most likely to have a significant impact on youth. At the same time, readers are cautioned that some of the findings we report may well not be characteristic of low-attendance settings.

easy-to-understand terms. In education, there are also benchmarks that are easy to specify and measure, such as high school graduation rate, attendance, and scores on national standardized achievement tests. Goals become trickier when one seeks to go beyond traditional constructs. Many school reformers emphasize the importance of promoting authentic student learning and deep understanding. While such goals may be desirable, they are not as easy to specify and measure. How clear are the goals in after-school centers?

Throughout its history over the past hundred years, youth or after-school centers have addressed an array of goals, from positive youth development, to problem prevention, to academic support and enrichment. All of these are relevant to these three centers. The centers are most concerned with psychosocial outcomes, both promoting positive development and preventing problem behavior, but are concerned enough with academic support that all youth are required to attend Power Hour (an hour during which staff are available to provide academic assistance). A look at the Boys & Girls Clubs of America Web site, under Who We Are, provides a good synopsis. Although the precise wording is freshened up a bit from time to time, the content has not varied significantly over the years of our involvement with the clubs:

Young people need to know that someone cares about them.

Boys & Girls Clubs offer that and more. Club programs and services promote and enhance the development of boys and girls by instilling a sense of competence, usefulness, belonging and influence.

Boys & Girls Clubs are a safe place to learn and grow – all while having fun.[3] (italics added)

These statements emphasize positive development, which, we agree, constitutes the top priority for these centers, as well as for many of those in the broader after-school field. The statements call attention to youth-staff relationships, activities, and programs that will promote positive outcomes.

Although fine for public relations purposes, there are potential problems in using this formulation to support high-quality implementation. For example, the statements imply that safety, fun, and developmental growth are mutually achievable. But sometimes these can be in conflict or be thought to be in conflict. One potential

---

[3] Downloaded from http://bgca.org/whoweare/ on March 16, 2009.

way to minimize such conflict is to have weak criteria for what constitutes developmental growth so that, for example, growth is essentially equivalent to having fun. Similarly, there can be a divergence between those who emphasize the importance of having caring adult staff in attendance and those who are dedicated to active efforts to instill developmental growth. Given that almost all staff will see themselves as caring, and we know that some of them in fact just hang out, it is not difficult to see how this situation can lead to a watering down of what constitutes developmental growth.

This discussion suggests that there is the potential for ambiguity and confusion as to the fundamental goal of these comprehensive after-school centers. In our assessment of the centers, we shall pay particular attention to how the goal of positive youth development is reflected in actual practice, to what practice tells us about how high the bar is for youth development.

In examining practice as a guide to understanding what youth development as a goal means at these centers, we shall pay particular attention to the extent to which staff focus on this goal. Research on school reform suggests that having a strong focus on student learning is a key feature of schools that have an organizational culture that supports reform efforts.[4] For after-school centers, this would correspond to an overriding emphasis on doing everything reasonably possible to promote positive youth development. This goal would serve as a constant beacon to guide staff interactions with youth and be key to planning activities and programs.

Program Development and Implementation

One critical characteristic of after-school centers is their capacity to implement high-quality activities and programs and to develop new programs as needed. We assess each center's capacity to do this by evaluating the quality of current activities and programs and by considering efforts to implement new ones. We include the quality of youth-staff relationships as part of this domain as mentoring is an important way to leverage those ties in order to promote youth development. In essence, this part of the analytic framework is concerned with how well the center's practices address their goals. Because these are comprehensive after-school

---

[4] Louis, Kruse, & Marks (1996).

centers, our assessment ranges widely over different programs, activities, and relationships.

Human Resource Development

It seems likely that whether an after-school center succeeds in providing effective implementation and achieving its goals will depend to a great extent on its ability to recruit, train, and retain a high-quality staff. Neither staff recruitment nor retention is straightforward, and the three centers took very different approaches to these issues. Training can be especially problematic. Extensive research on teacher training has revealed that short-term, one-day workshops or sessions have very little impact. What seems to be needed is ongoing consultative and training efforts over time that address issues that arise in real-time implementation efforts.[5] Alas, this finding has not stopped schools from continuing to do what doesn't work. Have after-school centers learned from the prior errors of schools or have they continued down the same path?

If anything, problems involving training are even greater in the after-school arena than in schools. The evidence base on effective after-school practices is thin. There is a good deal of folk wisdom, to be sure, but intensive research on these sites has only just begun.

Given these limitations, it would seem especially important to emphasize organizational learning. The extent to which an organization functions as a learning organization has received considerable attention in the lay and business literatures. This refers to whether there is a collective pursuit of knowledge and understandings that enable an organization to do its work better. In the absence of extensive technical knowledge, and problems in relying on one-shot workshops, after-school centers need to cultivate their own knowledge base. Many researchers who have studied school reform efforts have come to similar conclusions. They stress that to achieve meaningful reform (the organization's goal), intensive dialogue among teachers is essential.[6] So in addition to a more traditional concern with training sessions and supervision, we will also consider the extent to which organizational learning takes place, and especially the extent to which staff at a center talk with each other to learn how to do their jobs better.

[5] Berman & McLaughlin (1978).
[6] Louis et al. (1996).

APPLICATION OF THE ANALYTICAL FRAMEWORK
TO THE MIDWEST CENTER

Goals

The leadership and staff at the Midwest center agree that positive youth development is the fundamental objective. Within this context, Bob, the long-time director of the Midwest center, has two main priorities. The first is to pay most attention to the kids at his club who are most at risk. He encourages his staff to get involved – and stay involved – with those kids, regardless of how difficult they are to work with. The second priority is community outreach, focused on the epidemic of drug use in the surrounding neighborhood. Bob initiated collaborative programs with local schools, which are operated at school sites, some of which involved positive youth development activities as part of their prevention strategy. Several center staff are devoted to this outreach effort and work primarily at the schools.

The center-based staff have mixed reactions to their boss's priorities. They buy into the orientation to the neediest kids and disagree with the focus on community outreach. The disagreement is not about the intrinsic worth of that effort, but rather about what economists would refer to as its opportunity cost. If you prioritize, and devote significant funds to outreach, there is less attention and money available for in-center staff and programs. So the focus on outreach has its cost, and the center staff are aware of this and deal with its consequences on a daily basis.

Our concern in this book is on what happens inside the Midwest center. Given Bob's preoccupation with activities outside of the club, how well are the staff able to focus on the positive development of youth inside of the club? We will examine this via an analysis of implementation quality within Midwest, after which we shall return to consider the extent to which staff focus on what is manifestly its most important goal.

Program Development and Implementation

We now turn to examine activities, programs, and youth-staff relationships that took place at Midwest, after which we consider some efforts at program development that never got off the ground.

Game Room

The game room is the central space at Midwest, a multi-purpose space characterized by lively activity and generally friendly socializing. The majority of young people at Midwest can be found in this room. As a result, the room is often noisy and hectic, and there usually are a variety of activities going on at any one time. Here is a typical scene:

> *In the Game Room, there are approximately thirty to thirty-five children between the ages of eight and fourteen years. They are primarily Hispanic and about 30 percent of the children are African American. There is one Caucasian girl. The children are spread throughout the Game Room, involved in playing ping-pong, foosball, and assorted board games. There are two ping-pong tables on the west side of the room and across from them is a bench that lines the wall. A handful of children are seated at each ping-pong table's bench, waiting their turn to play the winner of the previous game. There are also kids sitting at various tables on the east side of the room, doing homework or playing board games.... There is hip-hop music playing from a radio that sits on a windowsill between the two ping-pong tables.*

Peace and order, however, do not always reign. Shouting and peer conflict, and several dozen kids running about, can at times lend the room the appearance of chaos, as a staff member noted after one such episode:

> *Our game room is so wild. It's the first thing you see, you know, and I've actually had parents tell me, "Oh no, I'm not taking my kids there – the kids there run wild." And it's true! When you walk in, the game room is chaotic and no parent wants to bring their kids there.*

From time to time, things could become overwhelming. Charlene, the primary staff person assigned to the game room, sometimes lost control of the room even when, as in the following instance, another staff person (Susan) was there to assist her.

> *At some point, Charlene turned off the lights.* [This usually means the staff is demanding the kids' attention and it usually is not a good thing.] *"It is entirely too loud in here! You need to stop yelling!" Charlene screamed. Some of the kids kept talking and Susan talked while Charlene was screaming. Susan continued to find out from the kids at the ping-pong table what had happened so she could mediate. "It cannot be this loud in here!" Charlene yelled. The kids at the ping-pong table continued to yell and talk about what had happened and Susan (who had*

her back turned to Charlene the entire time) continued to talk. Charlene
looked over at that ping-pong table, then at the kids (some of whom had
resumed talking), shook her head, rolled her eyes, threw her hands up,
and turned the lights back on. She sat back down at a table. [She looked
thoroughly frustrated. It was clear that she had not succeeded in
quieting the kids down beyond that moment.]

With lots of young people and little structure, the room could veer
out of control. Charlene is not especially skilled at maintaining
order, but it is unfair to attribute the problem entirely to her. We
return to this issue later in the chapter.

Although lack of control could be a problem, it should not be
overemphasized. Most of the time the kids were enjoying themselves and for kids that typically involves a lot of action and noise.
The social and recreational activities that take place there have considerable intrinsic appeal and act like a magnet to staff and youth
alike. There is a lot of energy, it is easy to interact informally, and
spontaneous opportunities for teaching, as we shall see, arise frequently. Kids are able to have fun without sacrificing safety, satisfying two important organizational goals.[7]

The positive draw of the game room presents Midwest with a bit
of a conundrum. The more time that staff spend in the game room,
the less time they have available for developing programs or other
duties. At the same time, the fact that there are not many engaging programs at Midwest is part of what draws kids (and staff) to
the game room in the first place. This is a dilemma that has been
endemic to Midwest for quite some time, but there is little pressure
from Bob to address it, given his greater attention to outreach rather
than in-center programming. The centrality of the game room to the
overall culture of Midwest provides an early hint that the emphasis
on safe fun can diminish the focus on positive youth development.
Safe fun is intrinsically worthwhile but it is not equivalent to development. Yet some staff may treat it as such, leaning to the view that
it provides experiences that are "good enough."

Youth-Staff Relationships

A focus on the development of young people should not be just
an abstract value, but instead a driving force that underlies both

---

[7] This issue is considered more extensively in Hirsch (2005).

relationships and formal programs. That is what we mean by a "focus." This was surely true of Manuel, one of the full-time staff members at Midwest.

Manuel is a soft-spoken man who has a quiet charm that is not apparent at first but reveals itself over time. He is short and slight, with a baby-face that sports a perpetual "five-o'clock" shadow. His shoulder-length hair is dark and silky and always pulled back into a ponytail at the nape of his neck. Manuel tends toward buttoned-up shirts paired with jeans, his shirt sleeves rolled up as if ready for hard work. At first sight he does not appear to be someone who would carry automatic authority with teens. Yet Manuel manages this task in the same calm way in which he approaches all his interactions, turning his full attention to the person in question and expressing himself in a firm yet caring manner. His large, dark eyes, always trained on the target of his conversation, help him keep the listener involved and focused. Manuel never raises his voice, but dispenses discipline and nurturing with equal aplomb. He is quick to break into a grin and volleys between concern and comedy, playing the clown as often as the counselor. His ability to work back and forth between serious discussions and playful interaction enhances his ability to discipline the teens when needed, as he comes off as neither the pal nor the principal, but somewhere in-between.

Manuel was not an especially good student in high school. He told us that in his freshman year, "I did horrible." He graduated from one of the better high schools in the city, but just barely had the required number of credits. He took college courses on and off, had tried out different majors, and was now looking toward a major that would reflect his interest in working with children.

There was nothing in this background to suggest that Manuel would have a talent for tutoring kids in math. He probably would not be able to get a job in a school as a math teacher. But, at the Midwest after-school center, it was clear that he had a calling for helping kids with math. It was an activity that he loved.

Marzelle came in and told Manuel he needed help with his math homework. He sat down and took out a tattered workbook. "That's your workbook? What happened to that, man, your dog chew on it?" Mateo [another staff] asked. "Man it's my good luck book! Ever since it got messed up like this I have been doing better in math and I do my homework now," Marzelle said grinning. Manuel got out a wipe board easel and set it up on the table next to me, facing Marzelle. He took Marzelle's

*workbook and looked at it. "Okay, so you have to figure out the surface
area. So what that means is, take this CD case. So the surface area of it
is the area of each of its side," Manuel said tracing each side of the case
with his finger, demonstrating to Marzelle "all added up and that is the
surface area. And you know that these two sides are the same so when
you know that area you can just multiply by two," Manuel continued.
He began to draw a cube on the wipe board and then deconstructed it
into each of its parts.*

The next day, Manuel followed up with Marzelle:

*Marzelle came up to the table and Manuel said, "Wassup man, you got
homework?" Marzelle shrugged and Manuel said, "Come on!" Manuel
whipped out a huge dry erase board and started writing equations.*

Manuel did not limit his teaching activities to math.[8] He started a
chess club (more on this later in the chapter) and was very active in
teaching both beginning and advanced tactics.

Manuel seemed quite focused on positive youth development.
The other Midwest staff did not demonstrate the same level of
commitment. This was reflected in social climate ratings made by
researchers during each site visit (at the conclusion of each visit, the
observer rated overarching characteristics of the center during that
observation). Midwest staff as a group were rated as engaged and
enthusiastic in their work on only 14 percent of site visits, as compared to 78 percent of visits to the West River club.[9] Manuel was the
only Midwest staff person who held his own with the West River
group in terms of both enthusiasm and orientation to teaching.

It is useful to compare Manuel with Mateo, the Midwest sports
director (who was Latino, like Manuel). At some other centers,
such as West River, gym and game room staff would be heavily
invested in teaching and promoting developmental growth, in
ways that went considerably beyond athletics (as we shall see in
later chapters). Mateo did not demonstrate that level of engagement. Yes, he would offer encouragement and advice (both during

---

[8] Additional examples of Manuel's work with Midwest youth on math are given
in Chapter 3 on Pocahontas.

[9] The data were treated as interval and analyzed via analysis of variance, with
Newman-Keuls post-hoc tests to clarify differences between specific clubs. The
results were not only statistically significant, $F\ (2,188) = 66.74$, $p < .001$, but were
the strongest between-club difference on any of the social climate variables. The
North River center scores on this variable (8%) were not statistically different
from those of the Midwest center.

open recreation time and team practices) and do his best to have boys include girls in basketball games. He was friendly and warm-hearted, and the kids enjoyed being around him. Mateo had been at the center many years, and several young people told us that their long time together gave the relationship a special significance.[10] Urban youth may well be better able to establish trust at younger ages, which would benefit their attachment to him.[11] Indeed, on our survey questionnaire, Mateo received the most nominations as the Midwest staff person to whom youth felt closest.[12] But too often he would sit at courtside doing paperwork, rather than being involved with kids, and a few times we observed him reading the newspaper in the game room. Hanging out can provide an informality and accessibility that can facilitate relationship development, but for Mateo this too frequently appeared instead to amount to time off. Moreover, he did not appear to use this hanging out as a foundation for developing deeper ties. He did offer guidance, but he did not do so with as much thoroughness as more committed or skilled staff at these centers. It is unfortunate that he did not draw on his popularity to mentor more actively.

These patterns are reflected in our structured observations of Manuel and Mateo. We made twenty-three observations of Manuel and twelve of Mateo over the course of the year. We should note that we could not undertake a formal observation if the staff person was not with the youth who were part of our study. The very fact

---

[10] The length of the relationship has been found to be critical to mentoring outcomes (Grossman & Rhodes, 2002), with relationships of one year or more especially valuable. At Midwest, and the other clubs, many youth had been coming to the site for most days for several years, so youth-staff relationships would score highly on this dimension (see Hirsch, 2005).

[11] Way (1998).

[12] Mateo's nominations appeared to reflect several factors: He was extremely likeable, he ran the gym (a favorite place in the club), and he had developed relationships over the several years he had worked at the club. Manuel had worked at the club less than a year at the time of the survey and was just beginning to get his "sea legs" in terms of comfort level and casualness in relationships with kids; he improved considerably in these areas over the course of the year (as can be seen especially well in the chapter on Pocahontas). We do not have an empirical answer to the question of whether the kind of companionship that Mateo offered would prove more valuable in the long term than the companionship plus active mentoring provided by Manuel, although we favor the latter. As will be seen in a subsequent chapter, even though Bill nominated Mateo as his closest staff person on the survey, by the end of the year, Manuel appeared to have made much more of a difference in Bill's life.

that we made nearly twice as many formal observations of Manuel than Mateo is due to Manuel's greater involvement with the youth who were in our study – and, indeed, Midwest youth more generally. When we examine the nature of their interactions, we see that Manuel is more likely than Mateo to provide instruction (39% vs. 25% of observation periods), communicate positively to youth (48% vs. 17%), and (in a sign of affection) have positive physical contact (39% vs. 17%) with them. Manuel, indeed, is the highest-rated of any of the staff at the three sites with regard to providing instruction and communicating positively to youth. Both Manuel and Mateo engage frequently in behavior management, as do most staff across centers; nonetheless, they are almost never coded for negative interactions with youth (4% for Manuel, 0% for Mateo). Their rate of negative staff-youth interactions is by far the fewest at any site. In these data, Manuel demonstrates the best ability of any staff person we assessed in this study to teach and communicate in a positive manner while at the same time maintain control without becoming aversive. This profile is quite consonant with an authoritative style of interacting with youth – high levels of both responsiveness and demandingness – that has frequently been considered the gold standard in research on parenting and has been found important to middle school teachers as well.[13]

Altogether, then, Midwest offered the potential for close relationships with adult staff. The quality of its mentoring, however, was due primarily to one person. Many youth did feel close to Mateo, but he had a more passive approach to mentoring and was not as focused on youth's developmental growth. Mateo had the potential to be a much more effective presence in the lives of these young people. We cannot help but wonder whether Mateo would have been more proactive with youth had he appreciated how much he was valued and the impact he might have been able to achieve.

Chess Club

The brainchild of Manuel, the chess club stemmed from his own love of the game. The chess club was a surprising and resounding

---

[13] For parenting, see Baumrind (1991), Maccoby & Martin (1983), Mandara (2006). Wentzel (2002) found that similar dimensions in the relationship between middle school teachers and students were associated with student motivation, social behavior, and achievement.

success, and spread like wildfire through the club. Manuel's own interest in and passion for chess was relayed to the youth and translated into their own appreciation for the game. Before the club officially started, Manuel played now and then with kids and staff who already knew the game and talked about what the club would do. This successfully introduced the game to the club and got kids interested in learning how to play.

The club began meeting in early February, and by late February chess was a daily activity at Midwest. Youth and staff were constantly playing chess in all areas of the club. And the games were not limited to youth and staff directly involved in the chess club. Boards would be set up in the game room, and there was such demand for games that youth would call "next," just as you would hear on the basketball court. The chess club itself had a strong core of participants, and Manuel was focused on teaching them specific skills and strategies. At first, the club met every day, but this objective was sometimes thwarted by Manuel's need to fill in for other staff.

Youth who played chess were engrossed in their games. Sometimes there would be two games going on simultaneously and at times a crowd of other youth would gather around to watch, suggest moves, and comment on moves that had been made. Nevertheless, even when there was a crowd, there was almost no disruptive activity. This made chess unique, as disruptions were commonplace during other club programs, such as Keystone and Torch (to be described in the next section).

The chess club involved kids of different ages, and Manuel took advantage of the combination of older and younger kids by having the youths teach each other through a combination of example and active participation. He would often have kids recreate the final stages of games to discuss things that could have been done differently. He would also demonstrate a variety of moves that they could have made in a certain situation and the actions that would have resulted from those moves. The young people learned as they played, making the activity entertaining and fun, as well as educational.

There was a chessboard in front of Manuel and the kids. Manuel was explaining to them about the end game and taking the king with the queen. He reminded them how they had talked about the beginning game and middle game and then he had them practice some end games, trying to checkmate each other. He would watch and then offer ideas for what they could have done differently. He switched around and had different kids play against different kids. He talked to them about different strategies for end games and how you blocked off portions of the board with your queen. As kids played, they would ask him about different moves or look at him for guidance. Manuel would remind them of things they had discussed in previous meetings and suggest different moves they could have made.

The chess club was the best program at Midwest. Led by an enthusiastic and knowledgeable staff member who was committed to teaching, chess elicited high levels of youth engagement, and involved them in a challenging, complex activity that led to significant learning.[14]

Keystone and Torch Clubs

Keystone and Torch Clubs are programs that are mandated by the national headquarters of the Boys & Girls Clubs of America. They involve similar activities, focusing on leadership development and community service, but are for different age groups (Torch is for 10–12-year-olds, Keystone is for teens). Torch Club had seven regular members, Keystone varied between seven and twelve. Both activities were run by paid staff members (Juan led Keystone, Manuel led Torch). The clubs sponsored and helped staff a sleepover at the club for younger children, a river cleanup, and a visit to a local nursing home to play chess with residents. Those youth who contributed the most to Keystone were invited to regional and national Keystone conferences – a sought-after perk. To help raise funds for the trip, and to help support other club activities, Keystone began and operated a store at Midwest in which youth at the site could purchase a variety of snacks and in which Keystoners could gain valuable business skills.

In evaluating the quality of program implementation, the first thing to consider is how regularly the programs met (program dosage). Presumably, if the program is a good one, youth will benefit from more frequent attendance. Although Manuel talked in the early fall of starting up Torch, he did not do so until February and even then was not able to have regular meetings. This was not due to

---

[14] We were able to observe youth improve their skills over time during actual game situations. In educational research, chess instruction has been found to improve students' cognitive development and academic achievement (Smith & Cage, 2000).

lack of conscientiousness on Manuel's part, but rather to the press of other commitments. The following interchange reflects this; it took place while Manuel was staffing the front desk because the staff person who normally does that was absent.

"How's Torch Club going?" I asked. He shrugged. "Could be better," he said. "Yeah? Why?" "I just don't have time to prepare for it. I have too much else to do and then I have to fill in for people, like this, and so I just don't have the time I need for it." I nodded. "Yeah, I was planning on sitting in today but I guess you won't be doing it here in the lobby, huh?" I asked. He smiled and shook his head. "Yeah. That's what I'm talking about. I am always having to fill in for someone and so I don't have time to do it," he said, shaking his head.

Keystone, by contrast, met every week throughout the year. We observed the group on a number of occasions, and talked to both Juan (staff leader of Keystone) and youth participants about it. Keystone meetings generally began with an icebreaker led by Juan. Youth's response to icebreakers in the first few weeks was positive, but then began to vary from enthusiastic participation to eye-rolling disdain. After the icebreaker, the meetings proceeded to discuss group business from current projects and activities, to planning special events, to discussing who would represent the group at conferences. At the beginning of the year, Juan led the meetings and came prepared with a typed agenda that he distributed at the start of meetings. After officials were elected by the youth, the Keystone president was supposed to be responsible for planning the agenda with Juan. In the winter, Roberta, the president, began to lead the meetings, sometimes without Juan's presence. Keystone vacillated between running smoothly, with youth engagement in activities (mostly elections or planning events like sleepovers), and being plagued by disruptions and youth non-responsiveness. A single meeting often see-sawed between these two extremes.

At times, Juan himself contributed to the disruption. In the following instance, Juan disrupts a group session led by Susan (another staff person).

While Susan was talking, Juan was goofing off from where he sat behind Susan. He was making faces and mouthing comments that I could not understand to Dude. Dude did the same thing back to Juan. [I was struck by this. Juan was acting like a teenager or something. Clearly, he was not helping Susan facilitate ...]

Overall, quality of program implementation was inconsistent. The program met regularly, it had a number of accomplishments to its credit, and it provided opportunities for youth leadership. At the same time, the value of the icebreakers diminished over time and, when they went poorly, the session started off on a bad trajectory. Many meetings were hampered by disruption, and Juan was not able to deal with this effectively.

Although we did not observe Torch Club on as many occasions as we did Keystone, it seemed to have some of the same problems. The degree of youth engagement in activities varied considerably, and Manuel often had difficulty managing the group process. As Manuel told us after one session, "this is so *not* easy."

The fact that Manuel had such difficulty with Torch Club is striking. After all, Manuel seemed to be a "wizard," according to McLaughlin et al.'s framework, at working with kids in chess club and in tutoring them in math.[15] But his wizardry seemed to have its limits. There appear to be two explanations for this discrepancy. First, there was the level of Manuel's motivation. He was assigned by Bob to run Torch, and he did not accept the assignment with boundless enthusiasm. By contrast, he started chess club on his own initiative and out of his love for the game. Although Manuel usually had a strong focus on youth development, his work with Torch suggests that his personal interest in the activity was important as well. Second, playing chess was a lot more engrossing to kids than the tasks they faced in Torch. The latter activities had less intrinsic appeal, so youth were more easily distracted and goofed off more readily.

Formal Educational Programs

There was a formal program for academic assistance (Power Hour) that was required for all youth, but it was run as a stereotypical study hall. Kids mostly did their homework on their own, and would only occasionally come up to the front, asking assistance from the staff person sitting at a desk. The staff person would help and then return to his or her paperwork.[16] It was no wonder that when

[15] McLaughlin, Irby, & Langman (1994).

[16] This kind of situation appears endemic to many after-school centers; see, for example, the initial evaluation of the 20th Century Community Learning Centers, where the academic assistance programs are similarly characterized as traditional study halls (Dynarski, et al., 2003).

a youth wanted help with schoolwork, they sought out Manuel in the game room and worked on things there, despite the noise and general commotion.

When Steven began working at Midwest in the spring, he took a more active interest in Power Hour. He would encourage youth to attend and discuss with parents whether their children had come and completed their homework. But Power Hour still functioned mostly as a study hall.

For most of the year, there was no educational program involving computers. After Steven came to the center, he began to do some teaching around use of the computer and was talking of offering a computer class for teens in the evening.

Programs That Were Not Supported by Midwest Leadership

Bob, the center director, supported Manuel's initiation of the chess club, but he discouraged several other staff initiatives aimed at developing new activities and programs. It is of more than passing interest that these other initiatives were targeted at girls and were led by female staff members.

Charlene was enthusiastic about getting girls together on a cheerleading team, a popular activity at several other clubs in the area.

> *"We tried to get a cheerleading team together and I'm like hold up, um, Bob, how we gonna get there? And he's like, well, there's no room on the van and we have no money for transportation. I'm like, how the hell are you supposed to have the cheerleaders then?! And then! We all know that the big thing for the girls to be on the cheerleading team is to have the outfit, right? So I tell Bob this – I went and found these cute pants at Target on sale that said Cheerleader down the leg. Mm-hmm, already went and did this. Went to Bob and he said, we don't have any money for that. Meanwhile, the boys get brand new, nice baby blue jerseys for the basketball team! So [name of other club] – since they closin' down or whatever, went through their old stuff. Found old maroon polo shirts and Bob said, 'oh, you can have those. That's the best we can do.' You believe that?! Uh-uh!!!" She shook her head in disgust.*

For most of the year, Bob also was not enthused about the efforts of Susan to start a psychoeducational group for early adolescent girls. Many of the clubs ran a program developed at national headquarters

called Smart Girls.[17] Indeed, during the gender equity initiative of
a few years prior, each club had been required to offer Smart Girls.
When we came for our first meeting at Midwest for the present
study, we saw that Smart Girls had been penciled in on the weekly
calendar as a regular offering. However, for many months, Susan's
efforts to get it off the ground received no support. Toward the end
of the year, Bob changed his mind and asked Jessie, another staff
person, to run the group, but the terms of his offer infuriated her.

> Jessie mentioned how Bob had just cut her hours. "And then he asked
> me to lead a girls program but he wants me to volunteer my time for it!"
> Jessie shook her head. "He asked the girls and they said they wanted me
> or Susan to do it and so he came to me and asked me to do it but as a
> volunteer." Susan looked annoyed: "I've been asking about doing a girls
> program since I got here and he has always put me off." Susan shook her
> head in amazement. Jessie nodded and shrugged.

This was not the only instance in which Susan had been thwarted in
her efforts to improve programming at Midwest. She noted that her
efforts to get the art room set up for use, which presumably would
be of greater interest to girls than boys, had come to naught due to
lack of support from Bob.

Thus, Bob provided little support for female staff who sought to
develop programs or activities focused on girls. However, because
none of the male staff other than Manuel tried to develop new
programs (it was unclear what would happen to Steven's interest in a computer class), we do not know whether Bob's actions
were specific to developing girls' programs or reflected a general
disinterest in change. Manuel was highly skilled and clearly Bob's
favorite, so it is understandable that Bob would support chess
club. But how he might respond to initiatives by other male staff
remains an unknown. As we shall see in the next section, Bob was
willing to support initiatives from regional headquarters for new
programs, operated by outsiders, that focused primarily on girls,
so some caution is warranted about interpreting his lack of support
for internally generated program initiatives for girls. Regardless of
the reason, Midwest was not good at new program development by
its staff and this appeared to shortchange female staff – and teenage
girls – in particular.

---

[17] This is a psychoeducational program that has a 110-page manual. An extensive
assessment of this program is provided by Hirsch (2005).

Programs Run by Volunteers or Other Organizations

There were three programs run on-site by volunteers and one program operated off-site in which several Midwest youth participated. The on-site programs included drama, dance, and mentoring; the off-site program was a peer jury run by the local police precinct in connection with the drug prevention initiative.[18] Each of the first three programs had received grant funding from external sources via efforts of the regional headquarters and were placed at several clubs. Following his usual practice, Bob supported headquarters in this effort by allowing the programs to be placed at his club, but that was the limit of his involvement.

We heard enthusiastic reports about the drama program from several youth, which primarily involved girls. They talked of exciting activities and were clearly committed to going to the weekly session. We knew that the girls would absolutely refuse to be interviewed for our research at a time when drama was scheduled. Unfortunately for our purposes, the drama instructor did not permit us to observe any session for more than a few minutes, believing that the presence of outsiders made the girls too self-conscious and detracted from their work. We obviously honored his request, and so cannot report how much challenge the activities presented and the kind of learning that may have taken place.

In contrast, there was remarkably little talk among youth about the dance, mentoring, or peer jury programs. In our experience over several years with a number of Boys & Girls Clubs, when a program excites kids, it generates "buzz." We did hear some positive reports about each of these programs, but the absence of any buzz leads us to suspect that the level of engagement (and, thus, benefit) was limited. Consistent with this, we heard practically nothing about these programs from paid Midwest staff. Usually if a program is generating enthusiastic youth participation, staff will talk about it with us, and either present it in a positive manner as a benefit to youth, or sometimes refer to it more ambivalently, in a manner that suggests competitiveness or jealousy. The fact that neither youth nor staff talked much about these programs suggests that their contribution to the center was modest, although we readily admit that our evidentiary basis for this conclusion is limited.

---

[18] The mentoring program involved community volunteers, not paid center staff.

HUMAN RESOURCE DEVELOPMENT

Buildings, equipment, and supplies are critical to after-school centers, but we consider the people who staff them to be their most important asset. If after-school programs contribute to youth outcomes, it is difficult to imagine a scenario under which the quality of after-school staff is not an important part of the equation. There are three dimensions of human resource development that we shall examine (social scientists prefer the term "human capital" to "human resource"). These include staff hiring, training and supervision, and the extent to which the Midwest center functioned as a learning organization. Human resource development means more than just the qualities of the people that are hired, but also how their knowledge and skill are developed.

Staff Hiring

We had been told years before by executives at the regional headquarters of these Boys & Girls Clubs that Bob was "old-boy" and nowhere was this more evident than in his hiring practices. Bob had worked at the clubs for decades and kept in touch with a number of the youngsters he had known from way back when, who had since grown into adults. Bob believed in becoming personally involved in the lives of club youth and in serving as their advocate. He did this for the young people at Midwest, and he was more than willing to continue in this role as his charges aged. This was reflected in his choice of staff. Three Midwest staffers – Manuel, Mateo, and Steven – had spent their childhood at clubs where Bob had been a staff member. Bob had known each of these individuals for fifteen-to-twenty years – indeed, for most of their lives.

Bob's old-boy hiring reflected one of his core beliefs, namely that you should go out of your way to provide personal help. It doubtless served as a clear statement to his staff, an act of role modeling, of what he expected of them with regards to club youth. This practice had benefits for youth. In our prior research, youth talked about how staff understood them because they were from similar backgrounds and this led to closer relationships.[19] The staff that Bob hired shared not only a similar background in terms of growing up or currently

---

[19] Hirsch (2005).

living in a similar neighborhood, but also in terms of attending a club as a young person. They thus brought to the center a level of understanding that could provide a solid foundation on which to develop effective programs and mentoring relationships.[20]

Beyond its potential benefits to youth, in hiring young men with whom he was so familiar, Bob had a much higher level of confidence than one would normally have with new hires that he could trust them to run the club in ways consonant with his values and style. After all, in essence he wanted them to recreate what he knew that they had experienced as youngsters themselves. This level of trust is important for anyone in a leadership position, but perhaps even more so for Bob, given that so much of his energy and attention was devoted to outreach efforts not located within the Midwest building. He could devote himself much more easily to off-site initiatives if he could trust that things would go as he wished on-site.

It will come as little surprise that the hiring practices at Midwest were not a big hit with the female staff. Charlene had originally interviewed for the education position that was filled by Steven. Charlene told us that she had gone through several interviews when, at the last minute, she was told that something had come up and was instead offered the position in the game room. That "something else" was Steven. She was quite displeased that she had not gotten the position for which she had originally interviewed.

Gender issues in employment went beyond a preference for utilizing the old-boy network. Several female staff told us that Bob had told them that he had refused to hire a woman because she was four months pregnant, even though this constituted illegal discrimination. The women felt shortchanged, believing that they were hired only to make the club look good in terms of employment statistics (in terms of hiring females and African Americans), and complained of being thwarted in every effort to develop new programs or even utilize existing resources.

Training and Supervision

Training and supervision are at the heart of human resource (capital) development. If youth workers are not given training and

---

[20] We are reminded of Kelly's (2006) emphasis on the cycling of resources within an ecological perspective.

supervision on site, they may not receive any at all. College or graduate programs that train youth workers are rare.[21] There are few consensual best-practices for working with adolescents that have been written about in any detail. There is as yet no dominant national association such as exists for pediatricians, psychologists, or social workers.[22] The employing after-school center therefore plays a vital role in developing staff knowledge and skills so that services improve in quality over time. Even if the professional infrastructure were to develop in the future, on-site staff learning would still be important to adapt outside practices to local conditions.

Unfortunately, training and supervision provided to Midwest staff ranged from none to minimal. Manuel, for instance, told us that regional headquarters had provided only one training session for staff about to start Torch or Keystone programs. In response to our query as to whether he had received any training, he told us:

> "No. Well, there was one training. Like for everyone who does Torch and Keystone. . . . But it just went over sort of the different areas that you are supposed to do, like community service and stuff."
>
> "So was it helpful?"
>
> He shrugged. "Not really."

Prior research has documented that one-shot, pre-implementation training is of little use for either educational or preventive mental health interventions, so Manuel's reaction is not surprising.[23] Manuel could have used ongoing training beyond the simple orientation that was provided. He might well have benefited from

---

[21] We are not advocating that all youth workers be college educated. Some individuals, like Manuel, have a natural affinity for this work but do not have college degrees. Moreover, classroom performance on exams and such might not be the best guide to who will actually be good in practice.

[22] For example, the National Association of Social Workers was formed in 1955 as a result of the consolidation of seven national organizations. It currently has 153,000 members. It is involved in establishing and maintaining standards of practice and provides services to members to protect and enhance their professional status. It has a code of ethics and publishes journals, books, and major reference works. There is as yet no comparable association in the after-school or broader child/youth work field. At present, there clearly is movement toward increased professionalization. There are a number of after-school organizations that have developed training materials and are discussing standards for professional certification and site accreditation.

[23] Substantial amounts of training and supervision over time needs to be provided (Berman & McLaughlin, 1978; DuBois, Holloway, Valentine, & Cooper, 2002; Fullan, 1991; Halpern, 1992; Robertson, 1997).

discussing how to design tasks that elicit enthusiastic, sustained youth engagement. He might also have benefited from discussions on how to handle disruptive peer interactions. But no such training was provided either at regional headquarters or at the Midwest center. Manuel at least did receive some training. Charlene received no training whatsoever in running the game room despite the well-known difficulties of that job.

This training need not be expensive. Indeed, it need not involve much, if any, outside consultation. Across the varied after-school centers in this region, there were any number of experienced staff who had accumulated expertise in working effectively with youth in various activities and programs. The centers could draw on this home-grown source of knowledge. And given the availability of this staff knowledge, there was the opportunity to provide periodic training and supervision to guide newcomers through difficulties encountered as they got further into program activities.

Bob could have addressed these gaps in training in his own supervision, but he did not. His supervision was limited to making sure that staff were at their assigned posts. Thus, if he saw Mateo hanging out in the game room too long, he might tell him that he was supposed to be in the gym. He was also involved in weekly planning done at staff meetings, checking up to see that tasks were being done. But we neither observed nor heard of Bob ever giving detailed feedback about how to do a task more effectively. As far as we know, he himself never provided supervision that was designed to increase the level of staff skills.[24]

Bob did have a second-in-command, a program director, who had frontline supervisorial responsibility for programs.[25] This person did not have Bob's out-of-the-club responsibilities and was focused, as Bob was not, on in-house operations.[26] Even if Bob did

---

[24] Bob did arrange for some specialized training, which backfired, in relation to the drug initiative. Staff resented being forced to go for an activity that did not directly relate to their own work but which instead was seen to serve Bob's own personal agenda. The fact that some of this training involved unpaid time did not help matters.

[25] There has been an emerging interest in distributed leadership models in educational settings (e.g., Gronn, 2000; Leithwood & Jantzi, 2000; Ogawa & Bossert, 1995; Spillane, Halverson, & Diamond, 2001; Wallace, 2002).

[26] The argument has been made to us by former executives at the regional headquarters that the club director had too many outside responsibilities (e.g., fundraising, interacting with the club's board of directors) to engage in the type of

not personally provide supervision, he should have provided leadership to make program supervision a top priority for the program director and to make sure that the supervision provided by the program director was useful. However, the program director did not differ in his supervisorial behavior from Bob; he would make sure that staff followed club rules but offered little feedback or guidance on the quality of staff work. Thus, although authority at the club was distributed beyond Bob, there was little leadership in terms of creating positive pressure for change and mentoring staff progress.[27]

Learning Organization

There has been increasing attention in the organizational literature to the notion of a "learning organization."[28] This refers to whether there is a collective pursuit of knowledge and understandings that enable an organization to do its work better. As such, a learning organization provides a continuous quality-control mechanism, always striving for improvement. In emphasizing learning at an organizational level, we seek to move beyond an emphasis on supervision to encompass a broader array of structures and processes. In theory, it is possible that Midwest could utilize alternative organizational practices to compensate for the inattention to supervision from Bob and the program director. In practice, though, this did not occur.

Perhaps the most compelling example of how Midwest did not function as a learning organization was in its response to Charlene's difficulties in maintaining order in the game room. As emphasized, the game room was the center of club life, but it had a tendency to veer toward being out of control. Charlene was not always able to maintain order and on occasion would become distraught over

supervision we have discussed. Instead, from their point of view, this should be handled by the program director at each site. Over our years of research, however, we have found that the best club directors have been actively involved in supervising program quality. Findings from research on effective schools likewise highlight the important role of the principal in providing frequent, personal monitoring of school activities (Levine & Lezotte, 1995).

[27] For the importance of these and related leadership functions in the educational literature, see, e.g, Heller & Firestone (1995); Leithwood & Duke (1999); Louis, Toole, & Hargreaves (1999).

[28] Important foundational works in this field include Argyris & Schon (1978); Cyert & March (1963); Nelson & Winer (1982); Nonaka & Takeuchi (1995); and Senge (1990). Collections of recent work can be found in Dierkes, Antal, Child, & Nonaka (2001) and Easterby-Smith & Lyles (2003).

conditions. Not only did Charlene receive no formal training in handling the game room, but she received very little in the way of consultation from other staff about how to handle developing situations more effectively. Almost all of the other staff had learned how to control the kids better than did Charlene. But they did not share their hard-won wisdom with Charlene. They neither went to her and talked as individuals, one-on-one, nor did they as a group sit down and problem-solve behavior-management strategies. Instead, their attitude toward Charlene was one of "sink or swim." They tended, in a rather macho manner, to view this as a sort of initiation ritual that you either passed or not on your own. Other staff would come to her assistance when things got out of control, because that was viewed as an intolerable situation, but they did not proactively work with her on how to prevent such situations from developing in the first place. This is similar to a tendency we have noted over the years, especially when we evaluated the gender equity initiative in the clubs, for staff to respond promptly to problematic situations but provide little proactive leadership to prevent their occurrence.[29]

The failure to work together as a learning organization was by no means limited to Charlene's troubles in the game room. Manuel and Juan had similar difficulties in running the Torch and Keystone clubs. But they never talked together about their common difficulties, nor did they brainstorm or collaboratively experiment with alternative approaches.

Training sessions that staff attended were not processed together afterward, diminishing their potential impact. For example, Manuel very much enjoyed attending a session at regional headquarters on counseling skills, but Juan felt it was a waste of time, that he was not a "counselor" and did not want to be. Discussing these divergent reactions might have helped clarify the mission of the club, their respective roles, the ways in which they might best address the needs of different types of youth, and how staff might complement each other in collective mentoring strategies.[30] Reflective dialogue in response to training opportunities can build the organization's capacity for high-quality program implementation. Indeed, it is quite possible that having staff discuss their responses to a training

---

[29] Hirsch (2005).
[30] The importance of shared vision and sense of purpose have been highlighted in school improvement studies (Louis et al., 1999).

session in this manner might ultimately prove of greater value than the training presentation itself. But no such dialogue ever took place.

Staff meetings, which generally took place weekly, could have provided still another venue for organizational learning. They could have been used, at least in part, as case conferences, discussing their understanding of a particular child, what worked best, what did not appear effective, and how they might do a better job with that child – and similar children – in the future. Case conferences of this sort are routine in medical and mental health settings, and there is no reason they could not be usefully employed in after-school centers. But staff meetings focused almost entirely on operational issues (e.g., planning for specific events), with occasional discussion of problems raised by a particular child. Case conferences were never held.

These case conferences need not be run by expensive outside consultants or require the kind of educational background provided by an advanced graduate degree. The staff at these centers are professional youth workers and have accumulated a lot of expertise. The case conferences would involve sharing that expertise, passing it on to others across the organization, learning from each other. That is what learning organizations do.

In some organizations, the lack of a group focus on learning together can reflect high levels of staff conflict and low levels of cohesion. This was not the case at Midwest. Staff were quite reasonable about helping each other out when needed. We observed several instances when they effectively coordinated responses in stressful situations with a troubled young person. Yes, they might get a big grumpy about needing to help out (particularly with Charlene), but the degree of dissatisfaction was not severe. They also got along socially, typically eating together at the club when they did not have to do so. Some of them did things recreationally outside of the club on their time off. They never tried to work together as a learning organization because it was not part of their culture and it never appeared to occur to them to do so.

Indeed, working together in this new way might have required them to develop new levels of trust. It is one thing to get along socially and hang out together. It requires a different level of trust to tell a colleague how to do something differently (and, presumably, better). Midwest staff would probably need to work at developing this level of support and require a level of support from Bob that did not exist.

Evaluation data might have provided a much needed stimulus to engage in learning. However, the site did not evaluate the quality of its program offerings.[31] In particular, there was no formal vehicle for obtaining youth input and feedback. Several years ago, during the gender equity initiative, regional headquarters had mandated the establishment of a Girls Council. The girls who participated in Girls Council at Midwest had argued for new programs. However, the Girls Council was disbanded at the conclusion of the gender equity initiative and no other mechanism had taken its place.

There thus was little attention to staff learning at Midwest. The failure of the two administrators to provide supervision directed at staff learning was matched by the lack of other organizational vehicles that could have served this purpose. Is it then a surprise that Midwest did not have a strong focus on promoting positive youth development?

CONCLUSION

In taking an organizational lens to the Midwest club, we were able to identify both strengths and weaknesses that are likely to translate ultimately into youth outcomes. Midwest subscribed to the overarching goal of promoting positive youth development. But what does an examination of its actual practices reveal in terms of its understanding of and commitment to this objective?

The club director, Bob, wanted to recruit staff who would care about and connect with troubled youth, and in this he succeeded. Both Mateo and Manuel, the staff members we studied most intensively, interacted positively with youth and maintained order in a high-energy setting. They had an easy way of relating, repeatedly expressed their interest and support to young people, and developed long-lasting relationships with them. The quality of affective bonds was high.

Manuel was clearly the star staff person at Midwest and he would be an asset to any after-school center. Beyond a positive approach to working with youth, he enthusiastically tutored all who sought

---

[31] Attendance figures were obtained and were a major concern of the regional headquarters.

his help in math and started the highly successful chess club, which consistently engaged participants and taught them complex, challenging skills. Manuel was comfortable and skilled in pushing young people beyond their comfort zone to explore new possibilities and to grow and learn.

The game room provided plentiful opportunities to have fun with friends – an important Boys & Girls Clubs objective. Such settings are of great importance to young people, and they are in short supply in these dangerous neighborhoods where gangs and drug dealers dominate city parks.

In taking a deeper look at implementation at Midwest, it is important to note that the glass is both half-full and half-empty. Yes, Mateo did care about and establish close ties with the young people, but he did little to actively promote positive youth development. He radiated concern and goodwill, but engaged in little active mentoring.

In a similar half-full and half-empty vein, Midwest sponsored several programs that offered youth the opportunity to explore different roles, learn new skills, and have some success experiences. But Keystone and Torch were not implemented terribly well and this likely constrained developmental gains that accrued from participation.

Thus, Midwest had some pockets of excellence, but almost all of them revolved around a single staff member. Should Manuel leave, or burn out, the developmental potential of the setting likely would diminish dramatically. Outside of the chess club, there was no program of consistently high quality. The work culture was more comfortable being reactive than proactive. There was considerable complacency about the quality of program implementation. All of these were substantial weaknesses and reveal a center that was not clearly focused on doing all that it could do to promote positive youth development. They could talk the talk, but frequently did not walk the walk.

Organizational flaws in human resource development appear to be a major contributor to weaknesses in quality of program implementation. These flaws explain why there was not more excellence at Midwest. Staff hiring was not geared toward identifying individuals who were skilled and passionate about specific activities that could promote development. Yes, it is important to have staff who are interpersonally adept. But cannot centers recruit staff who get along well with young people *and* are good at teaching specific skills? We shall see later in the book that the West River Club managed to do this quite well.

Once a staff member joins the center, it is important to have mechanisms in place that lead to professional growth and development. Even star staff, such as Manuel, can do better in at least some areas. But improvement mechanisms were scarce at Midwest. Neither the club director nor his second-in-command provided much direct training and supervision. Indeed, they provided no real leadership for focusing on the promotion of positive youth development as the center's overarching priority. They did not consistently encourage and enable the staff to focus on promoting positive youth development whenever they could. There were many occasions when Midwest staff were presented with situations that could have led to reflection and to new understandings and practices that could enhance youth development, but that did not happen. There was little awareness of the possibilities for functioning as a learning organization and no evident commitment to this objective. Yes, a new (and trusted) staff person like Manuel could bring to the center new interests and develop a program or activity around it (especially if it is a traditional, male activity such as chess), but there is nothing in how the organization functions that would otherwise promote, develop, and support efforts at new program development or upgrading existing programs.

In terms of the criteria stated on the national Web site, Midwest does well enough on having caring staff, and a safe place to learn and grow while having fun, but makes a much weaker showing with respect to "promote and enhance the development of boys and girls by instilling a sense of competence, usefulness, belonging and influence." A strong focus on the latter should involve having staff rally around and work actively, collaboratively, in constant dialogue, to keep pushing development. This was not true of Midwest. Rhetoric and reality did not match. Is the bar too low for what constitutes positive development at Midwest, or is the concept so spongy and ambiguous that most anything could pass muster?

In the next two chapters, we turn to case studies of Midwest youth. Given the profile of organizational strengths and weaknesses, it is likely that these two young people will benefit to the extent that their needs, interests, and interpersonal style are a good match to Midwest's particular strengths. As Manuel stands head and shoulders above other staff members, connecting with him will be important. Given that staff tend to respond more reactively than proactively, it is likely that Pocahontas and Bill will need to display some agency and initiative in order to activate the latent resources at Midwest. They may not receive help in specific domains unless they solicit it. Finally, it should not be surprising if the gender issues that characterize Midwest as a work site percolate down to impact youth in its after-school programs. In a twist, though, we shall see that gender stereotypes appear to be more harmful to Bill than to Pocahontas. At the end of the second youth case study (Bill), we shall conclude the section on Midwest with an overall integration of the most important things we learned across the organizational and individual (youth) analyses.

3

Pocahontas Joins the Tribe

We knew from the start that Pocahontas[1] should be in our study. Before we had any idea what the story of her year would tell, what changes – good or bad – might take place, we understood that we had to find a place for her in our research. Lively and vivacious one moment, sullen the next, the moody Pocahontas had one of the most stressful family backgrounds of any young person who attended the after-school centers. There was little doubt in our minds: Pocahontas would be a challenge for club staff. She was full of potential, yet at high risk for a host of bad outcomes, and we suspected that there would be a lot to learn from the experiences of this 14-year-old Latina girl. As it turned out, Pocahontas made dramatic gains, and her tale provides a compelling illustration of the boost that after-school programs can provide to troubled youth. Among the stories we will tell in this book, Pocahontas's is particularly revealing of the synergistic effects of programs, activities, and mentoring in a comprehensive after-school center. Pocahontas became extremely well integrated into the life of the center – she "joined the tribe" – and the security of that attachment provided a critical anchor for resilience and growth.

IN THE BEGINNING

Pocahontas's physical appearance and demeanor remind one that adolescence is on the border between childhood and adulthood. Despite her mature build and self-reliance, Pocahontas more often displays a childlike appearance, not accentuating her curves or

---

[1] Each youth chose his or her own pseudonym.

striking facial features as many of her peers do, but clothing herself in baggy t-shirts and jeans. Pocahontas has short, jet-black hair that curls around her chin and frames her expressive face. Bangs fall heavily over her forehead to just above her dark, piercing eyes, and large silver-hoop earrings are the sole accessories that accentuate her cheekbones and jaw line. Her eyes are the most expressive feature on her face, alternately sparkling with laughter and flashing with anger when provoked. Her facial expressions range from stony silence to exuberant joy to resentful anger. Pocahontas makes an entrance and always makes herself known in a room. She does this without the benefit of flashy clothes or make-up, but merely with the strength of her personality. Pocahontas emerges as full of life and energy, but is quick to shut down and pull her head into her shell when pushed or provoked. Anger can make her lash out, whereas disappointment and frustration make her turn inward. In quiet moments, when no one else is around, her eyes sometimes brim with tears and her tough exterior melts, revealing the lonely child that she hides inside.

In some respects, Pocahontas seems to reflect the common stereotype of the adolescent. This is a time of life that has often been characterized in the popular and clinical literature as one of *sturm und drang* – storm and stress. Raging hormones have typically been implicated as the culprit for these dramatic ups and downs. As researchers began to investigate this topic scientifically, however, it became clear that the picture of storm and stress was not applicable to most teens.[2] It does seem to fit Pocahontas, and although she was still in the midst of pubertal change, hormonal fluctuations would rank low on her list of life concerns.

Full of abandonment and death, Pocahontas's family life history was extremely stressful. Her mother had left her at an early age and had died a few years prior to the year of our research study. Pocahontas had little knowledge of why her mother had left or what had been the cause of her death. Pocahontas reported being very close to her father, but he, too, had died, just one year before we met her. Although she talked very positively of her relationship with her father, in ways that suggested that she idealized him, there is reason to wonder about the quality of their relationship. Her father, after all, had problems with alcoholism and had not always been available to

---

[2] Arnett, 1999; Douvan & Adelson, 1966; Steinberg, 1990.

her. Although the parental losses were clearly the most important, they were not the only ones that Pocahontas had suffered. During our time with her, a great-uncle with whom she was close committed suicide, shooting himself in despair over a long-term illness.[3]

After her father's death, Pocahontas went to live with an aunt, but it was not a good fit. Aunt Aurelia had three kids of her own to handle, one of whom was disabled. Pocahontas reported that Aunt Aurelia "hates my guts." Some complaints about Aunt Aurelia seem like the usual teenage issues around being treated unfairly, having no control over her own life, and being subject to endless warnings about getting pregnant. Regardless, Pocahontas consistently described the relationship in intensely negative terms and never told us of moments of affection.

Fortunately, Pocahontas had a grandmother with whom she was close, but oftentimes she felt alone in the world. When we asked her about the most upsetting thing that has happened in her life, she told us, while crying, that it was: "My dad being gone and not having anyone to talk to and not having anyone who I think loves me or [is] there for me." Indeed, whenever she talked about her father, Pocahontas would become very moved, often in tears, looking away without eye contact, hunched over, withdrawing into her own world.

Some young people have close friends who help them get through bad times, but not Pocahontas. She could act friendly with other kids, but "I don't got no friends – I mean, there are people I talk to, but no friends."

This, too, was a consistent theme. As Pocahontas admitted, she had plenty of "associates," kids she could chat or hang out with, but no real friends.[4] She also avoided many of these associates because they pressured her to do things she didn't want to do: smoke dope, drink alcohol, and have sex.[5] So, at the beginning of the year, with

---

[3] Loss of a parent due to death or separation during adolescence is a risk factor for the development of depression (Lutzke, Ayers, Sandler, & Barr, 1997; Roy, 1985) as well as suicidal behavior (Wagner, 1997).

[4] Many youth from low-income urban communities use the term "associate" in this way (see Loder & Hirsch, 2003; Way, 1998)

[5] Socializing and forming friendships with peers who engage in problem behaviors (also referred to as "deviant peers") is a well-documented risk factor in adolescence for the development of problems such as delinquent behavior, substance use, school failure, and teenage pregnancy (Fergusson, Woodward, & Horwood, 1999).

the exception of her grandmother, Pocahontas was socially isolated and felt emotionally all alone.

It should not be surprising that these losses and ongoing relationship stressors negatively impacted her school life. At the end of the last academic year, she had received failing grades ("F") in all of her courses. Her behavior in school was also problematic; Manuel, the club staff member with whom she would wind up spending the most time, told us that she had gotten into numerous confrontations with both teachers and other students. If Pocahontas kept following this path, there was the clear potential that she would wind up dropping out of school. Such a course would not be unfamiliar to her. Her father had been a high school dropout, and she told us of half a dozen associates in her neighborhood who had already dropped out of school.

Thus, at the beginning of our research, we knew that Pocahontas was able to be lively and engaging but was also moody and tended to wall people off. Our staff often felt that they had to "walk on eggshells" when talking to her. She was at clear risk of academic failure. That by the end of the year Pocahontas would wind up doing much better was far from preordained and did not, frankly, even appear likely.

POCAHONTAS'S YEAR AT THE AFTER-SCHOOL CENTER

In this section we trace important developments over the course of the year we spent in the after-school center with Pocahontas. Two realms will be considered: 1) Pocahontas's relationship with Manuel, and 2) Pocahontas's involvement in game room activities and club programs. The PARC profile for Pocahontas is shown in Table 3.1 (recall that PARC provides a shorthand way of describing the program, activities, relationship, and culture that characterize any particular involvement).

Closest Staff Relationship

On our initial survey questionnaire, Pocahontas named Manuel as the staff person to whom she felt closest, and he continued to be her closest tie over the course of the year. The closeness of this tie came through in all of our assessment procedures. When we had Pocahontas draw the map of her social network, in which she placed nearest to her own name those individuals to whom she felt

TABLE 3.1. *Pocahontas' PARC profile*

Starts at beginning of year

P: –
A: walk home together
R: Manuel
C: caring, protection, safety

P –
A math tutoring
R mostly with Manuel alone, occasional peer participation
C value education, nonjudgmental, patience, encouragement, insistence

P –
A talk about stressful situations (e.g., longing for deceased parents)
R Manuel
C emotional support, availability, nurturance, perspective

P –
A ping pong
R peers
C energy, enthusiasm, competitive, leadership role

P Keystone
A sponsor activities, raise money, decision making, trips
R Juan
C routinized, modest engagement, unclear goals, poor conflict resolution

P formal mentoring program
A academic support
R adult female volunteer
C minimal affective involvement, no links to club staff

Starts in middle of year

P peer jury
A clean up in club, help other staff with tasks
R staff noticed and commented on
C service to club, youth participation, youth recognition

Starts at end of year

P –
A join staff for dinner
R all staff
C family-like, responsiveness to youth agency

Note: PARC is an acronym for program, activity, relationship, and culture. Not all PARCs have a program component.

closest, Pocahontas placed Manuel right next to herself. When we had her rate how close she was to each of the individuals on the map, she gave Manuel the highest possible closeness score ("5" on a 1–5 scale). On our quantitative measures of different dimensions of youth-staff ties, Pocahontas's ratings of her relationship with Manuel were well above the sample averages for positive characteristics and below the sample average for negative aspects of the relationship.[6]

The significance and range of this relationship are revealed when we asked Pocahontas during our first interview with her what Manuel had said or done that made her feel close to him: "He's like a father to me. Every time I need someone to talk to, he's there for me and he understands me. We spend a lot of time together – he walks me home and I do my homework with him when I want."

Pocahontas begins by emphasizing the emotional dimensions of the tie, going so far as to say that Manuel is like a father to her – not a trivial comparison, and especially striking given her own father's premature demise a year earlier. Surely, Pocahontas could use someone in her life who gives her some of what a father might. One of the things that fathers can provide is safety, and she is quick to point out that Manuel walks her home almost every night. For her, the dangers she faces outside go beyond those that come from living alongside three gangs in a violent neighborhood. Pocahontas herself was threatened over the phone by an anonymous older boy. He told her that if he found her alone outside, he was going to chase and beat her. So she had good reason to be afraid, perhaps even of being sexually assaulted. Manuel's easy willingness to walk her the few blocks home – he never made it seem like an imposition, rather just as the most natural thing to do – assured her safety, made it possible for her to attend the after-school center, and probably gave their relationship a symbolic, father-like component.

Pocahontas refers as well to Manuel helping her with her homework. It is clearly something of importance to her, given that she includes it in her answer as to why she is close to Manuel. Nonetheless, it is referred to with qualification ("when I want"),

---

[6] On our scale measuring positive dimensions of her relationship with Manuel, her T-score was 63.96, which is notably higher than the ratings given by other youth to the closest staff tie. Similarly, her T-score for her rating of the negative aspect of her relationship with Manuel (= 43.99,) was less negative than the ratings of other youth of their closest staff tie. Detailed information about these measures is presented in the Appendix.

indicating some ambivalence. Some of this comes through in the following field note.

> *Pocahontas was sitting at the table on the side near the file cabinet. Manuel was sitting across the table from her. He was helping her with her math homework. "I just don't understand it! I don't like math!" Pocahontas was saying. Manuel encouraged her to keep at it and said "look at your notes, what does it say there?" He helped her work out the problems following the notes she had taken in class. At some point a teen girl came over and leaned over the railing. Pocahontas looked up at her. "Just give us a few minutes here, okay?" Manuel said. The girl nodded and walked towards the pool table. "I don't want to write this out all again!" Pocahontas said picking up a piece of paper with multiplication tables written out on it. "Well, Pocahontas, that's why you don't know it. You gotta write it out to learn it," Manuel said.*

This situation is not unusual. Pocahontas is grumbling and a bit whiny, protesting about not wanting to do math. Yet she keeps at it. Manuel stays with her, being quite patient. He helps her work on her multiplication tables, a task that they address on more than one occasion. Now you might think that a student in eighth grade should be well beyond this topic, should have mastered it years ago. But many urban students are lacking in basic skills.[7] There are probably not many resources at her school to help. At the after-school center, however, this is not a problem for her. Time, willingness, and a non-judgmental approach are there. One person helping another, and glad to do so.

Manuel tutors Pocahontas in more advanced math topics as well. In this field note, he helps her with an algebra problem.

> *Pocahontas brought her math workbook over to Manuel and asked him to check her homework. He looked it over while she played ping-pong and then brought out a black board that he set on the benches across the room. When Pocahontas was done with her ping-pong game he called her over to the black board, on which he had written a math problem. Bill and Raphael also went over and stood watching. Manuel had the [algebra] equation written out. Bill and Raphael began to do the equation and Manuel asked Pocahontas how she should do it. She took the chalk from Raphael saying something about how he'd better leave and he said "okay okay you're the toughest girl I know!" as he ran behind Manuel to escape Pocahontas. Pocahontas worked out the problem on the board with Manuel's guidance. He would prompt her with questions to figure out what the next step was and then let her know if she had done it*

---

[7] Low-income and minority children score disproportionately lower on standardized math tests (Schoefeld, 2002).

right or not. At the end he nodded and she said "so which one is that? Which did I get wrong?" He gave her the workbook and she corrected the problem and looked at the others. Bill asked to see the workbook and she gave it to him to look at.

Manuel's patience – and teaching style – is on display here again. He does not take the easy way out and just give her the answer. He gets her to think about how she should solve the problem. He continues to ask her questions to push her thinking and understanding. He then gives her feedback as to correct and incorrect answers. Manuel is teaching her not only the answer to a specific question, but a way to go about solving mathematical problems more generally. In getting her to talk about her approach to the problem, she also provides him with information that he can use to give her feedback beyond merely whether her answer was correct. To clarify the value of Manuel's tutoring, we asked Professor Miriam Sherin of Northwestern University, an authority on secondary mathematics education, to evaluate Manuel's instructional style as reflected in these field notes. She concluded that his approach corresponds quite well with recommendations by mathematics reformers that have often proved difficult to implement successfully in school settings.[8]

In this instance, Manuel and Pocahontas work on math in a wider social context. Two teenage boys are there. When Pocahontas comes to Manuel with the problem, Bill and Raphael don't leave. Yes, they do joke a bit with her, but only for a moment. They hang around and begin to work on the problem themselves. Bill asks to look at the workbook on his own after Pocahontas is done. Interactional processes of

---

[8] "Manuel's instructional approach seems to balance several key goals of reform: (a) he allows and even encourages/expects the student to take the lead in problem solving, (b) the student is expected to talk about her solution during the process, (c) the tutor/teacher facilitates learning with key questions and suggestions, and (d) Manuel's approach to working with Pocahontas seems to demonstrate that he believes both that understanding the process and understanding the solution are important for the student. So while he is willing to tell Pocahontas if her answer is right or wrong, even so, he wants her to understand how and what she's done to solve the problem.... While these are important goals, research finds that they are often quite difficult for teachers to implement. Thus, it's quite interesting that in this informal context, and I assume without much, if any, training, Manuel successfully develops an approach that incorporates these goals" (Sherin, personal communication, June 6, 2004). See Hufferd-Ackles, Fuson, & Sherin (2004) and National Council of Teachers of Mathematics (2000) for background.

this sort are not unusual at this site. Someone will begin an activity and others will become curious and join in. So Manuel gets to provide academic assistance to three kids rather than just one. And some kids get help who might not seek it out, as Pocahontas does, on their own. The fluid environment of the club facilitates these interaction patterns. There is no teacher ordering everyone to stay in their seats and keep quiet. Friendship and academics are not seen as separate worlds. In after-school settings, you can mix and match, draw on spontaneous expressions of interest, use friendship as an aid to learning.

This is not to say that in after-school centers, there is a miraculous transformation of young folk into die-hard students. Pocahontas is unusual in her steadfast determination to get better at math. But she doesn't always enjoy it and doesn't always appreciate Manuel's efforts to keep her going. When we ask Pocahontas what she dislikes about Manuel, she tells us it is that "he's always pressuring me to do my homework. He gets on my nerves." The emotional give-and-take happens with after-school staff, just as it happens with parents and with teachers.

Manuel addresses more than Pocahontas's math problems. He is generally encouraging of her doing well in school. Pocahontas's school guidance counselor recommended that she apply to one of the academically weaker neighborhood schools. But Manuel has higher expectations for her and encourages her to do well enough so that she can enter a better high school.

Manuel's relationship with Pocahontas extends considerably beyond a focus on school. As Pocahontas emphasizes in response to our query as to why she feels close to him, she finds Manuel to be someone she can talk to, someone who understands her. When we ask her on another occasion to give us an idea of personal stuff she talks about with Manuel, she tells us that it is about

> *how I feel in my house or when I'm sad because I'm missing my dad or my mom.*
>
> *How does Manuel respond?*
>
> *He tells me that that's the past and even though they passed away, I have to think about them and do this to make them proud 'cause that will make them happy.*
>
> *Do you wind up feeling better?*
>
> *Sometimes – I forget about it, don't think about it.*

Manuel does what he can to comfort and reassure her. Sometimes it works. But Pocahontas's losses run deep and reemerge again and again.

Birthdays are freighted with symbolic meaning, and it wasn't altogether surprising, given her background, that Pocahontas approached her birthday with ambivalence. About three weeks before her birthday, we asked her if she was having a party to celebrate.

> *"Because the people who are supposed to be there aren't going to be there so I'm not going to have a party," Pocahontas said. I asked her what she meant and she looked me in the eye and said, "My father was supposed to be there but he's dead. My mother was supposed to be there and she's not coming either, so I'm not having a party." Pocahontas's eyes started to tear up.*

Later that day, we find Manuel comforting Pocahontas in an unusual, father-like interaction.

> *"Want some lasagna?" Manuel asked Pocahontas. She wrinkled her nose and shook her head. "You know I don't like you Manuel!" Pocahontas said loudly. Manuel didn't respond. Pocahontas laughed and came over to Manuel and sat very close to him, with her legs folded up onto the chair. She was almost leaning on him. "Come on, it's really good," Manuel said. Pocahontas shook her head. "I know all you ate were those hot chips! Look at your fingers!" Manuel said. Pocahontas smiled to herself and then pulled out another bag of hot chips. "You know what that does to your stomach lining?" Manuel asked. Pocahontas said no and that she didn't care. "Did you eat at home?" Manuel asked. "No, my aunt didn't cook today, so it's on us. I ate cereal," Pocahontas said. "Come on, eat some of my lasagna. I made it!" Manuel said. [He was lying now, unbeknownst to Pocahontas.] She looked over at it and raised an eyebrow. "Come on, I'll buy you peanut M&Ms if you eat a bit," Manuel offered. Pocahontas immediately grabbed the plate and fork from Manuel and took a bite. She chewed slowly, as though the food tasted bad. "Is it bad?" Manuel said. Pocahontas grinned and said no and then started chewing normally. She put the plate down. "Come on, you have to finish it," Manuel said. "You tricked me! You said one bite!" Pocahontas said. "I'll buy you a dollar's worth of M&Ms," Manuel said. "You'll get me the M&Ms?" Pocahontas asked. Manuel nodded. Pocahontas went about eating the lasagna and finished the whole thing. "There, now you've had a real dinner," Manuel said. Pocahontas smirked at him and then opened up her hot chips and started eating them. Manuel sighed and shook his head and then went to get Pocahontas her M&Ms.*

This episode provides striking evidence of the bond between Pocahontas and Manuel. There is a familiarity and intimacy in their sharing the same fork and plate of food, and in the give-and-take between them, which has a family feel. It also reflects Manuel's concern and nurturance on several levels. The importance of an adequate diet is not a trivial issue for many of these youth, coming from very-low-income families. Pocahontas herself has complained of being anemic. So staff members tend to do what they can to help kids eat as well as possible. The deeper meaning is an emotional one. Coming only an hour or so after Pocahontas's sadness over the fact that her deceased father and mother can't be at her birthday, Manuel's sharing of food reassures her that there is still care and affection for her in this world. Manuel provides her with an emotional nurturance that helps sustain her psychological as well as her physical well-being. He's there for her when she needs him. In accordance with the significance and multifaceted nature of Pocahontas's relationship with Manuel, it is a central component in three of the six PARCs at the beginning of the year (Table 3.1).

Manuel is clearly committed to Pocahontas, but working with her has its challenges.

How easy is she to get to know?
Not easy at all.
Why?
It's kind of like with Bill [next chapter] – she comes off kinda loud and obnoxious, but later, if she wants, she'll open up to you.
What is the most difficult or challenging thing about Pocahontas?
Her stubbornness. She's very self-conscious. It's near impossible to get her to believe in herself. It's not impossible. It's just hard.
Has your relationship changed with Pocahontas at all?
It's just grown.
How?
She feels freer now to come to me when she has issues or concerns. She'll pull me aside – I need to talk to you. She tells me what's up and then I give her the pep talk.
Pep talk?
Yeah, whatever pep talk goes with what's on her mind.
Do you ever have one-on-one conversations with her?
Yeah. They're short though ... instead of back and forth, I let her talk because that's what she wants. Then I say what I have to say.
Does she listen?
Yeah, she hears me.

Manuel is Pocahontas's confidant and motivator, in addition to ful-
filling the roles of protector, tutor, and nurturer we encountered
previously. He tries to identify what she needs and adapt himself
to her style. He remains patient and sees that their relationship has
developed. His commitment to her springs in part from seeing the
good in her, her potential, as he makes clear when we ask him to tell
us the best thing about Pocahontas:

> *I like that she has a lot of love – a lot of love in her. She's a really good kid.*
> *I guess her circumstances are hard. But I see the brightness in her.*

As winter faded and the weather turned warm, Pocahontas and
Manuel continued to be close but spent less time with each other.
Pocahontas began to deepen her ties with other staff members.
She began to spend more time with Jim, another staff member, and
in describing a photo she took of the two of them together at the
club, asked us whether Jim looked like he could be her father. In
addition to dyadic ties with other staff, toward the end of the year
Pocahontas became part of group get-togethers of the staff at the
club. Manuel made it possible for her to join most of the staff members during their dinner break. Only a few of the young people at
the club were part of this group, making it a special experience. So
the intensity of Pocahontas's relationship with Manuel diminished,
but they remained close, and the tie provided entrée into a broader
group of adults who welcomed her.[9] In terms of Pocahontas' PARC
profile, we see how the PARCs that revolved around her relationship with Manuel set the stage for the emergence of one later in the
year that encompassed a broader cross-section of staff at the after-
school center (Table 3.1).

Activities and Program Participation

The game room was the center of activity in this after-school center.
Many activities were constantly taking place in the game room, but
first among equals was ping-pong. Kids were almost always playing it with energy and enthusiasm, and there generally was a line,
with everyone waiting for their turn. At ping-pong, Pocahontas was
the undisputed master. She played frequently. Although she had

---

[9] Hamilton and Hamilton (2004a) discuss how adult mentors can broker such
experiences for young people.

no shortage of challengers, it was well known that if you played Pocahontas, you were likely to get beaten. Her participation in this activity remained constant throughout the year and thus was a consistent part of her PARC profile.

Sometime in the spring, we began to notice that Pocahontas was doing serious cleanup in the game room. She washed windows and swept floors, as noted in this fieldnote:

> *"Ooh, these kids – they be making a mess! I used to throw candy wrappers like this on the floor or hide them like in here (she dug a wrapper out of a hole in the wall), but not anymore – because I have to clean it!" Pocahontas said loudly to me and Manuel. We nodded. Pocahontas went and got a broom from the hallway closest. She continued to sweep.*

A teenager doing chores without fussing, without being reminded? What is this? It turns out that Pocahontas was doing cleanup, and helping out at the front desk, in fulfillment of a community service requirement for a peer jury program at a local school. The club and school had developed a relationship growing out of a drug prevention initiative (see prior chapter) and one result of this was that club members, such as Pocahontas, were eligible to participate in the school's peer jury program. This involved hearing the cases of students who got into trouble at the school, and recommending what penalty, if any, should be meted out. Pocahontas participated in this weekly activity, though she was reluctant to talk about it in any detail, and did her community service at the club. Interestingly, we see in this instance a PARC that factored significantly in Pocahontas' year at the club in which the instigating element was her involvement in a program outside of this setting (Table 3.1).

In terms of formal programs at the club, Pocahontas was most involved with Keystone, but her involvement had both ups and downs. Keystone is a leadership program that operates at all Boys & Girls Clubs nationwide. The club sponsors activities for the whole club (such as dances or trips), goes to regional and national Keystone conferences, and raises money (typically through food sales) for its activities. As we noted in the prior chapter, sometimes Keystone meetings at this site went well, other times they fell flat. Over the course of the year, Juan, the staff person who led the group, grew less skillful in managing group process. Pocahontas participated as actively as most other youth – which meant that she occasionally skipped it because she found it "boring" – and was picked to go to a regional conference, which is an honor and sought-after perk. As it turned out, Pocahontas was unable to go because she had to take an important standardized test at school during the time of the conference. Juan became quite annoyed at Pocahontas for backing out of the trip. We had difficulty understanding this, because if Pocahontas did not take the standardized test, she might not be promoted to the next grade. So it was hardly a trivial matter. Pocahontas, in turn, was upset that she was treated so poorly by Juan over this incident and stopped coming to Keystone meetings. In contrast with her other PARCs (Table 3.1), Pocahontas' experiences in Keystone were less positive and did not deepen her level of involvement at the center.

Pocahontas and Juan were to have an additional falling-out. The club hires a number of members to work there during the summer, helping out with younger kids. Pocahontas applied for such a position, but was turned down by Juan. During the summer, we stopped by the club and asked if Pocahontas had been coming. Juan responded that

> *"Yeah, she's been around. She could have worked here this summer if she wanted to, but she bombed the interview. She came up to me and just said 'Juan, interview me because Bob [club director] won't let me leave until I talk to you about working here.' So I mean, what I was supposed to do? I interviewed her and she did okay, but it didn't seem like she wanted to work here at all. And I didn't want to make her do something that she didn't want to. So she didn't get the job. And then when she didn't get it, she was really upset. I told her, you know, if you want something, you have to go after it. You have to show that you want it and do something about it. But her attitude didn't let me know that she actually wanted to do it and so I told her that I didn't want to make her do something that she didn't want to do, and then have to be after her all summer because she didn't want to be working here." Juan shook his head. "I think it was really hard on her not getting it, but..." he shrugged.*

Manuel agreed with Juan's decision. He, too, thought that Pocahontas had not been serious in her application. At the same time, there were several other club youth who very much wanted that summer position. So, in the absence of a greater number of summer jobs, it seemed reasonable that Pocahontas would not be selected. Hence, although Pocahontas was awarded special recognition, such as joining the staff dinner group, this status was not given on a permanent basis but needed to continue to be earned.

The final PARC (Table 3.1) that began early in the year was her involvement in a formal mentoring program based at the after-school site. Adult volunteers were matched with program youth and got together one night weekly. Pocahontas was matched with a woman, but we were not able to find out much about their relationship. Like several other youths at the site, Pocahontas acknowledged the relationship, and once wore a t-shirt that the woman had given her, but had little enthusiasm for talking about it. Nor did Manuel communicate independently with the female mentor.

DEVELOPMENTAL GAINS OVER THE YEAR

We indicated at the beginning of the chapter that Pocahontas made dramatic strides over the course of the year. Now that we have traced her involvement at the after-school center, let us turn to look more specifically at her gains.

Perhaps the clearest indication of positive change came from her school. The year before, when Pocahontas was not in the club, she received all Fs on her report card and was repeatedly getting into trouble with teachers and classmates. Her most recent report card, during the spring, demonstrated remarkable gains. She now had three Bs, including one in math, and only one F. And she was beginning to get some As on specific assignments. Furthermore, her behavior at school had also made a dramatic turnaround: Pocahontas had just received an award from school for most improved behavior. These are quite substantial gains over a relatively brief period of time.

The quality of Pocahontas' relationships with adults improved considerably as well. At the start of the year, interactions with her were often difficult. She could be loud, angry, or withdrawn. As Manuel noted,

> *In the beginning, she had an issue with everybody. I think she didn't know how to talk to people. She started with that attitude with everyone.*

By the spring, she had calmed down considerably (though not entirely). She was more open and self-disclosing, and gave clearer cues as to what she needed, so that club staff – and our researchers – had a better idea of how to approach her. Pocahontas had clearly developed an exceptionally strong relationship with Manuel, one of the closest relationships we had observed in our years of research.

Pocahontas had developed good relationships as well with a number of other staff (both male and female). We heard less talk from her of being alone in the world.

There were several positive developments in Pocahontas' relationships with peers as well, though the gains here were not as strong. For much of the year, Pocahontas claimed that she had no friends. By the spring, when we asked her to draw the map of her social network, she put down two club youth to whom she was moderately close. She had begun to spend considerable time together with one girl, Rita. After dinner, they were often the only two girls in the club. But Pocahontas was ambivalent as to whether her relationship with Rita had gone from being "associates" to "friends." Pocahontas had also developed a romantic tie to another club member, but this caused some friction with Rita, who did not feel that Pocahontas treated him well. Indeed, Pocahontas often did ignore her boyfriend in the club, though in our experience this was not unusual for romantic partners. At several other clubs, we would never have known, from observing their interactions, that some individuals were romantically involved (and had been, in some instances, over a period of years).

While Pocahontas made tentative positive strides in developing friendships and romantic ties, she resisted peer invitations to engage in problem behaviors. She broke up with one boyfriend when he insisted they have sex. And she continued to keep her distance from associates in her neighborhood who drank alcohol, smoked marijuana, and had active sex lives.

In addition to resisting negative social norms, Pocahontas's behavior increasingly reflected the development of positive social norms. She willingly helped clean the club (more so than any other youth we had observed over five years), assisted at the front desk, participated in Keystone fund-raising activities, and regularly attended peer jury. In these activities, she demonstrated discipline, commitment, responsibility, hard work, and an ability to be a team player. Furthermore, as the year went on, she began to help younger children and assist staff when they were overwhelmed in the game room. Caring, too, is a positive social norm.[10]

---

[10] Pocahontas did not feel cared for by her aunt. She told us that her aunt was taking care of her only for the money. Although Pocahontas did feel cared for by her father when he was alive, the care she experienced at the club probably contributed to her being able to be caring to others.

In terms of the development of other aspects of the self, or personality, the profile is a bit more mixed. Pocahontas did seem to take some of Manuel's pep talks to heart, telling us that due to Manuel,

> *I'm gonna learn to believe in everything I do and never sell myself short for nobody, and don't let nobody bring me down ... he tells me how I should always appreciate what I have, and that I'm smart and never to give up, and that I'm a very capable person.*

Furthermore, as noted, Pocahontas had developed skills in emotional self-control; she no longer had major temper outbursts, for example, which involved storming out of a room. It is also possible that she became motivated to use skills that she already had; for example, she felt remorse that she went too far once with Manuel, and really upset him, and was determined to be more restrained in the future. Like most teenagers, she had more room for growth, but her gains in this area were impressive.

The situation is a bit more complicated in terms of the development of autonomy, an important developmental task of adolescence. Pocahontas was quite concerned with becoming as independent as possible. When we asked her about goals for next year, she told us that she wanted to be more independent. Indeed, she wanted to be able to get a job and make money, so that she would not have to rely on her aunt, and that she hoped to move out of her aunt's apartment and be able to live on her own when she turned seventeen. Her drive for independence derived not only from developmental pressure, but from her poor relationship with her aunt. Wanting to become more independent appeared to be more than merely talk. For example, we asked Pocahontas whether she was doing anything now so that she could become more independent. She told us, yes, that

> *[I'm] tryin not to need nobody's help.*
>
> *Like with what?*
>
> *Like Manuel with homework.*

Taking initiative and trying to do her homework on her own has its commendable side. However, given her extremely poor academic performance until recently, and some questionable basic skills, cutting herself off from adult help could prove terribly short-sighted. In order to further her long-term goals of independence, she may need to sacrifice some short-term independence. This is a difficult psychological dilemma, and not just for Pocahontas. It troubles many teenagers, who need to become more independent without sacrificing adult connections and support.[11] And it is not a dilemma just for adolescents. In research we have conducted with adults in terms of their own life situations, the same issue rears its head repeatedly. For example, the first author studied women, in their late twenties thru mid-fifties, who had recently lost their husband.[12] Many of these widows were quite reluctant to ask for – or appear to be asking for – help. So they would arrange to have coffee and chat, and during that chat their friend or relative might say or do something helpful, without the widow having to acknowledge that she had sought "help." Pocahontas, likewise, appeared increasingly concerned about what it meant to receive help, and it is possible that this may partially explain the decrease in her interaction with Manuel that we observed over the course of the year. So, yes, she was striving to become more independent, but that has both advantages and disadvantages.

POCAHONTAS IN THE MIDWEST AFTER-SCHOOL CENTER: STRENGTHS, SHORTCOMINGS, AND SYNERGIES

At this point we turn to a more analytical discussion of what we have learned from studying Pocahontas's year at the Midwest after-school center. We will begin by considering benefits she derived from the programs, activities, and relationships (PARCs) she formed. For Pocahontas, there were some important synergies among these different elements, and we shall do our best to understand the workings of these systems dynamics. We shall examine shortcomings in the after-school center as well: areas in which the club could have done better and could realistically make improvements. Our goal is to understand how being at the after-school center may have helped Pocahontas make such substantial gains over a short period of time.

It should be emphasized that in considering the strengths, shortcomings, and synergies of the club, we do so in relation to

[11] Grotevant & Cooper, 1998; Steinberg, 1990.
[12] Hirsch, 1980.

the specific circumstances of Pocahontas's life and psychological makeup. Pocahontas's life had been filled with a series of extraordinary losses and she often felt alone in the world, with little trust or sense of security. She was failing at school, and neither her teachers nor her aunt had high expectations of her. Pocahontas desperately needed psychosocial and educational resources to address these major gaps in her life.

Strengths

The Midwest center provided Pocahontas with an array of *activities* that were enjoyable and appeared to provide her a sense of competence. Pocahontas was the best at ping-pong, the central activity of the game room, which was at the heart of club life. She participated in Keystone, often working at the Keystone "store," selling snacks to center youth. She cleaned up in the game room. She occasionally relieved staff at the front desk, serving as a receptionist. She helped staff run the basketball tournament, even though she herself did not play the sport. She did well at all of these activities and exceptionally well in some. These displays of competence, explicitly recognized by others, provided a foundation for personal growth that had been lacking at school and in her aunt's home. For Erik Erikson, this sense of industry is a crucial developmental task.[13] Without it, the young person develops a sense of inferiority – an issue with which Pocahontas still struggled.

Judith Musick argued that a sense of industry or competence was critical to helping young adolescent girls avoid teen motherhood.[14] According to Musick, it is important to have "a sense that she is a person who gets things done and does them well, a person successfully growing up and into the wider world.... They provide the cognitive and emotional anchors to steady her.... Her sense of industry is her psychological insurance against a sense of inadequacy, hopelessness, inferiority – the sense that she will never amount to much" (p. 43).

In addition to providing the basis for developing competence and a sense of industry, activities at the after-school center enabled

---

[13] Erikson, 1963, 1968.
[14] Musick, 1993.

Pocahontas to become part of a peer group. There were kids her age with whom she could hang out, gossip, have fun, and explore new interests. The activities provided her a basis for getting to know these other youth and develop her ties to them. Moreover, her expertise at ping-pong gave her a valued place in the group. Although Pocahontas had a group of peers outside of the club, she tried to avoid them, as they engaged in risky activities; without her club associates, she did not have a peer group to be with at an age when such ties are so important. She may not have developed an intimate friendship with any of them, but being part of such a group is valuable in and of itself.[15]

Another major benefit of activities at the center is that they distracted Pocahontas from the emotional stresses associated with her parents' deaths and current living circumstances. Cognitive avoidance is one of the main strategies available to help us cope with potentially overwhelming emotions.[16] Even at the club, Pocahontas would occasionally dissolve in tears when thinking of her father, and some of her temper outbursts may have been a reaction to reminders of her parents' death or to ongoing tensions at home. Activities at the after-school center undoubtedly distracted her from obsessing about those troubles. The game room at the Midwest club was a constant whirlwind of action and interaction. It was busy and loud. There was too much going on to ruminate much about the outside world. Even our research assistants experienced this, telling us that no matter what was bothering them, be it academic deadlines or romantic issues, the troubles were left behind as they entered the fast-paced environment of the club.

Although distraction and avoidance do not initially sound like positive strategies, that is exactly what Pocahontas – and the rest of us – need when confronting overwhelming loss. We need some time and place to get out of ourselves and take a break from stress. Certainly, Pocahontas had lots of other potentially distracting activities available: She could have gotten drunk, or high on drugs, or lost herself in sexual escapades. These alternative avoidance strategies were readily available to Pocahontas; by no means would she have been the first to go down any of those routes. Instead, she distracted

---

[15] See Brown (2004) for a review of the literature on peer friendships and peer groups in adolescence.
[16] Krohne, 2003; Thoits, 1990.

herself by engaging in positive activities – clearly a better choice for her and for society.[17]

The *relationships* that Pocahontas formed with adult staff at the center appeared to play a critical role in her growth and resiliency. The relationship with Manuel was the key tie. The caring and affectionate relationship that Manuel provided addressed her basic needs for security, attachment, affection, belonging, and respect – needs that, many psychologists have argued, provide a necessary foundation for personal development.[18] In simple terms, Manuel was the parental figure that Pocahontas was desperately seeking. He nurtured her physically and psychologically, protected her against threats to her physical safety, supported her in multiple roles, and did not waver in his regard no matter what happened. Pocahontas learned that she could depend on Manuel, that he was always there for her. This provided her with what attachment theorists call a "secure base," or an emotional security, from which she could then explore the world with confidence.[19]

Pocahontas's use of Manuel as a secure base is evident both within and outside of the club. Within the center, as the year went on, she spent more and more time with other staff members, so that several adults effectively became part of her extended family. As she cultivated these ties, our field notes indicate that she would from time to time come back to Manuel and tell him affectionately, "I still love you," in a way that suggests the secure-base phenomenon.

Manuel's tutoring of Pocahontas in math, and general encouragement and support of her academic involvement, appears critical to her improved school grades. It is difficult to imagine what else might account for this improvement, given that Pocahontas herself attributes it specifically to Manuel's help with homework, and we are not aware of anyone else who either helped her with her assignments or was as encouraging of her ability to do well at school. The emotional tie that she had to Manuel likely played a major role in her receptivity to his tutoring.[20] Pocahontas could have gone to

[17] This would be considered a higher-level coping (defense) mechanism (e.g., Vaillant, 1977).

[18] Erikson, 1963, 1968; Maslow, 1968.

[19] Cassidy & Shaver (1999) provides a good collection of work in this area.

[20] Extensive research by Public/Private Ventures on mentoring relationships leads to the conclusion that a multifaceted relationship is important to the youth's receptivity to academic tutoring efforts (Sipe, 1996). See, also, Rhodes (2002) for a thoughtful discussion of mentoring.

the club's formal homework help sessions (Power Hour), but did not, choosing instead to seek out Manuel. For his part, Manuel was quite receptive to her desire for assistance and very patient and supportive.

The relationship that Manuel provided Pocahontas is much stronger than she likely would have been able to obtain in a typical stand-alone mentoring program. In those programs, mentors are assigned, sometimes on the basis of a presumed affinity that is never realized.[21] By contrast, at the after-school center, Pocahontas was free to seek out the staff person whom she was most drawn to on the basis of natural chemistry, giving her agency and ownership of the choice. The amount of time that Pocahontas and Manuel spent together and the consistency of his being there for her would rarely, if ever, be duplicated in a stand-alone program. The after-school center, and Pocahontas's almost daily attendance, permitted both a wider-ranging and more intensive relationship, and Pocahontas and Manuel made full use of those possibilities. Furthermore, the relationship was cross-gender, which is rare in stand-alone programs, especially for female youth with male adults.[22] It involved as well a certain amount of physical contact which, though completely nonsexual, would have been problematic in less public settings. This fatherly relationship was particularly important to Pocahontas at this point in her life.

Shortcomings

There are a number of programs and activities that the club did not offer that would have appealed to Pocahontas.[23] She loved to paint, and although the site did have an art room, no staff person was assigned to it and the room was rarely utilized. She enjoyed writing, in part as a way to express her feelings, but there was no vehicle that allowed her to pursue this interest. A youth newspaper that reported on activities at her club, or across the different clubs in the city, would have addressed this interest. Working on the newspaper would probably have improved her writing and

---

[21] Rhodes (2002).

[22] Bogat & Liang (2005).

[23] McLaughlin, Irby, & Langman (1994) provide examples of excellent youth programs.

computer skills. Being part of a team with other youth could have strengthened her peer ties.

A newspaper might also have avoided some of the difficulties that she and other youth experienced with Keystone. The latter program often did not have a clear goal. Funds were raised mainly so that some youth could travel to regional or national Keystone meetings, but not all youth could be funded, leading to conflict. The newspaper experience would have been more inclusive, with a more tangible, regular product.

In addition to skill development, and the satisfaction that comes from seeing something emerge from hard work, having more to do would have kept Pocahontas, and other kids at the center, from being bored. It may not be possible to eliminate periods of boredom when young people spend hours a day, four to five days a week, at a center. But they can be reduced. On many days, when Pocahontas tired of ping-pong, or didn't want to work on her math, there was little else for her to do beyond hanging out.

The Keystone program had difficulties that went beyond its goal structure. In theory, the program was designed to facilitate youth leadership. In practical terms, this translates to encouraging youth to express their own ideas and take responsibility for implementing them effectively. Some developmental theorists would interpret this as giving youth "voice."[24] However, when Pocahontas exercised her voice and, to us, responsibly informed Juan that she could not attend the conference because she needed to take an important standardized test the date of the trip, Juan reacted negatively, leading Pocahontas to stop coming to Keystone. Juan should have been more flexible and demonstrated better problem-solving skills. Sometimes the voice of youth will differ from the preferences of staff, and it is up to staff to provide adult leadership, to take the lead in resolving conflicts adaptively.

Synergies

As discussed in Chapter 1, the connections that exist (or could exist) between different PARCs is central to our understanding of the quality of comprehensive after-school centers. Pocahontas

[24] Brown & Gilligan, 1992; Harter, 1999.

provides an excellent example of such synergies. Our initial focus is on several positive synergies among different areas of involvements (i.e., PARCs) that were salient in characterizing her year at the center.

The most potent form of synergy is when "the whole is greater than the sum of its parts." This is a tough, and ambiguous, criterion. Our thinking about this issue has been influenced by work being done by complexity theorists in a wide array of domains, from physics to biology to economics.[25] Consider, for example, a chemical reaction. When you put enough of the right kinds of chemicals together, a reaction occurs spontaneously and new chemicals are formed. The new chemical is an emergent property of this interacting chemical network. The presence of a catalyst facilitates the development of the network. Stuart Kauffman used such an approach to theorize how elements of the primordial soup first came together to create life.[26] Our ambitions here are decidedly more modest, though by no means easy: to consider how the different aspects of Pocahontas's experiences at the Midwest Center became networked together in a manner that created emergent experiences. Had those experiences not become networked together, or interacted as part of a system, those emergent experiences would not have occurred (or are much less likely to have occurred). Specifically, we believe that had Pocahontas attended different after-school sites that allowed for only one PARC each, rather than a comprehensive center, certain critical experiences and developments would not have happened. Let us examine this argument step by step.

Pocahontas was involved in a number of activities and programs and interacted with all of the staff. As time went on, her involvement in activities with some staff were noticed more and more by other staff. Thus, all staff were aware of the time that Manuel and Pocahontas spent together, given that much of it took place in the game room and other staff were frequently nearby. Some of those staff members, in fact, told us that they had noticed that Pocahontas was interacting better with adults and youth and that she was more stable emotionally. All of us like to know that we are doing well

[25] For example, Arthur, Durlauf, & Lane, 1997; Kauffman, 1995. Much of this work is being done at the Santa Fe Institute. A popular introduction to this field is provided by Waldrop (1992).
[26] Kauffman, 1995.

at our work. After-school staff are no different and take satisfaction in seeing that they are having a positive impact on youth. In many instances, concrete evidence of having a positive impact is lacking, but it was available with respect to Pocahontas. The fact that other staff could see the evolvement of Manuel's relationship with Pocahontas, and the subsequent improvement in her behavior, probably increased their motivation to associate with her and contribute to her success.[27] Thus, positive momentum had been built and the pre-conditions for increased involvement of other staff had been put in place.

The catalyst for helping the reaction "catch fire" probably involved the service and help that Pocahontas increasingly provided to the club.[28] Over time, she did more and more for the club: selling snacks in the club "store" run by the Keystone program, cleaning up as part of her community service requirement for Peer Jury, helping out with younger kids, assisting with receptionist duties at the front desk, and running interference for staff when they became overwhelmed in the game room. This was a new role and one which she assumed willingly. Not many teenagers pitch in and do their chores without arm-twisting! The role was also performed in very public settings. It made life easier for staff (by sharing some of their duties) and contributed to the quality of life at the club.

As Pocahontas increasingly assumed this contributing role over time, it seems that the chemistry took off and staff responded by having her join their dinner group. This new PARC emerged as a systems-level response from the catalyzed network. A positive feedback loop had been generated whereby gains were reciprocated, leading to a new cycle of growth and development.[29]

---

[27] There is support for this thesis from a variety of research studies across the social sciences. Arthur (1994), who has made important contributions to complexity theory, has highlighted the importance of positive feedback, increasing returns, and self-reinforcing processes to explain economic phenomena. Social psychologists have found that persons may selectively identify or associate themselves with successful, high-prestige individuals or groups as a way of boosting their own self-esteem (Tesser, 1988).

[28] Lerner (2004) also emphasizes the importance of youth contribution. Whereas his analysis focuses on factors that lead to youth contribution, our analysis here considers the impact of youth contribution on catalyzing program staff. The complementary perspectives highlight the importance of this factor.

[29] Community psychologists have emphasized how resources can be recycled in settings (Kelly, 2006).

This kind of synergistic effect is unlikely to have occurred had these different PARCs not been networked together in the center. Do a thought experiment: Imagine that Pocahontas segmented her different activities across different sites, so that she went to Site X for math tutoring, Site Y for community service, and Site Z for leadership experiences, coming to the club only once a week to play ping-pong for two hours. Under those conditions – par-for-the-course for many suburban youth – Pocahontas probably would have had much less commitment to the club. Most likely, Pocahontas would not have volunteered very readily, if at all, to help out around the club. Would club staff have invited her, under those circumstances, to join their dinner group? Not likely. When she did all those activities at the same site, however, those same experiences now combined to lead to the invitation. At the Midwest after-school center, experiences combined to make the whole greater than the sum of its parts, whereas this probably would not have occurred if the very same experiences had occurred in different sites.

The symbolic and practical consequences of inclusion in the staff dinner group should not be underemphasized. For any teenager, being treated more like an adult, and being afforded quasi-staff status, is an important developmental milestone and sign of recognition.[30] For Pocahontas, in particular, orphaned and often feeling bereft of supportive kin ties, becoming part of the staff group likely gave her the experience of family that she craved.

Even in the fall, Pocahontas had indicated to us on a survey questionnaire that she considered the after-school center to be a "second home." In earlier research, we had found that having close, warm interpersonal ties was the main factor that led youth to consider the club a second home.[31] There is every reason to think that Pocahontas's strong relationship with Manuel played a major role in her experience of the club as a home. Indeed, it was at the center of three of her six PARCs at the start of the year. In addition, the center provided a place where many parts of her self could be at home: her enjoyment of ping-pong, her desire to improve her school grades, her varied moods, and so on. These varied elements combined synergistically to create this experience of home. It is unlikely that

---

[30] Coleman (1961, 1974) has written extensively on the importance of youth integration into the adult world.

[31] Deutsch & Hirsch (2002).

Pocahontas would have had this experience so fully in the absence of some of these elements.

Pocahontas' inclusion in the staff dinner group probably deepened even further her experience of the center as a home and of being part of a family there. Moreover, this deeper experience reflected her own agency, in repeatedly and voluntarily contributing to the center, and staff's positive response to her agency. Becoming part of the dinner group signaled an evolving system of reciprocity. As Pocahontas matured within the center, staff recognized and validated her development and new social identity. The increased reciprocity within this system of relationships made it a stronger social unit and made her bond with it more meaningful.[32] Thus, we can theorize, synergy among different areas of involvement in the after-school center led both to emergent actions and emotional experiences.

These synergistic effects were positive, in the sense that the different elements combined in ways that were advantageous to Pocahontas. There were no apparent negative synergies, in which elements combined in ways that were disadvantageous or unhelpful to her. However, there were missed opportunities for positive synergy. Pocahontas had a formal, volunteer mentor, but there was no communication between this woman and club staff and no linkages between this PARC and others. As noted, it is also possible that had there been additional activities such as newspaper or art, this could have led to helpful synergies in terms of Pocahontas's peer ties.

CONCLUSION

Pocahontas is clearly a success story. She made many positive developmental gains and avoided getting involved in a host of problem behaviors. Center activities and programs, and the relationships she formed there, all appeared to contribute to the remarkable turnaround she demonstrated in nine months. Her trajectory of improvement closely mirrored positive changes in her PARC profile from a tie to a single staff member and a few activities to a much broader set of relationships and activities. Pocahontas' own agency in this story of resilience and growth should not be slighted – her efforts

---

[32] In the social science literature, this would be seen as providing Pocahontas with increased social capital (see Coleman, 1990; Putnam, 2000).

helped catalyze latent systems of support and realize more fully the developmental potential of the setting. Particularly noteworthy were her persistence in seeking out help with her math homework and, later, the many service contributions she made to the functioning of the club.

Links to her life at school (school grades and behavior) and family (walking her home, and modest staff-family contact) helped embed Pocahontas' after-school experiences in the broader contours of her world. Center experiences were meaningful not only within the club, but carried over into the other important domains of her life. The center provided the core, a strong extended family, which helped her navigate through those rough and sometimes hostile environments. She developed a better and more secure place in the center community, which soothed her spirit and gave her hope of a meaningful future. This sense of belonging and making a place for oneself in society is important to all young people, but was especially salient to Pocahontas given her traumatic family history.

Pocahontas's experiences at the Midwest center illuminate features of that setting discussed on a more organizational level in the preceding chapter. Recall from Chapter 1 that organizational features of comprehensive after-school centers can make important contributions of center quality by influencing the quality of different programs and activities (i.e., PARCs). On the positive side, the Midwest center's concern with troubled youth, and emphasis on community links, were reflected in the attention Pocahontas received and in her participation in Peer Jury. In terms of organizational limitations, communication problems were evident in the lack of consultation between Manuel (or other center staff) and Pocahontas's formal, outside mentor. The lack of supervision – and, more broadly, quality control – could be seen in the downward drift of Keystone sessions over time, which led Pocahontas to quit the program. This drift might have been reversed with proper supervision or in-service sessions devoted to that program.

Gender biases in center leadership against girls (discussed in Chapter 2) did not, in this particular instance, play a major negative role in Pocahontas's experiences. Yes, Pocahontas probably would have enjoyed participating in an arts program and in a youth newspaper, both of which might be considered to be more female oriented. On the other hand, leadership's orientation toward girls and women may actually have worked to Pocahontas's advantage. One traditional role readily available to young girls is that of a "damsel in distress." Pocahontas fit this role well, with the deaths of her parents and unhappy life with aunt juxtaposed with her physical attractiveness and vivaciousness. If she were indeed cast in this role, which seems likely, as even some members of our research staff responded to her in part in this manner, it could have contributed to the mobilization of staff on her behalf.

Despite these qualifications, the story of Pocahontas is a powerful illustration of how after-school programs can benefit troubled youth. She drew deeply from the center's multiple resources and suffered little from its limitations. If all young people at comprehensive after-school centers benefited as much as Pocahontas did over a nine-month period, we would declare them a major success and be greeted by thunderous applause. We will have more success stories to tell, but none quite as clear-cut. And not all of our stories will be of successes.

As we seek to account for these differential outcomes, we shall rely extensively, as we did with Pocahontas, on a detailed examination and interpretation of each youth's PARC profile. The extent of developmental change is dependent not merely on each individual PARC, but on the linkages over time among PARCs. These linkages contribute in important ways, sometimes positively (as for Pocahontas) and sometimes negatively, to youth outcomes. Next, in Chapter 4, we will study the PARC profile of Bill, another youth at the Midwest center. We will then integrate in Chapter 5 our case study of Midwest as an organization with the case studies of Pocahontas and Bill to begin to elaborate a theory of after-school practice. We hope that this theory will help us understand – and improve – the quality of comprehensive after-school centers.

4

Bill: The Pros and Cons of Being One of the Guys

Like Pocahontas, Bill is a difficult character to miss. On the one hand, he is quintessentially "one of the guys," shooting hoops, playing ping-pong, and tossing around the term "gay" as his insult of choice. He can be loud and disruptive, with a history of school trouble for both fighting and academic failure. Yet closer observation reveals an intelligent boy with an introspective tendency and interests in social issues, chess, and history. The Midwest after-school center serves as a safe space for Bill, a place of moratorium where he escapes the pressure of gang activity present in his school and neighborhood.[1] His involvement in the chess club allows him to shine and develop relationships with staff. But Bill's story is also one of missed opportunity. He would have benefited from mentoring around his grades and school conflicts. Bill is not able to fully connect with the resources he needs because his demeanor feeds into stereotypes of male self-sufficiency. His one-of-the-guys persona winds up hurting him, hiding his need for the type of interpersonal support that Pocahontas was so successful in accessing. Bill's story illustrates a hidden danger of urban masculinity, especially in a setting such as Midwest, which is not oriented to proactive intervention.

AN INTRODUCTION TO BILL

Bill is tall and imposing, with toffee-colored skin. A large gold medallion hangs around his neck and his clothes of choice are sports

---

[1] Halpern, Barker, & Mollard (2000).

jerseys with baggy jeans, worn low to display his brand-name underwear. Bill demands attention, both by his physical stature and demeanor. Something about his presence sets him apart from other Hispanic boys at Midwest. He is not afraid to speak up and often dominates conversations. Bill at once engages you and holds you at bay, enjoying conversations but remaining guarded about what he reveals. In such ways, Bill is a typical fourteen-year-old male. As a freshman in high school, he has to negotiate new social territory. In a school plagued by gangs, posturing is part of what is required to keep him safe.[2] He reports having "too many friends to count" who have dropped out of school, gotten in trouble with the law, and are involved with gangs and drugs. He, too, has a police record as a result of a fight at school.

At the same time, there is something distinctly not one-of-the-guys about Bill. An edge of shyness peeks through his facade. Although he can strut with the best of them, at the beginning of the year Bill seemed uncomfortable around guys his age and older. He tended to hang out with boys and girls in the grade below him. Bill can be quiet and introspective, drifting off into the inner recesses of his mind. In one-on-one conversations, he is often reflective, letting down his masculine front. Bill is bright and prone to social commentary, such as when he announced that he would not be celebrating Thanksgiving because it is a celebration of Americans killing the Indians. "It's No Thanksgiving," he exclaimed, nodding emphatically to punctuate his point. The staff reacted as they often did to Bill, with shakes of the head and rolls of the eyes.

Bill's socio-intellectual bent is typically disguised under a masculine, "street" demeanor. This hinders Bill from fully benefiting from the club, as his needs are not always recognized. As noted previously, Midwest is not a particularly proactive organization. Staff respond well to crises but seldom identify problem areas that may be hidden from open view. This organizational shortcoming is a distinct disadvantage for Bill, as he hides behind his masculinity, not openly displaying his need for help.

---

[2] In a prior study, a club director told a researcher that he expected youth to display a certain "toughness" outside the club because it was necessary for their survival on the streets of the neighborhood (Deutsch, 2008). Others have discussed the ways in which "hypermasculinities" can be a reaction to fear and a means of gaining of respect (Barker, 1998; Goodey, 1998; Seaton, 2007).

Bill lives with his mother, aunt, and three female cousins. He reports a very close relationship to his aunt, whom he says he can confide in about anything.[3]

> *I tell her everything I do, no matter what. Whether it's good or bad ... [what I like about her is] that I can trust her. She won't judge me ... a little while ago I was talking and she gave me advice and told me about her past, what she'd done.*

Staff believe that Bill would not respond to personal, one-on-one conversations. They tried to develop ties with Bill through activity rather than personal conversations – a strategy in line with stereotypes of male friendship patterns as activity-based. Yet the quote above indicates a desire for and appreciation of personal interactions. In his interviews, Bill talks about how his aunt gives him advice and tells him about her past. She and one male friend were the people to whom he felt the closest. Bill was neither offered nor sought such relationships with staff at Midwest. It appears that staff attributed masculine stereotypes to Bill, assuming he did not want such relationships. Yet Bill indicates the importance of personal conversations in describing his attempt to talk to Dude, a fourteen-year-old club member and Bill's closest male friend at Midwest:

> *[I] tried seriously [to talk to Dude], then [I tried] joking around and his mind was somewhere else. Made me feel, like, if you talk to someone and they listen, but he was wandering off so made me switch to another topic. [Has this incident affected your relationship with Dude?] Kind of. I'd rather not talk to him about stuff that's important to me right now.*

Despite his desire for close relationships, Bill did not feel close to or trusting of either his peers or adults. He could "be himself" around peers but generally could not be his "real self" around adults.[4] In one-on-one interviews with researchers, however, Bill displayed a thoughtful and fairly open nature. He reported enjoying the interviews because they let him "get stuff off my chest." After his first

---

[3] Bill's aunt serves as a natural mentor for Bill. Although research points to the importance of natural mentors (see Zimmerman, Bingenheimer, & Behrendt, 2005 and Spencer, 2007b for reviews), it has also been suggested that a balance is needed between family and non-family natural mentors, especially in the realm of academic achievement (DuBois & Silverthorn, 2005a, 2005b; Sanchez, Esparza, & Colon, 2008).

[4] This information is drawn from Bill's scores on scales in the third interview.

interview, Bill was all smiles, exclaiming that the interview was "raw"[5] and encouraging Dude to do one too.

Bill is also capable of engaging on an intellectual level not advertised in his public persona. He chose his pseudonym after Bill Gates – not exactly the poster-boy for urban masculinity. Yet Bill has issues with trust. He is resentful of adults who don't trust him and often takes out this frustration on Juan, who Bill paints in stark opposition to a former staff member with whom he was close.

In line with the introspective side of himself, Bill admits that he worries a lot. His tendency to "think too much" is the aspect of himself that he likes the least. "I think too much, worry too much about everything that happens to me. Anything that happens to me I think about it the whole day." Bill would like to be calmer and not think as much. He tries to relax, do things with friends, or listen to music to take his mind off of things. Indeed, Bill sometimes seems to be somewhere else, going through the motions of activities but ruminating on other issues. He often acts out and is prone to being disruptive. His outbursts may reflect a desire to escape stress and distract himself from his overactive mind.

Bill does have a number of stressors. He has moved a lot and changed schools three times. In the twelve months prior to the first interview, his mother was seriously ill, Bill was physically attacked, and his aunt had her third daughter. He began high school, was suspended for fighting, and got a police record for a fight. Bill was failing two of his high school classes and was frustrated with his teachers, whom he felt didn't care whether or not the kids learned. He sees the kids as having more control over the classroom than his teachers. Bill wants to attend a "better" high school but does not make any effort to do so. He reports wanting to avoid staying back, but admits not doing anything to ensure that he will pass ninth grade. As a result of his fighting and poor academic achievement, Bill is at risk for school dropout and gang involvement.[6]

---

[5] Raw is a slang word for cool.

[6] Gang involvement has been associated with delinquency, hanging out with law-violating peers, detachment from school, low academic achievement and expectations, and feelings of low social control at school (Gordon, Lahey, & Rolf, 2004; Johnstone, 1983; Rizzo, 2003; Stoiber & Good, 1998; Thornberry, 1998; Vigil, 2003; Wood, Furlong, Rosenblatt, Robertson, Scozzari, & Sosna, 1997). Violent delinquency has been linked to gang recruitment and membership (Gordon et al., 2004; Johnstone, 1983; Stoiber & Good, 1998; Thornberry, 1998). Bill was environmentally and socially at risk for school dropout due to his being Mexican

Bill has been coming to Midwest since he was nine years old. He is one of the few teens there in both the afternoon and evening. Despite this, Bill complains that the club has declined in recent years and that there is less for him to do. Yet he was involved throughout the year in Keystone and the chess club. He also helped out with the Keystone store and did work around the club, including sweeping and monitoring the front desk. By the end of the year, Bill had scored one of the coveted summer jobs at Midwest, which would put him in a leadership role with younger members.

BILL'S YEAR AT THE AFTER-SCHOOL CENTER

The story of Bill in the Midwest club revolves around two main issues: 1) his involvement with the chess team, and 2) the club's role in risk management around violence and school dropout. Like Pocahontas, Bill benefited from a combination of positive PARCs, particularly chess club and the staff dinner group (see Table 4.1). These PARCs provided opportunities for developing relationships with staff and peers and a sense of validation and belonging. Yet unlike with Pocahontas, the PARCs did not address the important academic and psychosocial issues with which Bill was struggling and where he could have benefited from more direct adult involvement. Whereas some needs were met by the chess club, opportunities for intervention were missed in other areas, generally due to an interaction between the culture of the center, which influenced the culture of the PARCs, and Bill's personality.

Check-Mate: Bill Becomes King of the Club

Chess playing was a major theme in Bill's year at Midwest. In this section we first trace the history of Bill's involvement in activities at Midwest. We then focus on the chess club and identify key ways in which it met Bill's developmental needs.

American, from a poor, urban neighborhood, and living in a single-parent, low-SES household (Alexander, Entwisle, & Kabbani, 2001; Croninger & Lee, 2001; Gleason & Dynarski, 2002; Hess, 2000). He was at risk academically due to his failing grades, detachment from school, low academic self-esteem, peer alienation and anti-social behavior at school, and perceived lack of teacher support (Alexander et al., 2001; Croninger & Lee, 2001; Finn, 1989; Gleason & Dynarski, 2002; Hess, 2000).

TABLE 4.1. *Bill's PARC profile*

Starts at beginning of the year

P –
A basketball in gym
R Mateo, not particularly close
C success in tournaments, discomfort with peers

P Keystone
A sponsor activities, raise money, decision making, trips, staffing store, ran for elected leadership positions
R Juan, conflict and inadequate conflict resolution; Dude, close friendship
C routinized, modest engagement from peers, rejection, perseverance

Starts in the middle of the year

P Chess club
A playing chess, working with younger kids, playing against staff
R Manuel, younger peers
C high levels of engagement and focus, validation from adults and youth

P –
A helping out around club (staffing desk, cleaning)
R all staff
C noticed and appreciated by staff, youth participation and service

P –
A playing chess with staff (outside of chess club)
R Mateo, Manuel, other staff
C validation, belonging

P –
A game room
R peers, develops particularly close relationship with Dude, girlfriend
C mediator between youth, increasing comfort with peers

Starts at the end of the year

P –
A eating with staff
R Mateo, Manuel
C belonging, validation, family-like, responsive to youth agency

P summer job program
A hired as junior staff for summer
R all staff
C trust, validation

When we met Bill in the fall, his place in the club was uncertain. He was a steady member but had no distinct role. Bill appeared to be in the midst of his own identity exploration. He had confidence in his sense of self. Yet, in concordance with the developmental tasks of his age, Bill was trying on new roles and looking for validation.[7] Youth organizations can be a good place for such explorations, as they offer opportunities for achievement in a variety of areas and give youth a chance to "try on" roles and identities.[8] Bill is a good athlete and continually came out on top in basketball competitions. Yet he didn't seem comfortable with the older guys who played ball.

Bill named Mateo, the physical education instructor, as his favorite staff person. He had known Mateo longer than any other staff and said that Mateo asked about him when he didn't come to the club. He also liked that Mateo brought him food and gave him advice. Yet Mateo did not feel close to Bill, rating their closeness a 2 on a 1–5 scale.

> *In the beginning [Bill] was very quiet. He didn't talk to anyone. But as he got older, he started becoming more social with kids and staff. Before I couldn't hold a conversation with him, but now he'll talk … [Bill is] not very easy to get to know. You have to be a close friend to get to know him well.*

Similarly, Bill was popular with the younger teens but didn't appear close to his older club peers. Bill often asserted himself by joking and teasing. This sometimes frustrated other kids, including Dude who was frequently Bill's target.[9] During the focus group we held early in our research, Bill was extremely disruptive. He talked loudly over people, provoking Pocahontas to give up trying to participate after he cut her off numerous times. Despite his domination and aggressiveness, when he calmed down and participated in the focus group, he did so seriously and thoughtfully, revealing his more introspective nature.

---

[7] See Marcia's (1966; 1980; 1987; 1994) work for discussion of the four identity statuses that have been suggested to characterize adolescent identity development.

[8] Deutsch, 2004; Halpern et al., 2000; Larson, 1993; McLaughlin, Irby, & Langman, 1994.

[9] Humor may be a positive coping tool as well as a productive distraction from stressful situations (Abel, 2002; Fuehr, 2002; Lefcourt, Martin, & Ebers, 1981; Martin, 1996; Mishkinsky, 1977; Vilaythong, Arnau, Rosen, & Mascaro, 2003). Yet humor may also increase the risk of negative behaviors by allowing the individual to escape from, rather than confront, stressful life events (Nower, Derevensky, & Gupta, 2004).

Bill's attempts to assert himself were not always so destructive. He was an active member of the Keystone Club and wanted to take a leadership role. In the first few meetings, Bill signed up to help organize a sleepover, took a lead in an icebreaker activity, suggested an idea for a group project, and gave an earnest speech about how he would "live up to the responsibility" and "meet the challenge" of being Keystone president. Bill's candidacy is a good illustration of the balancing act he played between testing an adult identity and falling back on the clown his friends expected.

> *[The first candidate] finished her speech and Juan called Bill up [to give his speech]. "I think that if you gave me the responsibility I would live up to it. I would meet the challenge if you give me that responsibility." [One of the teen boys] said something and Bill began to giggle and continued on to say that he thought that he would be a good president.* [Bill seemed to begin by making a fairly serious point about himself, that he could be responsible if people trusted him and gave him the responsibility, but then seemed to lose momentum when he looked at his friends and got some feedback from them. He then began to laugh more and make more vague comments about being a good president.]

Despite multiple attempts, Bill was not elected to any leadership positions. His initial effort to display the mature, responsible side of himself was sidetracked by perceived negative feedback from his peers. Bill was frustrated by this failure and talked nostalgically about the group's former leader. Yet even in the absence of an elected position, Bill took an active role in the Keystone store. Bill and Dude staffed the store together nearly every day, forming a close friendship over the year.[10] Keystone served as a positive PARC in certain ways, as it allowed Bill to begin to serve the club and form a closer friendship with Dude. Yet Bill had a tense relationship with Keystone's staff leader, who often left conflicts in the group unresolved, and Bill received mainly negative feedback from group members, making it a potentially damaging culture for him. Thus, it appeared unlikely that, in the absence of other PARC possibilities, Bill would gain much developmentally. Yet Bill's actions throughout our first few months at the club made it clear that he was searching for a new role

---

[10] Dude was Bill's closest friend at Midwest, and the only club member to appear on Bill's social network map. Yet Bill rated his closeness with Dude only a 3 on a 1–5 scale.

at Midwest. He was looking to be given responsibility and wanted staff to recognize the leadership potential in him.

The opportunity for this recognition came in the form of a black-and-white board. Following Manuel's introduction of chess to Midwest, the game became one of the most popular pastimes at the club. It also provided Bill with a venue in which he could demonstrate skill and competence. He quickly became the club champ, beating kids and staff alike. The game allowed him to focus his attention and diverted him from the impulsive acting out that he used to take his mind off his problems. His domination of the chess board gave Bill a place among the staff, who began to treat him like "one of the adults."

It was around this period of time that staff began to allow him to remain in the club while they ate dinner. This was important to Bill. He praised Mateo for making this role possible.

> *Like when it's home time [Mateo will] let me stay. Let me eat in the game room. [Why does that make you feel good?] I'm not like a little kid. I'm part of the little staff group.*

Bill clearly prized this relationship and the trust Mateo had in him. Chess gave Bill the opportunity to prove himself to other staff members. The interaction below is an example of the type of validation Bill received for his newly demonstrated talent.

> *"Wanna play chess?" Manuel asked Bill. Bill nodded enthusiastically and went to go get the pieces and board. Bill returned with the chess board and pieces and set them up. "Hey, you gotta bring me your report card," Manuel said. Bill nodded. "Really, man. I don't care if it's all F's I gotta see it, okay? So bring it in." "Okay, I will," Bill said. Manuel nodded and they began to play.... Manuel continued to fill out the paperwork for the chess team as he played, while he was waiting for Bill to make a move ... [Manuel read the paperwork out loud, asking how the chess club might influence kids.] "It will help make stupid kids realize that they are smart," Bill said. Manuel looked at him with a confused expression. "You know, stupid kids may actually be smart." "Yeah, just wait till you get beat by one of those stupid kids!" Manuel said. Bill laughed and shrugged. "Yeah, that's what I'm saying. It may make us realize they're smart." As they played, Manuel would say "nice move" or "ah, man, that was a bad move." Bill would smile or say "okay okay enough with the bad moves! I get it!" Manuel would laugh and they would continue playing. Manuel won and Bill shook his head. "Man, I hate you Manuel," he said smiling. "Good game, man," Manuel said, putting out*

his hand. He and Bill shook hands. "Man, you played well. Do you want to play with the big pieces?" Manuel asked. "You mean your pieces?" Bill said, his face lighting up. Manuel nodded. "Yeah. I didn't know you had game or I would have been playing with you with those pieces all along!" Bill nodded and grinned. "Okay, go get them . . ."

During this interaction, Bill demonstrates abilities in two domains. He thinks about how chess can help kids at the club, assisting Manuel in developing the chess team. He says that kids "may make *us* realize they're smart [emphasis added]," aligning himself with Manuel in the club hierarchy. It is also possible that Bill is talking about himself, recognizing that through chess staff began to see him as bright. Bill also displays his talents. Even though Manuel wins, he compliments Bill, praises his playing, and acknowledges him as a peer in chess by offering to let Bill play with his personal set. Unlike Keystone, the person-activity-relationship fit in chess club was far more supportive of Bill's needs. He had found an activity in which he was talented and that let him take his mind off other issues. He found an adult who supported his participation, provided him validation for his skills, and encouraged him to become a leader in the activity. This PARC allowed Bill to feel both engaged and competent and to demonstrate his competence to others.

Yet the aforementioned interaction also illustrates a missed opportunity and points out how the culture of a PARC can be both positive and negative. Manuel asks Bill to bring in his report card, adding that he "doesn't care if it is all F's." This was likely an effort not to dismiss Bill's grades but to emphasize that, in line with regional club policies, Manuel needed to see Bill's report card. But it sends the message that Manuel is not concerned with Bill's improving his grades. Given the competence Bill showed in chess, Manuel could have taken this opportunity to explore with Bill why he did not transfer these skills to his schoolwork. This omission will be discussed in detail later.

Through chess, Bill found an identity in which he could shine, display leadership, and be accepted positively at the club. Over the year, Bill developed this identity, taking pride in his skills and using chess to focus his thoughts and take his mind off his problems. He played chess with staff members during their dinner hour and Manuel continued to provide both positive reinforcement and training. This resulted in recognition for Bill by both staff and peers. One staff member even said that he played chess on the computer until 4 A.M. after Bill beat him – a fact Bill repeated with pride.

Chess allowed Bill to develop an identity that incorporated both his needs for recognition and leadership and his intellectual abilities. Other kids at the club admired his playing and watched his games. Staff, especially Manuel, were adept at helping Bill expand his skills and recognizing when his frustration began to get the better of him. At that point they emphasized his competence, drawing him back into the game. Staff gave him the positive reinforcement he needed to keep at his newfound hobby. Bill's staying during the staff break was a poignant sign of inclusion. This separated him from other teens and made him feel "part of the little staff group." Bill's need to be recognized as a more mature teen was being met. Yet Bill had other needs that were not addressed despite the increased amount of time that Bill was spending with staff.

Fighting and Failing Grades

Bill had two problem areas which the club could have helped him address: re-occurring physical fights and failing grades. Both of these put Bill at increased risk for gang involvement and school dropout. Although there were warning signs, the staff did not heed them. They assumed that Bill could hold his own without their help, probably because Bill presented a self-assured and masculine front that was not consistent with needing or wanting help. Bill did manage to refrain from gangbanging and to stay in school. Had there been closer attention to these factors by staff, however, Bill may have been able to make gains in school grades and avoid fights.[11]

Keeping Bill in School
Bill consistently received C's and F's. This was despite apparent intelligence, as demonstrated by the nature and content of conversations he initiated about history and social issues. Bill reported high academic expectations for himself (he told us that he expected to attend college and pursue postgraduate education), but had low

---

[11] Researchers have emphasized the importance of broad-based programs and relationships, across environments, in promoting positive outcomes and helping youth avoid risky behavior (Stoiber & Good, 1998; Tolan, Gorman-Smith, & Henry, 2003). School dropout has been considered a developmental process that begins early and is interdependent with other problem behaviors (Alexander et al., 2001; Finn, 1989).

academic self-esteem. He wanted to be a better student, yet did not do anything to improve his grades or to avoid being held back. Bill had mixed academic self-efficacy, reporting having an easy time with tasks such as taking tests and figuring things out on his own, but difficulty with paying attention in class and completing written assignments. The fact that Bill had a positive overall sense of self-esteem and self-efficacy, but low academic self-esteem, may have put him at risk for dropout through a cycle of frustration, decreasing self-esteem, and eventual withdrawal from the catalyst for that frustration: school.[12] Bill's poor academic record was long-standing: he reported getting bad grades all his life. The combination of this history with his weak current performance, low academic self-esteem, and lack of effort put him at risk for school dropout.[13]

In addition to Bill's academic record, he was disengaged from school, adding to his risk for eventual dropout.[14] Bill felt his teachers did not care whether or not he learned, complaining that the environment at school was not one that inspired learning.

I think the kids have more control over the teachers than the teachers do over the kids and that's why they don't do well … I feel like [the teachers] don't care. In grammar school, they know the kids because there are only a few kids. But in high school, they don't care. There are more kids and they just lose interest, write work on the board, and don't care if you do it or not. [The teachers] just go to get their paycheck.

[12] This has been termed the frustration-esteem model of dropout, whereby a history of school failure leads to personal frustration and reduced self-esteem. In order to maintain a positive self-view, the student disengages from the source of her frustration: school (Finn, 1989). Bill had positive global senses of self-esteem and self-efficacy, but low academic self-esteem and a mixed sense of academic self-efficacy.

[13] Research has identified a number of cumulative academic risk factors for school dropout, including a history of poor grades, low academic expectations and self-esteem, disciplinary problems at school, spending little time on homework, lack of parental academic support, high absenteeism, and grade retention (Alexander et al., 2001; Croninger & Lee, 2001; Gleason & Dynarski, 2002). Bill's poor school performance, lack of effort, self-reported history of bad grades, and poor academic self-esteem put him at risk for dropping out of high school. Yet Bill did have high academic expectations. His mother was college educated, and Bill reported that his family was extremely proud of him when he graduated from eighth grade, an accomplishment that made him feel good. These factors could have served as a counterweight to the risk factors, especially if they had been combined with academic support from teachers and other adults.

[14] Finn (1989).

Midwest had the potential to serve as a more personalized setting, in which Bill came into contact with adults who cared about his learning and worked to help him succeed.[15] When Bill talked about Raoul, a former staff member, he referred to him as being like family, expressing the type of affective bonds we found to be common at many clubs.[16] Yet he did not transfer those emotions to other staff. As the story of Pocahontas demonstrated, Manuel was skillful in both working with teens on their schoolwork and relaying an attitude of general care. His ability to act like a father figure to Pocahontas appeared to increase his success as her math tutor. Yet Bill did not seek out Manuel, or any other staff, to fill either of those roles. Bill never did his homework at Midwest and, although Manuel asked him for his report card, no one consistently followed up with Bill about his schoolwork.

Keeping Bill from Gangbanging

As a fourteen-year-old Hispanic male living in an urban neighborhood with high levels of violence and gang activity, Bill was at risk for being the target of gang recruitment. Although recruitment and membership are two separate phenomena, they are linked. The presence of gangs, active recruitment, and higher levels of neighborhood social disorganization all increase the chances of a youth choosing to join a gang.[17] Bill's academic problems also put him at risk, as poor grades, school detachment, and low academic self-esteem are all associated with gang membership.[18]

Bill had a string of problems with fights at school, which led to a suspension and a police record. Such violent delinquency may increase not only the risk of Bill's being a target of gang recruitment, but also the risk that he will choose to join a gang.[19] Furthermore,

---

[15] Dynarski & Gleason (2002); Finn (1989).

[16] In prior research at the clubs, 74 percent of youth reported thinking of the club as a home. Those feelings were overwhelmingly due to psychosocial characteristics of the space, in particular relationships with staff (Deutsch & Hirsch, 2002).

[17] Not all youth who are recruited by gangs choose to become members. Yet being recruited and joining share some risk factors. Being recruited in and of itself can increase risk (Johnstone, 1983; Spergel, 1992; Thornberry, 1998). Bill's neighborhood had high levels of violence and gang activity.

[18] Johnstone (1983); Thornberry (1998).

[19] Gordon et al. (2004); Johnstone (1983); Stoiber & Good (1998); Thornberry (1998).

Bill was jumped on his way home from the club in the late autumn, losing his trademark medallion to the perpetrators. This shook him up; he was afraid to walk home alone from that day forward. Bill expressed this anxiety during an interview.

> *Yes [the violence in the neighborhood] affects you because sometimes you're scared to walk home at night, have to keep looking behind you, if you get robbed. I already got robbed before. [It's a] consistent issue.*

Bill's being a crime victim increases his risk of being recruited by a gang. It may also increase the attractiveness of gang membership to him. Joining a gang can be a strategy for gaining protection and managing fear.[20] It is notable that when discussing his fears with the researcher, he both opens up and remains guarded. His use of the second person (violence affects "you," "you're" scared to walk home) distances Bill from the neighborhood violence; yet he admits that he has been a victim. Similarly, he walks a line at the club between admitting his anxiety and keeping quiet about it.

Club staff took a hands-off approach to this area of Bill's life, never directly addressing his fears in a serious manner. The following excerpt demonstrates staff's interactions with Bill around his fear of violence.

> *At 6:00 P.M., Bill was still in the lobby. "Bill, what are you doing here? You gotta go home. Can't come in until 6:30," Maria said. "Can I use the phone?" he asked. "Use the phone at home, you gotta go now," she said. "I know I know that's why I want to use the phone," he said. "What? You'll go if you use it?" "Yeah, I want to call someone to come get me," he said. "Bill, just walk home," Maria said. "I live far. I don't want to. It's dark and I don't like to. I live far," he said. He repeated that he would have someone come get him. Maria shrugged ... and said he could use the phone.* [This was interesting because it seemed that Bill was really quite reluctant to walk home in the dark alone. He had said a few weeks ago that he lost his necklace from being jumped and I wonder if he was in fact jumped and is now fearful of walking home in the dark. It certainly appeared that way, as he was very reluctant to leave by himself.] *During the staff break ... Manuel and*

---

[20] Crime victims are more likely to be targets of gang recruitment (Johnstone, 1983). In addition, a prior victim may be more fearful and therefore prone to seek out the protections that a gang can offer. A sense of protection and belonging and assuaging of perceived threat and fear have been associated with gang membership (Li, Stanton, Pack, Harris, Cottrell, & Burns, 2002; Rizzo, 2003; Vigil, 1988; Wood et al., 1997).

Shawn were playing chess .... Bill came down into the room and stood next to Shawn, looking at the chessboard. "Bill, what are you doing in here?" Jesse said. "Watching the game," he said. Jesse bugged her eyes out at him. "Uh uh, it ain't 6:30, you gotta go home." "I'm waiting for someone to come get me," he said. "I'm just watching the game," he said, trying to stay in the room. "You fraid you'll be jumped?" Shawn asked. Bill nodded. "You scared to go home in the dark? Yeah, that Pocahontas, man, she's tough, fraid she'll jump you?" Mateo said. Bill laughed and nodded. Bill stayed and watched the chess game until it was over. He helped Manuel put the pieces away and then went back up into the lobby.

It is clear that Bill is afraid to walk home alone. In marked contrast to the staff's reaction to the threats directed at Pocahontas, no one walks Bill home or offers to arrange a ride for him. It is hard to dismiss the possibility that Bill's being male influenced this interaction. It seems counterintuitive to offer a strong, young, urban male an escort service. The staff seemed unable to accept that Bill, like Pocahontas, needs physical and emotional protection. Mateo's joking with Bill about being afraid of Pocahontas reflects the way in which many staff felt Bill was best approached: through humor. In an interview about Bill, Mateo said that "serious heart to heart talks wouldn't work. Joking, or casual conversation, maybe over a game, I think he would take that more to heart." The effect of the joking, however, may have left Bill feeling that it was not appropriate for him to be afraid or to ask for help.

A week later, Bill did begin to stay at the club during the dinner break. It is unclear, however, whether this was directly related to his anxiety about walking home, an issue which staff did not mention again. Bill himself did not always approach staff members about his problems. Mateo said that the first time he heard about Bill's school fights was when one of the researchers noticed a scratch on Bill's face, asked Bill about it, and mentioned it to Mateo, assuming that he, too, must have seen the scratch and known about the fights. Mateo then approached Bill and asked him who he was hanging out with at school. Bill told us that he did talk to Mateo about the fighting and that Mateo helped him think about changing schools. Beyond that conversation, however, there did not appear to be any intervention with Bill about this issue.

In contrast, Bill had no problems with fighting at the club. We never observed him physically threatening anyone or involved in any altercation. Mateo and Manuel both confirmed this, noting that Bill got along with everybody and never caused fights.

In sum, Bill sustained his participation in Midwest mainly due to his own initiative and desire to stay off the streets. The chess club helped carve out a niche for him and gave him a reason to keep coming to the club. Whereas staff could have done more to transform Bill's story from one of sustenance to one of improvement, in some ways Bill was able to meet important needs at the club.

DEVELOPMENTAL GAINS OVER THE YEAR

On the whole, Bill maintained his developmental status over the year and did not succumb to certain problem behaviors or outcomes for which he may have been at risk. Yet we also saw some developmental gains, especially in Bill's display of positive social norms and his relationships with peers and staff.

Like Pocahontas, Bill exhibited increased positive social norms throughout the year. He began to help staff clean up the club in the evenings. He also worked at the Keystone store and staffed the front desk. Despite his disruptive nature early on, he worked to demonstrate his responsibility. Like Pocahontas, his negative social behavior decreased somewhat over the year. In addition to helping out around the club, Bill also appeared to become a social force in his peer group. He formed closer relationships and sometimes appeared to moderate disagreements between his friends.

Bill's friendship with Dude is one of the clearest examples of the gains that Bill made in his social relationships at the club. At the beginning of the year, Bill seemed somewhat removed from his peers. He spent the majority of his time making fun of Dude and, although he would play basketball and ping-pong with some older guys, he did not seem comfortable with the older teens. During the year, Bill managed to form closer friendships and prove himself to staff, who gave him more opportunities to participate in new ways at the center.

Bill and Dude, by the middle of the year, were inseparable. Bill's aunt drove Dude home if she came to get Bill during the break. Bill would often check to see if Dude was around before deciding whether or not to stay at the center. When Dude went on vacation in the spring, he brought Bill back a present. Although at one time Bill felt that he couldn't talk to Dude about serious topics, he had a desire to do so, which in and of itself is an accomplishment for a teen boy prone to posturing. Dude was the only Midwest person who Bill included on his social network map.

Bill also developed a romantic relationship with a female club member. When there were conflicts between some female club members, including his girlfriend, Bill attempted to "stay out of it." He did his best to maintain his friendships with all the girls involved. Thus, Bill appeared to develop an increased comfort with his peer group at the club and pull back a bit from his provocateur role. These ties may have helped keep Bill involved at Midwest, diverting his attention from his "street" friends.

In addition to the other members, Bill began to develop relationships with a variety of club staff. Through the chess club, Bill strengthened his relationship with Manuel and even went to a conference with him in the spring. This was a big deal. Earlier in the year, Bill complained that staff did not give him the chance to prove himself. By spring, he was being given increased opportunities and responsibilities.

As mentioned earlier, Bill also interviewed for and got a summer job at the club. This was an important test for Bill, who doubted that he would get the job.

> *Bill started talking to me about how he wasn't sure if he was going to get hired because "people don't trust me and they think I'm a bad influence." I asked him what he meant and said that I trusted him. "I know! Thank you! But that's what people say," Bill said shaking his head. "I'm just glad [the job interview is] over."*

Thus, the fact that he got the job was an indicator to Bill that staff trusted him. Given Bill's distrust of adults, this was an important gain.

Chess also helped calm Bill down. When he played, he had an intensity that allowed him to deflect his worrying and focus on a specific and constructive task. Bill came to focus his energies intensely on the chess board, acting out less often.

Bill's resiliency played an important role in contributing to his developmental gains over the year. Bill sustained his participation at Midwest in the face of a number of factors that threatened to turn him away. Bill continued to try to gain a leadership role despite multiple rejections. He fought to be allowed to go on special trips. These efforts were not always supported by staff. Bill had to rely on his own personal determination to make Midwest a place that finally allowed him to grow and take on new roles and responsibilities.

Unlike Pocahontas, Bill did not make gains in his academic or social realms outside Midwest. He did not drop out of school or become involved with gangs, which are important outcomes that merit recognition. At the same time, his grades did not improve and he continued to have problems with fighting at school. His life outside the club neither deteriorated nor improved. In the next section we will discuss how the after-school center kept Bill from getting worse but failed to lead to developmental gains in these areas.

THE MIDWEST AFTER-SCHOOL CENTER AND BILL: STRENGTHS, SHORTCOMINGS, AND SYNERGIES

We now turn to a discussion of the strengths, shortcomings, and synergies of Midwest in dealing with Bill's needs. For Bill, the center played an important role as a hub of activity that kept him occupied and away from risky behaviors. The development of the chess club was successful in engaging Bill and providing him with needed assistance. Through such activity the center helped Bill avoid gang activity. There were also important synergies in the ways in which staff used chess as a means of involving Bill in other center programs and in addressing issues in his life. There were also shortcomings in Midwest's efforts to address Bill's academic struggles and school fights and unrealized synergies of which a more proactive center may have been able to take advantage.

Strengths

The most important resource that Midwest provided for Bill was the chess club. Chess provided Bill with a number of needed supports. It gave him the attention and recognition that he craved, especially as he began to surpass staff members in his skills. It also allowed him to focus his energies on a constructive activity, serving as a distraction from his outside stressors, much as we saw club activities do for Pocahontas.

The chess club, as structured by Manuel, had a number of strong design features that enabled it to serve as a positive setting. Manuel had youth of different skill levels play each other, fostering co-operative peer learning. He also monitored those games, providing scaffolding for the less expert members and reinforcement for the more skilled youth. He had youth replay parts of games, reviewing moves that could have been done differently and reinforcing skills recently learned. Manuel repeatedly recognized Bill's progression in the game and encouraged him to play against both youth and staff. The chess club could have been designed and implemented in a very different – and less satisfactory – way, without any or all of these features. The manner in which this particular chess club was designed and implemented provided the type of environment that Bill needed to develop leadership skills, confidence, and, ultimately, a new role at Midwest. Like Pocahontas, Bill benefited from Manuel's strengths and energy.

In addition to giving Bill an opportunity to display his skills, chess also provided a venue for developing relationships with staff. Bill's increased involvement with Manuel, Mateo, and Steven led to his spending more time with the adults in the latter part of the year. These relationships opened up possibilities for deeper discussions of Bill's life and an opportunity for greater mentorship. By the early spring, Manuel had come to believe that Bill was a kid who he could influence and began to speak to him about more personal issues.

Bill's involvement with chess also kept him off the street. Earlier in the year, Bill complained that there was not much for him to do at Midwest. Membership in youth organizations decreases during adolescence worldwide.[21] It would not have been surprising if Bill had stopped coming to Midwest as the activities available grew less exciting to him; he sometimes left if the chess club wasn't going to meet. Ceasing coming altogether would have left Bill with his "street" friends, some of whom were involved in high-risk behaviors.[22] The chess club may have prevented such an outcome. Chess's role in solidifying Bill's identity at the club should not be overlooked, especially in relation to the potential risk of gang involvement.

Bill's consistent involvement with Midwest appears to be a form of self-preservation, a means of keeping himself out of trouble and distracting himself from outside problems. This is similar to the way

---

[21] Cotterell (1996).

[22] Associating and having unsupervised time with delinquent peers may increase the risk of gang involvement (Gordon et al., 2004; Rizzo, 2003; Thornberry, 1998).

in which Pocahontas used the club as a place where she could keep away from friends who pressured her to engage in unwanted activities and escape her feelings of loneliness and isolation. Bill, too, had a number of stressors that weighed on him. The energy of the club served as a distraction from problems for Pocahontas; so, too, did chess provide an adaptive means of cognitive avoidance for Bill, focusing his attention on things other than his problems.

Bill's use of the Midwest center as a place to escape the issues of gangs and violence is highlighted by Bill's description of his club friends who, he says, are more childish than his outside friends. His friends from the neighborhood and school he describes as both more mature and more "street." One of the benefits of a youth center is that it can be a place for "kids to be kids."[23] Furthermore, it allows deferment of the decision of whether or not to join a gang. Having an identity linked to an organization can help teens avoid the recruitment activity of gangs.[24]

Bill was exploring and seeking out new roles. Gangs may support such identity work, offering leadership opportunities, the chance to demonstrate responsibility, and clarification of age and gender roles, which both come to the fore during adolescence.[25] All of these issues were salient to Bill, as demonstrated by his activity at Midwest. Bill's active search for increased responsibility and leadership, combined with his delinquency and fear of crime, could have led him to gang membership as a means of resolving his identity issues. Bill was also from a father-absent home and had little attachment to school – two additional risk factors.[26] Midwest had the opportunity to meet some of the needs that Bill could have sought through a gang: institutional attachment, social control, positive adult relations, a definite role, and a vision of and path to a competent adult identity.[27] Both gangs and after-school programs have been talked about, by

[23] Hirsch (2005).
[24] Halpern et al. (2000).
[25] Gangs offered Bill opportunities for achievement, leadership, social support, and both group and individual identity, including a responsible, masculine identity (Li et al., 2002; Spergel, 1992; Vigil, 1988, 2003). His high levels of self-questioning and alertness to social situations as well as characteristics associated with mainstream success (e.g., intelligence) can put him at further risk (Cartwright, Howard, & Reuterman, 1980), especially as he received negative feedback from adults (Johnstone, 1983).
[26] Johnstone (1983); Stoiber & Good (1998); Thornberry (1998); Wood et al. (1997).
[27] Johnstone (1983); Spergel (1992); Vigil (1988, 2003); Wood et al. (1997).

both members and researchers, in the language of home and family, underscoring the similar needs that these two divergent social organizations can meet.[28]

Shortcomings

The major shortcoming of Midwest was undoubtedly the staff's inability to address Bill's school issues, both social and academic. Despite a greater attention to schoolwork than we saw at many other centers, the staff at Midwest did not engage Bill in such activity. They seemed resigned to the fact that he was doing poorly. Other than seeking to review his report card, they did not take any steps to help him improve his academic achievement. Bill could have benefited from a more direct homework program for teens. The afternoon homework program was geared toward younger kids, and there was no formal program in place for the teens. Yet such a program could have been implemented. When standardized test time came about, Steven led group review and preparation sessions for the teens. This type of group program could have been part of the regular evening activities at the club, encouraging students to do their homework in a social setting. In fact, when Manuel helped Pocahontas and others with math homework in the game room, Bill sometimes got involved. He enjoyed looking at other kids' homework and talking through the problems. Thus, he may have taken part in a homework program, particularly if it drew on his interest in socializing. Despite the fact that Bill had developed a closer relationship with Manuel through the chess club, that relationship was not leveraged to bring him into this other PARC from which he would have likely benefited. Bill may have responded to staff proactively asking him to work with them, as Manuel did with Pocahontas.

In addition to his grades, Bill had a number of fights at school throughout the year. Bill said that he talked to Mateo about it. Nevertheless, despite some initial discussion toward helping Bill think about changing schools, there was not any follow-up to see if Bill was successfully negotiating the social situation at high school. We recognize that finding time to go to a youth's school is asking a

---

[28] Branch (1999), Clark (1992), Deutsch & Hirsch (2002), Flannery, Huff, & Manos (1998).

lot, given many competing demands. Yet the organizational structure of Midwest could have better supported such efforts, as we will discuss later in terms of unrealized synergies.

We suspect that Bill would have benefited from involvement with Midwest's mentoring program. Perhaps if he were able to develop a close, long-standing relationship with an adult who could address some of the issues in his life, he would have been able to transform his story into one of positive momentum. During the year of the study, Bill did not have a mentor because there were not enough to go around.

Staff could have helped nurture the mature and thoughtful side of Bill. For example, following a Keystone discussion about the inappropriateness of using religious or ethnic labels as slurs, Bill suggested that Keystone do a skit about somebody making a religious slur as part of an educational project on which they were working. Juan neither acknowledged nor followed up on Bill's suggestion. It seemed that Bill had been pigeonholed by Juan, and perhaps other staff as well. As a result, his attempts to display the mature and introspective side of himself were not always recognized.

Synergies

Bill's story has some elements of positive synergy, yet it is also a tale of missed opportunities. Whereas Pocahontas benefited from the staff's multi-pronged approach and made gains in a number of areas, Bill showed less drastic improvement. He became more integrated into the club as an emerging leader, as Pocahontas did, but did not transfer this success to other areas of his life, as Pocahontas was able to do.

Positive, Realized Synergies

For Pocahontas, her increased participation in varied club activities, and evident academic and developmental gains, was the catalyst for her being accepted into the staff dinner group. For her, this emergent action, and associated experiences, was the culmination of her effort. Bill also joined the staff dinner group. The combination of his participation in the chess club and his concerns for his physical safety appeared to be the catalysts for this inclusion. Because these two situations emerged within weeks of each other, it is impossible to tell whether only one or both led to his inclusion. However, for Bill, joining the staff dinner group was more the beginning rather than the end of the story of how synergies led to emergent actions.

The combination of Bill's chess-playing abilities and his remaining in the club while staff ate dinner appeared to give Bill that sought-after opportunity to demonstrate his maturity and potential. Staff members were able to get to know Bill outside of his interactions with his peers. The combination of his involvement in the chess program and integration into the staff dinner group appeared to spark a reaction that allowed him to develop a new role at Midwest, something of which Bill was clearly in need. This was a case of positive synergies between PARCs, wherein relationships and competencies developed and demonstrated in one PARC influenced relationships and activities in another PARC.

In the chess club, Bill evolved into a leader naturally, demonstrating his skill and ability to play with both adults and kids. He did not have to fight for a position; rather, he used his natural talents to take on the role of club champ. Having an activity in which he was intrinsically engaged helped bring out his strengths and competencies.

Moreover, when Bill was engaged in a game, his focus never strayed from the board. This was in stark contrast to his participation in Keystone, where he often had to be chastised for talking or goofing off. Chess allowed him to demonstrate that he did have self-discipline. This may have led staff to be more inclined to give him a chance to prove himself in other areas. His abilities in working with the younger members were also highlighted through his chess playing. He showed that he could interact in a positive way with younger members, rather than always being a provocateur.

This emerging role worked to integrate Bill into Midwest's more official leadership structure. After he started to stay in the evenings, Bill began to help staff clean up and watch the front desk. By the end of the year, Bill had gone to a conference with Manuel. Once he began to be integrated, the synergies appeared to kick in, pushing him into multiple new roles and relationships.

For Bill, the culmination of this process, at least during our year at the center, was when he was hired to work at Midwest during the summer. This was indisputable evidence of staff recognition of his leadership abilities. As a paid staff member himself, he now had a new – and highly valued – social status. This new status reflected a natural desire for a place in the adult world, while at the same time allowing him to maintain his connection to other club youth.

The difference in the nature of the culminating, emergent experiences for Bill and Pocahontas reflects their different developmental needs. With the loss of her parents and other important adults, Pocahontas craved a deep experience of family, which was realized via inclusion in the staff dinner group. Bill, on the other hand, was most concerned with securing a position of leadership and adult recognition, and for that need the crowning moment was his summer job appointment. It is also possible that differences in the sequencing of events played a role. Pocahontas had made steady, gradual improvement over the course of the year, and her culminating experience came afterward. Bill became part of the staff group before he had done as much work, over as long a period; it was not until the time the summer job application came around that he had put together a similarly sustained record of accomplishment.

As with Pocahontas, it is difficult to imagine Bill's positive trajectory had the center not offered a comprehensive after-school program. Earlier in the year, Bill had disengaged from the sports activities. He had been rejected for a leadership role in Keystone. Had the center offered only one (or both) of those activities, there is a good chance that he would have then dropped out of the after-school program. However – to his credit – Bill persisted in trying out different activities. When chess club – a new program – was started, this persistence paid off handsomely.

Unrealized Potential Synergies
Within Bill's year at the center, there are multiple examples of unrealized synergies, potential interactions just below the surface, waiting for someone to tap into them.

Given his high level of chess skill, the staff could have talked to Bill about ways in which some of those skills and analytical abilities could transfer to the classroom. Bill did join the chess club at school, the sole instance of which we are aware in which there appeared to be a transfer of gains from the club to school. This new school involvement could have served as a springboard for examining additional opportunities at school that might make sense for Bill. Participation in extracurricular activities at school could motivate him to remain in school and start a process of reevaluating his relation to school more generally.[29] Unfortunately, these possibilities were not explored by club staff.

Another unrealized potential synergy involved the possibility of making his participation in chess contingent on increased academic effort and possibly even better grades. A weaker, though potentially still effective, contingency might have limited the extent of his participation in chess pending academic improvement. This might have inspired Bill to work harder at school in order to be able to participate in an activity that he thoroughly enjoyed and which was a primary source of his leadership role. When done well, this strategy can succeed. At one center in our earlier research, the physical education director instituted a rule making gym time contingent on grades. This approach succeeded at least in part because of the strength and popularity of that individual staff member.[30] There are clear potential risks to implementing this kind of contingency contract. The timing of implementing this approach would be an issue, as it might have short-circuited the positive momentum Bill was building; perhaps it had a greater chance to succeed once his gains at the center had been consolidated. Of course, there is always the possibility that Bill's grades would not improve, leading to a downward trajectory that could include dropping out of the club, increasing his distrust of adults, and joining a gang. The danger that such a plan could backfire is real.

A case conference on Bill could have provided a venue for staff to work together to develop a plan for addressing Bill's academic and social issues. Mateo felt that Bill did not respond well to one-on-one, serious talks. Yet Manuel was developing a closer relationship with Bill through playing chess and felt he could talk to Bill about personal issues. With some leadership, Manuel and Mateo could have developed a team approach to getting Bill to improve his grades and desist from fighting, combining their efforts based on each staff person's strengths and relationship with Bill.

For Bill to truly benefit from this kind of effort on the part of club staff, one staff member or an outside consultant would likely have had to play critic, or "devil's advocate," to the rest. The only way

[29] Participation in school-based extracurricular activities has been found to decrease rates of early school dropout among those at high risk (Mahoney & Cairns, 1997).

[30] Hirsch (2005).

a case conference would have worked for Bill at Midwest was if someone could push the organization to move beyond seeing Bill as "one of the guys." This would require a capacity for critical self-reflection that was needed but not evident.

One prevention strategy that has been suggested for at-risk youth is closer ties between the different environments in their lives, especially between school and home and home and neighborhood.[31] Midwest had the potential to foster such linkages. Midwest had a team of experts – the drug outreach staff – whose skills and knowledge were not realized for in-house kids and staff. The outreach workers had ties to school personnel and had experience in working with schools. There was thus a possibility for teaming with the outreach workers and school staff that had considerable potential for benefiting Midwest youth. In addition to benefiting the kids, this kind of teaming could have helped the two sets of staff feel more like one unit and reduced the tensions that existed between them (and between the club director and the in-center staff).

Similarly, had the center worked on developing a skit about social issues, as Bill had suggested, they could have made use of the expertise of the drama club leader. There were good resources available to Midwest, but it was part of their culture that they were not particularly oriented toward seeking out other adults as resources.

Negative Synergies

Until this point, we have discussed actual or potential positive synergies, positive in that they did (or could) work to the benefit of youth. However, for Bill, there was also a negative synergy at the club, one that worked to his detriment. For Bill, the lack of a proactive orientation to intervention among staff, combined with the difficulty of seeing beyond gender stereotypes about urban male teenagers, combined to diminish the ability of staff to assist him in regards to physical safety and to establish more open and revealing relationships with him. This overall culture influenced the culture of individual PARCs. Even in those programs and activities that had generally positive cultures of youth engagement and support for leadership, staff tended to take a more

---

[31] Stoiber & Good (1998); Tolan et al. (2003).

hands-off approach when it came to directly intervening in problem areas outside the direct purview of the activity, especially
with boys.

Overall, the story of Bill is one of a teen boy exploring his identity and testing different pathways to a successful adolescent role.
Midwest came through for Bill in the form of the chess club. This
activity gave Bill opportunities to be a leader, demonstrate competence, and focus his attention away from the stressors in his life. It
gave Bill a role in the center and more successfully integrated him
into the culture of Midwest. Without chess, Bill's story would likely
have been different.

At the beginning of the year, Bill was frustrated by staff's lack
of trust in him and his inability to gain a leadership position. He
was bored and felt there were few activities to engage him. Had
Manuel not begun the chess club, it is likely that Bill would have
dropped out of the center or significantly decreased his attendance
by the end of the year. This would have left him on the streets,
hanging out with friends who were involved in some risky activities. Gangs could have become attractive as a means to meet the
needs that he ultimately met through the chess club. Midwest provided a haven from the streets and a space for identity exploring.

In addition, the chess club provided Bill with an opportunity
to develop a close relationship with a staff member and served
to strengthen an existing relationship. At the start of the year, Bill
named Mateo as his favorite staff person. Yet during the year, he
undoubtedly benefited more from his relationship with Manuel,
developed through chess. His involvement in chess also appeared to
strengthen his tie with Mateo, as he began to play chess and eat dinner with him and the other staff. Thus, the development of the chess
club provided Bill with a venue for deepening both his engagement
in the center and his relationships with multiple adult staff members. Staff began to recognize and reward him for his competencies
in a manner that he had not experienced through involvement in
other activities at Midwest.

Whereas Bill's year at Midwest had some positive, likely preventative, effects, there were limits to the benefits he received from
his participation. Although being "one of the guys" was part of

what drew youth and staff to Bill, it also limited the resources this particular center could make available to him. Bill did not receive maximum benefit from the center in part because staff didn't view him as "needy." Pocahontas wore her heart on her sleeve. The damsel-in-distress role, a female archetype, benefited her in terms of getting help from staff. Bill, on the other hand, was left mostly to his own devices. Staff enjoyed playing chess with Bill and appeared to take pleasure in their interactions with him. However, they were not able to see him as a teenager in need of assistance. There is no archetype for the urban male in distress. Such a character is supposed to handle his problems on his own. In our previous work on a gender equity initiative at these (and other) centers, we found that it was precisely such gendered assumptions that restricted the opportunities available for both boys and girls.[32] Staff need to view youth beyond their gendered bodies and not fall back on gendered stereotypes or assumptions in their interactions with and programming for teens.

Overall, the organizational shortcomings of Midwest translated into limits on the help that the center was able to provide for Bill. The staff's orientation away from proactive intervention, their failure to learn together how to do a better job, their difficulty in seeing other adults connected with the center as resources, and the blinders put on by gender stereotypes all played a role in restricting the depth and breadth of support Bill received and the developmental growth he made at Midwest. Interestingly, the gender stereotypes that served as shortcomings for Bill were strengths for Pocahontas, and allowed her to gain more from the center than Bill did. This highlights an important point. The developmental support provided to youth by comprehensive after-school centers is dependent not only on features of the organization or characteristics of the individual youth, but on the fit and interaction between the two.

In the next chapter we synthesize the lessons learned from Midwest and focus on what we have learned across these three chapters. By considering the individual youth's narratives in the context of the center case study, we begin to build a theory of how comprehensive youth centers operate as both complex organizations with multiple components and people and as settings that

[32] Hirsch (2005).

serve individual youth. In Midwest, we saw how individual youth trajectories were sometimes promoted and sometimes held in stasis by the interaction of organizational and individual youth features. Both Pocahontas and Bill appeared to be somewhat proactive youth who were able to seek out what they needed at Midwest. Yet other youth may not have been as lucky, and we consider how the features that prevented further gain from the youth we studied may have been holding Midwest back from reaching its potential as a center for positive youth development.

5

Putting It All Together: Midwest Center

At this point, it is time to take a step back and consider what we have learned by our several studies of the Midwest after-school center. We hope in these mini-chapters – including the ones that follow the case studies of the other centers – to contribute to an integrative understanding of how comprehensive after-school centers influence youth outcomes. As part of this effort, we pay particular attention to distinctive features of comprehensive centers. Centers of this sort are complex organizations, and our analytic framework seeks to integrate both organizational and person-level factors. Grounded in the experiences of Pocahontas and Bill, as well as the organizational-level study, our objective is to abstract broader insights from those accounts. We therefore need to shift gears somewhat and consider what more general principles may be at work, which we can then reexamine in future chapters.

In Chapter 1, we introduced the concept of a PARC (program, activity, relationship, culture) to capture the multifaceted aspect of youth engagements at these centers. For both Pocahontas and Bill, this proved to be a very useful concept. For both of them it was critical to find one PARC that meaningfully engaged them. A meaningful PARC anchored their continued participation in Midwest and fostered developmental growth. Pocahontas found this with Manuel around math, Bill with Manuel around chess. In these instances, the person was an adult staff member; it may be possible for a peer to serve in this role as well, but our research was oriented toward youth relationships with adult staff, so we are not in the best position to address this question.

The advantage of a comprehensive center is that many potential PARCs are available. If the site had offered Torch Club only, it is much less likely that either Pocahontas or Bill, or any other youth, would have made such a connection, given Manuel's modest enthusiasm for the activity. At after-school sites that offer one activity only, youth will either sink or swim on the basis of their fit with that one PARC offering. There are many more opportunities to find a fit at a site that offers multiple activities.

The problem with Midwest was that there were few high-quality PARCs that were actually available. Manuel, on his own initiative, developed strong PARCs around math tutoring and the chess club. Those activities served as the basis for the development of excellent relationships with a number of youth over the course of the year. By contrast, Mateo, who initially had closer relationships with youth than Manuel, was never able to develop any strong program or activities, and the benefit that youth gained from him was more ambiguous. Nor were any of the other staff able to offer strong PARCs.

The analytic framework presented in Chapter 1 posited that organization-level factors impact a center's programs, activities, relationships, and culture. Our research at Midwest did indeed suggest that the gap between the potential and the reality of the PARCs could be traced in large part to organizational failures. Training was minimal to non-existent. Supervision was limited to making sure that staff were at their assigned activities and not goofing off; beyond that, we saw no evidence that club leadership attended to the developmental quality of any program or activity. This impacted staff behavior in various programs and activities, and likely accounts for the high levels of lackadaisical performance, excessive joking around, and resentment.

Manuel's successful launch of the chess club suggests a possible strategy to circumvent these limitations: hire staff who already have strong interest and skill in an activity that should translate well to the after-school center.[1] If this were done, staff hiring practices could be made into an organizational strength, and this strength might offset other organizational weaknesses. Of course, it would then be necessary to follow through and support staff in new program development, something which Bob (club director) did for Manuel only. Indeed, Bob actively discouraged new programming for girls. So even though there may be multiple organizational

[1] Hirsch (2006).

routes by which centers can foster strong PARCs, Midwest did not consistently pursue any of them.

Although quality of implementation frequently left much to be desired, the other activities at Midwest did play an important synergistic role in the benefits that Pocahontas and Bill ultimately derived. Given that they were able to find a core PARC in which they were meaningfully engaged and which led to personal growth, the other activities were able to play a secondary yet not insignificant role. For both Pocahontas and Bill, their participation in a wide range of activities reflected a very substantial participation in the life of the club. It may be especially important that both young people gave back to the club, contributing service.[2] They not only participated in the life of the club; they helped make the quality of life there better for all. The fact that the different activities were interwoven in the culture of the center gave meaning to those additional activities. Indeed, the cultural meaning attached to these engagements offered both youngsters an opportunity to step into leadership, adult-like roles and identities in a family-like setting. This was quite important to both Pocahontas and Bill, as it is to most adolescents. The synergistic effects of those additional activities likely outweighed their value when considered solely as independent activities. Indeed, over time, the synergistic effects of participation in the culture of the center may come to equal or surpass benefits derived from any one activity, particularly if the PARCs are not of high quality, as was the case at Midwest. There appear to be fewer available synergies at after-school centers that do not offer a wide array of PARC options.

Even if synergistic effects emerge as especially valuable over time, the developmental potential of the site is likely to principally reflect the quality of the individual PARCs. We emphasize in this book systems-level or synergistic effects both because we believe they are important and because they have received so little attention previously. In this context, we do not believe there is sufficient justification for positing that synergies are more important than the sum of individual PARCs, though this is an interesting question for theory and research to consider in the future. It is also interesting to consider whether synergistic effects on development will be stronger when the PARCs are stronger.

[2] Lerner (2004) similarly paid special attention to youth contributions.

Our analysis highlights how centers may or may not contribute to enhancing development, but an important part of their mission is also to prevent or ameliorate problems. We saw troubling signs that they may sometimes be missing the mark in this area with respect to Bill's getting into fights. This is another area where the lack of strong organizational procedures is implicated. There were no comprehensive case conferences or systematic, regular reviews of individual youth. Either of these might have provided a vehicle for alerting staff to youth behavior that might otherwise fly below the radar. Although we suggested that the inattention to Bill's particular issue may reflect a cultural blind spot at Midwest, once that blind spot is identified, its potential relevance could be routinely considered – indeed, it could be part of a checklist of factors to consider – in subsequent reviews of youth.

Here again we find another instance in which a center can develop an organizational mechanism to compensate for some of its limitations. All organizations are weak in some area. An important task for leadership is to identify those weaknesses and find ways to eliminate, ameliorate, or compensate for them.

Youth Agency

At this center, it was important that youth exercise agency in seeking out meaningful person-activities. Despite initial setbacks (e.g., in running for president of Keystone), Bill persisted in exploring all of the options open to him at the club. He kept trying, again and again, and eventually his effort paid off. Given that the culture of the club was to be reactive rather than proactive, such effort was important. Bill did not make such an effort regarding academics and failed to benefit from the center's resources. The only staff member who demonstrated much proactive effort was Manuel, and his launching of the chess club made all the difference to Bill. Youth agency may be less critical in centers in which staff are more proactive.

The response of staff to the exercise of youth agency and commitment is crucial. Positive, supportive adult feedback helps validate these emerging roles and identities. Both youth also received validating feedback from their peers (for Pocahontas, particularly in relation to ping-pong, and for Bill, particularly in relation to chess).

Staff are unlikely to always respond positively to youth. In instances when adult staff either do not provide validation or go so far as to reject youth in their agentic behavior, youth may not only fail to benefit, but may actually suffer. The more staff and activities, the greater the potential rejection that youth may encounter at a site, leading to poorer outcomes. Both Pocahontas and Bill received some rejection from Keystone, but remained resilient in the presence of actual or hoped-for rewards in other domains of center life. After-school programs that involve fewer activities provide fewer paths to both support and rejection. Thus, centers that reject youth across multiple PARCs may have a more serious negative impact than single-focus after-school programs. Unfortunately, we will need to elaborate on this point in our consideration of the North River center in subsequent chapters.

A Familial Environment and Identity Development

Beyond the quality of implementation, and explicit support or rejection, the ability of staff as a group to provide a familial type of environment was important to both Pocahontas and Bill. At Midwest, the staff got along well with each other. They were able to coordinate their responses effectively in troubling situations. The cohesiveness and comfort of staff with each other can provide the foundation for these types of synergistic, familial experiences.

In comprehensive settings, youth have the potential to express different parts of themselves with staff in different activities. This encourages the articulation and differentiation of identities. Becoming part of a harmonious staff group provides the social context for integrating the identities expressed across staff. Identity integration is important to some theorists of adolescent development, such as Erik Erikson.[3] To the extent that the articulation and integration of multiple identities has developmental implications, well-functioning comprehensive settings may have distinct advantages.

[3] Erikson (1968). The value of identity integration for adults is discounted by postmodern theorists, though whether there is a distinct advantage (or not) to efforts at such integration during adolescence has not been addressed.

As we turn to consider the North River and West River centers, we shall find that they differ from Midwest on important organizational dimensions. The youth at those centers also bring with them their own distinct personal histories and interests. The study of these additional youth and settings will enable us to reconsider and refine this initial theorizing and come to a more complete account of comprehensive after-school centers.

NORTH RIVER CENTER

6

A Study of Organizational Dysfunction

The North River after-school center is a large structure that sits in the middle of a wide street dotted with dilapidated buildings and a smattering of newly renovated homes. Club staff monitor the entrance, ensuring that only club members, parents, and approved visitors enter. The neighborhood around North River is not very safe. The streets feel deserted, and there are few businesses within walking distance. Staff members often warn visitors not to walk in the neighborhood alone; their final words are always some version of "be safe out there."

Our initial survey questionnaire provides a good indication of the youth (age ten and older) who come to the club. The survey was completed by 112 youth ages 10–17, with an average age of 12.8. The sample was 97 percent African American. Only two youth indicated other races (White, Hispanic). Sixty-three percent of the youth who completed the survey were male. It was a high-poverty sample, as 89 percent reported receiving free or reduced-price lunch. On average, youth reported coming to the center three days per week, and 25 percent reported that it was their first year at the center.

North River was distinct among the centers we studied for its nearly exclusive focus on control of youth's movements. We were struck by the palpable air of authority that characterized the center. There seemed little room for kids to be kids. Structure can be important in neighborhoods with high levels of violence, such as North River's. Yet the exclusive attention to control created an environment largely devoid of spontaneity and fun and absent any focus on youth development.[1]

---

[1] Structure and supervision are both important features of effective after-school programs (Little, Wimer, & Weiss, 2008; Mahoney, Larson, Eccles, & Lord, 2005).

The order and control exerted by North River's management team extended to staff as well as youth, leading to a fairly negative atmosphere. Our researchers' ratings of the center's social climate, made at each site visit, are telling. Staff conflict was observed on 23 percent of the visits, nearly twice that of Midwest and ten times that of West River. This was mostly due to conflicts between staff and leadership, as there were few instances of conflict between program-level staff. Staff complaints were heard on nearly half (42%) of our visits (compared to one-third and one-fifth of visits at Midwest and West River, respectively) and staff cooperation was only observed on four (5%) occasions. Furthermore, whereas staff engagement and enthusiasm were observed less frequently at North River, staff low involvement and negativity were observed twice as much as at the other two centers. Finally, youth at North River participated in decision making significantly less than youth at the other two centers, reflecting its authoritarian culture. Unlike other centers, the appeal of North River, for youth or staff, was not obvious.

As might be expected, North River did not function well as an organization. The climate felt compartmentalized and authoritarian, with little active programming. Rather than fostering the types of best practices that have been suggested for after-school programs,[2] North River appeared to foster many of the "practices to avoid."[3] The club directors seemed to have little concern with youth development and focused almost entirely on behavior management. To sum up the overarching mood of the center, one researcher made the following comment on her first visit to North River: "This was a very different experience than the other clubs. There did not seem to be any organized activities and as far as I could tell the staff seemed to see their jobs as nothing more than babysitting."

GOALS

The goal of North River is order above all. Every young person is to be in his or her assigned physical place, obeying staff directives.

At North River, however, a premium was placed on structure at the expense of, rather than within, engaging programs.

[2] Eccles & Gootman, 2002; Mahoney, Larson, Eccles, & Lord, 2005; Moore, Bronte-Tinkew, & Collins, 2010a

[3] Moore, Bronte-Tinkew, & Collins, 2010b

Whether or not the youth are having fun or engaging in activities that promote positive youth development – the stated mission of the clubs – is not a priority for club leadership.

The center director is a formal man who insists on being called "Mr. Jones" by all club members, staff, and volunteers. When he emerges from his office, youth and staff stick to the rules. Although Mr. Jones occasionally jokes around, his presence is generally one of authoritarian leadership. Youth programming is secondary to structure in his goals for the center.

The program director, Joanne, gives off an initially warmer vibe than Mr. Jones. She interacts more with the youth and is apt to joke around, especially with the teens. But she can also be a strong disciplinarian and expects staff to play by the rules. If a staff member is having trouble disciplining a youth, s/he often sends the child to Joanne, who instills a sense of obedience in the kids. Although she is more likely to make exceptions to rules than Mr. Jones, Joanne believes that all programming should be structured and does not trust in staff's abilities to run unstructured activities.

The staffs' visions often conflict with that of the center's leadership. Staff members are more concerned with the personalized experience of the youth than either Mr. Jones or Joanne appear to be. Program staff have the most daily contact with club members and tend to value flexibility over structure. Their expressed goals appear more aligned with the national organization's focus on positive youth development. Some staff seem more inclined to take youth input into account, or to have a slightly more youth-driven approach to programming.[4] Despite this, all staff uphold the ordered nature of North River and "fall in line" as far as adopting the center's authoritarian style. Even new staff members are quickly enveloped by the culture of authority and complaint.

PROGRAM DEVELOPMENT AND IMPLEMENTATION

Appearance is paramount, and Mr. Jones displays little concern for the process below the surface. The attention to discipline at the expense of youth development can be damaging to youth[5] as well as

---

[4] See Larson, Walker, & Pearce (2005) for discussion of the benefits and challenges of both adult-driven and youth-driven approaches to programming.

[5] Moore et al., 2010b.

to staffs' abilities to successfully work with the kids. It also impedes implementation of several programs.

In the afternoons at North River, youth rotate from program area to program area on the hour. The upside of the rotation system is that youth have the chance to engage in a variety of types of activities each day. Yet even with the variety, youth cannot freely choose their activities at any given time. Staff express frustration with the rotation system and find it difficult to maintain the quality of certain programs within the rotation structure. This disconnect between the staff and leaders' goals for the center, along with a lack of communication between the administrative and program staff, led to some serious conflicts.

Within program areas there was little structure or staff-led activity. Outside of the formal club programs, youth generally engaged in free-play within each area. Half-way through the year, an easel was erected in the front lobby to display the daily activities. Despite this, there was seldom a match between the activity listed and the activity observed.

This combination of structured rotation with unstructured activities meant that the youth who attended North River in the afternoon (those ages thirteen and younger) had opportunities neither to make decisions and express autonomy nor to engage in purposeful, engaging activities – two factors characteristic of positive youth development and linked to effective after-school programs.[6]

In the evenings, the teens were free to choose their own activities. Here again, however, there were few organized or structured options. The teens most often hung out in the gym, with the boys playing basketball and the girls chatting on the bleachers, or in the game room, where they played pool and other table games. Some organized activities did meet periodically, yet conflicts with club leadership marred the teens' year at the center – an issue that will be discussed in-depth later.

---

[6] Engaging, purposeful activities that focus on skill-building and work toward mastery have been identified as features of effective programs (Birmingham, Pechman, Russell, & Meilke, 2005; Larson, 2000; Little et al., 2008). Durlak, Weissberg, & Pachan (2010) found that after-school programs were most likely to be effective when they used skill-building approaches including "a sequenced set of activities to achieve skill objectives ... [and] active forms of learning." In addition, contexts that provide structure but also allow for youth to exercise autonomy and express their opinions have been identified by researchers as supporting positive youth development (Eccles & Gootman, 2002; Mahoney, Larson, Eccles, & Lord, 2005).

Like other clubs, North River staff took kids on a number of trips during the year. In addition to the large, overnight trips to conferences, there were fairly regular trips to the movies. These often occurred during school break weeks, when the center was open all day. In addition, there were trips to a local entertainment complex, a roller-skating rink, and professional basketball games. North River also participated in inter-club events such as the games room tournament and basketball league.

Gym

The gym at North River is Scottie's domain. A middle-aged African-American man, Scottie dominates the gym with the same type of authoritarian rule that characterizes the club as a whole. His main goal appears to be to maintain order in a space that is prone to some level of chaos. Scottie has mixed relationships with youth, some extremely negative and others very positive. The two youth case studies (Chapters 7 and 8) demonstrate both of these extremes. Youths' experiences in the gym appear to be dictated by the nature of their relationships with Scottie. In general, younger club members and teen girls spend much time sitting on the bleachers and teen boys typically play basketball on their own. Despite earlier efforts to institutionalize girls' gym time at the centers[7], no specific programs for girls existed during the year of our study. Occasionally Scottie would attempt to get teen girls involved by scheduling a gym night or setting up a volleyball net, but no effort was put into recruiting girls to play or to sustaining such opportunities over time.

There is little interaction or teaching between Scottie and youth of any age around recreational activities. Despite the fact that Scottie is the recreational staff member at North River, his interactions often do not include explicit discussion of recreational activity. Of the seven staff members who were observed during structured observation periods across the three clubs, Scottie had one of the two lowest counts for including recreational content in his observed interactions with youth, despite the fact that the gym is typically the center of recreational activity in a club. He also had the lowest count for providing instruction in a skill or activity.

[7] See Hirsch, 2005.

Scottie planned specific activities for the younger members each afternoon. Yet youth engaged in that activity pretty much on their own, without any guidance or encouragement from Scottie. Scottie spent the majority of his time monitoring behavior or keeping score. It was not uncommon for much of a group's gym time to be spent sitting on the bleachers – rather than enjoying themselves on the gym floor – while Scottie attempted to establish quiet and order. We spent a lot of time in gyms at Boys & Girls Clubs, and the youth at North River seemed to spend less time being active and having fun in the gym than their peers at other centers.

Game Room

Like the gym, the game room is characterized by free play and attempts to retain order. Occasionally there are pool, table tennis, and board or video game tournaments. Mid-way through the year, the game room was revamped, with new equipment and the addition of board games. In the corner of the game room is a television with a video game station. This is a popular area when open, and sometimes staff play video games with the kids. As is true across the club, the main staff activity in the game room consists of monitoring kids' behavior. This appears to be driven by the leaders' expectations. For example, one afternoon, two staff members – Daniel, who ran the educational programs, and Sean, who oversaw the front desk – were monitoring the game room. Mr. Jones had told them that they each had to stay on one side of the room. This impeded their abilities to effectively engage with the kids.

> [W]hen Mr. Jones walked through [the room for a third time] Daniel had just begun to walk across the room to the other side to problem solve for a boy who had come over to him and told him that another boy had taken his place in line. As he got three-quarters of the way across the room Daniel saw Mr. Jones come in and turned to the boy and said "I have to stay at that side of the room. You need to go tell Sean what happened and he'll take care of it." Daniel walked back over to where I was standing. [Daniel seemed to be very aware of Mr. Jones' expectations of how the game room was supposed to be monitored. He clearly changed his behavior when Mr. Jones came. It seemed a shame to me, and rather bureaucratic, that Daniel couldn't help the little boy because he was on the opposite side

of the room and it was clear that had Mr. Jones not come in then Daniel would have helped him anyway.]

This is a great example of the mindless emphasis on order and control at the North River center. Mr. Jones puts the staff in a straitjacket, even when it comes to behavior management, one of his primary concerns. Of course, this culture is even more problematic in terms of enabling fun and positive youth development.

Keystone and Torch Club

Two of the only structured programs for youth at North River were Torch Club (for the younger kids) and Keystone (for the teens). Both of these programs were led by staff who were well liked by the youth, Daniel (Torch) and Michelle (Keystone). Yet both programs got a late start and were impeded by organizational issues at the center.

Torch Club did not have its first meeting until the end of March, about six months after it should have begun. To make matters worse, the recruitment efforts for Torch Club once it was started were sub-par. The first meeting was scheduled for a Friday. Early that week staff announced to kids that there would be a Torch Club meeting on Friday and that they were looking for kids to participate. Daniel was given the materials on how to run Torch Club on Thursday, the day before he was expected to run the first meeting. The national organization's description of how Torch Club should be run and the expectations of North River's leadership were not consistent. Rather than target specific youth based on staff recommendations, as recommended by the program materials, North River's leaders told staff to make a general announcement to youth. Seven or eight youth attended the first Torch Club meeting but the second meeting was cancelled because no one showed up. Daniel continued to try to attract kids to Torch Club meetings but had difficulty finding a weekly meeting time that fit with the club's rotation schedule. He also did not want to force youth to attend, as he felt that club leaders wanted him to do. As of May, Torch Club had not fully gotten off the ground and Daniel seemed to feel thwarted rather than supported in his efforts.

Despite being one of the only structured activities for teens, Keystone did not have a staff member to lead it until part way through the year. The club therefore missed the first regional conference. Although on the surface this may not appear significant, regional conferences were a big deal for the teens. Keystone conferences were a chance for the youth to travel out of their neighborhoods and cities and meet other Boys & Girls Club members from around the region. Thus, staff often used the opportunity to attend conferences as an incentive to increase teens' active participation in Keystone. When Michelle was hired in November, she was given the task of leading Keystone. Although she was able to eventually get the club up and running, she, like Daniel, was frustrated by a lack of training and support from club leadership.

> *Like, for Keystone, I did not know what I was doing. At all. I still don't even know what I'm doing ... I ask a lot of questions – that's how I learn. But like, Joanne and I really were not getting along until about December. I used to ask her all these questions about Keystone because I didn't know how to do it and I think she took it the wrong way – like I was trying to get her to do all the work.... But I just really didn't know what to do.*

Despite Michelle's difficulties, by January Keystone had about a dozen regular members and had updated its charter to a higher status. The club ran a number of projects including a Valentine's Day dance and a diversity food fair. Girls and boys shared participation and leadership in Keystone. Overall, the youth at North River appeared to be more involved in meetings than the kids at Midwest. There were fewer disciplinary issues or transgressions with teens talking to each other during meetings. The youth were somewhat more active in terms of helping plan and implement projects, and seemed more invested in Keystone's activities. This was one of the few places at North River where youth engaged in activities that required collaboration in working toward a goal.

> *The main foci of the Keystone meeting were the diversity project and the Valentine's Day party. Michelle said that they had one month left until the diversity project and that they would hold the food festival on the day of the club open house. She suggested that they charge parents and community members $5 to eat, since it would be like a buffet where they could try food from all different regions of the world. Michelle said that the countries that she was thinking of were Italy, Mexico, America, Africa, and China. [One of the girls] said that she wanted to do China. [One of the boys] said that Michelle had said France the week before.*

*"No, she said Italy or something," Tweetie said. "No, she said France,"
[he] repeated. "No I said Italy," Michelle said. He shook his head. "You
said France." "Well, if I did it was a mistake. I meant Italy. It's easier." She said that they would have to go up on the computers to do
research on each country and would then get poster board to make [a
sign] for each booth with information about the country. She then said
they would have to choose restaurants for each place to cater the food. "I
think we need to meet more than once a week," Tweetie said. Michelle
nodded. "Yeah, I told Chris that he would have to cover the game room
for me for the next few weeks so I could be up in the computer room with
you guys doing the research," she said.*

This excerpt is typical of Keystone meetings. Michelle largely
directed meetings and activities in terms of overall planning but
she also emphasized that the events were youths' responsibilities
and she was there to help rather than do it for them. The teens felt
comfortable speaking up and expressing opinions and suggestions.
Despite its success in terms of active youth involvement and over-
coming a late start, Keystone also fell prey to scheduling conflicts.
There was some difficulty in the beginning finding a good time for
the teens to meet. Later in the year there were nights when Keystone
was listed on the board but did not meet due to outside events or
field trips. The issue of communication between leadership and staff
was one that plagued North River, frustrated many staff, and sometimes made it difficult for programs with regular meeting times to
maintain consistency when the timing of conflicting events was not
shared ahead of time.

Formal Educational Programs

Daniel was hired as the education director in the winter. When he
was hired, he began to run Power Hour, a national Boys & Girls
Club program that provides homework help and tutoring to club
members under the age of thirteen. It ran daily on the same hourly
rotation schedule as the rest of the club. Initially, Daniel ran Power
Hour on an as-needed basis, having kids sign up for hourly slots. He
took only a certain number of kids at a time. Once a youth finished
his or her homework, the kid could return to the regular program
area and the next kid on the list went up to Power Hour. In this manner all youth who needed help could get it and youth were not stuck
in the room after they had finished their work. Daniel was informed,

however, that he had to stick to the rotation schedule of the rest of the club. This appeared to make Power Hour less efficient. Whereas once all the kids in the room were doing homework, the rule that kids could not leave meant that Daniel had to find ways to entertain the kids who finished their homework before the hour was through.

> *There were about 10 kids in the room.... A group of girls were sitting at the table in the center of the room. Daniel was talking to them about some worksheets they were doing on rhyming and couplets. [Daniel's assistant] had one or two boys on the side of the room. At a table at the other side of the room about 4 boys were playing Uno ... [The boys playing Uno] were laughing and talking and when one got near Uno he would get up and do a little dance and pump his cards in the air, displaying his hand to me proudly.*

The presence of youth who did not need homework help meant that the room was not as quiet or as focused as it had been earlier in the year, leading to distractions for youth doing homework or getting tutoring. There was no homework help in the evening, although Daniel planned to start a homework program for teens.

The computer room was the other area at North River that included an educational component. In the afternoons, however, kids mostly played computer games of their choice. The instructor, Mr. Marshall, typically monitored the room passively, responding to inquiries from kids and providing help where needed. He described his vision for the computer room as follows:

> *See, I have them playing these computer games that require thinking and logic. Cause if I just get up there and lecture, they're not going to listen and I am going to lose their attention.... So I try to get them games that they enjoy that are at the same time teaching them the skills I need them to acquire so that I can then move on and teach them things that I want them to know. And that is why, you know, I don't tell them how to do things. Cause if they just come running to me asking me how to do it then that doesn't help them. They gotta learn to think it out for themselves. So I help them when they need it but I make them think about it and figure it out.... I begin with teaching about the concept of the computer.... And I teach them basic troubleshooting cause something is gonna go wrong and so they have to know how to fix it so they don't get frustrated. And I teach the basic parts of the computer, you know this is the monitor, this is the keyboard.... But before I can move on to teach them the more advanced skills I have to get them to a certain level of thinking and that is what the games are for.*

Mr. Marshall did talk kids through problems when they approached him with a question. Rather than telling them how to do something, he would ask a series of questions to get them to the right answer, scaffolding them to actively think and arrive at the information they needed to solve the issue. Yet despite occasional focused programs, such as one for Black History Month, the younger members were observed almost entirely playing computer games with only occasional incidents of learning, which were initiated by youth when they encountered a problem. Some youth, such as Beyonce, reported enjoying their time in the computer room but likely would have benefited from more structured programs or classes. In the evenings, teens would come into the computer room now and then to surf the Internet or work on school papers or projects for Keystone, but no formal programming was evident.

Swimming

The swimming program finally got up-and-running in the spring, although the aquatics instructor, Chris, had been hired in January with the promise that the pool would be in working order in a month. The program was supposed to focus on swimming lessons, but the organization of the club as a whole made this difficult, as youth had to rotate with their age groups and there was, therefore, no possibility of arranging swimming lessons by skill level.

Cheerleading and Basketball

During the winter, there was a boys' basketball team, comprised of many of the teen boys who came to the club in the evenings. Rockwell coached the team, which practiced during the week and had weekly games at other clubs. Many of the teen girls traveled with the boys to the games to support them. A group of girls began a cheerleading team on their own, with the goal of eventually cheering at the boys' games. The girls began to create and practice cheers in the corner of the gym or in the auditorium, when they were allowed to use it. Eventually, the club found a volunteer coach for the team. But the girls never got uniforms, and there was tension between the coach and the girls, who thought the coach did not respect the ideas they had come up with prior to her involvement.

The situation between the teens and North River's leadership blew up after a boys' basketball game later in the winter. Following a loss to another club, Mr. Jones chastised the team and called them losers. The incident occurred while the team and the cheerleaders were on the bus on the way back to the center from the game. One of the program staff described the incident to a researcher.

> *I then asked … how the game went … [the staff member] just closed his eyes and shook his head slowly. He told me that Mr. Jones had called the teens losers and gone off on them … "It was like Jekyll and Hyde – I had never seen that before. You know, [one staff person] said that he's used to it and [another] said he's seen it plenty of times, but you know, that was my first time. I never seen anything like it," [the staff person] said. He said that Mr. Jones called the cops on some of the teens from his cell phone after making the bus driver stop the bus … [because] Mr. Jones had felt that the boys were going to assault him. "I knew the police wouldn't come…. And then, he was tryin' to kick them off the bus. Get a taxi back or something. He was tellin' the bus driver to open the doors and I was telling the driver to keep them shut. You can't be doin' that – cuz they still in our possession! … I could not believe it. I could not believe it. You don't tell kids they're losers – it's so hard to get them involved and now they won't even want to try…. And then he went back to normal as if nothing happened…. All I know is that he needs to apologize to those kids. I don't know what's going to happen if he doesn't," [he] said. I asked him how the kids seemed to react. He shook his head and said they were upset and that some of them had been crying, most of them yelling back at Mr. Jones.*

This story was repeated to us by multiple youth and staff over the weeks that followed. Even staff were upset by Mr. Jones's behavior. Mr. Jones demonstrated a failure of leadership on multiple counts. He appeared oblivious to the emotional impact of his words on the youth. His use of demeaning language and ridicule was in direct contrast to the organization's positive youth development framework. He also failed to maintain control of the situation on the bus. His threat to leave the teens in a neighborhood that was likely unsafe, and possibly the territory of gangs from rival neighborhoods, was irresponsible to say the least.

Not surprisingly, the majority of boys reacted by quitting the basketball team. The cheerleaders also disbanded in response to how the boys had been treated. For a few weeks, most of the teens avoided North River. We never saw any signs of Mr. Jones processing the event with the youth. While other staff discussed with us the impact of the incident on club members, there appeared to be no leadership taken in proactively addressing the issue or assessing its impact on the youth. Despite the event's emotional impact and the lack of follow-up on the part of club leaders, the teens eventually returned to North River, although a high level of tension remained and most boys still boycotted the official basketball team.

This incident is a serious indictment of the center leadership and the culture they created. It threatened the safety of the young people and was anathema to the values of positive youth development. Moreover, to the best of our knowledge, this incident never became known to the regional headquarters and speaks poorly of their oversight of this center.

Junior Staff

One of the most popular programs at North River is the Junior Staff program. Junior Staff are club members ages thirteen to eighteen who intern at the center, assisting regular staff in their program areas. The junior staff program is a national BGCA program geared toward career advancement and youth development. At North River, junior staff members are allowed to come to the center in the afternoon even if they are over the age of thirteen. Junior staff sometimes float from area to area, depending on who needs help, but most often are assigned to a particular staff person or area. Many youth stick with the staff member who is their favorite. Junior staff tasks range from helping line up the younger kids and bringing them from area to area, to taking attendance, to helping the coach and keeping score of games. Many of the junior staff also come to the center in the evenings, when they hang out with the rest of the teens. Although this is not a structured program, as youth do not meet together in a group, it gives many members an age-appropriate role and a sense of belonging and purpose in the club.[8] Younger kids sometimes talked about how they "can't wait" until they are old enough to be junior staff. We saw some youth transition into the role of junior staff, a transition that seemed to be accompanied by pride in and an attachment to their new position. The junior staff program appears to be successful in transitioning members from

[8] See Deutsch, 2008.

afternoon to evenings and to give older youth a purpose for continuing to come to the club. Youth organizations have historically had difficulty retaining the participation of adolescents. The junior staff program successfully taps into the desire of adolescents to take on more responsible positions within a familiar setting in which they are already known and is the most successful program at this center in terms of promoting positive youth development.

Programs Run by Volunteers

There were a number of miscellaneous programs at North River throughout the year that were run by outside volunteers. These included a hip-hop class, a drama class, and a mentoring program. Like Midwest, the mentoring was run by the regional Boys & Girls Club headquarters, which brought in mentors on a weekly basis. An outside volunteer taught the hip-hop class, which ran for part of the year in the afternoons. It met weekly and involved mainly girls between the ages of seven and ten. We also heard a lot of talk about a public speaking class, run by a popular African-American adult who showed his face around the club now and then. The class had taken place in prior years, but we did not see evidence of it the year that we were at North River.

Once cheerleading disbanded, drama was the only program at North River other than Keystone that involved teen girls. It met weekly and was run by a woman from a local university. Despite interest from teen girls and commitment on the part of the leader, the group faced difficulties with consistent meetings and interruptions in their programming. The volunteer leader said that she would sometimes show up and find other people in the auditorium, where the drama group was scheduled to meet. Although the leader liked the kids and thought that they had great potential, she told us that she was frustrated by the lack of organization and communication at the club and saw it as impeding her ability to run a successful program.

Again, the issue of communication between club leadership and staff posed a problem for the maintenance of an otherwise successful program. The club was at risk of losing the program altogether due to the instructor's frustrations with the club. This would have meant the loss of one of the only programs that involved teen girls.

Staff-Youth Relationships

Much of the interaction between staff and youth revolved around order and discipline. Center leaders placed a premium on behavior management rather than on youth development, activities, or youth-staff relationships. In general, the relationships between youth and program staff seemed fairly good, although not necessarily close. There were some exceptions. Certain youth, especially some of the older ones, had very close-knit relations with staff members. Michelle appeared to develop relationships with both the younger and older girls within a few months of being at North River. Rockwell seemed to be bonding with some of the teen boys. This may in part reflect the fact that until Michelle and Rockwell arrived, there were no younger program staff.

Overall, the social climate ratings made by researchers indicated higher levels of staff negativity and lower levels of staff enthusiasm and engagement at North River than at the other two centers. Although the program staff reported enjoying their work with the kids, this was not always evident in their behaviors. North River had the highest frequency of negative staff-youth interactions.[9] North River also had significantly fewer peer-like interactions between staff and youth – perhaps a reflection of the fact that the staff person who was the focus of targeted observations at North River, Scottie, was substantially older than youth and than the staff who were the focus of observations at other centers.[10] In fact, the staff members North River youth listed as their favorites were all substantially older than staff at other centers, likely because North River's younger staff members were all new when the surveys were conducted.

Despite a general lack of engagement of staff in youth activities, every now and then, moments of interaction emerged. These bursts of joint activity occurred most often in the evenings when the staff and youth were not tied to specific rooms and staff may have felt freer to join in and play games with the teens.

---

[9] The difference between North River and Midwest was statistically significant, but there was no significant difference between North River and West River.

[10] At North River, Scottie and Joanne were the two staff who were named most frequently by youth as their closest staff person. However, because Joanne was the program director, she seldom interacted with the youth and was only observed with a target youth once. Thus, the observational ratings for North River represent Scottie's interactions with youth.

*I went into the game room, where there were about a dozen girls and a dozen guys playing pool, video games, and just milling about. Sharon, Chris, and Sam were getting ready to play around the world ping pong and Sharon handed me a paddle. As we were playing [two teen guys] joined in. Eventually Tweetie and some other girls came out of the gym and some of them joined the game, including Tweetie, while the rest stood and watched. Rockwell came out and was watching but declined to play. All the kids and Sam, Sharon and Chris were all laughing and teasing each other and rooting each other on as they ran around the table. [*This was one of the first times that I had seen really active interaction between staff and youth in a sustained playful and fun activity here. All the staff were actively involved and the kids were either playing or watching. Everyone seemed to be really enjoying themselves.*]

There were also a few youth-staff dyads rife with discord. Some of these conflicts were fairly open. These often resulted from the staff's reactions to the youth's behavior and what was perceived to be unfair punishment of the youth. Other conflicts were more covert and based on a long history of tension. Over the course of the year, extreme conflicts emerged between center leaders and teens.

The friction between youth and leadership at North River is illustrated by a subtle incident that took place following the youth Christmas party, at which kids received pre-wrapped gifts. After the party, Mr. Jones addressed the young kids' complaints about some of the gifts.

Kids were talking and Mr. Jones said "You all can take it home to your parents if you want to complain. We ain't your parents. Complain to them and maybe you'll get what you want. We do the best we can. I'm sorry if you didn't get something you like but we do the best we can. So you should be grateful."

Although not outright hostile, Mr. Jones's reaction to the youth was also not responsive. He could have proposed a way to engage the kids in problem solving, such as forming a youth council to suggest presents for the following year. Such an approach would have been more aligned with the positive youth development focus of the organization. Yet instead of emphasizing youth as having capacities to be developed, he treated them as problems to be fixed. As seemed the norm at North River, the kids for whom the party was being given were not given any agency in deciding what they wanted from it.

Scottie is a good example of the contradictory beliefs and behaviors of North River's staff. Whereas he had a very close relationship with some youth, he had highly negative interactions with others, as indicated by his having the highest percentage of negative interactions of any staff member across the three centers. It was routine to hear Scottie complain about the juniors (youth aged eleven to thirteen) as acting like babies. He constantly grumbled to researchers, in front of the kids, about youths' inability to follow directions, listen, or stay still and quiet. The root of some of his frustrations was made apparent during a visit to the gym during dismissal time one afternoon.

> *Scottie looked up at me and shook his head and said, "Why they leave me all alone in here? ..." He frowned and peered out into the game room. "Now see, why he have her doing that now? And look at them! They have nothing to do but they leave me alone with these kids. All the staff supposed to be in here," Scottie said. His tone was somewhat upset – it sounded more hurt than anything ... Kids would come up to Scottie and start to ask him something but once they started talking, Scottie would say, "Be quiet. Be quiet. Be quiet," so that they could never finish what they were asking. Other times, when the kids would call Scottie's name, he would say, "Do not say my name. Uh, don't be calling my name." There were some kids, however, that he allowed to get a drink of water and he had me escort one of the younger girls to the bathroom.*

Yet at other times, Scottie used kids' misbehavior as teachable moments. He and Victoria (at West River) had the highest number of observations coded for expressing goals and expectations for youth. For Scottie, this may have stemmed from dual concerns with behavior management and providing youth with fatherly "life lessons." The following interaction occurred one afternoon when Scottie had the juniors watch a movie in one of the club's multi-purpose rooms because the heating was broken in the gym. The members were talking and lounging against the wall as Scottie was trying to get them to sit down and be quiet. Scottie warned them that their "clownin'" would get them in trouble in high school in more ways than one.

> *"Now some of you are eighth graders – you 13 and going to be goin' to high school next year. Well, now things are different in high school. You go in there tryin' to act hard and there will be sophomores, juniors, and seniors there, waiting for you who already hear that you a freshman and you actin' hard.... All the clownin' around you did in grade school ... you can't be doing' that in high school. There are gangs, girl gangs too,*

some that are even worse than the boy gangs," Scottie said. Some of the kids snickered.... "Oh, you think it's funny now until some of you end up one of their girlfriends.... I think we ought to take you girls down to [a women's penitentiary], show you what 'hard' is, what actin' 'hard' can get you. Yeah, I think it'd be good for you.... You know what 'the big house' is? ... when you turn 18 you will be tried as an adult. Now the worst three high schools ... are the most violent. But it happens everywhere.... Now, I'm telling you this because I want you to know that things are going to be different when you get to high school. Johnny, do your brother say it's a joke?" Johnny (a club member) shook his head seriously. "No, it aint' no joke.... There will be some of you who will be approached by gangs. And it happens, kids who went here who are now in gangs. Some cut, stabbed, beat, some of them dead. One day we closed down the club and walked over ... to look at the bodies, all covered up, dead from a shooting, some of them kids from this club. It ain't no joke.... When I ... see some of the kids who used to come here who come up to me it makes me so sad, when they come up to me and say, "Hey, Mr. Scottie! Could you help me out with a cup of coffee?" Scottie paused and looked around the room and then kept talking, "'Shoulda listened to you when you was tryin' to help me out. Shoulda listened to what you said. 'I'm telling you now because it's different when you get to high school.... When you get to high school I hope you become leaders, because if you become followers you will go down the drain."

This example demonstrates the strengths of having staff members who are familiar with and have a history of involvement in the youths' communities, something on which the North River center was strong. Scottie was one of only a few staff members across all the clubs who was observed discussing past experiences with the youth, likely an indication of his long history at the club. In this instance, Scottie drew on his experiences with other North River kids and in the local schools to provide some natural mentoring. Nonetheless, Scottie's approach may not have always been engaging to youth. Indeed, the researcher who observed the previously described interaction noted that whereas she was moved by Scottie's tale of former club members, most of the youth had their heads down on their desks and did not appear to be engaged in his narrative. In fact, Scottie frequently lectured youth on the future, something that we will explore more in Tweetie's case study. Because we observed Scottie after he had been working at North River for many years, we do not know whether his didactic approach was a result of the overall climate at North River, his experiences with losing other youth to the streets, or simply his personality. Regardless, for all his grumbling, underneath the gruffness, Scottie appeared to truly care about the kids' futures.

In fact, Scottie sometimes expressed fondness for the kids, and was particularly supportive of the teens and critical of Mr. Jones after his blowout with the teens.

> *I mean, that just is not the way you speak to kids. That's what happens when someone doesn't really interact with kids all that much and just doesn't know how to speak to them. Joanne too. She comes in here and sees a guy and girl leaning on each other on the bleachers and she's all yelling and saying what's going on they can't do that in here. And they weren't kissin' or nothing. Just sitting there … [because they do not interact with the kids] they don't know how to talk with them. I mean, you gotta give respect to get respect. [Other staff and I] we all grew up around here and were here when they were all gangs in the clubs. But they was never no fights cause they knew this was a place where you gave respect. But no boy wants to be made to look bad in front of all his friends. And no girl neither. You don't want to have someone call you out in front of all your friends. You gotta respect them.*[11]

In fact, of all the staff observed across centers, Scottie had the highest percentage (5.7%) of observations coded for supporting youth leadership, the same percentage of observations that were coded for negative interactions. This likely reflects the fact that Scottie nearly always had a junior staff person with him during observation periods. Scottie had close relationships with those youth who served as junior staff with him, although he had highly negatively charged relationships with other youth.

The tension between program line staff and club management appeared to filter down to staff's interactions with youth, with negativity spreading like wildfire, even to new staff. The atmosphere at North River highlights the importance of organizational practices to the daily experiences of youth at after-school centers.

---

[11] This idea of bi-directional respect – needing to give respect to teens to have them respect you – has been cited as important by teens in other studies of youth centers. In those studies, the teens discussed respect both as an important dimension of their own personalities and as an important factor that differentiated their relationships with staff at after-school centers from those with adults in other contexts of their lives. Both youth and staff saw the importance of bi-directional respect in supporting youth participation as well as adult authority in after-school centers (Deutsch, 2008; Deutsch & Jones, 2008).

HUMAN RESOURCE DEVELOPMENT

As should already be evident, North River was not a model for best practices in organizational management or human resource development. Rather than support and nurture staff to reach their potentials, North River appeared to squash enthusiasm for working with young people and impede staff's attempts to improve programming.

Staff Hiring

A number of new staff members were hired during our time at North River. In addition, volunteer or temporary staff people were brought in to run specific programs that youth wanted, such as drama and cheerleading. These new staff members had the potential to increase both the variety of activities and the number of natural mentors available to youth. Yet management's attitude toward staff once they were hired, characterized by a lack of trust, high levels of control, and little to no staff autonomy over their program areas, not only diminished the effects of new staff on the center's activities and culture, but also made it difficult for North River to retain program staff. Although there was a core group of long-time staff members, newer staff appeared unhappy with the structure of the club. Many of them expressed uncertainty about how long they would stay. One staff member indicated that this was the culture at North River: "What's sad is they expect [staff turnover. Some kids asked me], so, when are you leaving? And I was like I don't know. If you get rid of [one of the leaders], I'll stay longer!" The laissez-faire attitude to staff turnover could be particularly damaging to youths' experiences at the center, as close and consistent youth-staff relationships is a common feature of successful organizations.[12]

Training and Supervision

Staff received little training, although they were expected to do their jobs the "right way." At North River, this meant primarily maintaining order. Staff training is a problem on a regional basis and one that we heard about continuously over the years. Training sessions

---

[12] Hirsch, 2005; Little et al., 2008; Moore et al., 2010a; Rhodes, 2004.

appear to focus mostly on orientation and overriding issues but seldom go in-depth on teaching needed skills to lead a particular program or to work effectively with youth. A number of staff reported being given duties and programs, including nationally chartered programs such as Torch Club and Keystone, without any training or preparation. The lack of training also extended to the general issue of how to manage a program area effectively.

> *"When you were hired for this position, were you trained or orientated to how to do this?" I asked. She shook her head. "So how did you know what to do?" I asked. "I winged it," she said. "I mean, when I came in, they said, oh, there's some manuals in case you don't know how to play the games and want to read the rules but I already knew how to play all the games," she said. "So aside from the technical aspects of like, knowing the rules, were you given any direction on how to deal with the kids?" ... [she] shook her head. "Yeah, I just winged it. I did not know what I was doing. I mean, we had a games room training in November or January," she said. I asked her when she came on and she said in October.*

Even Joanne expressed a desire for more training from regional headquarters.

Supervision of staff focused on adherence to structure and rules. Rather than helping staff grow into their jobs, management's supervision often impeded staff's abilities to make program improvements. Program staff saw a need for flexibility in their on-the-ground tasks that was not supported, and was often punished, by club leadership. When staff took initiative to solve a problem but, in doing so, violated a club rule or structure, they risked chastisement from above. An example of such a situation took place during the winter, when the heat was broken in the gym. Scottie took a group of kids into the auditorium to watch a movie during their gym time.

> *I heard Mr. Jones' voice say, "Where's Scottie – he in here?!" Scottie looked up and said, "Yeah, I'm in here. I took my group in here because we ain't got no heat in the gym and we ain't moved nothin' – these tables was already like this. I just had them sit down – we ain't pulled no chairs out." ... "No, you can't be doing that. You can't just take them in here," Mr. Jones said, glaring at Scottie. "Well, we ain't done nothin' wrong and there ain't no other room to go to," Scottie said. "[Orange] room," Mr. Jones said in an angry tone ... Mr. Jones stormed out of the auditorium, shaking his head ... Scottie shook his head. "I got the Juniors next and they a big group. They ain't gonna fit in the [Orange] room – it's a small room! He don't know that – he don't realize what a big group they*

is. And it's cold in the gym – we ain't got no heat and I am not going to put children in there...It's times like these that make me not want to be here – when you have someone like that. Shoot, if he don't care, then why should I care?" Scottie said in an angry and frustrated tone.

This was not the only example of staff attempts to be proactive being punished instead of rewarded. Rockwell volunteered to coach the boys' basketball team. Yet rather than being thanked, he was told by the club director that "the team needs a 'real' coach." Rockwell was angry about this reaction: "I'm thinking, if you wanna get your ass out there and try and coach those kids, go ahead. But I've been busting my ass and doing all of this by myself. Ordering the uniforms, the cheerleading uniforms – no one's been helping me...I really like working with these kids. Especially the teenagers. But I'm not used to other people I work with not being professional." North River was in danger of losing Rockwell because of club leadership, not youth. In fact, he left at the end of the year.

Learning Organization

It is difficult to imagine an organization less inclined to engage in organizational learning. The focus on hierarchy and order impeded cooperation and did not encourage staff members to try new things. Rather than turning conflicts into teachable moments or opportunities to grow, the organizational lens was placed squarely back on structure and discipline. The management's treatment of staff then bled down to youth.

Due to the strict rotation system, staff were isolated and had few consistent, daily opportunities to work together or learn from each other.[13] Staff meetings could have provided such opportunities, but

---

[13] Such staff isolation is reminiscent of the experiences of classroom teachers, who may have few opportunities to collaborate across subjects or grades. Educational researchers have suggested, however, that increasing teacher collaboration may be important for improving schools, teacher satisfaction, and student outcomes (Johnson, Berg, & Donaldson, 2005). The effects of teacher collaboration on student outcomes may come through teachers improving their pedagogical practice by learning from their peers (Goddard, Goddard, & Tschannen-Moran, 2007; Jackson & Bruegmann, 2009) or due to teachers sharing knowledge and information about students, which helps teachers better address children's needs (Hart, 1998). Both of these factors are applicable to after-school program staff, who may benefit from both the practical skills and youth-level knowledge of their colleagues. Yet collaboration requires trust between the members of the school community (Johnson, Berg, & Donaldson, 2005), something that was absent at North River.

meetings did not appear to be held consistently. Staff reported that staff meetings occurred "theoretically" once a week, but that in reality they went "in spurts" and staff were not always told about them ahead of time. Part-time staff did not attend at all. When meetings did occur, they were led by Joanne and focused mainly on scheduling issues and program planning. Mr. Jones would generally come in at some point during the meeting to discuss anything that he had on his agenda. Staff report that they sometimes discuss youth but, like at the Midwest club, it tends to be when one staff person brings up a particular kid with whom they are having difficulties. At such times, one staff member reports, the meeting "really just turns into a bitchfest," with other staff talking about how that kid drives them crazy too. So instead of fostering a culture that focuses on promoting positive youth development, staff meetings if anything tended to reinforce a culture of negativity.

Despite the hierarchy at North River and the overall isolation of staff, program staff did on rare occasions call on each other to support their decisions.

> *Daniel called a little girl off the bleachers and told her she shouldn't have hit the boy next to her. "But he hit me first!" she said. "I don't care. That's what we're here for. You tell us. You don't go and hit him. I'm here to help you stay out of trouble," Daniel said. The girl folded her arms and continued to grumble and protest that he had hit her. "Okay, but it's not okay to just hit someone back. You tell us if someone does something to you," Daniel repeated. Albert then repeated this message loudly, to the whole group. "All of this back and forth stuff has got to stop. If someone does something to you you tell us. That is what we are here for. And it shouldn't be taking this long to quiet all of you all down." Daniel walked by and Michelle called him over. She asked if he was disciplining the girl he had pulled out of line and told him that she needed to fill out a discipline form for that girl also. They chatted briefly and quietly (Michelle held a clipboard up next to their faces so the girls nearby couldn't hear what they were saying) about each of their problems with the girl, comparing notes. They agreed to write her up together.*

It should be noted that this episode involves collaboration but not organizational learning. Collaboration can serve as a foundation for organizational learning, or be an outcome of organizational learning, but it need not involve any organizational learning at all, and that was true at the North River center.

As suggested by the preceding excerpt, staff reported that they generally felt supported by other program staff. One staff person, who had been at the club for more than twenty years, described the program staff as "like a family." The feeling of support between program staff did not extend to their relationships with the two center administrators. We have previously discussed the predominantly negative relationship between Mr. Jones and center staff; it should not be surprising that there was also considerable negative feelings and a lack of trust toward Joanne, the second-in-command. As one staff member told us about Joanne,

> She's vindictive, she makes everything personal, she's paranoid, and she – I just don't think she's professional! ... She thinks we're out to get her or something...We're told, she's our supervisor. We have to go to her first ... [Joanne is] so paranoid that she freaks out if we don't go to her first because she thinks we're trying to go above or around her, you know?].... But like, I would never go to Joanne because I don't trust her. And I feel like if you were to go to her with a problem, she'd use it against you later.

Given the extraordinarily high levels of conflict and distrust, it is not difficult to understand why almost no organizational learning was evident at this center. Overall, this center was an organizational disaster. There was conflict over management styles, lack of communication, disagreements over program structure, lack of training, lack of support for programs, and perceived incompetence of administrators by staff and perceived incompetence of staff by administrators. The center's culture and dynamics impeded the realization of core national and regional values on the importance of fun and positive youth development.

CONCLUSION

Our year at North River was marked by one of the most explosive incidents we observed over our years in after-school centers. The incident did not come as a complete surprise. North River's culture was one of conflict and blame. Mr. Jones had an authoritarian leadership style and, after being disrespected during the bus ride home from a losing basketball game, the young people finally rebelled.

Sometimes a crisis can be a catalyst for positive change, but this did not prove to be the case at North River. The incident was never processed, most of the youth eventually returned to the center, and the culture did not change.

One of the great failures at North River was that there was no outside oversight to step in and overhaul the center. There was a Board of Directors for the center and the center was part of a regional group of Boys & Girls Clubs. But if they ever learned about this incident, or understood the pervasive negative culture at the center, we never heard about it and it certainly never resulted in any action. Mr. Jones could be quite charming and articulate. We suspect that he presented the operations of the center in a very positive light, and the visitors never spent enough time at the center or had extended conversations with anyone else at the center to learn otherwise. An alternative perspective would likely have been provided only by parental complaints or by site visits by external reviewers. We shall return to this need in the concluding chapter in the book.

The other factor that might have attracted attention from the Board or regional headquarters was if youth had left the center in droves. But they returned. Given the pervasive negative climate, why did they do so?

There were several factors that help explain why youth kept coming to what was a rather low-functioning after-school center. North River played an important role in the local community. In a neighborhood that was fraught with violence and crime, the club provided a safe place for kids. Parents could trust that their kids were safe inside its doors. Teenagers who wished to avoid the local gangs and violence on the streets knew that North River provided a safe haven to be with their friends. The structure and order imposed from above at North River served a purpose in a community in which a lack of management of youth could prove dangerous.

There were also a number of close, familial-like relationships at the center. Scottie, for all his negative interactions and griping, also had very tight-knit, fatherly relationships with a number of youth. In addition, the long history of some staff provided a stream of consistent relationships with adults who knew the youth and their families. The addition of a number of younger staff who appeared more energetic and interested in cultivating new activities for youth provided additional opportunities for such relationships to develop.

Even in the absence of a focus on positive youth development, the presence of these relationships provided some incentive for youths' continued participation.[14]

There were also two acceptable-to-good programs: Junior Staff and Keystone. And new programs and activities were periodically added or restarted, providing at least a glimmer of hope for a fresh start.

Unfortunately, the return of disillusioned youth to the center probably reinforced the belief that the center was a good place for youth. The Boys & Girls Clubs are a powerful brand in the after-school world and in many of these communities. Powerful brands can promote complacency, a satisfaction with things as they are, a sense that they have a handle on what to do, that there are no real alternatives.

Yet beyond being a safe physical space and providing access to relationships with non-familial adults, North River provided few developmental benefits for youth. The organizational structure and management styles of the club leaders were major barriers to North River's moving forward. Even new staff were quickly indoctrinated into the culture of behavior management and hierarchy, ensuring that "new blood" had little impact on either center or staff practices.

In the next two chapters we will read about two youth who had very different experiences at North River. In both cases, the young people had some positive interpersonal ties at the center but were also negatively impacted by the center's culture.

---

[14] Relationships with adults have been found to be a key feature of successful youth programs and one that is often listed as an important factor by youth themselves (Deutsch & Hirsch, 2002; Hirsch, 2005; Little et al.,2008; Moore et al., 2010a; Rhodes, 2004).

7

Undercutting Tweetie: The Trials and Tribulations of a Youth Leader

Tweetie is the type of teen you just can't miss. A gregarious, attractive fifteen-year-old,[1] she makes her presence known in a positive way, taking on leadership roles and acting as a friendly emissary to center visitors. Tweetie started coming to North River in the third grade. Three of her siblings also attend the club, making Tweetie and her family a center institution. She knows all the staff well and has an especially close relationship with Scottie, who serves as a big brother and father figure to her. Tweetie is a constant presence at North River and is involved in many club activities. Yet despite her deep involvement in the center and her close relationship with Scottie, Tweetie's year was plagued by roadblocks. A number of incidents thwarted her natural leadership potential, including conflicts with staff and activities that were dropped. These roadblocks appeared to decrease her attendance at the center. Further, and perhaps more importantly, such undercutting experiences likely dampened potential positive effects of her involvement with North River. Tweetie did not make many gains over the course of the year. She was a high-achieving youth from the start, but multiple opportunities for her to develop her leadership skills at the center were not realized. Tweetie avoided getting involved with the gangs and violence that were prevalent among the girls in her neighborhood, but we can only imagine what gains she may have made if she had received greater, active support from North River.

---

[1] Tweetie was fourteen at the beginning of the study but turned fifteen in the middle of the year.

IN THE BEGINNING

A petite girl, Tweetie makes up for her small stature in personality. When she strides through a room, her broad smile and friendly "hello" precede her. Tweetie changes her hair style often and always looks fashionable. Yet she is not prone to sitting and talking about hair or nails, as, she complains, other girls do too frequently. Rather, she is drawn to activities, especially ones in the gym. Everyone at North River knows her – a fact in which she takes pride. And Tweetie's social prowess does not end at the center doors. Her social network map and lifeline are chock full of friends.[2] She takes pride in the fact that "everybody looks up to me and the kids are like 'Hey Tweetie' and everybody knows me." Tweetie is president of her school's student council and over the years has been involved in a number of activities both in and outside of North River.

At school, Tweetie has participated in track, basketball, volleyball, cheerleading, and drama and has been on Honor Roll continually since fifth grade. Her lifeline is sprinkled with moments of accomplishment and good times, such as winning first place in track, going to concerts, and happy family events, including reunions, skating parties, and family members having babies. She has been dating a fellow club member for about three years and has close relationships with a number of female friends as well as her mother, siblings, aunts, cousins, nephews, and nieces. Yet Tweetie's life has also been marked by difficult times, including the deaths of a family member and a fellow North River member over the past year.

Tweetie has a long history of involvement in programs at North River. The center and some of its staff hold a valued place in her heart and life. Tweetie says that Scottie knew her from "before I was born." Her first stop at the center is always the gym, where she checks in to say hello to Scottie before going about whatever other activities are on her plate that night. She also lists other staff with whom she had positive relationships over the years, including a former program director and a public speaking instructor.

---

[2] Tweetie has strong peer skills. She scored somewhat above the sample mean on peer relations self-efficacy (T-score = 53.82) and on peer-trust (T-score = 56.69). In addition, she scored a full standard deviation below the mean on peer interpersonal sensitivity (T-score = 40.41), meaning that she is less sensitive to negative aspects of peer relations than other youth. Yet she does have some difficulties, and clearly holds high standards for herself, as she scored about half a standard deviation below the mean for peer self-esteem (T-score = 45.67).

Tweetie says that when she first started coming to the club, as a young child, she did not want to try any new activities. "When I was real little I used to hate how little kids have to play basketball and stuff. I hated doing it all ... I just liked sitting down." In his interview, Scottie also mentions this:

> *When she first come she didn't want to try. She felt she couldn't do it. So I work with her ... I guess she trusted me, cause she tried. Even though she didn't like it she participated. She plays the sports now.*

As one of the most active teens we saw at any center, it is hard to imagine this younger, uninvolved Tweetie. But both she and Scottie mention this when talking about how their relationship has changed.

Over her years at North River, Tweetie participated in Torch Club, Smart Girls, a mentoring program, and played on girls' basketball and softball teams. She took classes at the center, including the public speaking class, the instructor of which she reports as being an "inspiration" to her. Thus, when we first came to North River, Tweetie was one of the most involved and active adolescent members. In fact, when asked what outcomes she wanted to avoid in the coming year, Tweetie reported that she wanted to avoid coming to the club less in high school. During the year we observed her, Tweetie was involved in Keystone, drama and law enforcement classes, and the cheerleading team. Thus, she seemed primed to make the most of her eighth-grade year at North River.

Scottie and Tweetie have a close relationship, and Scottie has nothing but positive words for her. "[She is a] very sweet, very kind person. She listen when you talk to her ... and she respects me. Nothing disrespectful in my presence." Joanne, the program director, sees Tweetie differently. Rather than viewing her dominant personality as having leadership potential, she feels that Tweetie "has a stubborn streak in her. She's very opinionated.... She can become quite disrespectful ..." Although we did not directly observe Tweetie in any such interactions with Joanne, we were aware of conflict she had with club leaders. When Tweetie felt that she or other club members were being treated unfairly, she apparently engaged in interactions that could be read as disrespectful to the adults involved. Joanne's words are an ominous foreshadowing of Tweetie's year at North River. Despite Tweetie's enthusiasm for sports and interest in a variety of programs, she was continually shut down by club leadership. Her attempts to organize the girls and initiate new activities were thwarted, sometimes directly, other times more subtly. As the year went on, it became more and more unclear what would keep her involved or what gains she could make from her participation in North River's programs. At every turn, Tweetie seemed to face adversity in her attempts to create a more creative and active environment for her and her peers.

Despite the stumbling blocks put in her path by North River's leaders and programs, Tweetie came to the center about three days a week throughout the year. She considers North River a second home, and her relationship with Scottie, who serves as both a protector and a preacher to her, is particularly kin-like. Yet by spring, it was unclear whether there was enough at North River to sustain her interest or support her development in the years to come.

TWEETIE'S YEAR AT THE AFTER-SCHOOL CENTER

Tweetie's experiences at North River encompassed two areas: her relationship with Scottie and her involvement in, and attempt to start, a variety of activities. The former was a clear asset. The latter could have been a supporting factor, but instead became problematic due to conflicts with the center's leaders and overall culture. This is reflected in Tweetie's PARC profile (Table 7.1), which indicates a pattern of lack of developmental support within the context of programs and activities despite close relationships with Scottie and some peers.

Closest Staff Relationship

Scottie serves as a father figure to Tweetie. She puts him in the inner circle on her social network map and always goes to see him when she arrives. Tweetie says, "I knew Scottie for years. He like an uncle or something. He's somebody you can look up to." Scottie reciprocates this, recognizing their family-like tie. "I'm like a big brother. She sit and talk to me about things. I think she considers me a father figure as well." In fact, Scottie knows Tweetie's biological family fairly well. He even paid Tweetie's siblings to do some chores for him, saying that he knew "they could use the money."

Tweetie and Scottie's was one of the closest bonds at North River. Whereas we went months without knowing that Tweetie was dating

TABLE 7.1. *Tweetie's PARC profile*

Starts at beginning of year

P –
A hanging out in gym
R Scottie
C family-like, caring, protection, advice, educational goals

P cheerleading
A organize and lead practices, choreograph cheers, cheer at boys' games
R peers, coach, program director, director
C initially: peer responsiveness to youth agency, energy, enthusiasm; later: lack of responsiveness to youth agency, conflict with staff and administrators

P drama class
A drama-related activities
R peers, instructor
C unknown

Starts in middle of year

P Keystone
A attending and leading meetings, decision making, organizing activities, planning community event
R peers, Michelle
C youth-driven, engagement, peer leadership

P –
A playing sports in gym
R Scottie, peers
C frustration, lack of support from peers and staff

P boys' basketball team manager
A organizing, leadership, going to boys' games
R Scottie, male peers
C peer leadership, activity

P –
A helping Scottie with younger kids
R Scottie, younger kids
C combination of support and autonomy, responsibility, trust

Starts at end of year

P Girls gym night
A sports
R Scottie
C lack of participation, lack of staff and peer support, frustration, never really implemented

a fellow club member, we recognized the relationship between Scottie and Tweetie immediately. Their kinship was obvious in public words and actions. Tweetie's first activity in the club was often saying hi to Scottie, which she'd preface with an announcement such as "I'm gonna go talk to the old man now." This recognition was mutual. One afternoon when Tweetie entered the gym, Scottie acknowledged her presence with "Oh, there's my lil' sister!" Their relationship had many kin-like qualities, as demonstrated in the following field notes.

> *Tweetie was one of the first teens to come [into the club]. She carried a shopping bag with her and handed it to Scottie, who was sitting at the front. [Tweetie sometimes brought Scottie food for dinner.] "This bread is frozen!" Scottie said. "It was the only bread they had. And it's frozen cause I was outside with it!" she said laughing. Scottie shook his head. "Put it in the oven or something," Tweetie said smiling and walking into the club.*

> *Tweetie came in and said hi to me and said "I am going to go talk to Scottie." She walked over to the other side of the game room, where Scottie was standing near the doors to the gym. After a couple of minutes I went over and stood with them. "Cause you know you got a bunch of big brothers here," Scottie was saying. "If anyone give you any trouble you just call me. You 911 me and I'm down there with the rest of your big brothers.... You know you can tell em they can't be messing with our little sister."*

These instances are typical of their daily interactions, which range from little-sister-like hassles to fatherly concern. Scottie takes a protective stance toward Tweetie, and she willingly sits through his sometimes lengthy and preacher-like monologues on life. Theirs is a relationship built on a mutual sense of obligation and care.

Scottie also actively mentors Tweetie around issues of school and future plans. Even within the busy environment of the club, Scottie always finds time to talk with Tweetie one-on-one. When asked what he typically talks to her about, Scottie responds:

> *School, major, what she's gonna do with her life, boys, friends, how to carry herself, things she shouldn't do.... Make boys respect you. Long time for boyfriends – get an education, good job.... Like, she wanted to be a lawyer. I told her ... decide what kind of lawyer she want to be. Look it up, then print it up and then bring it down [to me to look at].*

He gives advice to Tweetie about

> *... life, school, job, love life – tell her don't have no young men hittin' on you. Respect you. Ain't no pullin on ya – if you can't get along, leave them alone. (And how does she respond?) Very well. She smile,*

listen well, if she don't understand, she say, "Scottie, what you mean by that" and I explain.

It would be easy to dismiss this as an adult overstating his influence on a teen. Indeed, Tweetie does rate their relationship slightly less positively than does Scottie (she gives it a "4" while Scottie gives it a "5" on a 5-point scale), but both ratings reveal a close bond. And Tweetie does confirm Scottie's wide-ranging mentoring role.

[I have talked to him] about boys … club stuff, people at the club. I be talking to him about what schools I'm going to. He be givin' me advice about what school I should go to, the good schools … [It is important] cause it's like my future.… He just tell me how it is. Cause I ain't got no father figure in my life or nothing.

Academics is an important part of Scottie and Tweetie's relationship. Although there was little, if any, direct school support for teens at North River, Scottie was an ardent advocate for Tweetie in the realm of academics. They shared an interest in law that helped Scottie talk to her about choosing her schools and classes. During our year at the club, Tweetie was making the choice of what high school she would attend in the fall. This was a constant topic of conversation for her and Scottie.

Scottie asked her where she was going to high school and she said she didn't know yet. "Well, what you want to do? You got to decide what you want to do, you know, what you want to major in and what you want to be and see which high school is best for that." "I want to be a lawyer," Tweetie said. "Okay, so you got to see what high schools offer law classes." Tweetie nodded.

Scottie also addresses broader life issues. These conversations sometimes lean toward monologues, however. At times, Tweetie's strong respect for and commitment to Scottie appears to keep a conversation going in spite of diminishing returns.

When I entered the gym Scottie was in the middle of talking to Tweetie. "You can't just play one sport. You gotta have something to fall back on. I knew this one guy, ya see, he went to college on a scholarship … so like he was playing football on scholarship … but he hurt his knee and couldn't play football anymore so he had to leave college.… You gotta have more than one thing, diversify. You can't count on one sport to get you through college. Then you'll have nothing to fall back on …" Tweetie is listening and nodding.… "What's your grades? You get A's and B's? So you must be like a 3.0 or something?" Tweetie nods. "That's good, that's good . . ." Scottie then asks Tweetie about what high school she is going to go to and they briefly discuss different high schools, with Scottie commenting on which are better than others. . . . Scottie mentions the military as a good way to get money for college and tells a story about his cousin. "You know he was in Desert Storm. . . . But he been all over the world. And we got a girl at [local high school] who went into the Marines and we get postcards from her from all over. . . . Man, it's a great way to see other places and to get money for college."

This conversation reflects much of what we see as both the strengths and shortcomings of their relationship, which we will discuss in the "shortcomings" section.

Tweetie's relationship with Scottie provides more than support and academic mentoring. Scottie also recognizes Tweetie's developing need for autonomy and her innate leadership skills. Rather than infantilize her, as he easily could do given his protector role, he encourages her autonomy and gives her opportunities to take on more responsibility. He recognizes her need for both support and independence and appears able to balance these two, sometimes competing, developmental demands.[3] As noted in Chapter 6, Scottie was observed supporting youth leadership more than any other staff we observed across centers. He did have negative relationships with many youth, and focused a lot on behavior management. Yet when youth formed close relationships with Scottie and served as junior staff with him in the gym, he would foster their taking on leadership roles to an even greater extent than other staff we observed.

There was ample occasion for such interactions, as Tweetie spent a good deal of time with Scottie in the gym. One afternoon, Scottie talked to her about the problems he was having with the twelve-to-thirteen-year-old group. These kids were only a couple of years younger than Tweetie. Yet he asked her to take some of them to another program area, assigning her to a supervisory role. He then pulled Tweetie aside to talk to her about the discipline issues. Scottie also provides opportunities for Tweetie to take on more formal leadership roles, such as the basketball team manager, which will be discussed later.

Scottie's relationship with Tweetie spans a range of life domains and provides her with needed support. Their close bond is an

[3] Steinberg, 1990.

important asset in terms of Tweetie's involvement in the club. In fact, the relationship domain of Tweetie's PARC profile is dominated by Scottie, who appears in all but three of her eight PARCs. The question remains, however, whether this mentoring relationship would have been enhanced by participation in a meaningful activity, notably missing from Tweetie's PARCs. There was little opportunity for joint activity, which may have limited the benefits Tweetie could reap from her relationship with Scottie as she got older and began to visit the center less often.

Activities and Program Participation

Despite a lack of organized activities for teens, especially early in the year, Tweetie made the most of North River's programs. In addition to being a leader in Keystone, a national Boys and Girls Club service program for teens, she managed the boys' basketball team, started a cheerleading team, and tried, whenever possible, to participate in girls' gym night. These activities fostered leadership skills and further integration into the center, including giving her a role as an effective youth organizer. Yet some of the activities, especially the latter two, also had clear costs. Her agency was thwarted by club leadership and organizational factors that kept her from receiving their full benefits.

At the beginning of the year, Tweetie was involved in a drama class at the center and spent a lot of time hanging out with Scottie in the gym. Yet perhaps the most important activity for Tweetie that fall was the cheerleading team that she started. The scenario below showcases Tweetie's leadership skills and ability to fire up her peers.

> *The girls went to the far side of the gym along the side lines and Tweetie began to line them up.... Tweetie got them into formation and they began to do a cheer.... Tweetie stopped a few times and said "don't wait for me, just keep going." She also commented that people weren't being loud enough.... For the next 45 minutes they practiced the old cheer and began work on two new ones.... The girls would work together, with [another girl] and Tweetie generally giving the ideas for cheers and the other girls giving input and working them out together.... When they developed a new clapping and stomping routine girls who got it immediately would break off with a smaller group of girls and they would teach it to each other in groups, then do it in a circle together, and then try it in formation.*

Tweetie got the group going, kept them on task, and provided ideas. Yet she did not overpower them; she served as an effective facilitator. The activity gave her a chance to be creative while being a leader.

Initially a success, the cheerleading team took a nosedive when club leadership intervened. First, when the girls' uniforms didn't arrive as scheduled, it was a big disappointment, and the girls seemed very annoyed by the setback.

> One of the cheerleaders ... said that they were not cheering tonight because they did not get their uniforms. "The boys' basketball uniforms came and ours were supposed to come at the same time but they didn't. So we said we ain't cheering cause what are we gonna cheer in?" At that moment I heard [the club director] saying something to other cheer-leaders, further down the bleachers. "The cheerleaders aren't cheering?" he asked. "What we gonna cheer in?" Tweetie asked. "These?" the girl sitting next to her said, pulling at her jeans.

The trials and tribulations of the cheerleading squad did not end with the uniforms. In what initially seemed to be a supportive gesture, the center got a coach to work with the team. Unfortunately this only seemed to undermine the girls' own initiative. The coach did not connect with the girls. A number of girls quit the team after the coach called some of their behavior outrageous. On top of that, the coach did not appear to be capitalizing on the fact that the girls had begun the team and choreographed a number of cheers on their own. One girl told me that "[the coach is] having us do a bunch of cheers that we don't like. And she won't let us do any of ours."

Originally begun from Tweetie's enthusiasm and organizational abilities, the cheerleading team had the potential to be an asset for development. Instead, it turned into an exercise in frustration, as Tweetie came up against barriers imposed by club leadership. Rather than reinforcing her initiative, it shut her down.

In the late fall and early winter, at the same time that Tweetie was struggling with the cheerleading team, there was a major alterca-tion between the center director and the boys' basketball team. On the bus ride home from a game that the team had lost, Mr. Jones called the boys losers. The cheerleaders, who had been at the game, were on the bus and witnessed the altercation. The situation became explosive when the boys began to yell back at Mr. Jones and he threatened to kick them off the bus. This caused a particular rift in

Tweetie's relationship with North River because her brother was on the basketball team and she felt personally attacked by Mr. Jones.

> *Scottie said to me quietly, "Mn-hmm, you missed the mess on Wednesday." I asked him how the basketball game had gone, guessing this was to what he was referring. "Oh, the game was fine. We lost, but they played good ... [the club director] called the kids 'losers'!! ... Tweetie went off on him – told him that he don't be callin' her brother no loser."*

To top off the conflict, one of the other cheerleaders had gotten into a fight with a girl at the center where the basketball game was being held. As a result, Mr. Jones told the cheerleaders that they could no longer attend the basketball games. This was almost a moot point, however, as the teens went on strike following this incident, threatening not to return to the club.

> *Shelby [one of Tweetie's friends] was in the gym and I asked her about the cheerleading team. "Oh, a bunch of us quit," she said. "Why?" "Mr. Jones said we couldn't go to any games so we quit. I mean, what we gonna do if we can't go to games? And he was telling all the team that they were losers and stuff. So we were mad. And you know, the coach, I don't know. She was supposed to be here tonight, but I don't know if she's coming. We were going to meet with her and tell her we were quitting. She's having us do a bunch of cheers that we don't like. And she won't let us do any of ours. So I don't know. Maybe we'll stay but...."* *I asked why she had trashed their cheers. "I don't know. And she has us doing a bunch of other cheers that we don't like." Shelby shook her head and shrugged. "And if we can't go to games then. I don't know what's going to happen." I asked her if they would consider just cheering for themselves, or if maybe Mr. Jones would change his mind. She shrugged and said she didn't know. "But you didn't even cheer at that game. So why did he say you can't go to any more and call you losers?" "Nah, the basketball team lost so he was calling them losers. But us, my sister and Tweetie were sitting on the bleachers and then you know some guy there called my sister a B and she got mad and jumped up and they got into it and so now Mr. Jones said that we can't go to anymore games. But I mean he called her a B what was she supposed to do?" She shook her head. Tweetie came by while Shelby was telling me the story and she corroborated it. I asked if they would consider having the cheerleading team or make it a dance team just for themselves even if they couldn't perform. She shrugged. "I don't know, maybe." "Cause you guys were doing so good! You got yourselves all together and made up the cheers. I mean, you guys were really doing well and had done it all yourselves!" She nodded and shrugged and said they would talk to the coach when*

she came. Shelby told me that actually they had not been planning on
coming back to the club at all because they were all so angry about what
Mr. Jones said. "I mean, we weren't gonna come back at all." "Why did
you?" She shrugged. "I don't know. Nothing to do at home, I guess."

Having "nothing to do at home" is not the sole source of motivation
you would want for attracting adolescents to a youth center. Yet in
reviewing Tweetie's PARC profile, it is apparent that there was not
a tremendous amount of activity that would attract her to North
River directly over the course of this year. The breakdown of the
cheerleading team, the club director's conflicts with the teens, and
the center's overall inability to successfully capitalize on the enthusiasm and energy of some of its members reflect the organizational
issues discussed in Chapter 6 and foreshadow the negative synergies discussed later in this chapter.

One bright spot in Tweetie's PARC profile during the year was the
Keystone Club. Although Keystone got off to a slow start at North
River, this did not stop Tweetie from taking full advantage of it once
it was on its feet. She took on an active role in the group, serving as a
leader and getting things done. When faced with a looming deadline
for a community diversity fair for which there was still much work
to do, Tweetie suggested that the group meet more often. Michelle,
the staff member in charge of Keystone, responded positively to this
suggestion and indicated that she had requested staff help so that
she could assist the teens with research for the project. Tweetie even
came to the club early to do research on the computers and paint
posters for the fair. Rather than having to be asked to get things
done, Tweetie took initiative and encouraged other club members
to help. Michelle supported the youths' autonomy, as well. During
a meeting in which they were planning a Valentine's Day dance, she
took careful notes on what the teens said, allowing them to brainstorm but indicating where and when certain ideas would not work
due to administrative restrictions.

Tweetie said members of the North River club should get in free.... As they
discussed the various details Michelle took notes on what was said. "Okay,
so it will be from 7–10 and North River members will get in free but it will
be all club members invited ..." [Michelle summed up.] The kids wanted
to let in people who weren't club members but Michelle said [the program
director] wouldn't go for that. "Now this is your project. I mean, I will
help out but I am not organizing the party for you. If you want a party you
gotta do it. If you don't do it, then there won't be a party."

Tweetie had a positive relationship with Michelle, naming her as one of the staff she liked on her club timeline. Yet their relationship did not appear to be particularly close. Tweetie did not mention Michelle in any other interview and did not put her on her social network map. It is possible that their relationship may have grown over time. Scottie had been at the club as long as Tweetie had and Michelle was brand new. Yet at least during this year, Tweetie's PARCs appeared to feature *either* a close relationship *or* an engaging activity, rather than offering both within the same program. Keystone was one area that offered promise of a more complete PARC if Michelle (and Tweetie) stayed long enough to deepen their relationship.

Tweetie's leadership skills were further honed through her position as manager of the boys' basketball team. It was Scottie who tapped her for this. Tweetie didn't appear to start this position until the winter, after the cheerleading team disbanded and during ongoing difficulties with getting the girls' gym night going, issues that will be discussed later. In the spring, while talking about the variety of sports activities she used to do at the center, Tweetie noted a contrast to the current situation. "Things are crumbling around here. They're just kind of falling off." Scottie's giving her a distinct role with a team provided her with something concrete to do in the face of a "crumbling" situation. Furthermore, it provided her extra time with Scottie. Her role as team manager meant that Scottie allowed Tweetie into the gym during team practices when the space was off limits to other teens. Along with Keystone, this activity was a small bright spot in the midst of an increasingly bleak PARC profile.

As noted in Chapter 6, there was no sports program for teen girls during the year we were at North River. This left Tweetie holding the ball, literally.

Tweetie said that it was time that the girls get on the [basketball] court. "Why don't we ever get to play?" One of the guys said something about how she could go ahead. "I ain't kiddin'" Tweetie responded. "I'm serious!" The guy shrugged and wandered off onto the court, where two separate half court games were taking place on either end of the court. Tweetie said that it was about time the girls get to play but that the guys never take them seriously ... "Come on. We're playing ball," she said to Shelby, who looked at Tweetie with her eyebrows raised. Tweetie marched out to the further end of the court, with Shelby following her. They went out onto the court and got the ball from the guys playing there. Two more girls joined them and they just started running around and shooting the ball, usually without even dribbling. The guys who had been on the court left after a few minutes and went to the other end of the bleachers. However, within 5–10 minutes the guys on the other end of the court saw that the guys had vacated the other end of the court and started playing full-court basketball, just running right down the court and into/over the girls' game without any acknowledgment that they were doing it. The girls stayed put for a few minutes, just moving over when the guys came down to their end, but after about the third or fourth time they gave up and left the court.

Tweetie showed impressive initiative given the circumstances. But even her determination could not keep the girls going. Constantly battling the boys for space took the joy out of the game. The girls needed a staff member to back them up.

Scottie did at times try to involve the older girls in the gym. Yet his efforts were minimal and not consistent enough to succeed. Furthermore, they were not supported by leadership. The reoccurring problem of boys overtaking the gym was common across centers, and was one of the reasons that girls-only gym nights had been implemented previously.[4] The lack of a girls' night seemed especially frustrating to Tweetie and reflected her overall experiences of activities at North River, which tended to thwart rather than support her initiative and enthusiasm.

Tweetie came into the gym and leaned against the wall next to me. "Can I have a basketball Scottie," she asked. Scottie shook his head. "Uh uh, only one out there at a time. The other night there were two balls out and the guys could not handle it. They were throwing the balls everywhere ..." Tweetie sighed and leaned against the wall. "I thought it was girls' night," she said. "That's the only reason I came," she added. "It was supposed to be but you're the only girl who signed up," Scottie said. Tweetie shook her head. "Man, they never want to do anything except sit around and talk," she said nodding to the girls who were gathered on and around the bleachers talking to each other and to the boys. "I wouldn't have come otherwise. I just came cause I thought it was girls' gym night. There's nothing to do otherwise. It's boring," she said. I asked how often they were supposed to have girls' gym night. "This was supposed to be the first but I guess we won't have it now since no one signs up," Tweetie said. She shook her head.

---

[4] Hirsch, 2005.

Tweetie's weariness and frustration are clear. She is annoyed at both the club and her peers. The lack of engaging and autonomy-supporting activities at North River during the year of our study affected Tweetie's participation in the center and may have prevented her from making further gains as a developing youth leader.

DEVELOPMENTAL GAINS OVER THE YEAR

There were no clear-cut developmental gains for Tweetie over the course of the year. Yet Tweetie was starting from a strong position as a good student and active peer leader, both in school and at the center.[5] In contrast to youth discussed elsewhere in the book, who had room to grow both socially and academically, it would have been difficult to quantitatively measure any growth in outcomes for Tweetie. Over the year, she continued to get good grades and be on Honor Roll, stayed involved in activities even in the face of frustration, and was student body president. Yet that does not mean that there was not room for development. Tweetie scored below the mean for our sample on the peer self-esteem and overall self-efficacy measures in March of the study year. This was a surprise. Given how confident Tweetie appeared, her position as student council president at school, and the initiative she demonstrated in starting new activities at the center earlier in the year, we would have expected her to score above the mean on these measures. The fact that she didn't suggests to us that she may have been negatively affected by the climate at North River, which continually thwarted her leadership attempts over the course of the year. She would have to overcome what she experienced at North River that year to continue on the pathway on which she had begun, let alone to develop further.

This was in contrast to Tweetie's report of North River's influence on her in the past. As noted earlier, Tweetie credited the center for her current level of activity. And Tweetie wanted to retain a connection with the center despite her frustrating experiences during the year. Tweetie was afraid that, with the demands of high school, her attendance at North River would decrease. She was trying to manage her time to make sure she would stay involved at North

---

[5] As noted, Tweetie had high scores on most of the peer relatedness scales. In addition, she scored at or above the mean on both academic self-efficacy (T-score = 55.39) and academic self-esteem (T-score = 51.22).

River. This active desire could suggest that Tweetie perceived North River as having a positive impact on her. Yet it could just as easily reflect a sentimental attachment to the center based on what it had meant to her in the past and its long-time position as a safe base in her life.

At the least, however, Tweetie's participation at North River may have had a preventative effect. Tweetie's neighborhood was rife with violence, including a lot of gang activity and physical fights between girls. The center was a safe haven. Tweetie herself was known to prevent fights at the center, getting staff to break up impending fights between girls. It would have been more difficult for Tweetie to take such a proactive role on the streets, without the support of the staff, particularly Scottie.

Thus, no specific positive developmental outcomes are evident for Tweetie during the year in which we observed her. Her history of participation at North River suggests that the center had provided her with developmental supports in the past, but currently, the main developments we saw were negative. We now turn to the specific strengths, shortcomings, and synergies we observed over the year, which often kept her from receiving maximum benefit from the center.

TWEETIE IN THE NORTH RIVER CENTER: STRENGTHS, SHORTCOMINGS, AND SYNERGIES

Strengths

Although there were obvious negative aspects of North River's culture, which will be discussed later in the chapter, the fact that it is a comprehensive after-school center was a strength for Tweetie. Her assets could be drawn out by the setup of the club. The center being a multi-age program, Tweetie was able to benefit from being a role model to younger youth and integration into the social fabric of the center. She enjoyed her position, acting as a caretaker for younger kids and peer leader among the teens. Yet this required staff to capitalize on Tweetie's abilities and the opportunities inherent in the multi-age center, which did not often happen in a structured way. Her family's long involvement with, and her own prominent place in, North River meant that both staff and youth knew Tweetie. Many also knew a lot about her family and what was going in her life outside the club.

Staff could monitor her and track her progress. Most staff recognized Tweetie as a distinct individual who brought unique abilities to North River. Scottie, in particular, kept tabs on her.

Because the club offered a variety of activities, at least in theory, the potential existed for Tweetie to explore and build capabilities in different areas. She appeared to benefit from this aspect of the center in her early years at the club, although this was less, if at all, evident over the year of the study. The multiplicity of roles and activities offered by a comprehensive center such as North River allows for the emergence and support of multiple identity domains.[6] In contrast to more targeted programs, comprehensive centers offer youth a number of different areas in which they can succeed and receive validation. As Tweetie noted, this diversity of activity did not come naturally to her, especially in sports. Being forced to rotate to the different activity areas as a young kid seems to have made her more open to trying new and different activities as a teenager. Given that she did not have a natural proclivity for sports, it is possible that without the forced rotation she would not have spent time in the gym and would have missed out on the opportunity to develop her relationship with Scottie, which was clearly an asset to her. Yet as Tweetie shifted from childhood into adolescence, North River was not able to provide continued support for exploration and validation.

At times, however, North River did buttress Tweetie's leadership skills. When programs were working well, her leadership was recognizable across activities, from cheerleading to Keystone. Activities are most effective in promoting positive youth development when they provide intrinsic, interesting opportunities for initiation and leadership on the part of youth and move along a temporal arc that culminates in an end product.[7] For Tweetie, Keystone and the early days of the cheerleading team clearly met these criteria. In Keystone, she was actively involved in meetings, giving ideas for new projects and working on them independently outside of group meetings. She saw the end result of this work in events such as sleepovers and the diversity fair, activities that Keystone planned and in which Tweetie was instrumental. In cheerleading, Tweetie drew on her natural interest in the sport to rally her peers and engage them in developing and practicing routines. Their performances were

---

[6] Dimitriadis, 2001; Hall, 2001; Halpern, Barker, & Mollard, 2000; Hirsch, 2005.
[7] Larson, 2000.

a rewarding end product, and when the possibility of performing was removed, interest in the team dissipated. The leadership skills Tweetie developed in Keystone and cheerleading, before the latter disintegrated, may have transferred to her school life, where she was student council president. It is possible that North River and her relationship with Scottie, over time, helped Tweetie develop the initiative and engagement we observed and encouraged her to take on leadership roles outside the center. Although we have a chicken-and-egg problem here, as we were observing Tweetie at North River while she was student council president, the opportunity to enact and receive validation for her skills in a non-academic environment could have been an asset. Yet the lack of recent, steady support dampened this potential.

Tweetie's relationship with Scottie was a particular strength of the center. It kept Tweetie linked to North River even in the face of frustration and boredom. More importantly, Scottie provided some of the only opportunities that supported Tweetie's developmental needs. When Scottie asked Tweetie to help him with the younger kids, he was treating her as both a confidante and role model to other youth. Thus, he was supporting her developmental need for autonomy within the supportive bounds of his relationship with her.[8] Tweetie's respect for Scottie, his deep care for her, and their mutual sense of obligation gave her an established place in the social network of the club. He was one of few adults on her social network map, and one of only six club people, the other five of whom were youth. The one other club adult Tweetie mentioned as important to her was a part-time speech coach. Although she said he was an inspiration to her, we never saw him at the club. He also did not appear on her social network map or her club timeline. Yet the fact that Tweetie named another adult male highlights a significant factor that makes her relationships with center adults distinct from those she could have formed in formal mentor programs.

Tweetie says that she does not have a father figure outside of Scottie. Yet Scottie and Tweetie would likely not have been paired in a stand-alone mentor program. Formal mentoring programs generally use same-sex pairings; male mentor-female mentee relationships are extremely rare.[9] Although we have no reason to believe

[8] Deutsch, 2008.
[9] Bogat & Liang, 2005.

that Tweetie would not have benefited from a same-sex match, her relationship with Scottie served a specific need. His protector role would probably not have been mimicked by a female mentor.[10] Scottie is able to infuse his protector role into the broader context of their relationship. This can be seen during a conversation in which Scottie and Tweetie were discussing high schools to which she was applying: "Well, [that school is] just down the expressway from here so if anything happens you know just 911 [and] I'll be there right away. Me and your big brothers ..." Scottie weaves talk of physical safety into their discussion of schools, emphasizing both the protector and academic mentor aspects of their relationships. Tweetie's bond with Scottie, set in a dangerous neighborhood, undoubtedly provides a needed sense of security.[11] Furthermore, Scottie and Tweetie come from similar backgrounds. He can relate to her in ways that a formal mentor from a different background likely could not. Scottie also mentors Tweetie in a range of life domains. He has access to these various parts of her life because of the depth of their involvement. He knows her family, sees her on an almost daily basis, and watches her interact with friends, boyfriends, and other adults. This gives him ample opportunity to address these issues in a natural way. Yet there were drawbacks to their relationship and Tweetie's participation at North River overall.

Shortcomings

Tweetie's relationship with Scottie provides a vehicle for discussing the pros and cons of mentors from the same socio-economic background as youth. If we think back on the excerpt earlier in the chapter

---

[10] Research indicates that female mentors often provide more psychosocial mentoring relationships, whereas male mentors tend to provide more instrumental types of relationships (Bogat & Liang, 2005). Tweetie and Scottie's relationship appeared to combine these two components. The academic conversations they had were somewhat instrumental in the sense that they were focused around a specific task – choosing a high school. The protective nature of their relationship, although quite psychosocial, was also fairly reliant on the gendered nature of their relationship, for example, a big brother-little sister or father-daughter type of physical protection.

[11] In prior work at Boys & Girls Clubs, relationships with staff were found to have a greater positive effect, specifically on self-esteem, for youth who live in more violent neighborhoods. The effect size for club staff was twice that of the effect size for closest adult kin and four times that of closest tie to a school adult (Hirsch, 2005; Pagano, 2001).

in which Scottie talked to Tweetie about diversifying sports participation and the military as a means to pay for college, we can see
many of the strengths as well as shortcomings of their relationship.
On the one hand, Scottie is adept at using culturally distinct forms of
communication, telling stories as a way of making his point.[12] Yet at
times this storytelling seems to devolve into a monologue. Although
Tweetie is listening, she is not involved in the conversation, mostly
staring out at the basketball court, occasionally nodding or saying
"yeah" in response to certain points. The researcher who observed
this interaction noted that "towards the end it started to feel more
like Scottie was just enjoying talking."

In addition, some of his academic advice may be narrow. It is
not clear how emphasizing being diversified in sports can help
Tweetie, whose level of sports participation would not qualify her
for sports scholarships. Even if she were an athlete, focusing only
on sports may still jeopardize her chances of making it through
college. The strength of Scottie's position is that he is familiar with
the local high schools and has a history to which Tweetie can relate.
He is realistic about how she can get money for college and has
specific stories about local peers to provide her with meaningful,
relevant examples. Mentors from outside the neighborhood would
likely not understand the constraints Tweetie faces. As a result,
their advice may seem impractical. On the other hand, Scottie has
limited access to the colleges themselves. He is aware of certain
routes to college but has not had direct experience with the chan-
nels of authority in higher education. An outside mentor may have
insider knowledge of college culture that could give Tweetie a leg
up in a way that Scottie's advice cannot. Although it may still be
early for Tweetie to be considering college, a balance of these two
approaches could be optimal for helping Tweetie achieve her educational goals.

The lack of activities for teen girls was a clear shortcoming for
Tweetie. This led to boredom, frustration, and possibly disengage-
ment from the center. When Tweetie did take a stand, she was not
supported. This thwarting of her initiative may have dampened her
sense of self-efficacy. The fallout from the cheerleading team did
not appear to be compensated for by her role as manager of the
boys' basketball team. Given her energy and initiative, she should

---

[12] Hirsch, 2005.

have taken on more leadership roles throughout the year at North River as she prepared to enter high school. In contrast, however, her role as a leader appeared to decrease, as did her attendance. This is not surprising. The continual buildup of thwarted attempts could be expected to wear her down and make her less likely to put herself in leadership positions at the center in the future. The lack of encouragement for girls, and for girls' sports in particular, was a significant drawback. Tweetie clearly wanted, and would have benefited from, girls' gym night as well as organized girls' sports teams. Furthermore, she would have benefited from additional activities, like Keystone, that drew on her leadership skills.

This lack of activity was also a shortcoming in terms of her deriving maximum benefit from her relationship with Scottie. We talked earlier about the person-activity interaction, whereby the combination of a rewarding activity and a strong relational connection provides positive developmental support. Companionship alone may not be as effective as a combination of emotional support and focused mentoring.[13] According to our PARC model, it is the combination of programs, activities, relationships, and culture that produce the context for optimal developmental opportunities. For Tweetie, her main interaction with Scottie revolved around informal discussions during Tweetie's visits to the gym. Although he did give her delineated leadership roles, the bulk of their time together was simply "hanging out."

This is not necessarily a bad thing. Elsewhere we have argued that "hanging out" is an oft-neglected part of relationship development in after-school programs.[14] It offers opportunities which structured activities cannot due to time and activity constraints. But when "hanging out" is all there is, it leaves important resources untapped. Tweetie did not benefit from the added engagement of programs or activities and the relationship was not supported by the overall culture at the center, which focused on structure and hierarchy and discouraged both youth and staff from taking initiative or leadership. It seemed only a matter of time before Tweetie tired of sitting on the bleachers listening to Scottie talk to her about school. Although their discussions about high school choices could be considered focused mentoring, we do not know what will happen to their relationship

[13] See Chapter 5 for discussion of the person-activity.
[14] Hirsch, 2005.

once Tweetie enters high school. When the school choice conversation is no longer applicable, to what will they turn to keep their relationship going?

It is quite possible that they could find other areas of life and academics around which Scottie could provide focused mentoring. Tweetie looked up to Scottie and appeared to tolerate him even at times when his monologues ran long. Girls tend to benefit from relational development, and "meaningful conversations" may be one route to developing and maintaining intimacy.[15] Scottie and Tweetie's conversations could have had many of the benefits of joint activities. Furthermore, because of their kinship connection, Tweetie may have continued to rely on him for support. But if Scottie and Tweetie had a specific activity in which they were involved together, the probability of their interactions carrying on through high school may have been increased. Such an activity connection would have provided a more specific reason for Tweetie to continue to seek him out when other demands on her time would be increasing. In addition, if more of her activities at the center provided a culture of youth leadership, and more of her relationships were embedded in activities with cultures of leadership, her experiences in North River that year may have been quite different.

Synergies

There were a number of synergistic interactions that influenced Tweetie's experiences at North River. The bulk of these were, unfortunately, negative, although some positive synergies were also observed.

Positive Synergies

Scottie's making Tweetie manager of the boys' basketball team is one of the few positive synergies we observed. Given the lack of structured activities for teen girls, and Tweetie's natural proclivity for organizing and peer leadership, the management position was a good fit. It built on her skills and gave her a role with duties and responsibilities, something that she took seriously. Scottie even said that if he were the program director, he would pay Tweetie. We see this as a synergistic occurrence because it was the interaction of

---

[15] Bogat & Liang, 2005; Rhodes, 2002.

Tweetie's own personality (her agency and responsibility), her close relationship with Scottie (and his ability to recognize her needs), and the overall culture of the club (which offered few structured activities for her) that led to her taking on this position. Had Scottie not recognized and tapped Tweetie's leadership skills, or not realized that she needed more opportunities for formal roles, it is likely that Tweetie would not have had this leadership opportunity.

A prerequisite for positive synergies is that staff members support youth's participation in multiple, sometimes competing, programs. Youth benefit the most when staff are aware of the various roles that youth play in different activities and support them in being able to take advantage of the variety of opportunities that a comprehensive center can offer. One of the few other positive synergies we observed at North River was Michelle's ability to support Tweetie's leadership activities even when they competed with her participation in Keystone.

> *While we were doing the interview Michelle came in at some point to get a video game. "You're going to miss the meeting," she said. "Meeting tonight?" Tweetie asked. [I had noticed a sign that said there was a Keystone meeting from 7–8.] Michelle nodded. "Yeah. But I know you're the team's manager and all that so you gotta go with them," Michelle said grinning at Tweetie.*

In a less positive situation, Tweetie may have been asked to choose between participation in Keystone and managing the basketball team. This may be a particular strength of comprehensive youth centers, as Michelle was aware of the importance of Tweetie's role with the basketball team and had an interest in supporting this other center activity. In addition, because Tweetie and the other Keystone members came to the club regularly, it was possible for Michelle to catch them up on what they missed or be flexible in rearranging meeting times when necessary.

The final positive synergy for Tweetie was the positive response she received from her peers on the cheerleading team and in Keystone. In Keystone, this was supported by the staff leader. In cheerleading, it was in opposition to the adult leader. Yet in both cases, Tweetie was initially validated by her peers, who responded positively to her ideas and encouraged her leadership. The cheerleading team, however, eventually dissolved, and this was followed by lukewarm at best – and hostile at worst – peer response to

Tweetie's attempts to get the girls to participate in the gym. Thus, the positive peer response did not seem enough to counterbalance the negative synergies that emerged over the course of the year.

Negative Synergies

There were two major areas in which negative synergies abounded. Both came in the interaction of Tweetie's strong personality with club programs and organizational structures/leadership. Scottie was able to capitalize on Tweetie's leadership capabilities, moving her toward opportunities to enhance these skills and appreciating her as a distinct individual. Other staff were unable or unwilling to do so. As a result, the center often clashed with, rather than supported, Tweetie's needs.

Tweetie came to the center with a strong personality that made her a natural peer leader. Yet Joanne, the program director, saw her as a troublemaker: "She has a stubborn streak in her. She's very opinionated. Has her own sneaky side to her." Rather than use Tweetie's opinionated nature as a force to develop, club leadership tended to shut it down. Because she saw Tweetie as having a "sneaky side," Joanne seemed unwilling to support her initiative. She appeared to view it as a challenge to her own authority. This limited Tweetie's ability to act on her ideas and organize her peers.

The conflicts between the club director and the teens, and the girls and the cheerleading coach, worked together to create an overall negative climate for Tweetie. Rather than being validated for her leadership skills, Tweetie was reacted to negatively by staff and neutrally by peers. Despite Scottie's attempts to help her, conflicts with staff shaped her experiences in the late fall and early winter. Rather than having the teen girls rally behind her and keep the cheerleading team going, they all quit. This was not in response to Tweetie, but was rather in response to the adults. Yet the fact that Tweetie could never get other girls to join her for gym time and faced active resistance from her male peers meant that she was not receiving support for her initiative from any side. The synergy of these various negative experiences and relationships was particularly bad because it crossed domains, permeating her activities and relationships at North River.

Tweetie needed opportunities to flex her leadership skills and participate in different activities. At times, she even joined in with younger kids, apparently just to have something more structured to do. It was clear that she was getting bored. Whereas other girls seemed to be content with sitting on the bleachers and socializing, Tweetie wanted to be doing something more active. This need was impeded both by a lack of programs and the expectation that the girls would not participate in other activities even if given the opportunity.

> *Scottie was sitting on the bleachers with Tweetie [and a bunch of girls] ...* "You know, it's real important to be active. You got to exercise and stay active!" *Scottie was saying to the girls. Some of the girls rolled their eyes at Scottie.* "Wednesday night, is girls' night in the gym," *Scottie said. Most of the girls left. Tweetie shook her head and said* "They won't come. ... I'm active – I'll do things here! But other girls – they act like they too good to do it. They won't play."

On the one hand, Scottie faced a real difficulty in getting programming for girls. Staff members reported that the center leadership did not support programs financially. This made it difficult to initiate and sustain innovative programs. On top of that, the girls did not take quickly or easily to girls' night in the gym. Even Tweetie was frustrated by her peers' lack of participation in sports.

At the same time, however, girls' gym night was never sustained long enough to rally support. The one or two times that they tried it, Tweetie would show up ready to play. When no other girls came, Scottie would reopen the gym to the boys. When given the chance, Tweetie tried to get girls involved. Her leadership skills and desire for activities likely would have led her to drum up participation had she had access to the gym on a regular basis. With the support of staff, her chance of success would have been greater. As it was, her initiative was not validated but, instead, led to frustration. She was involved in a negative feedback loop that, over time, was likely to shut her down and both push her out of North River and inhibit her from taking on further leadership roles. Not only did she see her own efficacy fail, but she saw her mentor, Scottie, unable to make change, as well. This likely enhanced her disappointment and reinforced her feelings of powerlessness within the club.[16]

---

[16] According to Bandura (1986), we receive information about our own self-efficacy from four sources: performance attainments, vicarious experiences of observing the performance of others, verbal persuasion, and physiological states. Tweetie clearly had negative experiences in terms of observing the outcomes, or lack thereof, of both her own attempts to impart change and Scottie's attempts to develop new programs. Therefore, her self-efficacy in terms of her ability to make change within the club was likely to be negatively impacted. As noted earlier, her overall self-efficacy score was below average (T-score = 45.51), which

CONCLUSION

Tweetie's story is a potent example of the interaction of a youth and her context. She demonstrates the complex nature of developing centers that meet the needs of diverse youth. On the one hand, Tweetie's personal psychological strengths poised her to receive maximum benefits from a comprehensive after-school center. On the other, some of her traits interacted negatively with North River's culture and leadership, leading to less than optimal experiences for Tweetie. In another center, we can imagine how her initiative would have been rewarded instead of thwarted. We believe that a center such as West River could have led to more obvious developmental gains and enhanced her already positive trajectory.

Tweetie did not appear to make any gains over the course of the year. In fact, it is possible that her experiences at North River were decreasing her sense of self-efficacy. We would have expected her to develop over the course of her eighth-grade year, to grow into more of the leadership roles that she appeared ready to take on at the beginning of the year. Despite her trials and tribulations, Tweetie continued to come to North River. Her attendance began to drop off at the end of the year, however. And her sense of global self-efficacy was less than we would have expected given her early signs of competence. It appeared that North River, while having supplied Tweetie with some positive support and opportunities in her youth, was not able to successfully transition to meet her new needs as an adolescent. North River's focus on discipline and order was not well suited to the increased autonomy that teenagers require. The center was unable to respond appropriately to the sense of empowerment that Tweetie was displaying when she attempted to start the cheerleading team. Despite the fact that youth development is part of the mission of the center, and that positive youth development includes nurturing and responding to youth voice, North River consistently shut down Tweetie. This may have been their biggest shortcoming. Had they been able to harness Tweetie's voice, she likely could have helped North River provide more engaging activities for her peers.

is surprising given her strong leadership abilities and initiative. Yet it is reasonable to assume that she would not put much hope in being able to change the culture of the center. This may have increased the likelihood of her giving up on North River as well as depleting her own sense of self-efficacy.

Ironically, in how they handled Tweetie, they were in fact treating her as one of the adults. The staff's relationships with club leadership were marked by power struggles and suspicion, as discussed in Chapter 6. Thus, the program and club director's treatment of Tweetie mimicked how they reacted to the staff. They did not – or could not – recognize that Tweetie needed a balance of adult support *and* opportunities to enact her autonomy.

Tweetie's persistent connection to North River in the face of its inabilities to support her overall may be in part due to her strong bond with Scottie. Scottie provided Tweetie with both emotional and instrumental support. Their kinship may have kept Tweetie involved even after she began to be frustrated by the lack of activities. Here again, we can see the impact that one person can have. Within the context of a center that had few assets to offer, Tweetie found a mentor who supported her across a variety of life domains.

Tweetie and Scottie's relationship also demonstrates the unique interaction of youth and centers. Beyonce, who you will read about in Chapter 8, had a distinctly negative relationship with Scottie. Their relationship kept North River from being as positive a place for Beyonce as it could have been. With Tweetie, the same adult has precisely the opposite effect. This highlights one of the greatest challenges that comprehensive youth centers face. No one center can be all things to all youth. Rather, it requires a combination of staff and leaders who can recognize the diverse needs of individual youth and work to meet those needs in ways that are appropriate and targeted. The needed synergies of different staff for different youth are likely best achieved at a comprehensive center that has a variety of staff who lead different activities and who may be able to connect with very different types of youth. Yet this also requires strong leadership and organizational support for an environment that creates positive synergies through coordinated relationships and activities.

North River lacked such vision. The center leadership was focused primarily on discipline and control. There was little individualized attention paid to youth unless, as in Tweetie's case, a staff member happened to develop a close relationship with a child. In the absence of organizational support, the synergies that occurred between youth and the centers were often negative. Staff and leadership often worked at odds instead of in concert. Thus, whereas

Tweetie found support from Scottie, the benefits she reaped were not buttressed outside the gym. Rather, both she and Scottie often found themselves butting their heads against the center's proverbial walls. Tweetie's individual strengths and her relationships with Scottie did more to create a positive experience for her than the culture of North River did. Tweetie was an adolescent poised to take advantage of the benefits of a comprehensive youth center. Yet North River fell short, not living up to its potential.

8

Beyonce: A Good Friend Is Hard to Find (and Keep)

Beyonce hardly fits the profile of risk that we have come to associate with young people living in low-income urban neighborhoods. Risk for school failure? Beyonce has made the Honor Roll the last two years and counts reading as one of her favorite pastimes. Risk for becoming involved in a gang or behaviors such as substance use, premature sexual activity, or violence? It is difficult to envision any of these scenarios on the immediate horizon for Beyonce. In fact, whereas all of these activities typically arise in the context of relationships with peers, what is most outstanding about Beyonce is her overall lack of positive or rewarding ties with other youngsters her age.[1] Rather than getting in with the "wrong crowd," Beyonce is experiencing great difficulty getting in with *any* crowd. It is precisely these distinguishing characteristics that make the experiences of this ten-year-old African-American girl during her year at the club so instructive and important. As we shall see, Beyonce's story illustrates how after-school centers can be of significant benefit to youth whose greatest liabilities have little in common with prevailing stereotypes of urban risk. It is equally vivid in highlighting how limitations in programs, organizational practices, and mentoring can lead centers to fall well short of the mark in responding to the needs of such young people.

---

[1] Peer relationships are an important influence on social skills, behaviors, and values throughout the course of development (Damon, 1990; Harris, 1998); poor peer relations in childhood also are associated with increased risk for maladaptive outcomes (e.g., psychopathology) during adolescence and adulthood (Kupersmidt, Coie, & Dodge, 1990).

IN THE BEGINNING

Beyonce's appearance is emblematic of the uneven rates of physical development that typify the transition to adolescence. A growth spurt during the past year has left her easily one of the tallest girls in her age group at the club. Otherwise, her slender, somewhat gangly physique holds little hint of her evolving maturity. Her mostly straight black hair falls slightly below her shoulders and frequently is braided in a ponytail. Rarely, if ever, do we notice her experimenting with more characteristically ethnic hairstyles sported by other African-American girls at the clubs. Her clothes, furthermore, trend toward neatly pressed polo shirts and khakis. Not surprisingly, she is accused at times by youth at the club as acting or talking "White." Her voice has a whiny, high-pitched quality to it which at its most pronounced can remind the listener of the sound of fingernails on a chalkboard. Completing Beyonce's appearance is a pair of wire-rimmed glasses. They are a bit oversized for her and often slip part-way down her nose. Truth be told, there is a somewhat "nerdy" quality to Beyonce. It is difficult to imagine her fitting in readily in most peer settings, let alone one in which her demeanor and dress are so out of step with prevailing norms.

As noted, Beyonce does well in school, having made the Honor Roll both this year and last. This is no small feat when one considers that she has transferred schools twice during this period.[2] Her current school, furthermore, is one of many in the city designated as "failing" according to the performance guidelines of the federal No Child Left Behind Act.[3] Contrasted with her academic resilience, Beyonce appears vulnerable to both social isolation and conflict at school.[4] By her own report, she does not enjoy positive relationships with her classmates. Indeed, she says she has no

---

[2] Children in urban areas who change schools frequently tend to perform less well academically (Ingersoll, Scamman, & Eckerling, 1989; Temple & Reynolds, 1999).

[3] More than half of the schools in the city in which the research was conducted failed to meet performance guidelines of the No Child Left Behind Act during the 2002–2003 school year.

[4] It is well documented that youth who are resilient in one domain, such as academics, may nonetheless experience significant adaptive difficulties in other domains, such as their social relationships (Luthar, Cicchetti, & Becker, 2000).

friends at school. And her relationship with her primary teacher seems ambivalent at best:

> *I feel good [about school] but sometimes the teacher drives me up the wall. [Why?] She makes me angry. She always yells at people. And I just don't understand it. Cause she doesn't like it when people yell at her.*

Beyonce lives with her mother and an older aunt only a couple of blocks from the center. Her mother works full time and earns an income that keeps their home free of the most serious manifestations of economic deprivation. Nor have Beyonce or her family been confronted with other types of traumatic or chronic stress that are relatively commonplace in the lives of other youth attending the club. Yet, Beyonce's development might be regarded as having been compromised by at least one aspect of her home life. Although she has three brothers and two sisters, none of them live with her and she sees them only occasionally. This situation takes away any opportunities that Beyonce might have to hone her social skills through day-to-day interactions with siblings.[5] For better or worse, it is the adults in Beyonce's family system who seem to figure most prominently as sources of companionship. Indeed, when drawing her social network, she makes a point of noting that both her mother and an aunt, with whom she enjoys a close relationship, are like "friends" to her.

Both socially and emotionally, Beyonce is in many respects a very challenging youngster. With adults, she tends to come across as eager to please, at times to the point of being cloying, clingy, and even manipulative. When asked what she likes most about herself in an interview with one of our research team, for example, she smiles at the interviewer in a manner that does not seem entirely sincere and replies, "That I'm here with you."

As we shall see, not all adults who Beyonce encounters at the club are subject to these putative gestures of adoration. Indeed, her feelings about staff and peers alike tend toward simplistic black-and-white extremes of either an idealized halo or intense dislike. When asked to rate her relationships with individual staff on a

---

[5] In a national study of more than 20,000 children, teachers rated students who had at least one sibling as better able to form and maintain friendships, get along with people who are different, comfort and help other children, express feelings in a positive way, and show sensitivity to the feelings of others (Downey & Condron, 2004).

wide range of characteristics, her responses rarely waver from the extreme positive or negative end of the scale depending on her over-all feelings about the person involved. It is hardly surprising, there-fore, that there is an emotionally volatile quality to Beyonce's social interactions. Indeed, it is not unusual to see her quickly transition from the most syrupy to the most surly of demeanors, often with a flair for the dramatic in which her feelings seem to be exaggerated for effect.

Anyone who has spent time around a budding adolescent will find much to relate to in these descriptions. Yet, other aspects of Beyonce's behavior and emotional makeup clearly deviate from what is typical of this stage of development. To some extent, sim-ple immaturity may be the culprit. The lack of perspective taking, nuance, and abstraction in her processing of social experiences is such that even relatively benign and isolated encounters can become fodder for strong negative reactions toward others. Her capacities for self-reflection appear similarly underdeveloped.[6] When probed for an answer to the question regarding what she likes most about herself, for example, she responds only with, "I like golf. It's a good sport."

And when asked what she likes least about herself, she seems at a loss, "I'm really not sure."

Other aspects of Beyonce's attitudes and behaviors could have more troubling origins. Even at the relatively young age of ten, it may be possible to discern the roots of later personality dysfunc-tion during adulthood.[7] For Beyonce, it would hardly be a stretch to be concerned in this regard about her tendencies to cling to adults, to alternate between extremes of idealizing and rejecting others, to gravitate toward emotional drama, and to provoke others in ways that are passive-aggressive.

It may be unreasonable to expect even the most effective after-school center to fully address the needs of a challenging youth such as Beyonce. In her case, although she has been attending North River since third grade, this clearly has not been sufficient to avoid the delays that have emerged in her social and emotional develop-ment. Nor has it been enough to provide her with the one thing that

---

[6] Typically, by Beyonce's age, youth have acquired the capacity to engage in self-reflection and can communicate likes and dislikes about themselves within multiple areas (Harter, 1999).

[7] See Geiger & Crick (2001).

any ten-year-old girl needs and wants: a best friend. As Beyonce's year at North River unfolds, however, we will see how the seeds of her earlier experiences there are able to take root and allow her to cultivate a satisfying, albeit short-lived, friendship.

BEYONCE'S YEAR AT THE AFTER-SCHOOL CENTER

As we consider Beyonce's year at the after-school center, our focus will be on important developments taking place in her relationships with peers and staff. Both sets of relationships figure prominently in her PARC profile, which is shown in Table 8.1. As it illustrates, Beyonce's experiences with other youth as well as adults at the center were decidedly mixed, with both positive and negative elements.

Peer Relationships

We find Beyonce's relationships with peers at the club to be troubled throughout the year. Conflicts with other youth occur on a regular basis and she must endure a widespread lack of peer acceptance.[8] The following field note from an end-of-year pizza party that we held for the youth who participated in the research speaks to the social exclusion and isolation that was commonplace for Beyonce:

> *The kids joked around with each other in good fun. The only exception was a general dislike and disdain for Beyonce. [The joking ended here – clearly, it was difficult for the other kids to tolerate her.] Beyonce had been eating at a separate table and I asked why she was sitting by herself. "Oh, well, since you're over there, I'll come over there," she said to me. She got up and moved over. Jasmine and the other kids looked at me and mouthed, "Why did you do that?!"*

At the beginning of the year, Beyonce is most often observed in solitary activity, isolated from her peers. Over time, however,

---

[8] Peer acceptance refers to the overall extent to which youth are liked or well received by others their age in a given setting, such as a classroom or after-school program. Peer acceptance is not synonymous with friendship (Asher, Parker, & Walker, 1996). Youth who are high in peer acceptance still may not have close friends and those who are low in peer acceptance may nonetheless have some friends. Peer acceptance and friendships thus each may be important in determining the overall quality of a youth's peer relationships and for this reason are considered separately in our discussion of Beyonce's year at the club.

TABLE 8.1. *Beyonce's PARC profile*

Starts at beginning of the year

P –
A informal, unstructured
R peers
C lack of respect, some harassment, close monitoring by staff protects against more overt victimization

P gym
A informal sports and games
R Scottie, highly conflictual, lacking in warmth or validation
C emphasis on discipline and control; avoidance

P –
A informal socializing
R Sharon, advice and guidance concerning relationships with peers
C validation and appreciation of her strengths

Starts in the middle of the year

P –
A informal, unstructured
R affiliation with a loosely knit group of less popular girls
C superficial, limited

P –
A informal, unstructured
R close friendship with same-gender peer (Angel)
C some sharing and discord, not maintained

Starts at the end of the year

P Power Hour
A homework
R Daniel, positive
C structure and routine with adult supervision

---

we begin to see her in the company of a small, loose-knit group of girls with whom she seems to get along reasonably well. These girls, although not overtly rejected, tend to be overweight and fall relatively low on the hierarchy of peer groups at the club. This development undoubtedly offers Beyonce a certain measure of welcome social acceptance. Yet, for the most part, her relationships with these girls appear superficial and limited. Of the ten persons she includes in her social network map (which was completed near the end of the year), for instance, only two are youth at the club. Nonetheless, she does highlight the importance of her relationship with one of these youth, Angel, who she describes as "her best friend in the whole world."

Beyonce tells us that she first met Angel at school when she was in the third grade. It is not until they both began attending the club the following year, however, that they began to get to know each other and, this year, by Beyonce's account become close friends. When interviewed about her significant experiences at the club, Beyonce focuses on this friendship:

> "She's my best friend. I didn't really have any friends stick until her. [Why not?] Because they just weren't the right ones for me. I hadn't met the right friend for me. Like, one girl, she would be my best friend one day and not the next. But with Angel it has stuck."

When we conduct our wrap-up interview with Beyonce, she is preoccupied with an impasse that has occurred in her friendship with Angel:

> I don't know what I did to make Angel mad, but she and I used to be best-est friends in the world and she gave me this necklace. And if she doesn't like someone I wouldn't play with them because that would offend my friend. But I don't know what I did to make her mad but she's rolling her eyes at me and not talking to me and I wish she would be my friend again. I don't have many friends at school and just 4 friends here. And I'll be moving soon so it will be more difficult to make new friends and I really wish she would be my friend again.

On a return visit to River North in the summer, Beyonce informs us that she and Angel patched things up, although their friendship is no longer active:

> [So what ever happened with you and Angel? I know that you were arguing. Did you make up?"] After the argument we decided the key to being best friends wasn't arguing so we just shook hands and forgot about the argument and become friends. But I haven't seen her in a long time.

Relationships with Staff

Beyonce's relationships with staff figure no less prominently in her year at the center. Their potential to influence the success or failure of her efforts to make positive connections with peers is especially noteworthy. Youth receiving mentoring from adults in programs such as Big Brothers Big Sisters may exhibit significant improvements in their relationships with peers.[9] In these programs, however, youth and mentors are likely to spend relatively little time together in the actual presence of the youth's peer group. By contrast, peer interactions are one of the most salient features of most after-school centers. As such, in these settings, relationships with staff offer rich potential for direct, "on-line" (i.e., immediately available) mentoring of youth in how to handle different situations involving peers.[10] Staff also may spend considerable amounts of time with youth in programs and activities that are geared specifically toward promoting positive peer interactions. For Beyonce, however, as we will see, there is limited fulfillment of these possibilities.

As can be seen in Beyonce's PARC profile, it is not only that staff support and mentoring lags in this area. There is also is a relationship between Beyonce and one North River staff person, Scottie, that is itself highly problematic. It will be recalled from Chapter 6 that Scottie is the staff person with primary responsibility for overseeing activities in the gym. As the year begins, Beyonce spends a significant amount of time each day in this part of the center and thus interacts with Scottie on a regular basis. This is necessitated by the set rotation of youth through the gym and other activity areas at North River, as described in Chapter 6. It would not be difficult for any observer to realize quickly that Beyonce and Scottie's relationship is highly conflictual, with issues of discipline at the center of most of their disputes. The following field note from a member of the research team is illustrative.

> *Beyonce got out of her seat and asked if I would ask Scottie if she could sit closer to the television [on this day Scottie had moved youth to the television room because the heating was not working in the gym]. I asked her why she wouldn't ask him. She said, "Because I know he's just going to say no! I just want you to ask!" Scottie walked over and said, "Uh, Beyonce, get in your seat!" Beyonce hurried to her seat. Scottie frowned and said to me, under his breath, "She lucky we let her do anything, the way she been actin'." I asked if Beyonce was misbehaving. Scottie*

---

[9] An evaluation of the Big Brothers Big Sisters program found that youth who were randomly assigned to receive mentors through the program reported improvements in the quality of their relationships with peers over an eighteen-month period, compared to youth in a no-mentor control group (Tierney & Grossman, 1995).

[10] Hirsch (2005).

nodded and said she had been talking back to him. Scottie got up again and as soon as he did this, Beyonce ran over to me and asked if I would ask Scottie for her if she could move up. I asked her where her glasses were and she said somebody had accidentally stepped on them but new ones were on the way. Scottie came up from behind her and I motioned for Beyonce to ask. She asked if she could sit closer to the television and Scottie barked no at her. Beyonce sat back down, pouting. Beyonce then started leaning forward in her chair (she was sitting in it backwards). "Uh, sit up straight, young lady!" Scottie said. Beyonce continued to lean forward. "Beyonce, sit up straight!" Scottie said again. Beyonce leaned her chair back down so she was sitting straight. She started to lean forward again, closer to the screen. Scottie reached over and slammed her seat back down so that she was sitting straight. Beyonce whipped around and glared at Scottie. "You know I can't see!" Beyonce said, loudly. "What'd I tell you about mouthin' back to adults?!" Scottie said in a loud and irritated voice … Scottie sat down, rolled his eyes, and said to me, "Can you believe I talked to her mama on Friday?!" "What'd she say?" I asked. Scottie shook his head and said, "She said, 'I'll talk to her' and look at how she actin'!"… Something must have happened (that I didn't see) because suddenly, Scottie yelled, "Beyonce, go stand in the corner!" Beyonce turned around with a surprised look on her face. "Go stand up there! In the corner!" Scottie said. Beyonce got up and stood by the television. "Get in the corner. You don't need to be hearing no sound!" Scottie barked. Beyonce stood off to the corner, still squinting at the television.

These types of interactions between Scottie and Beyonce are nearly an everyday occurrence. It is not surprising, therefore, that Beyonce's ratings of the negative aspects of her relationship with Scottie are far higher than the sample average. In fact, they are almost off the chart.[11] Consistent with the global and polarized manner in which Beyonce perceives many of her relationships, she uses the most extreme rating ("5" on a 1–5 scale) to describe the frequency of each possible negative aspect of her relationship with Scottie.

Scottie, for his part, also has very little positive to say about Beyonce. When asked directly about her best qualities, he makes reference only to qualities that she once exhibited, but he no longer sees.

---

[11] On the scale measuring negative aspects of her relationship with Scottie, Beyonce's ratings correspond to a T-score of 84.90, which is extremely high relative to the ratings that other youth gave to staff who were not their closest tie.

When I first met her [3–4 years ago] she was a very sweet young lady, did what you asked her, easy to talk to. [and what's best thing now?] It's hard to say.... Those mood swings – if she don't feel like listenin' she turn her head at you, nose up, and make faces.

When asked to rate his feelings of closeness to Beyonce (on a 1–5 scale), Scottie uses this as a further opportunity to comment on the decline in their relationship.

It used to be 5. Now it's 2 because her attitude changed.

Notably lacking are any feelings of warmth or appreciation of Beyonce's positive qualities. Scottie's exclusively negative style of engaging Beyonce, furthermore, makes it unlikely that his guidance or advice will be heard.[12] Indeed, in her interview ratings, Beyonce generally disavows the presence of any mentoring facets to their relationship.[13] When we ask Scottie what he talks about with Beyonce, the closest thing to mentoring that he describes is prescriptive advice about how she should relate to authority figures:

Her attitude and her behavior. [What kinds of things?] Learn to respect adults like she do her mother. Respect all adults.

Missing is any attention to the area in which Beyonce is ostensibly most in need of help – her peer relationships. This omission is not for lack of opportunity, as illustrated by the following field note:

Beyonce and another girl were continually hitting each other in the gym and sometimes stood up and chased either other, yelling at each other ... "He hit her," Jamal said pointing at Beyonce. "Listen to Jamal and turn around and be quiet," Scottie said to Beyonce. "He lies, you said so!" Beyonce said. Scottie shook his head and told Beyonce to turn around in her seat and to be still and quiet. She sighed and turned and folded her arms across her chest. "That's why I don't like him," Beyonce said quietly, turning to me.

[12] Rhodes (2002) theorizes that the dynamics through which mentoring relationships can promote positive developmental outcomes are unlikely to unfold without a strong interpersonal connection, specifically one characterized by mutuality, trust, and empathy. Research supports this assertion (see Rhodes, 2005).

[13] On the scale measuring mentoring aspects of Beyonce's relationship with Scottie, her ratings correspond to a T-score of 23.10, which is markedly below the ratings that other youth typically gave in this area to staff who were not their closest tie.

Despite the potential to capitalize on this situation by mentoring Beyonce in her peer relationships, Scottie turns it into one in which the focus is on obeying his directives.

At this stage of their relationship, Scottie has little confidence in his ability to reach Beyonce. We see this clearly when he is asked to describe the strategies he finds helpful in working with her:

> *That's a hard one. When she don't wanna be bothered, which is 95% of the time ... she doesn't really give you the opportunity. You find yourself thinking you are the wrong person.*

Under these circumstances, the best approach for a young person such as Beyonce can be an "exit strategy" of seeking out alternative settings.[14] In this way, it may be possible both to avoid someone with whom one has a problematic relationship and to come into contact with new persons who offer opportunities for more rewarding interactions. It is noteworthy, therefore, that later in the year, Beyonce elects to stop including gym in her daily rotation of activity stations at North River. In its place she substitutes Power Hour. As discussed in Chapter 6, this program was initiated relatively late in the year and involved youth spending time completing their homework under staff supervision. This change in Beyonce's daily routine effectively brings to an end her daily conflicts with Scottie. It also serves to introduce her to a new staff member, Daniel, the education director at North River who is given responsibility for Power Hour. We did not have the opportunity to observe their interactions directly. As such, we have limited knowledge of this element of Beyonce's PARC profile. Still, she does include Daniel on her social network map (completed after she began to attend Power Hour), describing him as a "friend." Juxtaposed against her aversive experiences with Scottie, Beyonce may be primed to experience even relatively benign or neutral encounters with staff in a positive light.

The contrast becomes accentuated in the portion of her PARC profile that focuses on her relationship with another staff person, Sharon. Like Scottie, Beyonce has known Sharon since she first began attending the club approximately three years ago. In a further parallel to her relationship with Scottie, she and Sharon appear to be less close now than in the past. The reasons for this change are

---

[14] DuBois & Felner (1996).

very different, however, from Beyonce's escalating pattern of conflict with Scottie. Sharon currently works only part time at the after-
school center. In addition to taking away the opportunity for daily
interaction with youth at North River, Sharon's part-time status
and other responsibilities prevent her from leading any programs
at the center. These constraints are highlighted by her comments
when she is asked to rate how close she feels to Beyonce (on a 1–5
scale):

> When she first came here, I was [working full-time and] running
> programs. Now I no longer run programs. I don't interact [with Beyonce]
> as much as I used to. Maybe a 2.

Given these considerations, we are somewhat surprised to find
that Beyonce identifies Sharon as the staff member at North River
with whom she has the closest relationship. We become even more
intrigued when she rates their relationship as having a notably
strong mentoring dimension.[15] It occurs to us that Beyonce's nom-
ination of Sharon as her closest tie could have more to do with limitations in her relationships with other staff at the center than with
the strength of this tie per se. Likewise, given Beyonce's tendency
toward extremes in how she describes her relationships, we are
reluctant to take her reports of receiving mentoring from Sharon at
face value. Our interviews with both Sharon and Beyonce, however,
reveal that their relationship does indeed include significant guidance and support. This includes advice from Sharon about how to
handle difficult interactions with peers at the club:

> [Think about whether you ever talk about personal stuff with Sharon?
> What kinds of things do you or have you talked about?] About what I
> don't like about other kids ... [How does Sharon respond?] She reacts
> nicely. She says "That's OK. Don't worry about it. Walk away or go tell
> someone. And people who talk to you aren't your friends. [Do you wind
> up feeling better? If so, how?] I just do the instructions she tells me – it
> really helps.

It is clear, furthermore, that Beyonce experiences Sharon as an ally
and protector in the peer arena.

---

[15] On the scale measuring mentoring aspects of Beyonce's relationship with Sharon,
her ratings correspond to a T-score of 61.83, which is approximately one standard deviation above the sample average for youth ratings of the staff with whom
they had the closest tie.

She [Sharon] says that she will always protect me and watch over me when the kids are messing with me. [How does this make you feel good about yourself?] It makes me feel good that I have someone on my side.

Their relationship also appears to provide Beyonce with a much needed source of positive regard from an adult within the club setting. When we ask what kinds of things Sharon has said or done that makes her feel close to her, Beyonce highlights the compliments that she has received from Sharon about her appearance and behavior:

She says I have nice hair and clothes. She tells my mother I've been really good in the club.

When asked to describe Beyonce, Sharon likewise takes this as an opportunity to extol the many virtues she sees in her personality and behavior:

She's a very bubbly person – very exciting – very intelligent. Cheerful. Happy go lucky kid. Mischievous – there's a sneaky part about her. Overall, a pretty good kid.

This type of validation has the potential to carry over to Beyonce's peer interactions at the club, bolstering her feelings of confidence that they too will take a positive interest in her. (Recall, too, that Sharon described Tweetie in Chapter 7 as "sneaky." This appears to have been a general descriptor she used for many youth without necessarily intending a negative connotation.)

How is it that Sharon is able to make these inroads with Beyonce, a youngster who by any measure would not be categorized as easy to mentor? It is not simply that Sharon manages to avoid conflicts or disagreements with her. Beyonce, for her part, freely volunteers that there are times when she does not feel close to Sharon and that "sometimes she [Sharon] has an attitude problem." Sharon likewise acknowledges difficulties in their relationship, but also describes how she works to strategically deal with these challenges:

[Were there any times you and Beyonce weren't getting along?] Yes – many! [How did you get over that?] I um, find things that interest her. She's more productive when she's helping out [and] when she has attention. She likes to be a helper, likes to talk a lot. Like to express herself. Give her a platform to do it on – let her be part of the process.

She elaborates on these strategies when asked later in the same interview what she finds "works" with Beyonce:

> *If you're trying to be the authority figure – it doesn't work. If you approach her as a friend or confidant, just give her advice and not boss her and/or tell her what to do.*

Sharon's approach with Beyonce is thus youth-centered (i.e., focused on being responsive to Beyonce's interests, needs, and personality) and egalitarian (i.e., peer-like interactions with minimal appeals to authority that might clash with the growing desires for autonomy and self-direction that are the hallmark of youth of Beyonce's age). This orientation to interacting with Beyonce is in marked contrast to Scottie's authoritarian attempts to deal with her.

At the same time, there is also clearly a goal-directed quality to Sharon's interactions with Beyonce as she seeks to help her problem-solve and become involved in meaningful projects. These qualities align well with those that found to be characteristic of more beneficial and long-lasting relationships between adults and youth in formal mentoring programs.[16] Issues relating to gender also may facilitate Sharon's relationship with Beyonce. Recall, for example, how Beyonce embraces the validation she receives from Sharon about gendered aspects of her appearance (e.g., hair). Sharon likewise tells us that she and Beyonce often engage in "girl talk." Indeed, as a female staff member, Sharon may represent a particularly credible

---

[16] In qualitative research on relationships established in Big Brothers Big Sisters mentoring programs, Morrow and Styles (1995) identified two major types of relationships with different patterns of interaction, which they labeled *developmental* and *prescriptive*. As summarized by Keller (2005), "Mentors in developmental relationships ... believed they should meet the needs of the youth by being flexible and supportive, incorporating the youth's preferences, and building a solid relationship. In contrast, mentors in larger category of prescriptive relationships typically viewed their role as being an authority figure.... These mentors initiated their matches with goals for transforming the youth and began their attempts to address difficulties in the youth's life early in the relationship" (p. 89). Developmental mentoring relationships tended to last longer and were more likely to be described in positive terms by youth as well as mentors (Keller, 2005). Hamilton and Hamilton (1990) distinguished between mentoring relationships that were primarily either *social* or *instrumental* in their orientation. For social mentors, the primary goal was relationship development. For instrumental mentors, the aim was to help the youth accomplish a task or goal in an area of interest to the youth by providing advice, guidance, and explanations. These relationships were less likely to terminate early and appeared to be more beneficial to youth. Sharon's relationship with Beyonce appears to incorporate the strengths of both developmental and instrumental orientations to mentoring.

source of guidance for Beyonce in her struggles to develop friendships with other girls at the center.[17]

This potential notwithstanding, we did not observe or hear of Sharon providing Beyonce with any direct assistance in handling the problems that arose in her friendship with Angel. Perhaps owing to her part-time status at the center, Sharon thus was apparently not able to capitalize on a prime opportunity to provide Beyonce with on-line mentoring in the area of her peer relationships. Nor to our knowledge did any of the other staff with whom she interacted at the center offer this type of support.

DEVELOPMENTAL GAINS OVER THE YEAR

Beyonce's year at North River saw her make significant, albeit modest, gains in the area in which she was most lacking at the start of the year: her peer relationships. As we have noted, by the year's conclusion she had cultivated a loose confederation of a few peers with whom she spent a considerable amount of time. Their relationships, although not particularly close, were nonetheless largely absent of overt conflict. These ties thus represent the emergence of a pocket of peer acceptance for Beyonce in an environment in which only isolation and rejection from peers were evident earlier in the year. Yes, Beyonce still had a long ways to go. Many of the other girls remained scornful of her. But the gains she made represented important first steps.

Importantly, Beyonce also developed a friendship with another girl at North River.[18] This relationship had its share of conflict and appears to have been short-lived, as is so often the case with friendships during early adolescence. Yet, it was nonetheless Beyonce's first close friendship and thus a milestone accomplishment for her.

There are also some indications of improvement in Beyonce's relationships with staff at North River. Gains in this area are most directly attributable to Beyonce eventually being able to minimize day-to-day contact with Scottie. In this respect, what we observe is more a reduction in the level of conflict she experiences with staff

---

[17] See Bogat and Liang (2005) for an in-depth discussion of gender issues in mentoring relationships for youth.

[18] Some research (Bagwell, Newcomb, & Bukowski, 1998) suggests, in fact, that having a close friendship during childhood is more important to long-term development and well-being than is overall acceptance by peers.

rather than a growth in positive dimensions of these ties. Beyonce's relationship with Sharon does not seem to deepen or intensify during the course of the year, and there is only limited evidence of her beginning to broaden her base of support to include other club staff.

Beyonce's gains in social functioning with peers and adults at the center are clearly circumscribed. It is not surprising, therefore, that her responses on several measures we administer during the latter part of the year suggest a psychological toll from her ongoing interpersonal difficulties. These data speak to Beyonce's lack of confidence in her ability to handle different situations with peers as well as to her pronounced feelings of mistrust and inadequacy when interacting with other youth.[19] Added vulnerability stemming from a fear of being hurt or criticized by adults is also apparent.[20]

Beyonce does, however, hold out hope for positive change.[21] This is poignantly illustrated by her response when she is asked what she "expects" for herself in the coming year and what she is doing to help realize these goals:[22]

> [Next year, I expect to be...] to be a better person around kids and to tell what they do to me. [What am I doing now to be that way next year...] I'm trying not to hit them when they hit me back but I can't help it 'cause you get very angry when someone hits you for no reason.

These comments also convey Beyonce's awareness that she needs to interact more appropriately with peers and strengthen

---

[19] Beyonce's score on the scale assessing her self-esteem in the area of peer relations corresponds to a T-score of 36.78, which is well below the sample average. On this scale, she disagrees with statements that would signify a sense of satisfaction with her acceptance by peers ("I am as well liked by other kids as I want to be"), the number and quality of her friendships ("I have as many close friendships as I would like to have"), and her social skills ("I feel good about how well I get along with other kids").

[20] Beyonce's T-score on a measure of interpersonal sensitivity in relationships with adults was 62.15, more than a standard deviation above the sample average.

[21] The benefits of hope and optimism have received increased attention in recent years from the burgeoning field of "positive psychology" (Seligman & Csikszentmihalyi, 2000).

[22] This portion of the interview involved asking youth about their "possible selves" for the coming year. Youth who report more positive and adaptive possible selves have been found to exhibit better adjustment in areas such as self-esteem, behavior, and academic performance (Knox, Funk, Elliott, & Bush, 1998; Leondari, Syngollitou, & Kiosseoglou, 1998; Oyserman & Markus, 1990).

specific social skills (i.e., impulse control, anger management).[23] Her capacity for insight and optimism are assets that could help Beyonce make strides forward in her peer relationships. Indeed, without some awareness of her current limitations and a sense of hope that things can get better, Beyonce might well not respond so favorably to the guidance that figures so prominently in her relationship with Sharon.

More generally, however, we discern little change in Beyonce's personality over the course of the year. Rather, she continues to come across for the most part as an immature and difficult youngster. Chief among the liabilities that remain salient in our observations of Beyonce at the club is her inability to regulate her feelings and impulses in a wide range of social situations with peers and adults alike.

Academically, Beyonce's success at school continues as she ends the year with a B+ average. She also neither reports nor shows signs of potential involvement in risky behaviors, such as gangs or drugs. Clearly, she still lacks the kind of involvement with peers that, alas, can be a starting point for the emergence of such behaviors in adolescence.

BEYONCE IN THE NORTH RIVER AFTER-SCHOOL CENTER: STRENGTHS, SHORTCOMINGS, AND SYNERGIES

We now turn to an examination of strengths, shortcomings, and synergies as they pertain to North River and Beyonce. The advantages that involvement in an after-school center offered this youngster should not be overlooked, especially in view of the signs of progress she exhibited in certain areas during her year at the club. Yet, there were clear shortcomings in how well this center both responded to Beyonce's needs and capitalized on the assets that she brought to the setting. Moreover, the most prominent synergies involve the club's shortcomings and thus likely served to compound missed opportunities for developmental growth during Beyonce's year at North River.

---

[23] The capacity for self-understanding and personal insight has long been emphasized as important within the psychotherapy and counseling literatures. More recently, these abilities have been conceptualized as a core component of emotional intelligence (Goleman, 1997) and, relatedly, as "intrapersonal intelligence" within Gardner's (1993) theory of multiple intelligences.

Strengths

Two primary strengths stand out when considering the role of an after-school center such as North River for Beyonce. First, her attendance at this after-school center provided her with the opportunity to establish and maintain a significant mentoring relationship with a concerned adult. This relationship was cemented in the foundation of a long-term relationship that encompassed Sharon and Beyonce's mutual involvement in the club over a period of several years.[24] During this time, Sharon had developed a nuanced understanding of Beyonce in which recognition of the challenges presented by this budding adolescent was tempered by an appreciation of her more child-like ebullience and desire to please adults. These latter qualities were likely in greater relief earlier in Beyonce's development and thus might well have been overlooked had the club environment not afforded Sharon an opportunity to become acquainted with Beyonce at a relatively young age.

A second strength of North River is that certain features of this setting were advantageous for Beyonce's peer relationships. Like many after-school centers, the club offered exposure to a diverse group of peers. Thus, despite her significant social liabilities, in this environment Beyonce was able to establish relationships with a few girls who accepted her. She also was able form a close friendship. Either of these feats might not have been possible had her after-school time been restricted to a setting less rich in opportunities to interact with peers.

The intensive adult oversight and monitoring that was provided at North River during the after-school hours is a further advantageous feature of the setting for Beyonce. As noted in Chapter 6, fights among older teen girls broke out with some regularity at North River during the less structured evening hours. It is not unreasonable to assume that such incidents also might have occurred with younger girls had there been less intensive adult supervision of their interactions. Had this been the case, Beyonce's conflictual pattern of interactions with other youth at the center easily could have led her to become the target of more severe acts of aggression. Her experiences with peers at North River were undeniably rocky and unfulfilling in many respects. Yet, we never witnessed or heard

---

[24] The benefits of longer-term mentoring relationships for youth are well documented (Rhodes, 2002).

about any instances in which Beyonce was seriously victimized by other youth while at the club.[25] Given her lack of social wiles, we could easily imagine the after-school hours being more perilous for her had she been left to fend for herself in a less structured and well-supervised context.[26]

Shortcomings

Scottie's interactions with Beyonce are a glaring shortcoming in the experiences of this youngster at the North River after-school center. Both the negative emotional intensity and often derogatory content of Scottie's responses to Beyonce are clearly outside the boundaries of acceptable conduct for staff persons who are charged with fostering the development of young people. North River as an organization lacked systematic mechanisms for ensuring that staff lived up to minimal expectations of appropriate behavior in their interactions with youth. These might have included a process through which youth or their parents could share concerns regarding staff behavior. Had such a mechanism been in place, it might have served as a catalyst for Beyonce or her mother to initiate some intervention by the club in the situation. It could have represented, moreover, a meaningful avenue for youth involvement in the club and contributed to a culture of accountability.

An equally prominent shortcoming is the failure of Sharon and Scottie to problem-solve together how to deal with Beyonce. Had they worked as a team, Sharon might have been able to encourage Scottie to experiment with some of the strategies she had found to be successful in her relationship with Beyonce. Such exchanges also might have contributed to a positive reframing of Scottie's highly personalized and negative perceptions of some of Beyonce's more challenging behaviors. Communication and problem-solving

---

[25] In this context, our focus is on physical forms of victimization. Beyonce clearly experienced other forms of negative treatment by peers at the club, which are noteworthy and can be considered social or relational forms of victimization (Crick, Casas, & Nelson, 2002).

[26] Youth are at highest risk of being victims of violence in the four hours following the end of the school day (Snyder & Sickmund, 1999). Those youth who are unsupervised during these hours are especially likely to be victimized (Pederson, de Kanter, Bobo, Weinig, & Noeth, 1999).

between Scottie and Sharon (and potentially other staff) concerning Beyonce, furthermore, could have led to greater consistency in the behavior management strategies used with her at the club and thus enhanced their effectiveness. A center culture that emphasized collective responsibility for youth – a concept introduced in Chapter 1 – could have fostered cooperative efforts among staff in responding to Beyonce's needs. Structured mechanisms for communication among staff could have been valuable as well. These include dedicating portions of staff meetings to sharing and planning approaches to working with difficult youth such as Beyonce.[27] Supervision of staff in principle could have afforded similar advantages. It seems likely, however, that its effectiveness would have been undermined at this center by the often negative and punishing nature of the director's own interactions with youth and staff.

A final shortcoming of North River in addressing the needs of Beyonce is the scarcity of structured programs at this after-school center. A program focused on the development of social skills could have helped Beyonce learn and practice more effective strategies for handling conflicts with peers and for making and keeping friends.[28] One promising candidate in this regard would have been Smart Girls, a structured psychoeducational program for young adolescent girls developed by Boys & Girls Clubs of America and thus designed specifically to fit within the club environment.[29] Beyonce also could have benefited from consistent involvement in a structured program that capitalized on one of her strengths, such as her academic skills or interest in computers. Beyonce's quick gravitation to Power Hour when it was introduced late in the year at the center speaks to the potential appeal of this type of programming for her. North River's drama

---

[27] Staff planning meetings can be held up to several times a week in middle schools to provide teachers and other school personnel charged with responsibility for the same group or "team" of students the opportunity to coordinate instruction as well as to plan for the needs of individual students (Alexander & George, 1981). Greater amounts of common staff planning time in middle schools have been linked to improvements in student behavior and achievement (National Middle School Association, 2004).

[28] One recent evaluation of after-school programs found evidence of stronger effects on problem behavior outcomes for programs that placed greater emphasis on instruction in social skills and character development (Gottfredson, Gerstenblith, Soule, Womer, & Lu, 2004).

[29] For a detailed description of Smart Girls, see Hirsch (2005).

club also would have represented an intriguing potential tie-in to Beyonce's strengths, given the theatrical quality that we observed in many of her interactions with others. This program was plagued by implementation difficulties, however, and limited to teens. Had Beyonce been able to enjoy sustained involvement in a structured program at North River, the adult leader might have become another mentor for her. Especially in view of the limits on Sharon's time, this is something that surely could have added value to her experience at this after-school center.

Synergies

Unfortunately, when after-school centers fail in multiple ways to be responsive to participating youth, this increases the likelihood that different shortcomings will combine synergistically in a manner that compounds their ill effects. This clearly is evident in the case of North River and Beyonce, whose PARC profile is characterized by a number of interrelated unfavorable experiences and missed opportunities. The most prominent negative synergies that we observed involve the culture and organizational climate of the center and the opportunities that existed for Beyonce to receive effective mentoring from staff. The center's rigid adherence to rotating youth through set activity stations posed unavoidable constraints on the abilities of youth to seek out those staff with whom they had positive relationships and, conversely, to avoid those with whom they did not. It is this latter consideration that figures so prominently in Beyonce's year at the club. Regardless of the extent of her difficulties with Scottie, had she not been essentially forced to spend substantial time with him each day, the distress that this relationship engendered for her largely could have been avoided. Likewise, with more freedom to chart her own course of activity, Beyonce could have intensified her efforts to seek out staff and activities that provided more promising contexts for mentoring (e.g., Power Hour with Daniel).

Several facets of North River's broader organizational culture likewise may well have exacerbated the limitations of staff in providing mentoring to Beyonce. What stands out in this regard is the marked level of disenchantment among staff with the center's administrators, as discussed in Chapter 6. We can speculate that conflicts with center leadership diverted staff time and energy from youth and that the quality and level of their engagement with them suffered as a consequence. At one level, staff irritability with center leader-ship may have simply decreased their resiliency in dealing with youth who themselves often exhibited irritating behavior. Further, the constant pressure to maintain order to avoid the wrath of the center director would lead to less patience with kids. These types of repercussions would be especially damaging to young persons such as Beyonce who are in need of relatively more intensive mentoring.

There also are missed opportunities for positive synergy at North River that could have worked to the benefit of Beyonce during her year at the center. Those that strike us as most prominent pertain to the ways in which greater availability of the different types of struc-tured programs referred to previously could have enhanced staff mentoring of Beyonce. Given that interactions with peers would have figured prominently in most of these programs, Beyonce's participa-tion could have substantially expanded the opportunities that staff persons had to provide on-line mentoring to her in this critical area.

CONCLUSIONS

In earlier chapters, we emphasized the difference that individ-ual staff persons were able to make in the experiences of both Pocahontas and Bill at the Midwest after-school center. In the cur-rent chapter, we see further evidence of this theme, albeit on a much more limited basis, in Beyonce's relationship with Sharon. Sharon's approach to working with Beyonce is closely aligned with the fea-tures of formal mentoring relationships that appear most likely to yield significant dividends for youth in different areas, including peer relationships.[30] This relationship, moreover, illustrates the ways in which youth may be able to establish longer-term ties with staff at after-school centers that typically are not feasible in the con-text of more structured or time-limited interventions.

At the same time, by any objective measure, Beyonce exhibited only limited gains during her year at the club. Those occurring in her peer relationships, although noteworthy, were neither sub-stantial nor fully sustained. Nor could we detect evidence of sig-nificant growth in other related areas of her development such as her social maturity. We can speculate that more noteworthy benefits might have accrued if Sharon had worked full time at the center or

---

[30] DuBois, Holloway, Valentine, & Cooper (2002); Tierney & Grossman (1995).

perhaps there had been a structured program available to serve as context for enriching her mentoring of Beyonce. These circumstances might have been especially helpful if Sharon had used greater contact with Beyonce to capitalize on opportunities to provide her with on-line mentoring in areas such as her relationship with Angel. We are skeptical, however, that the difference would have been sufficient to meet all of Beyonce's needs. The typical youth who is matched with a single adult volunteer in a formal mentoring program has been found to exhibit only modest developmental gains.[31] For those youth who present challenges similar to those encountered with Beyonce, even these benefits are often elusive.[32] Even allowing for the potentially significant added value of more frequent contact, longer-term ties, and unique opportunities for on-line mentoring that may exist within the environment of an after-school center, it would seem unwise to us to place exclusive reliance on a relationship with a single staff person.

A more promising scenario would be one in which a youth such as Beyonce receives support and guidance from a collection of staff members at an after-school center – a *personal mentoring network* of staff each with a significant relationship to the youth. This idea is consistent with our conclusion in Chapter 5 that the manner in which several staff collectively provided a familial type of environment at the Midwest after-school center was important for both Pocahontas and Bill. Our discussion in the present chapter builds on this observation by highlighting the potential advantages of establishing formal mechanisms for staff communication and problem solving. As our discussion of the missed opportunity for collaboration between Scottie and Sharon illustrates, such mechanisms could potentially go a long ways toward enhancing the quality of the relationships that youth cultivate with staff in after-school centers. Clearly, if having a personal mentoring network is important to youth in these settings, our case study of Beyonce suggests that it is not only the size of the network that matters. Rather, it is also the ability of the staff involved to work together and thus function as a coordinated group in addressing the needs of the young person involved.

In Chapter 5, we discussed how it was important for both Pocahontas and Bill at the Midwest after-school center to find

---

[31] DuBois et al. (2002).
[32] Rhodes (2002).

one person-activity that meaningfully engaged them and provided opportunities for mentoring from staff. Beyonce's year at
North River lacked any type of comparable experience. This is not
surprising given the relative dearth of available programs at this
after-school center and the limited freedom that youth were granted
in how they spent their time there. Just as a significant person-
activity proved instrumental in helping Pocahontas achieve real
progress in an area where she had struggled (math), we see how
the absence of an analogous opportunity compromised Beyonce's
ability to make headway in her own area of difficulty (peer relationships). A person-activity, in fact, likely would have afforded
staff a wide range of valuable opportunities to provide Beyonce
with direct, on-line mentoring in her interactions with peers. Our
analysis of Beyonce's year at the club adds further to our theorizing in this area by underscoring how organizational features of
after-school centers may be critical in determining whether youth
succeed in finding rewarding person-activity niches. These include
the diversity of available activities or programs with the center as
well as the degree of latitude that exists for youth to explore these
possibilities. Facilitating conditions in these areas were conspicu-
ous by their absence at North River.

Nonetheless, Beyonce did find her way toward the end of the
year into Power Hour, an activity that clearly tapped into her
strengths and offered the potential for a meaningful tie with a staff
person. Her exercise of agency in capitalizing on this opportunity
is reminiscent of Bill's persistence in exploring different options
open to him at the Midwest club. We noted that youth initiative
in that context was especially important because of the reactive nature of the club environment. At North River, there was the
added barrier of organizational practices that constrained youth in
pursuing different activity options. In this type of center, whether
fairly or not, the exercise of youth agency may be especially critical. This is suggested in the case of Beyonce not only because her
efforts were pivotal for becoming involved in a rewarding activity at North River, but also because the pursuit of this opportunity served to extricate her from a highly averse relationship with a
staff person. In comparison, it will be recalled from Chapter 7 that
Tweetie's efforts to effect change in the same after-school center on
a broader scale were largely thwarted by club leadership. Our case
study of Beyonce's year at North River indicates that when youth in

this environment exercised agency focused more narrowly on their individual needs – in ways that were acceptable to staff and center leadership – it could prove beneficial despite the club's formidable barriers to more systemic change.

Still, it would be a mistake to conclude that Beyonce's experiences at North River were immune to fallout from higher-level administrative difficulties that plagued the club. The changes we have discussed to organizational practice or culture that might have benefited Beyonce all would require a strong commitment from staff. Yet, staff morale and trust had been greatly eroded stemming from their pervasive disenchantment with club leadership. We strongly suspect that this situation would have served as an insurmountable obstacle to any initiative to support a more well-orchestrated response to the needs of Beyonce and other youth at the center. As we turn in subsequent chapters to consider the West River center, it will be useful to keep in mind the role of leadership influences within after-school centers. Unlike North River, these chapters will illustrate the potential for leadership practices to radiate to the experiences of individual youth in ways that are positive and beneficial.

9

Putting It All Together: North River
and Midwest Centers

As we did with the Midwest center, we will now take a look back at the overarching themes and lessons learned from our three studies of North River. Whereas each case and the organizational-level study are informative on their own, our goal in this chapter is to present a more complex analysis that synthesizes and expands on important concepts not only from within North River, but also from within Midwest.

North River had many areas of failure. One of the notable differences between Pocahontas and Bill, the youth presented from Midwest, and Tweetie and Beyonce, the youth presented from North River, was the inability of either Tweetie or Beyonce to find a complete PARC in which she was truly engaged. A complete PARC features three components: 1) a program or activity, 2) a relationship, and 3) a cultural dimension. The benefit of a PARC is that the whole can be greater than any of its parts. In other words, although a strong relationship with a staff person is important, the overall PARC will be stronger and likely have more benefits when that relationship is in the context of an engaging program/ activity and supported by a culture that promotes youth development. At Midwest, we saw how complete positive PARCs provided Pocahontas and Bill with developmental supports beyond that which they would have received with one or two of the components alone. In the case of North River, in the absence of any complete PARC, neither girl reaped such benefits.

Tweetie had a strong relationship (Scottie) without any program or activity and had a strong activity (Keystone) that had the potential for developing a relationship but had not done so yet. Her potential strongest PARCs (cheerleading and girls' gym night) never fully materialized. In the first case, center leadership thwarted the program's potential through a combination of neglect (not ordering uniforms, not listening to what girls wanted from a coach) and active conflict with the group members (Mr. Jones' altercation with the teens, the coach's disagreements with the girls). In the second case, the potential of a girls' gym night was hampered by staff and leaders' lack of attention to recruiting girls and developing activities that would sustain their interest. Tweetie may have been particularly able to benefit from a complete PARC in the gym, as she already had the foundation of a relationship with Scottie, who supported her leadership as well as served as a father or older brother figure to her. That relationship had the potential to continue to grow if it were supported by a program and culture. Yet without such surrounding structures, we were unsure what the continued benefit of that relationship would be as Tweetie matured.

Beyonce, on the other hand, had two relationships (Angel, a peer, and Sharon, a staff member), neither of which were situated in a larger PARC. At the end of the year, she attempted to attach herself to a PARC (Power Hour) and reported developing a relationship within it. It was not clear at the end of the study whether or not this relationship had grown or whether Beyonce had reaped any other benefits from her participation in Power Hour.

The absence of engaging PARCs limited the availability of developmental opportunities for Tweetie and Beyonce. It also restricted the opportunities for and benefits of mentoring and strong peer relationships, which for Beyonce would have been particularly important. As noted in Chapter 5, comprehensive centers can provide multiple opportunities for youth to make connections with staff and to find meaningful programs that offer opportunities for growth, belonging, identity exploration, meaningful relationships, and the demonstration of competency. Where few PARCs are available, youth are left to "sink or swim," as was the case at North River.

The failure of North River to offer strong positive PARCs was a result of organizational failures. Similar to the situation at Midwest, staff members were neither well trained for the programs assigned to them nor provided with encouragement or support to start new programs. Yet what differentiated North River from Midwest was North River's pervasively negative culture. Whereas at Midwest there was a general lack of support for staff initiative, particularly in the realm of girls' programs, at North River there was active belittlement of staff ideas. This was an important difference. Absence of support might make it less likely that staff will take initiative. But the active discouragement from and fear of center directors at North River almost guaranteed that no staff would take the initiative to start programs stemming from their own or youths' interests, as Manuel did at Midwest. This culture of negativity permeated North River and quickly infected new staff. High levels of mistrust between administrative leaders and program-level staff ensured that staff members were not going to risk trying something new. Furthermore, when staff did jump in to provide youth with activities, such as Rockwell's taking on the coaching of the boys' basketball team, their efforts were often belittled, if not downright crushed. Volunteers, who also would have provided opportunities for new and engaging PARCs, were frustrated by what they perceived to be a lack of support, communication, and organization. The consequence of this was that both Tweetie, who was poised to reap benefit from a comprehensive youth center, and Beyonce, who could have benefited from strong peer and adult relationships, made few, if any, gains over the course of their year at the center. Any development that did occur appeared to be almost in spite of North River's culture and organizational practices rather than because of them.

Another notable point of difference between Midwest and North River was the experience of the individual youth in terms of their role within the center. At Midwest, both Pocahontas and Bill benefited from two cultural aspects of the center: they were provided with leadership roles that had importance in the life of the center and they were enveloped within a familial environment in which some sense of communal responsibility and care existed. Two major facets of North River's culture prevented either such synergy from emerging at the center.

First, youth agency was thwarted at North River. The sole opportunity for youth to give back to the center in a meaningful way was through the junior staff program, which indeed seemed to be the most successful program at the center. Yet rather than capitalize on youth's love of this program and look for other meaningful ways that youth could contribute to the center both before and after they were of an age to be junior staff, center leaders appeared uninterested in creating other opportunities for youth leadership and participation. Attendance and behavior management seemed to be their sole concerns. Tweetie's attempts to build new programs, such as cheerleading, were thwarted, removing opportunities for both an engaging PARC and a meaningful role in the center. In Chapter 5, we pointed out that youth agency – and staff's positive response to such agency – was important for youth's finding meaningful person-activities at the Midwest Center. At North River, youth agency was also important, but youth were oftentimes prevented from exercising any agency. The leaders' focus on structure left little room for youth to exercise any autonomy. It also ensured that staff would respond negatively to youth agency, as they risked chastisement from club leaders if they were perceived as allowing any behavior that strayed from the carefully controlled rotation and behavior management system. Thus, not only were youth unable to seek out the types of opportunities that Bill and Pocahontas found at Midwest, but most attempts to exercise agency were punished rather than rewarded.

Second, staff at North River spent much of the day isolated from each other due to the center's rotation system. This limited opportunities for staff members to share information or collaborate. The high levels of conflict between staff and leadership also contributed to a culture of distrust. Staff meetings were sporadic, did not include part-time staff, and could turn into "bitch fests." On top of that, there seemed to be little incentive for or interest in organizational-level learning. All of this combined to create an atmosphere in which the positive synergies that we observed arise at Midwest, although somewhat limited in nature, were missing altogether. Not only were there missed opportunities for positive synergies, but the only synergies that did emerge were negative. In Beyonce's case, the rotation system amplified her highly conflicted relationship with Scottie, creating a tense environment in which she not only had to spend time with someone who distressed her but was also not able to seek out other, more supportive activities and relationships. For Tweetie, the absence of complete PARCs was reinforced by leadership's discouragement of youth autonomy, leading to an atmosphere in which her potential was impeded rather than enhanced.

As indicated in Chapter 5, the strength of comprehensive youth centers is in their abilities to offer multiple PARCs that allow for youth to seek out activities that fit their interests and needs. On the flip side, if a youth is rebuffed across multiple PARCs, it could be more damaging than experiencing rejection in a single domain. Such appears to be the case at North River. This was particularly evident with Tweetie. As Tweetie's efforts at leadership were rebuked in multiple areas, she became increasingly disengaged. Imagine if Tweetie had been at a center that offered not only Keystone but also support for cheerleading, drama, and girls' gym night. Imagine if Scottie and Michelle were supported by club management in giving Tweetie leadership roles and had the opportunity to discuss Tweetie's efforts with other staff, who could have been encouraged to recognize Tweetie's role in the center. We suspect that had Tweetie experienced success rather than failure across multiple domains, she would have had a more positive developmental trajectory. If North River offered multiple *strong* positive PARCs, it may have served as more than a place for her to stay out of trouble and could have enhanced her strengths, thus promoting positive youth development.

Furthermore, for both youth, mentorship opportunities were hampered by the structure of the club. Both Beyonce and Tweetie could have benefited from staff members having opportunities to share information with each other and develop programs to engage youth in meaningful activities of their choosing. This strategy was successful with Manuel, Bill, and Pocahontas at Midwest. We suspect that, had it been supported by leadership, it could have worked at North River, too. The lack of proactive support for mentorship was particularly discouraging because North River actually had a potential strength in the area of staff. Because it had a number of older, long-time staff, there were people who knew the community and youth's families well. Yet club leaders did not capitalize on this strength. There was no effort to use such community knowledge to train newer staff, who were well positioned to develop the type of peer-like relationships we saw at other centers.

Our study of North River makes evident the importance of oversight for after-school settings. Had regional headquarters conducted any spontaneous site visits or talked confidentially with program staff and youth, they likely would have identified the issues which we observed. The center's strong membership, historic place in the community, and perhaps certain long-time staff, some of whom were known by youth's families, enabled North River to conduct business as usual and not reflect on its practice. Although center-level autonomy is certainly important, such autonomy must occur within bounds.

North River staff members also could have benefited from interacting with and learning from staff members at other centers. Consider the initial enthusiasm of Michelle, Daniel, and Rockwell, for example. These new, young staff seemed ready to develop new activities and excited to work with youth. They appeared to do a good job when they had the opportunity to lead activities in which they became meaningfully engaged (e.g., Michelle with Keystone, Daniel with Power Hour, Rockwell with basketball). Yet, in each case, there were barriers or discouragement from center leadership. On top of that, the long-term staff at North River were older and suffered from the years of tension and conflict that existed between them and club leadership. Had the new staff members met young, engaged staff from other centers, they may have been able to generate new ideas and been pushed to engage youth more proactively than the culture at North River encouraged. Instead, they were enveloped in an atmosphere that dampened their enthusiasm and dissuaded them from taking a positive approach to the youth with whom they worked.

It should be evident here that ultimately a broader, more system-wide lens for considering after-school centers and programs, including inter-organizational linkages, is likely to add value. In terms of systems issues, our emphasis in this book is on adding organizational-level analyses of selected issues that have in the past received little attention in relation to after-school settings. We readily acknowledge that this is but a first, though hopefully useful, step.

The following chapters on the West River center will provide a point of contrast to North River. Whereas North River suffered from a lack of effective leadership, West River had a strong organizational culture that supported staff and youth's efforts and development. In some places where North River struggled, it could have learned from West River, had a more general region-wide atmosphere of organizational learning encouraged such practices.

WEST RIVER CENTER

10

The Jewel in the Crown

At the time of our earlier research, West River had the reputation as the best Boys & Girls Club in the region. During the intervening years, it had gone through a rough spell, with lots of administrative and staff turnover. However, as we came to know the center during this second study, it was clear that West River had gotten back on its feet and was again a beacon of excellence.

The West River Center is in a large, free-standing building. It has a gym, game room, and multiple meeting rooms spread out over two floors. The neighborhood is primarily African American, although other groups have come to reside there in increasing numbers. Retail establishments mix in with single-family homes and apartment buildings, including several public housing units. Although there is less violence here than around the other two clubs, nearly all the young people who attend tell us that they do not feel safe in the neighborhood.

Our initial survey questionnaire, completed in the fall by ninety-eight youth, reveals the demographics of youth ages ten and up who attend the club. The sample is primarily African American (89%) and Latino (9%). Most are in early adolescence (average age = 12.6 years). Almost all of the families are low-income (85% qualify for free or reduced-price lunch). Most have been coming to the center for years (only 15% started attending this year). The great majority attend three to four days per week for two to three hours each day.

During each of our site visits, we rated the presence or absence of different qualities, and it is clear from these ratings that we found West River to be a much more positive place than either Midwest or North River. West River was significantly more likely than the two other centers to be rated during our visits as demonstrating staff cooperativeness, staff enthusiasm, positive staff remarks about youth or the club, youth enjoying their time at the site, youth making positive remarks about the club or staff or other youth, and parents being in attendance.

We now turn to our analytic framework for understanding West River as an organization, examining their focus on positive youth development as an overarching goal, quality of program development and implementation, and human resource development. In each of these areas we would expect superior performance at West River, and that was exactly what we found.

GOALS

As discussed in Chapter 2, the organization's goals as set forth by the Boys & Girls Clubs of America include safety, having fun, and positive youth development. West River subscribed to all of these. What particularly distinguishes this center from the other two is their strong focus on promoting positive youth development. West River differs from North River in that youth development is a top priority, which was not the case at North River. West River differs from Midwest in that club leadership and most staff focus on this objective, whereas this was true for only one staff person, Manuel, at Midwest.

As in the prior chapters that consider these centers as organizations, we will best come to appreciate West River's focus on positive youth development through considering their actual practice. As we will see, this focus is evident in a wide range of activities, from sports to structured programs to personnel decisions.

PROGRAM DEVELOPMENT AND IMPLEMENTATION

Our focus will be on programs led by paid staff (there were nine staff at the center, including the director). It should be noted, though, that there were a large number of volunteers at West River, and their participation substantially increased the range of activities available to youth.

Game Room and Gym

The game room is one of the main settings for having fun at West River. Pool (billiards) and ping-pong are the two most high-profile activities. As is typically the case, the excitement ebbs and flows, although the noise level rarely descends very low. Disputes do occur, as in most youth games, but are kept under control. In the game room, as throughout West River, safety is maintained. Ben, the staff person in charge, knows how to keep things within bounds. Ben spends a lot of his time joking with the kids and participating in their activities, but it is clear that he is an adult and serves as referee and judge when needed. Because the game room tends to be the least structured setting in the center, Ben estimates that he spends more of his time on discipline (75%) than do the other staff members (who provided estimates of 10–20%).

The young people rotate through the game room on a set schedule. Although both West River and North River rotate youth through various activities, at West River youth can opt out of the rotation in order to participate in a specific program that meets at that time. This implementation of a rotation system provides flexibility and sensitivity to youth choice, which was not true at North River.

At Midwest, young people would congregate in the game room because there typically was not much interesting stuff going on elsewhere, but that is not so at West River. Perhaps nowhere is this contrast as evident as in the gym. The gym at West River is physically larger than at Midwest, but the more important difference is in how the sports director at each center interacts with youth.

Nelson, the sports director at West River, is highly focused on helping youth improve their skills and raise the level of their game. Basketball is the most popular activity, and Nelson always finds an opportunity to do some coaching, even when kids are just informally playing with each other. Here is an example of how he seeks to encourage and provide tips about how to play better:

> During the game Nelson kept close track of what was going on, commenting on each player's moves and commenting when they took shots. Whenever one of the taller boys would get the ball, Nelson would yell "just shoot it – you know you can make it from there – just do it!"… Nelson yelled "Shaun, Shaun, man, you are bigger than he is, you can put that ball over your head and he can't get it. Don't crouch down on the ground, use what you have!"

Nelson had this type of engagement regularly. In this he differed from Mateo, the sports director at Midwest. Although popular,

Mateo as often as not would sit at courtside doing paperwork or reading a magazine rather than be actively coaching. At North River, Jimmie would more likely be found chatting with youth on the sidelines than coaching those who were playing ball. So it really is only at West River that the gym director had a consistent focus on actively promoting positive physical development.

Dance

Victoria was a twenty-something, athletic African American known for her big smile. She ran several core programs at West River and the dance program was her favorite.

Victoria's dance team was not for the lazy or indifferent. It was a competitive, high-energy group, and Victoria consistently sought to bring out the best performances. At the beginning of the school year, there are tryouts for the team for two days. At the end of each day, a certain number of youth are cut. Those that are cut on the first day are the C-team, those that are cut on the second day comprise the B-team, and those that are left are the A-team. The A-team gets to compete against groups from outside the center. If someone on the A-team is ill or not able to attend a competition, someone from the B-team or C-team takes their place.

Competition – both within the team and against other teams – continues throughout the year. There are some contests where only some of the A-team can participate and those spots need to be earned.

> Victoria emerged out of her office at this point and said, "OK, y'all are going to be practicing for a while here tonight cause we just have three more days before this competition on Friday. They respect us, but the only way they gonna keep respecting us is if we keep performing at a top level. So, I can only have ten of you guys on stage at a time, so today we are going to start figuring out who those ten people are gonna be. So I what I want to happen is to go through each song and have two people go up and perform for me at a time so I can see who knows which dance the best and I can put you in.

Getting – and keeping – youth engaged is an important priority in any program, and competition is certainly one vehicle that can be used effectively to accomplish this.

Victoria constantly coaches the girls and boys on the team on how to improve.

> *In the middle of the dance, she [Victoria] stood on her chair and yelled,*
> *"Alecia, Fatima, I can't see your energy, I can't see you smiling. You*
> *know the steps but you gotta have attitude!" Whey they finished the*
> *dance she said that they did a good job except that Alecia needed to*
> *perk up or else no one was ever going to pay attention to her and that*
> *Fatima needed to stop flailing her arms. At this point, Victoria and*
> *Fatima stopped in the middle of the floor and Victoria literally held one*
> *of Fatima's arms behind her back while making her perform the dance*
> *moves so that she would get used to not having her arm flailing.*

In addition to verbal exhortation and instruction, and physical guidance, as in the above example, Victoria would also model desired
steps, particularly when the youth were first learning a new dance.

> *She would lead the group through the various steps and then stand back*
> *and watch them do it slowly. If anyone made a mistake she would walk*
> *behind them and guide their body through the steps until they got it*
> *correctly on their own.... Victoria was working very hard to teach the*
> *dance to the youth and finally she said to them, "OK, I want y'all to sit*
> *down and I am going to do this for you so you can see hot it's supposed*
> *to look and then I want you all to copy me." She started the music and*
> *began to dance. Although I had seen her dance when she was teaching, I*
> *had never seen her "perform" before and she was extremely talented, so*
> *much so that everyone clapped when she was finished. All of the youth*
> *stood up again and practiced the dance a few more times.*

Victoria freely dispensed lots of praise when things were done
right or better than before. But she did not hesitate to insist on high
standards.

> *Then Victoria moved into the next song and asked for those perform-*
> *ers to step up. The exchange of kids was really slow and Victoria got*
> *irritated because some of them had stopped to talk or grab a snack off*
> *the table. She said, "Hey, I'm not dealing with a bunch of babies here.*
> *Get going, we got a performance in two days!"*

Victoria also would seek to improve dance skills by occasionally
bringing in outside teachers to teach them other dance forms such
as ballet and tap.

The dance group was a source of considerable pride to youth,
staff, and community members. There often was an audience, even
for daily practices, which at various times included other youth just
wanting to watch, parents, or outside friends and acquaintances. It
was not unusual to have parents attend competitions, whether in

dance or a sport like basketball, but this was one of the few groups where you might find parents observing on a routine basis. Thus, the dance group was a high-profile activity and one that was characterized by a clear and consuming focusing on promoting youth skills and competence. The instructor had high expectations and employed a variety of motivational and teaching techniques.

Smart Girls

Smart Girls is a structured, psychoeducational program for early adolescent girls developed by the Boys & Girls Clubs of America national headquarters. The program, which is documented in a 110-page manual, includes a total of 32 sessions across five domains: lifeskills (problem solving, communication, and coping skills), know your body, eating healthy and fitness, accessing the health care system, and role models and other mentors. During our earlier research on a gender equity initiative at these centers, implementation of this program was mandated. Unfortunately, the quality of implementation often left much to be desired, as we documented in detail in an earlier book.[1] During this study, West River was the only one of the three centers to offer this program. It was run by Victoria, who we previously met in connection with the dance group.

At most centers, Smart Girls had a reputation for being a special and somewhat secretive place, some of which reflected the requirement that things talked about during the group had to be treated as confidential. Victoria did her best to emphasize the special nature of the group when she welcomed new members.

> "[Y]ou gotta get a tattoo cause we're a secret society and stuff. So you have to get a Smart Girls tattoo – you know on your neck or on your back." Brittany interrupted, "what about a tattoo?!" Victoria responded with "You know I am just playing – you don't have to get a tattoo but remember that we are all smart girls here and we are all important to each other. We are helping each other become strong women!"

Unlike many Smart Girls leaders, Victoria demonstrated a good command of the material and generally had little difficulty in having the group address the objectives of any particular session. In this session, the focus was on dealing with threats to self-esteem.

---

[1] Hirsch (2005).

This discussion included one about the different people who influence you, [including] your Mom, TV, friends, boys, etc. Along these lines, Victoria talked with the girls about all the things in the world that seem to mediate against having a positive self-esteem, things like television and always seeing skinny girls with rich guys on MTV cribs.... [She] continued talking about the importance of having good self-esteem so that you can resist the people who put you down and listen to the people who pull you up.... Victoria talked about "Prince Charming standing down on the corner in his Timberland boots, saggin', with his hat cocked to the right" who get in a relationships and says to a girl, "it you an' me against the world." Particularly how this can affect a girl's self-esteem if he beats her or gets involved with drugs or even leaves her, and how sometimes he might leave her with a baby.

In accord with the program, Victoria comprehensively addressed a variety of threats to their well-being, including many tough situations that girls from this neighborhood could well encounter. She did not hesitate to address even highly personal issues and she did so in a reassuring way, pointing out ways to cope effectively. She was a supportive presence, promoting resilience and growth. When done well, these centers provide one-stop shopping for mentoring, and Victoria used Smart Girls effectively to enhance her ability to mentor these early adolescent girls.

Like most Smart Girls instructors, Victoria was able to generate considerable discussion among the girls. She also was unusually thoughtful about how to handle some of the more difficult process demands of the program. For example, there are a number of sessions that feature youth role plays. When we reviewed this program more systematically in prior research, we found that few staff prepared youth for those situations.[2] Victoria, instead, would first take the role players out into the hallway to go over with them what they needed to do.

Torch Club and Keystone

Both Torch and Keystone were active in planning a number of high-profile events at West River throughout the year. These groups provided numerous opportunities for youth to assume leadership role. The main activity for Torch Club (for those ages ten to twelve) was the Cadet Olympics (the cadets were ages six to eight).

[2] Hirsch (2005).

Victoria started by saying, "Well, guys, this is going to be an informal planning meeting where we need to talk about our Olympics for the cadets. Cause we really need to start planning – we have to get it into [regional] headquarters by March. That means we have to plan AND have the event and write it up so we can get a reward by March. So today we need to plan what activities we want them to have, what kind of food we want, and who is going to be in charge of what. So I want you each to think of an activity for me that we can have the cadets do." They started going around the circle and suggest 20 meter dashes, the long jump, frog hopping, vertical jumping, and triple jump. Victoria started asking whether they could have a dancing section but Yolanda yelled out, "No, no, Victoria, this is sports, not some dance competition!" Victoria laughed and agreed with her and asked if anyone could think of anything else. She said that it was a good start and that they needed to think about what type of food they wanted at the banquet afterwards. . . . Michael spoke up and said that he knew a really good and cheap pizza and wings place that he could bring the menu in from. "Perfect – thank you, Michael – that will be your job to present to us why you think that is the place we should order from!"

We can see that there was lots of opportunity for youth to participate in problem solving and decision making. They didn't hesitate to disagree with Victoria when she tried to make a spot for dance, her favorite activity. The Olympics involved a good deal of advance planning in which they could develop skills in project management and assume varied responsibilities. The Cadet Olympics were a success and although Torch members were involved in some other activities, the group began to meet less frequently after the Olympics as Victoria became increasingly involved with dance competitions (Torch had met irregularly before Victoria took over the group in mid-year).

Our observers rated different aspects of the center during each visit, and West River got the highest ratings for youth voice (i.e., expressing their own opinions), as reflected in the prior field note. However, there were also many occasions when staff acted in a directive manner. This happened a number of times with Keystone, the leadership group for teens that was directed by Vanessa.

. . . Vanessa began to assign jobs for the evening to everyone: some people had to blow up balloons, some had to start covering the wall of windows in the game room with black paper, and some had to find the material for the cadet's activity. When she was listing who would do what, DeJuan yelled out that he was doing balloons, but when she got down to his

activity, she assigned him to finding garbage bags. "No, I am doing balloons," he responded back. She then again responded with "No, you are not, you are going to find garbage bags to put the balloons in!" He finally slumped in his chair and did not make any sort of move to go anywhere to find balloons. When Vanessa brought the balloons back in, no one made any sort of move to go and do their jobs and everyone just began to blow up balloons instead.

Indeed, Vanessa often had trouble controlling the group as they were easily distracted and often bent on socializing rather than working on a project. They also were not always satisfied with her leadership or their roles. The following field note documents what happened at the first Keystone meeting after the group had run a sleepover for younger kids.

[Vanessa] went on to say that she really appreciated all of their hard work at the sleepover and was proud to announce that they made over $500 for Keystone. Everyone nodded with excitement and approval. Anna interrupted at this point and said "but I've got some complaints: wasn't this supposed to be a Keystone sleepover? And weren't we the ones who were supposed to be running it? Why were other people telling us what to do, you know? We planned this and then we have people telling us when to go to bed, how to scoop the ice cream, where to be when. I was read mad especially when VOLUNTEERS from other clubs are telling us what to do and they don't even know me!" Vanessa was just staring at her, then she said, "Well don't we have some opinions. Well, Vanessa has some opinions, too, Miss-I-know-everything. First of all, I wanted to THANK the volunteers, as they were where they were supposed to be – at the correct post and doing their work when many of you were not! In addition, everyone was stressed. I know I may have snapped at many of you more times than one, but that's what happens under stress. You all know I had to go out and get food four times during the night and in the morning, and that I had one staff member just not show and that I had kids who had to stay here in-between cause their parents didn't want them going home and coming back! No, everything did not go perfectly and wonderfully and I am sorry if many of you did not have fun; how-ever, we accomplished our goal of making money for Keystone that will support us in our different activities. [Other complaints by youth were aired, including some concerning the behavior of Vanessa's boyfriend at the overnight. Vanessa suggested some ways that things might be done differently next year. She then successfully transitioned into a discussion of a forthcoming out-of-state trip for Keystone members.]

It is not unusual for things not to go as planned in sleepover or other large youth events (ask any parent). When the youth who had planned the event did not like how aspects of it turned out, they felt it was OK to voice complaints with some vigor. It should be noted that they raised significant issues, rather than some of the silly matters that were discussed in Keystone at Midwest. Vanessa does not shrink from addressing the situation, but tries to universalize the phenomena in ways that minimizes blaming. By the end of the meeting, the young people have vented and believe that they have been heard at least to some degree, and are then able to move on to other topics. Nonetheless, there is a persistent dynamic in Keystone of youth feeling disrespected and not given sufficient responsibility, which ultimately may be key criteria for successful youth programs.[3] Moreover, although we can appreciate the mutual assertiveness, one can question whether Vanessa reacted too strongly and sarcastically to Anna.

Torch and Keystone at West River had a number of success stories to tell and provided opportunities for leadership, skill development, and peer ties. They were not, however, an unblemished success. Torch met irregularly and Keystone had problems with staff leadership. We now turn to another West River program that had implementation problems.

Dental Health

During the year the center began a program for youth ages nine-to-twelve to teach them about dental health. The program was sponsored by a national dental organization that had recently funded a community dental clinic. The program had a written manual and sessions were designed to be offered weekly. Nelson was selected by club leadership to be the instructor, although he clearly had no interest in the activity. Many sessions, Nelson would simply "forget" his program manual at home. The time that was supposed to be spent on the curriculum was generally utilized as open gym time. When Nelson did bring the manual to sessions, he would read or paraphrase haltingly; there was little discussion, and it is likely that the material simply went in one ear and out the other.

[3] Deutsch (2008).

Academic Support

Like every other Boys & Girls Club, West River had a Power Hour. This was a scheduled hour during which youth could receive tutoring or help with their homework. At this center, it was held in the library. It mostly functioned as a stereotypical study hall: Youth were supposed to work on academic material, but generally did not do so, instead gossiping among themselves. The staff person was more concerned with keeping the noise level from rising too loud than with offering academic assistance, although that was provided on occasion if specifically requested by a young person.

Youth at the center were also required to bring in their report cards when issued. A staff member would look these over and typically give a sentence or two worth of feedback.

> *Today was report card day and Victoria came out of her office and sat down at a table with Tareesha, Maria, Tommiana, and Micere. One by one she asked for their reports cards and then looked them over, making comments like, "OK, you don' better here, but you gotta get this up to at least a C." When she got to Tommiana, she shook her head and said, "OK, this isn't bad, but get it up to all A's and B's. Good work, you are doing better." Tommiana just shook her head, sad down and started whispering with Maria.*

The only follow-up that we observed or heard of would occur at the next showing of report cards.

It is difficult to imagine that either of these initiatives had much impact on youth's academic performance.

Youth-Staff Relationships

The emphasis at West River on program implementation did not detract from the quality of youth-staff relationships. Staff at this center received our highest ratings on a number of measures in this domain. On a quantitative measure of mentoring, youth rated the West River staff more highly than the staff at the other two centers and, despite the small sample size, this difference reached statistical significance in the contrast with Midwest.[4] Youth also

---

[4] As in all statistical analyses we report in the book, we used a significance level of $p < .05$.

rated their relationships with staff at West River to have the fewest negative interactions, though this difference did not reach significance. On our structured observational measure of youth-staff interaction, West River staff were recorded more frequently than staff at other centers as providing emotional support, having physical contact (a positive measure denoting warmth and friendliness), providing choices for youth, and discussing plans for future activities (all of these results were statistically significant). In interviews, Nelson, Victoria, and Ben all affirmed that they considered themselves as mentors to youth at the center and were comfortable in that role. Staff here clearly had active, positive relationships with youth and this type of relationship was the rule rather than the exception.

HUMAN RESOURCE DEVELOPMENT

As in the prior organizational chapters, in this section we consider hiring practices, training and supervision, and the extent to which the center functions as a learning organization. Given that West River does a much better job at program implementation that the other centers, it should not come as a great surprise to find that there are some distinctive aspects to their human resource development practices as well.

Staff Hiring

When we talked with Joe Bryant, the center director, at the beginning of the year, he made it clear that he had made wholesale staff changes when he took over the club the prior year. He wanted committed staff with good skills and did not hesitate to fire those who did not measure up. In this respect, West River was unlike the other two centers, where there was no recent history of terminating staff.

This approach was also adopted by Natasha, the program director and second-in-command. West River had a large volunteer contingent but not all of those worked out well. Some volunteers were very engaged with youth, but others abused their position by playing pool and foosball in the game room instead of supervising, or playing basketball instead of refereeing a game. Natasha told us on more than one occasion of volunteers she had to dismiss because of poor performance. Natasha was well known for her high expectations and ran the center by the motto "If Mama ain't happy, ain't nobody happy." At the same time, she strove to keep the atmosphere light-hearted and fun; for example, she was known to make up little songs and ditties and sing them over the loud speaker that is heard throughout the club.

West River did share with the other two centers an emphasis on hiring some staff who had neighborhood connections. Both Ben and Victoria had grown up and still lived in West River's neighborhood. They knew several of the youth's parents based on that connection. Both saw themselves as potential role models for getting an education and good job. Ben had been a member of the center in his own youth.

Training and Supervision

West River provided more training to new staff than the other centers, but there were mixed reactions to it. Training consisted almost entirely of job shadowing. A new hire would shadow one or more veteran staff for a week, observing what they did and having the opportunity to ask questions and discuss issues. This can be a useful way to transmit what theorists in organizational learning refer to as tacit or implicit knowledge, the often unspoken understandings that are frequently at the core of how an organization functions. A new hire can actually see how to approach and handle situations that may be difficult to describe in a written manual.

Staff who had been hired under this training regimen were split in their reactions to it. Some thought this system worked great and was all that they needed. Others found it to be insufficient preparation. There was some tendency for those who grew up in this neighborhood to respond favorably whereas those who grew up elsewhere found it lacking. Perhaps those who grew up in these circumstances came to their jobs with a greater understanding of how to deal with these youth and only needed a few pointers on how to apply that knowledge in this particular setting. Unfortunately for those who wanted more than job shadowing, nothing else was forthcoming.

West River leadership consisted of more active supervisors than their counterparts at the other centers. Despite his myriad responsibilities outside of the club, Joe Bryant, the overall director, regularly made the rounds of different programs and activities and was acquainted with all staff and many youth. Natasha, the second-in-command, stayed on top of what everyone was doing and did not hesitate to intervene when something was not going as desired.

> *Natasha pulled Nelson off to the side and I moved in a little bit closer so that I could hear what was going on. "Why aren't you doing your program? Your program area is to be doing Dental Health [Nelson had been directing a sports activity] – we get money from them!" Nelson looked at her and shook his head, "look, I am sorry – I can't do it – I don't have the book [program manual]." Natasha looked back at him and said, "well, when you gonna remember it?".... Nelson agreed that he would certainly remember the book next week and she replied that he better cause the club wasn't going to get any funding if they didn't put on the programs that were asked for.*

We were not able to observe whether Natasha ever commented on how skillfully Nelson read from the manual when he did bring it. In general, he read directly from it rather than paraphrase, and his reading was rather on the dull side. Of course, if he knew his boss was observing and evaluating him, on those occasions he might have read with a bit more energy. There was no instance in which we observed Natasha provide this more in-depth type of supervisorial guidance for any program or activity.

Learning Organization

Job shadowing was the main vehicle for promoting organizational learning. Staff meetings were held regularly, but most of the staff found them boring and tried to get out of attending if they could. Those meetings typically focused on operational issues rather than on organizational learning.

Of course, given the generally high level of program implementation at this center, one might argue that West River was doing just fine without the need for an organizational learning initiative, that the focus on hiring top staff and firing those who did not perform was all that was needed. Although we agree that their personnel-hiring policies provided important benefits, there were several important areas in which West River could have made important improvements.

We have noted that there were implementation problems with Torch and Keystone in the other centers, and West River was not immune to these. Sometimes they met irregularly, sometimes there were issues with the group dynamics, and sometimes there were tensions regarding youth exercise of leadership. The latter is especially salient to Torch and Keystone as they are supposed to be settings to develop youth leadership. Yet there are occasions when youth assertiveness makes staff uncomfortable. This is a key tension within many youth programs, but particularly for those, like these centers, that subscribe to a positive youth development model. The answers are not going to be found easily, but West River did not provide opportunities for staff to discuss and problem-solve these issues.

The conundrum regarding youth leadership was not limited to those two programs. Some of the staff felt that youth voice needed to be developed and listened to throughout the center. Nelson was the most vocal about this.

> *The club could be geared more so where the kids run it and choose the programs it runs and we oversee it. They [leadership] are geared more to numbers rather than quality.... We call ourselves youth development but we tell them what to do and they will look for someone to tell them their whole lives.*

Discussing these sets of issues could provide the foundation for continual improvement and strengthening of programs and activities. These are tricky issues to think through, and much experimentation is probably needed. It is something that needs to be done if we are serious about youth voice and leadership. But these discussions never took place.

There are all kinds of fruitful discussions that can take place as youth centers strive to do better. Case conferences around specific young people are one of those. Had the staff held such conferences, and considered Tommiana, whose case study we will present shortly in another chapter, they would have recognized that there are a decent-sized number of young people at the club whose needs were not adequately recognized and addressed. West River is an active and fast-paced environment, and it is not easy to stand out in the crowd. There are young people there who can get lost in the shuffle. If there were regular case conferences covering an assortment of youth at the center, the staff might be better able to recognize this dynamic and consider how to address it. But no such conferences took place.

CONCLUSION

Compared to the other two after-school centers, West River has a much greater capacity to deliver high-quality programs and activities. In large part, this reflects a much more consistent staff focus on promoting positive youth development. There is a similarity to the Midwest Center in that one staff person plays a central role in emphasizing this approach; at Midwest it was Manuel, at West River it is Victoria. But there are several other staff at West River who do this as well, whereas at Midwest there was only Manuel. Nelson plays a particularly important role in this regard in his role as sports director. Sports is a very prominent activity at these centers, and Nelson is constantly seeking to enhance youth athletic skills. In addition to their specific programmatic responsibilities, West River staff readily see themselves as mentors to young people. There is thus a consistency and depth to the focus on positive youth development that drives staff-youth interactions.

The focus on positive development does not come at the expense of fun or safety, two other overarching goals of Boys & Girls Clubs. The game room at this site is just as lively as at the others. Safety and order are not compromised. At North River, the center director was so focused on order that there was little room for positive development. At West River, they did not see this as a forced choice and instead focused on both. This complementary focus is similar to the concept of authoritative parenting, which is generally considered to represent the gold standard in raising adolescents.[5] Authoritative parenting combines a concern with high expectations and careful monitoring of behavior with an emphasis on responsiveness to young people, warmth, and open communication. In a similar vein, organizational consultants Thomas Peters and Robert Waterman concluded that the best-run private companies manage to avoid a

---

[5] Mandara's (2006) review of the research indicates that authoritative parenting is the gold standard for minority families as well.

false dichotomy between X and Y, and instead aim to do both X *and* Y.[6] The West River center is a great example of how a safe and highly organized environment can be created that is consistent with an emphasis on positive youth development.

The human resource development policy at West River provided strong support to the focus on positive youth development and the implementation of quality programs and activities. The center director was committed to hiring staff who had strong people skills, a youth development orientation, and a good background in the types of activities that are featured at the center. They provided more training than was typical at these clubs. The job shadowing helped transmit tacit or implicit knowledge – the kind of knowledge that it difficult to convey adequately in written form – of how to deal with the young people who attended the center. The administrators routinely monitored staff performance to make sure that they were doing good work. Staff who did not meet high standards were terminated.

Despite the comparative strength of the human resource policy at West River compared to the two other sites, there was still room for significant improvement. There was no training beyond the initial, one-week job shadowing. There were no case conferences on individual youth (or types of youth), no discussions on how to deal with problems and tensions in Torch or Keystone (two core programs), and no consideration of broader issues concerning youth voice and leadership. A focus on organizational learning could have enhanced West River's many strengths and provided a mechanism for continual improvement. The director then might not have had to rely so heavily on firing and hiring staff, but could have a wider range of options available for making changes. West River has gotten many of the basics down, but it needs to strengthen its organizational practices if it wishes to strive for a higher order of excellence.

[6] Peters & Waterman (1982).

11

Midnight: A Teen Father Stays the Course

It might come as a surprise to many observers to find a youth such as Midnight frequenting a comprehensive after-school center. As a seventeen-year-old, this African-American young man is well beyond the age when most youth stop making a habit of attending after-school programs.[1] Nor, as a teen father, does he fit the profile of avoidance of risk behavior that might be expected of older youth who do remain engaged in after-school centers. Coupled with the challenges of parenthood, Midnight has struggled academically and at one point been expelled from school for truancy. The risky and illegal behaviors that are modeled by many of his peers, furthermore, clearly would make it easy for him to gravitate toward a more dangerous life on the streets. How is it, then, that Midnight has ended up being such a reliable presence at the West River center and an enthusiastic participant in several programs there? This puzzle is made all the more intriguing by the fact that he must travel by bus forty-five minutes to get to the center each day. As we shall see, Midnight's story offers a potent example of how after-school centers can benefit older teens, even those who already have experienced significant setbacks and thus may be passed over by programs with a focus on prevention. His year at West River is remarkable, too, as a demonstration of how a lack of support tailored to the individual needs of youth, in Midnight's case his academic difficulties, can be a formidable weakness of after-school centers.

[1] The Public/Private Ventures study of Boys & Girls Clubs (Arbreton, Bradshaw, Metz, & Sheldon, 2008) found that the average frequency of attendance at clubs dropped by about 50 percent as youth moved from middle school to high school.

IN THE BEGINNING

Even a casual observer at West River would likely be quick to take note of Midnight. Although average in build and stature, his disarming smile, good looks, and gregarious personality coalesce to create a certain radiance that attracts, if not demands, attention from peers and adults alike. Most days, he dons a baggy pair of jeans or dungarees that, in conformity to popular style among his peers, sit a few inches below his waist and periodically require adjustment to accommodate either his physical activity or the admonishment of a staff person. Notably absent are any indications of gang affiliation or more expensive accoutrements of hip-hop culture, such as designer clothes or shoes. Midnight's appearance, as we shall see, is emblematic of the reality that his priorities as a dedicated teen father lay elsewhere.

As noted, Midnight is parent to a young child. His daughter, Kenya, was born the summer before the school year during which the research was conducted. Although no longer romantically involved with Kenya's mother, he reports that they see each other regularly and get along well. Contrary to the popular stereotype of male lack of responsibility when it comes to teen fatherhood, Midnight sees Kenya nearly every day and is actively involved in her caretaking. Indeed, he speaks readily of the pride and enjoyment that he derives from being a father: "When my daughter was born it made me feel real good. I am having so much fun watching her grow up."

Now in his third year of high school, Midnight's grades are poor – mostly Ds and Fs – and have been throughout high school. Two years ago, his academic difficulties were punctuated by his explusion from school in the wake of his chronic truancy and overall apathy toward school work. Although reinstated and now attending an alternative school, as noted above his grades continue to be problematic. One immediate consequence of Midnight's poor academic performance is that he is not able to participate on sports teams as he did earlier in high school. Interestingly, he is not without interests that might be tapped to spur greater motivation to do well in school, as he describes himself as enjoying both history and writing poetry. He complains, however, that there are no more history classes for him to take and that English is his least favorite subject. Socially, Midnight reports having several friends at school and liking most of his teachers. Yet, he includes none of these persons in his network map of significant ties.

Midnight lives with mother and stepfather and is the oldest of four children in the home. His youngest brother Maurice, age thirteen, also comes to West River, and Midnight describes their relationship as very close. In fact, he views himself as a role model for Maurice – a theme that we will see echoed in his relationships with other youth at the club:

> *My little brother has the greatest influence [on my behavior] because he wants to be just like me. So I have to use his motivation to be like me to keep me going and keep my being a good person.*

He reports having generally close and positive relationships with members of his family, including a sixteen-year-old sister whom he finds a reliable source of support. Within the past year, this sister became pregnant and an older adult brother was convicted of car theft. When Midnight was twelve years old, he also experienced the death of a younger brother from cancer. Not long thereafter, his grandmother died, which he describes as a very difficult experience for him and his entire family. Midnight's mother, a high school graduate, works at a hospital. Her shifts regularly have her returning home late at night, thus making her unavailable to Midnight and his other siblings during the after-school and evening hours. His biological father has relocated to another state and does not appear to have maintained a relationship with Midnight.

Midnight started coming to West River approximately two years ago, at age fifteen. The club is situated partway between his new school and home; as noted earlier, getting to the club requires significant travel time, as does the return trip home. He has nonetheless maintained a pattern of coming to the club nearly every day after school. Outside of the club, Midnight likes to play sports with friends and go the movies. On the weekends, he says that he likes to "party" with his friends and associates. He reports that nearly all of these peers belong to gangs and that many are involved with drugs. Midnight himself denies gang involvement. When asked, however, he confirms that gangs are a significant problem in his neighborhood and that he must constantly negotiate perceptions of whether he is involved in this type of activity:

> *Yes. [Why?] Cause it's always how someone looks or dresses. They always think you are in a gang or something like that.*

Later in the year when completing the photography project for the research, he offers the following reasons for not taking a picture of his neighborhood:

> *I don't like any place in my neighborhood. I don't like anyone or any-place there.*

Thus, at the beginning of our research, we knew that Midnight was a charming and gregarious older teen. Despite facing many adversities, he had remained engaged with his family and school and been remarkably conscientious in undertaking his responsibilities as a father. His academic difficulties, questionable peer affiliations, and potential to be caught up in gang activities within his neighborhood clearly continued to serve as potent sources of risk for school dropout, involvement in illegal activity, and victimization.[2] Understanding the role the club played in helping Midnight avoid these possible outcomes, while also bringing into relief his strengths in areas that offered potential avenues for a successful transition to adulthood, will be important as we turn to an examination of his year at West River.

MIDNIGHT'S YEAR AT THE AFTER-SCHOOL CENTER

As we consider Midnight's year at the after-school center, our focus will be on both his relationships with staff and his participation in different activities and programs at West River. His experiences in both of these realms are salient in the PARC profile for Midnight, which is shown in Table 11.1. The central theme of Midnight's year at the club is one of stability and continuity rather than change. Accordingly, we do not attempt to align the different units of his PARC profile with particular periods of time during the year.

Relationships with Staff

Midnight's closest staff tie at West River is with Victoria. He first met Victoria nearly ten years ago when she lived next door to his

---

[2] Research consistently indicates that youth such as Midnight who experience multiple risk factors are at particularly high risk for negative outcomes (Moore, 2006). At least part of the explanation for this appears to be that different risk factors can potentiate one another in their effects such that, when experienced in combination, they have an especially pronounced impact (Rutter, 1979; Sameroff, 2000).

TABLE 11.1. *Midnight's PARC profile*

P	dance
A	dual role as participant and assistant leader
R	Victoria, encouragement, opportunities for responsibility and leadership
C	non-judgmental, fun, pro-social
P	Keystone
A	sponsor activities, raise money, decision making, trips
R	Vanessa, socialization with friends
C	engagement and valuing of older youth
P	–
A	fatherhood, caring for baby
R	noticed and appreciated by staff, admonitions to not get girlfriend pregnant
C	non-judgmental, peer support, accommodating
P	–
A	mentoring younger youth
R	younger youth, facilitation and coaching from staff
C	cross-age peer interactions, engagement and valuing of older youth, lack of formal role

family in his old neighborhood. After his family moved, there was a hiatus in which they did not see each other much until Midnight began coming to West River regularly last year. Both describe their earlier relationship in fond terms, with Midnight adding that they still often enjoy talking about the "old days" when they see each other at the club. Close ties like these with non-parental adults have been highlighted in research as a protective factor for youth from urban neighborhoods.[3]

It is clear, however, that since being reconnected with Victoria through the club, Midnight's relationship with her has taken

---

[3] In one recent longitudinal study (Molnar, Cerda, Roberts, & Buka, 2008), youth from urban neighborhoods who reported greater ties with non-parental mentors were found to have significantly lower levels of aggression and delinquency. This same research, however, found evidence that access to mentoring and other individual-level resources may confer benefits only in the presence of supporting neighborhood-level resources. This latter finding underscores the potential importance of urban youth having opportunities for daily involvement in an after-school center as a complement to whatever personal resources they bring to this type of setting. In Midnight's case, this interplay is especially salient as his access to West River served to revitalize his earlier personal relationship with Victoria.

on added depth and significance and become quite close.⁴ The catalyst for this has been Midnight's participation in the dance program that Victoria leads at the club. Midnight, in fact, at one point in our interviews with him refers to her simply as his "dance choreographer." Yet, it is readily apparent when talking with either of them that their relationship is much more multifaceted than this description might suggest. When asked what he likes about Victoria, for example, Midnight is quick to underscore the importance of their overall friendship and the ways in which she serves as a role model and source of inspiration for him: "She's my friend, also a good motivator, a great dance teacher, a positive leader." When completing his social network map for the research, furthermore, he puts Victoria as close to himself as his girlfriend,⁵ commenting how much he cares about her and how he has known her "forever."

Victoria expresses similarly fond feelings for Midnight and an appreciation of his strengths:

He is a positive person, you never see him upset. He is very helpful and a hard worker if he is into something. [What is the best thing about Midnight?] His personality. He is a genuinely nice person. He gets along very well with other people.

Midnight's close tie with Victoria is manifested in their playful and affectionate interactions with one another, as illustrated in the following field notes that were recorded on two separate occasions:

After one dance, Victoria told the girls to sit down and took Midnight and the two other boys to the front to practice their steps. She slowly went through step by step and when they did not understand she put her hands on their hips or their arms or legs and would physically move them

---

⁴ When completing his social network map, Midnight rated the closeness of his relationship with Victoria as a 5 (Extremely) on the 1–5 scale, a rating that he otherwise reserved for family members and his girlfriend. Victoria similarly rated her feelings of closeness toward Midnight as a 4/4.5 on the same scale. Likewise, on our measure of youth-staff relationships, Midnight's ratings of his relationship with Victoria on the mentoring sub-scale of the instrument were highly favorable even when compared to those that other youth assigned to the staff members with whom they enjoyed their closest relationships (T-score of 59.05).

⁵ When constructing their social network maps, youth were told that the distance they position different members of their networks from themselves should reflect their feelings of closeness with those persons.

in the correct way. At one point she was dancing with Midnight and yelled over her shoulder, "don't worry Monique [Midnight's girlfriend], I'm not flirting – just teaching him to dance!"

At the end [of a dance routine], Midnight jumped over and started giving [his baby] kisses and tickling her. Victoria yelled, "Okay, enough of the baby talk – let's do this again with everyone!" Midnight got up but as he walked by Victoria he gave Victoria a little push. Victoria said, "Hey now there – who's in charge here?" He laughed and got back in line.

The familiarity that Victoria was able to cultivate with Midnight opened up avenues for their relationship to also incorporate more direct and probing forms of mentoring.[6] The role of trust – an important component of any relationship – in allowing for this is illustrated by Midnight's response when asked whether he learns things from Victoria:

Yes, leadership and communication skills. [Is this important?] Yes, if I'm not goin' to take it from a male role model, I might as well take it from a female. From my experiences she is more trustworthy than Nelson and Ben (male staff members at West River).

When interviewed, Midnight, in fact, describes getting advice from Victoria on a near daily basis and regularly discussing personal matters with her. Repeatedly, he cites Victoria as an important source of support and guidance in helping him fulfill his responsibilities as a father, succeed in school, stay out of trouble, and pursue his goals for the future. Within the academic realm, for example, he notes that Victoria takes the time to help him with his school work and has actively assisted him with seeking out scholarships. Despite the challenges he faced in school and as a teen father, Midnight also scored above average on our measure of overall self-efficacy (i.e., confidence in his abilities),[7] an asset he succinctly credits in part to Victoria's support: "When I say I can't, she shows me how."

A final important component of Midnight's relationship with Victoria is that the flow of support is not unidirectional. On several

---

[6] Research indicates that youth are likely to be more receptive to a directive orientation in mentoring relationships when the mentor has first taken the time to first build a solid relationship with the youth (Keller, 2005).

[7] Midnight's score on the measure of overall self-efficacy corresponded to a T-score of 57.42.

occasions, we observed her seek out his assistance. The following field note is illustrative:

> *Midnight walked in and Victoria yelled, "Hello sir." He said "Hi" and walked over to where she was sitting. Victoria told Midnight, "This is the last week to be learnin' things cause next week we start the program, so you got to know everything by then." Midnight said, "OK" and started working with Daniel [another older teen]. After about fifteen minutes, Victoria said, "Alright misfits in the back, Midnight you work with them." The boys started jabbering amongst themselves and Victoria said, "That's you Shawn, Derrick, Andre." One of the boys triumphantly said, "She did not call me," but Victoria heard this and said, "Oh yeah, you too." Midnight took these four boys to the back of the room and started working on the boys' moves, while the girls and Daniel stayed in the front and started going through a dance for the Christmas program.*

She also was generally receptive to Midnight's own initiatives to be of help, as seen in this field note:

> *When Natasha got up and left, Victoria looked and said, "kay kay y'all I am working over here so how bout all of you work hard out there?" Midnight walked up to her and said "maybe it would help if we could watch that movie [a video of one of their recent performances] so we could see what we are doing right and what we are doing wrong." Victoria responded, "oh that is such a good idea – will you go and talk to Reginald?" Midnight went to the computer room and two minutes later was pushing a TV in on a cart, with Reginald in tow with a camcorder and cords to connect it to the TV. Victoria yelled out, "kay let's watch this movie cause Midnight was so nice to remember. Let's see how hot you all look in your outfits!" All of the youth began to crowd around the TV. . . . As we were watching Midnight continually got embarrassed saying, "why don't none of you all tell me I look like that?" Monique kept laughing and everyone kept making comments about Midnight's pants falling down around his knees. Victoria came up behind Midnight during the movie and put her arms around his shoulders and leaned in on him and laughed along with everyone else.*

When we interviewed Victoria, we discovered that these types of interactions were the outgrowth of a conscious strategy on her part:

> *[How do you go about trying to influence him [Midnight]? What kinds of methods do you use?] Just discussions and just trying to talk to him. Give him leadership and responsibility. [What do you find works? What do you find doesn't work?] It works well to give him leadership positions and then feedback.*

The element of discussion and feedback in Victoria's approach is noteworthy as it aligns with research indicating the value of sharing and reflection within mentoring and service activities for adolescents.[8]

During the course of the year, it seems that Midnight's relationship with Victoria deepens and becomes increasingly important to him. Compared to his previously noted description of her as a "friend" earlier in the year, at the end of the year he describes their relationship in more intimate terms:

> *I am very close to her ... I see her as my very, very close friend. I could talk to her about anything.*

Midnight included only one other staff member, Vanessa, in his social network map. Yet, it is clear from our observations and interview data that he enjoyed positive relationships with essentially all club staff and that these were an important part of his experiences at West River throughout the year. Midnight's interactions with other staff frequently served to reinforce messages that he received in his relationship with Victoria. As illustrated in the following field note, for example, staff took an active interest in Midnight's role as a father and expressed appreciation for the commitment he displayed to his daughter:

> *Midnight walked in at one point and came over and said hi to Nelson and I. He sat in between us and I told him how jealous I was that [other field observer] had gotten to see his baby girl last week. Nelson started laughing and put his arm around Midnight saying, "that boy loves his baby more than he will ever love another woman," and started laughing.*

Likewise, staff often offered admonitions to Midnight about having another child with his current girlfriend:

> *As Midnight and I were sitting completing the interview [for his Photography Project], Vanessa walked up and said, "What are those pictures of?" Midnight responded "me and my girl!" Vanessa said, "Hey, why aren't there any pictures of me in there?" Midnight responded, "Well you ain't been here cause you been dealing with your stuff if you know what I mean!" Vanessa said, "Yeah, well you know – I got stuff goin' on – will jus don't be goin' and getting that girl of yours pregnant now!" Midnight laughed and said, "Oh, no."*

[8] For mentoring, see Nakkula and Harris (2010); for service learning, see Conway, Amel, and Gerwin (2009).

Further mirroring his relationship with Victoria, Midnight's interactions with other staff also served as constructive opportunities for him to exercise leadership and responsibility at the club. We see an example of this in the following field note:

> As Ben left Natasha had all of the boys stand up. She began to lead them in stretching exercises. Midnight took notice of this and broke away from this volleyball game and walked over saying, "No no no that is not the way to do it!" He put his arm around Natasha and said, "Let me show them how to do it!" She laughed and nodded her head in agreement. He had them line up in a perfectly straight line and lead them in jumping jacks and push ups. He had them all counting together and loudly in unison low voices. Natasha was almost rolling on the floor with laughter and amazement. She came back over to me just shaking her head and said, "Well, looks like Midnight is our newest staff member" and shrugged her shoulders laughing.

We will see later, too, when considering Midnight's role as a mentor to younger children at the club, how multiple staff were important in supporting and guiding these efforts.

Finally, there is reason to believe that the two male staff at West River, Nelson and Ben, served as significant role models for Midnight. Midnight's interview responses when asked about each of these staff are informative in this regard:

> [What do you like about Nelson?] He's a good motivator, positive minded, and good athletics director and cares about everybody. [And now Ben. What do you like about him?] He's fun to be around, good worker, everybody respects him.

We can thus see the potential for Midnight to learn from the examples set by these staff in several important areas. The caring and considerate manner in which Nelson and Ben interact with others is likely especially valuable for Midnight to see modeled in view of gender stereotypes that do not necessarily encourage such behaviors among males.[9] As we turn to consider the programs and activities that Midnight participated in at West River, we will see that these staff served not only as role models for him, but also as valuable sources of guidance and feedback in a variety of contexts.

---

[9] Qualitative research supports the importance of emotional intimacy as a theme in male mentoring relationships (Spencer, 2007a).

Programs and Activities

Midnight was involved in a range of different activities and programs at the club. Dance, which he participated in on a daily basis, though, was clearly the activity that he relished above all others. He participated in all of the group's performances and was highly conscientious about attending practices and keeping up with what was expected of him in this program. The following field note, which includes a brief exchange between Midnight and a member of the research team, provides a glimpse into the commitment to this activity that he sustained throughout the year:

> *I was not familiar with the dances [being practiced] so they were apparently new in the last couple of weeks. Midnight was not as familiar with many of them and so stood toward the back for a couple of them and watched for a few times through and then could join in and dance as well. After a few runs with the whole group Victoria asked them all to separate and she had groupings of boys and girls perform.... As they were running through, I pulled Midnight aside and asked him if he would have time to talk. He said he really needed to work on these dances because he was behind but as soon as he knew them he would be able to.*

As already described, dance offered Midnight a steady diet of opportunities for exercising leadership and responsibility. This required, however, that he be able to move between the dual roles of participant and facilitator as the situation warranted. He showed remarkable initiative as well, always being quick to jump in whenever he saw an opportunity to help direct or assist the group. As he could be quite insistent in these overtures, they sometimes were a source of a certain amount of tension in his relationship with Victoria, as illustrated in the following field note:

> *[A CD is stuck in the stereo that is used during dance practices] Midnight commented, "I take my stereo apart all the time – I can do it"... Victoria said, "Well, until we get [a] screwdriver we can't do anything. Midnight go get Mr. Johnson and tell him we need a screwdriver in here if we are going to have dance practice.... Midnight walked back into the room with the screwdriver and Victoria said, "'Kay hon', hand it over." He insisted that he could do it. "C'mon Victoria, just let me try." She replied, "Um, that would be no" and took the screwdriver from him.... When Victoria was finished getting all the screws off the back, she tried to pull the back piece off but it wouldn't come off. Midnight said, "See Victoria, I told you – you should have let me do it for you – it*

would be all fixed by now." Victoria responded, "Midnight, shut your mouth." He replied, "You have to take off the side ones as well – look, here they are attached at the bottom. Victoria sighed when she saw that he was right and began to take off the other ones.

Such issues were always able to be negotiated, however, and, as we have seen, dance as a whole was instrumental as a catalyst for the evolution of an increasingly close relationship between Midnight and Victoria.

Dance also served as an outlet for Midnight to engage in a fun and relaxing activity with peers. As such, it functioned as a powerful alternative to partying with friends outside of the club and the numerous risks that this entailed. Midnight formed several new friendships with other club members through dance as well, thus providing an added social dimension to this activity for him. These social ties and the significance that they held for Midnight were revealed to us, in part, through his Photography Project. One of his photos featured several youth with whom he had established friendships through the dance program:

> *[These are] my dance idols: Alan, Mercury, Shana, and Latrice – Total Domination. The whole group admires them cause they are so perfect and almost there. They are all my friends.*

And, in at least one instance, we see that his participation in this activity was a vehicle for forging a close friendship with another older teen at the club:

> *[Tell me about this photo?] He is my close friend and my co-dancer. Everything I do he likes to do. I thought I would never meet anyone who could dance like me and he gave me [illegible word] when I met him.*

We know less about the PARC that involved Midnight's participation in Keystone, an activity that he joined at the beginning of the year. He did not hold one of the formal leadership positions in this program. According to staff, however, he was an active participant and had a significant amount of responsibility in the group. He also included Vanessa, the staff person who led this activity, in his social network map.[10] Clearly, too, the group's activities, such as the trip to visit colleges, provide a valuable opportunity for Midnight to be supported in planning his future.

---

[10] Midnight rated the closeness of his relationship with Vanessa a 3 on a rating scale of 1 to 5.

When asked during one of our interviews[11] what he is doing to work toward his future goal of being in college, for example, he is quick to highlight his participation in Keystone. Research, in fact, suggests that involvement with Keystone can foster self-confidence and leadership ability,[12] benefits we suspect may well have accrued for Midnight.

Throughout the year, we are struck as well by the active role that Midnight assumes in offering guidance and support to younger club members and thus serving, in effect, as an older peer mentor to them.[13] The following field note, along with others shared previously, illustrates Midnight's comfort and ease in interacting with younger charges at the club:

> *They ran through the [dance] routine several times, with many of the preps tripping over themselves.... While this was occurring, Midnight and Shana [another older teen] were putting on a "skit" for all of the little kids to one of the newer songs where guys and girls have to dance together. He was pretending to try to pick her up by dancing and she was responding with her own dances. All of the younger preps were laughing and pointing. Summer [a younger child], who was sitting on Monique's lap, kept yelling, "that's your boyfriend, that's your boyfriend." Monique just smiled and moved in her seat to the music.*

With Midnight's penchant for garnering group attention and being "on stage," one might question whether his mentoring of younger children at the club extended to more personal, one-to-one interactions with them outside of the limelight. Yet, as illustrated, by this field note, it is clear that he had ample capacity to assume a more intimate, caretaking role when the situation called for it:

> *As we were doing the interview [with Midnight], a younger girl walked by to leave. Midnight called out to her, "Melinda, are you goin' home?"*

---

[11] The manner in which Midnight linked his participation in Keystone to his goal of attending college was revealed in the portion of our interview that asked about his possible future selves.

[12] Swigert & Boyd (2010).

[13] Many formal mentoring programs assign older youth to mentor younger children (Karcher, 2005, 2007). In comparison, Midnight's mentoring role with youth at West River evolved as a more natural outgrowth of his interactions with them in different programs and activities at the club.

She said yes and Midnight replied, "Wait five minutes. Monique and I are gonna be goin' that way, we'll walk you home." We finished up and Midnight left with Monique and the girl.

This is not to say that Midnight was without his rough edges as an aspiring mentor. As illustrated by this field note, at times his manner of interacting with younger club members clearly lacked the sensitivity that would be desired:

Midnight and Victoria and I [research team member] when through several other drills with the girls teaching them defensive moves and how to shoot free throws. By the end of the period there were only about ten girls left who were in line and trying.... Midnight was playing one on one against Brianna and whenever she was in his way, he simply picked her up and moved her so he could make a shot. She was getting very frustrated and at one point just kicked him in the leg and left the game.

As such, it is important to note that although staff such as Victoria recognized and generally were appreciative and encouraging of Midnight's mentoring of younger children at West River, they also were not hesitant to redirect his interactions with them when necessary and in so doing provide feedback that could cultivate his skills as a mentor. This type of coaching is illustrated in the following field note that was recorded when observing Midnight engaged in playing volleyball with a group of younger children at the club:

Midnight was attempting to give tips on techniques and was not hesitant to yell, "lazy girl!" when one of the girls wouldn't run or dive for the ball. Every once in a while Nelson would glance over and yell a pointer or two to one of them like, "keep your eyes on the ball – move towards it – get down low!" and then turn his attention back to the boys in front of him. He would also yell out to Midnight to keep his mouth clean as Midnight had a tendency to swear while playing.

As was the case in this example, Midnight's interactions with younger children often occurred alongside club staff who were engaged in guiding and supporting these youth in the same activity. Midnight thus had opportunity throughout the year to further hone his skills in this area by drawing on West River staff as role models.

Our account of Midnight's year at West River would be incomplete, too, without taking note of the manner in which his experiences at the club intersected with his role as a father. As noted, he routinely brought his baby daughter to the club in the after-school hours. In no instance did we observe him encounter any barriers or resistance to doing so. To the contrary, as is apparent from field notes already shared, both staff and peers at the club actively accommodated and supported Midnight in caring for his daughter and always were seen to do so in an accepting and non-judgmental manner. Midnight, as we have noted, took his responsibilities as a father very seriously. As such, rather than rely excessively on the support that was available to him at the club, he was able to utilize the setting as an arena to practice his skills as a father. As any parent knows, changing diapers is a bellwether of one's willingness to get one's hands dirty (sometimes literally!) in caring for a young child, thus making the following field note recorded during a break in dance practice particularly noteworthy:

> *Midnight used this opportunity to grab his daughter and the diaper bag and change her diaper on one of the tables. He was very careful with her, and very loving.* [Field observer note: It was interesting to see how he and Monique interacted in taking care of her, as Monique is not the mom. It was clear that Midnight was the primary caregiver and had the most responsibility for her, even though Monique was watching her as he was in dance practice.]

DEVELOPMENTAL GAINS OVER THE YEAR

As alluded to previously, in most respects Midnight's year at West River may be best characterized as one of stability rather than growth. First, however, we shall consider the ways in which he may indeed have progressed in his development over the course of the year. Within the academic realm, Midnight's grades in school show a slight trend toward improvement. Compared to the Ds and Fs he reported at the beginning of year, in our end-of-year interview with him he reports receiving a C in one class (English) and Ds in the others. We also can conclude with some confidence that Midnight's positive relationships with staff, especially his deepening tie with Victoria, have served to fortify his self-confidence and solidify his emerging sense of personal identity.[14] We expect similar gains have

---

[14] Midnight scored above average on a general measure of identity relative to others in our research sample (T-score = 61.76).

accrued, too, through his active involvement and leadership in club activities and meaningful engagement with younger children.[15] These facets of Midnight's year at the club, in fact, map quite well against the building blocks that have been suggested to be critical both for positive youth development generally[16] and for workforce readiness specifically.[17] We see evidence, furthermore, of an impressive level of maturity in Midnight's responses when asked toward the end of year about the vision that he holds for his future: "a good father," "college freshman," "own apartment," and "professional dancer." No less impressive, the list of what he most wants to avoid includes "bad health insurance" and "all altercations between me and my daughter's mother's family," laudable ambitions that clearly are not what one might expect to hear from an adolescent father who is still immersed in navigating his own development.

Yet, when asked in our end-of-year interview what he has gotten out of coming to West River, Midnight emphasizes how it has been instrumental in helping him steer clear of harmful outcomes: "It gave me something to do, other than standing outside [and potentially getting involved in] drugs and other illegal stuff." His perspective is hardly surprising when one considers the gravity of the consequences that could easily have befallen him had he become involved in the risky activities that are commonplace among his peer group outside of the club. These include not only incarceration, of course, but also serious injury or death as a victim of violence.

---

[15] Available evidence suggests that cross-age peer mentoring programs can benefit the youth who serve as mentors in areas such as empathy, self-esteem, and school connectedness (Karcher, 2007). Midnight thus may have derived significant benefits from his supportive interactions with younger children at West River.

[16] In one widely used framework, positive youth development is conceptualized as consisting of "Five C's": Competence, Confidence, Connections, Character, and Caring (Hamilton, Hamilton, & Pittman, 2004). Lerner (2004) proposed adding a sixth "C", Contribution. The dimension of Contribution can be manifest in contributions to one's family as well as to groups and organizations in one's community, both of which are clearly evident in the case of Midnight.

[17] One widely referenced framework divides workforce readiness skills into three main domains: Learning and Innovation Skills; Information, Media and Technology Skills; and Life and Career Skills (The Partnership for 21st Century Skills, 2009). Midnight's experiences at West River, which revolved around exercising leadership, responsibility, and initiative, seem particularly well aligned with strengthening skills that this framework identifies as important within the domain of Learning and Innovation: Creativity and Innovation, Critical Thinking and Problem Solving, and Communication and Collaboration.

No doubt for him, the prospect of such outcomes is all the more unwelcome because of the implications that they would have for his ability to parent his daughter. Taking stock of these considerations, the premium that Midnight places on simply staying the course (i.e., avoiding negative developments) during his time at West River is easily understood.

MIDNIGHT IN THE WEST RIVER AFTER-SCHOOL CENTER: STRENGTHS, SHORTCOMINGS, AND SYNERGIES

We now examine the strengths, shortcomings, and synergies of West River for Midnight. The center's success in engaging an older youth such as Midnight, a teen father no less, in regular attendance throughout the year is clearly remarkable and merits our attention. At the same time, there is ample room for improvement in how well West River took advantage of the opportunities that were afforded by Midnight's high level of engagement, especially with regard to supporting his efforts to secure a positive future for himself and his daughter. The most prominent synergies had the effect of accentuating these strengths and shortcomings and thus amplifying their importance when considering Midnight's year at West River.

Strengths

Three key strengths stand out when considering West River as an after-school center for Midnight. First, the center provided a "safe space" for him to simply have fun and recreate with peers. When we think of safety, our thoughts typically go first to issues of physical well-being. Taking into account the menacing aspects of Midnight's neighborhood, the risky behaviors of his peers outside of the center, and the reality that violent juvenile crime is concentrated in the after-school hours,[18] the significance of West River as a "safe haven"[19] for him seems difficult to overstate. Unlike many after-school programs, as a comprehensive center, West River was available to Midnight on an everyday basis. Without this level of access, the center's potential as a protective setting for him clearly would have been significantly diminished. As an older adolescent, the varied opportunities

[18] Snyder & Sickmund (1999).
[19] Gambone & Arbreton (1997).

that Midnight had to exercise leadership and responsibility at West River were likely one of the keys to the center's success in keeping him off the streets and out of harm's way. On a more subtle level, West River likely also afforded Midnight a significant measure of psychological or emotional safety as a place where he knew he would be accepted by peers and adults alike. In view of the reality that many teen fathers can feel stigmatized by broader society,[20] the non-judgment and supportive reception that Midnight could expect at West River is especially noteworthy.

The mentoring that Midnight received from center staff is a second significant asset of the setting. Staff members were clearly appreciative of this teen's strengths and his need to be granted a certain level of autonomy – factors that typically are crucial in forging a solid relationship with any older adolescent.[21] Capitalizing on their foundation of good rapport and trust with Midnight, staff also conveyed clear expectations about his need to fulfill his responsibilities as a father and to avoid a pregnancy with his current girlfriend. We will have more to say about the consistent messages and support that Midnight received from staff when discussing synergies that characterized his year at the center.

West River also served as a medium for the cultivation of Midnight's exceptionally strong mentoring relationship with Victoria. This relationship was facilitated by Midnight's family having been neighbors of Victoria at an earlier point in his development. This obviously was a serendipitous coincidence, although it is worth noting that it was made possible by virtue of the center's practice of drawing on the immediately surrounding community as a source for staff.[22] Midnight's involvement in dance at the center, furthermore, served as the primary catalyst for deepening his relationship with Victoria. For older adolescents in particular, mentoring relationships with adults may take root most readily in the context of instrumental support that helps them learn specific skills and experience a sense of accomplishment.[23] Had there not been an

---

[20] Davies, Dix, Rhodes, Harrington, Frison, & Willis (2004).

[21] Darling (2005).

[22] In formal mentoring programs, it is typical for the adults who are paired with participating youth to reside outside of the youth's immediate neighborhood, thus making shared social connections that might facilitate the development of the relationship an unlikely occurrence.

[23] Darling, Hamilton, & Niego (1994); Keller (2005).

activity offering at the center that provided this type of opportunity, it is reasonable to expect that Midnight's relationship with Victoria would not have flourished in the manner that it did.

Finally, we also should take note of the opportunities that Midnight experienced at West River to explore potential career interests and to develop skills important for workplace readiness more generally. It is not clear that he possessed the talent to realize his dream of becoming a professional dancer. Yet, through Midnight's many positive experiences in dance at the center, this activity helped instill the confidence he would need to pursue other, perhaps more viable careers in this arena. In view of Midnight's readily apparent aptitude and penchant for youth work, the steady diet of opportunities that he had at West River to help facilitate activities involving younger children under the tutelage of adult staff is significant as well. Such situations do not necessarily arise in more age-segmented after-school settings, nor, when they do, is it likely to be routine for there to be a similar level of attention among staff to mentoring the efforts of youth such as Midnight. More broadly, we also see how the culture, activities, and staff at West River flexibly accommodated this older adolescent's proclivities to assume responsibility and exercise leadership. This attribute of the center, along with those aspects that engaged him in the development of skills such as problem solving, communication, and teamwork, offered a strong foundation of preparation for eventual entry into the workforce.[24]

Shortcomings

What stands out most as a weakness in considering the experiences of Midnight at West River is the lack of focused attention to supporting his success in school. Like nearly all of the other older youth at this after-school center, we never observed him doing school work. Nor did this emerge as a significant topic in discussing his activities at West River with either him or staff. For

---

[24] The skills that were fostered through Midnight's experiences at West River overlap considerably with those that have been referred to as the "4 Cs" required for workforce readiness in the modern economy: critical thinking and problem solving, communication, collaboration, and creativity and innovation (The Partnership for 21st Century Skills, 2009).

many youth, the lack of an academic dimension to time spent at an after-school center might not be all that noteworthy. But for Midnight, with his persistent pattern of poor grades in school, it clearly is a source for concern. Without a formal program or activity to help ensure regular time spent on homework, it fell to either staff or the culture of the center as a whole to offer support and encouragement for attention to academics. For Midnight, Victoria clearly was the staff person at West River best positioned to wield this type of influence. It appears that Victoria did, in fact, discuss school-related concerns with Midnight on a fairly consistent basis and at one point even helped him look into applying for college scholarships. Lacking from their relationship, however, are more direct and potentially powerful forms of academic support and expectations, such as tutoring or perhaps even making time on homework a condition for participation in dance.[25] Unfortunately, we also see no evidence that academic assistance was a part of his ties with other staff. Nor was the culture at the center, at least as it pertains to older youth, one that we can expect would have prompted Midnight to prioritize putting effort into school work while there.

With his aspirations to attend college and concern with providing for his daughter, Midnight also likely would have been receptive to more structured forms of assistance directed toward helping him plan for his future. He garnered some support in planning for college from Victoria and through his involvement in Keystone. Ideally, though, West River would have offered Midnight the opportunity to be engaged in a broader array of activities geared toward preparing him for a successful transition to adulthood. Job readiness training, for example, could have complemented the benefits that Midnight was gleaning through the informal, staff-like responsibilities he assumed at the center. No doubt, a paid internship, perhaps focused on assisting Victoria in teaching dance or working with younger children at the center, would have been valuable as well. This would have formalized and documented his role at the center in a way that would have made it more understandable to potential employers.

---

[25] There is considerable support for the beneficial effects of tutoring on academic achievement (for a review, see Elbaum, Vaughn, Tejero Hughes, & Moody, 2000).

Synergies

Two positive synergies, each involving Midnight's relationships with center staff, stand out to us in considering his experiences at West River. The first of these is a remarkable level of consistency in how different staff interacted with and supported this older teen. We see no evidence that this was the product of intentional staff planning or coordination. Nonetheless, as discussed in Chapter 10, the culture at West River encouraged staff to value the strengths of youth and take an active interest in their lives. Accordingly, we can reasonably credit the overall staff climate at the center as helping foster the common threads of communication and support that are interwoven into Midnight's relationships with multiple staff. Whatever factors were ultimately responsible, Midnight's relationships with staff at West River were such that they undoubtedly reinforced one another in ways that enriched the mentoring he received there. Our observations earlier in the chapter suggest, in particular, that these ties likely fostered an overall sense of being positively regarded and valued by adults at the center as well as a depth and consistency of guidance that otherwise would not have been possible.[26] This aspect of Midnight's year at the center clearly is very much aligned with our concept of collective mentoring.

A second beneficial synergy revolves around this youth's relationship with Victoria. As noted earlier, collaborative engagement in a meaningful activity or project appears to be one of the most powerful catalysts for the development of a strong mentoring tie between an adult and older adolescent. Certain PARCs may be especially well suited to filling this role. For Midnight, this was the PARC that revolved around his participation in the dance program at West River. Had it not been offered as an activity at the center, we can easily imagine that his relationship with Victoria would not have evolved to reflect the emotional depth and wide-ranging forms of support that it did. Conversely, the enthusiasm and impressive level of commitment with which Midnight embraced dance likely was facilitated by his previously established relationship with

---

[26] Nakkula and Harris (2005) proposed a framework in which relational/affective and instrumental/goal-oriented features are mutually important in determining the quality of mentoring relationships for youth. Midnight's collective ties with staff at West River reflect both of these strengths.

Victoria. Without their history of friendship outside of the center, for example, he might not have felt nearly as comfortable exerting a leadership role in this activity and, even if he had, such overtures could well have met with a much less favorable response from the staff person in charge. Midnight's involvement in dance, in turn, was clearly facilitated by the accommodating and non-judgmental culture of the West River center when it came to his status as a teen father. In another after-school setting, it cannot be assumed that either adults or peers would have been so welcoming and supportive of his parenting role. By, in effect, setting the stage not only for his comfortable participation in activities such as dance, but also his supportive interactions with staff in these contexts, the culture of West River was a critical element of the positive synergies involving activities/programs and staff relationships during his year at the center that we have highlighted.

A notable missed possibility for synergy is the lack of an apparent linkage between West River and Midnight's school.[27] Whereas a system was in place for younger children to bring their report cards to the center, this was not the case for the older teens. Nor, to our knowledge, was there any direct communication between center staff and Midnight's teachers. Greater information sharing along these lines would have enabled staff such as Victoria to offer Midnight more effective academic support and might have alerted them to a need for more intensive forms of assistance (e.g., tutoring) in this area. A stronger linkage between the center and Midnight's school likely would have been useful, too, for coordinating efforts to assist him with postsecondary transition planning. This could have led West River staff to reevaluate the appropriateness of college enrollment as an immediate goal for Midnight based on his current level of academic performance. Likewise, their observations could have provided those at his school (e.g., guidance counselor) with greater awareness of potentially viable career paths or employment options for him. The

[27] Within the widely influential developmental-ecological model of Urie Bronfenbrenner (1979), an after-school center and the youth's school would each be considered microsystems, whereas the quality and types of connections that exist between these settings would be part of the mesosystem. Bronfenbrenner hypothesized that development generally is enhanced when communication occurs across the different contexts that are salient in characterizing the mesosystem for a given youth.

potential impact of these various unrealized opportunities for more integrated support across center and school settings is clearly amplified in the case of Midnight because of his relatively long-standing history of academic difficulties.

CONCLUSIONS

We began this chapter by posing the question of what factors were responsible for Midnight – an African-American teen father from economically challenged life circumstances – demonstrating such a remarkably high level of participation in the West River after-school center. It is a question that resonates with concerns that are paramount for the broader field of after-school programming, where success with engaging older adolescents has been hard to come by and where rates of program participation have been historically lower for both minority youth and those from lower socioeconomic families.[28] As we saw in Chapter 10, the West River center noteworthy for its strong leadership, staff focus on positive youth development, and capacity to offer high-quality programs and activities. With Midnight, we see how the center was able to draw on these foundational strengths to both engage and benefit a youth who is representative of an underserved group in after-school programs.

With direct relevance to this issue, Public/Private Ventures recently produced a report focused on recruiting and retaining older African-American and Hispanic males in after-school programs.[29] Based on a review of available literature and interviews with staff from ten programs identified as successful in engaging middle- and high-school-aged ethnic minority (African-American and/or Hispanic) males, several factors emerged as important for retaining such youth in after-school programs over time. Three of these closely parallel those that stand out as important for sustaining Midnight's participation in the West River center: offering programs relevant to older minority youth in terms of interest, cultural issues, and economic needs; empowering youth by giving them

[28] Wimer et al. (2006); Deschenes, Arbreton, Little, Herrera, Grossman, & Weiss (2010).
[29] Kauh (2010).

responsibilities and opportunities to lead; and providing a nurturing environment in which youth feel they are cared for and valued
in multiple ways.

Our analysis additionally highlights mentoring from staff as a
potentially influential factor for engaging older youth in after-school
centers. Echoing themes from prior chapters, we see how both the
strong mentorship from a single staff person (Victoria) and from staff
collectively figured saliently in Midnight's experiences at West River.
Good mentoring, especially when it comes to older teens, may be as
much art as it is science. Indeed, what stands out most to us in considering the positive relationships that Victoria and other staff at West
River forged with Midnight is not any particular technique or strategy that they deployed, but rather the manner in which they deftly
managed to weave into their interactions with him both validation
of his strengths and potential on the one hand and valuable guidance
and clear expectations for his behavior on the other hand. Clearly,
at least with this particular youth, staff demonstrated an impressive
mastery of knowing when to simply encourage and when to step in
and offer direction.[30] Their ability to do so enriched not only their
individual relationships with Midnight, but also the overall developmental value of his experiences at West River. From an organizational
perspective, the consistent mentoring that Midnight received at West
River may be credited in significant part to the center's emphasis on
hiring staff with strong skills for working with youth, as well as its
focus on promoting positive youth development.

Clearly, though, Midnight's year at West River was not without
noteworthy missed opportunities. Chief among these is the lack
of support at the center for addressing his ongoing academic difficulties. As much as anything else, graduating from high school is
a key determinant of whether older adolescents such as Midnight
will enjoy a relatively successful transition to adulthood or, alter-
natively, fall prey to any of a host of negative outcomes that jeopardize their futures (and, in the case of Midnight, the long-term

---

[30] Midnight's relationships with West River staff appear to illustrate what
psychologist Reed Larson (2006) has referred to as "motivational scaffolding."
Motivational scaffolding is a process through which adult mentors can benefit
youth by communicating caring and acceptance while concurrently conveying
realistic expectations and helping them set and work toward personally meaningful goals.

welfare of his daughter as well).[31] Likewise, the center was not well-equipped to provide the types of more formalized vocational training or employment opportunities (e.g., apprenticeships) that for at-risk youth especially can function as valuable bridges to the world of adult work.[32] Such considerations raise fundamental questions about what types of services and supports it is realistic or appropriate for after-school centers to provide for youth. It is not unreasonable to expect that West River might have been able to offer some of the programs and activities that were lacking in Midnight's experiences at the center. Yet, as is illustrated by this case study, the needs that are identified for any given youth may be diverse and call for relatively specialized forms of assistance (e.g., those appropriate for a teen father in the case of Midnight). This reality suggests to us the value of pursuing strategic partnerships with other youth serving organizations and institutions (e.g., schools, job training programs) that have the complementary skills and resources. As we have pointed out, such arrangements offer a rich potential for positive synergies that extend beyond the four walls of an after-school center.

[31] The costs of not earning a high school diploma include, but are not limited to, lower future earnings and a higher likelihood of being unemployed in adulthood, as well as increased risk for incarceration (Steinberg, Johnson, & Pennington, 2006).

[32] Hamilton (1990); Halpern (2009).

12

Tommiana: A Contest between Closeness and Competition

Tommiana is a somewhat typical twelve-year-old girl. With a number of friends and some close adult relationships, including with West River staff, she is active and involved in multiple activities at the center. Dance is Tommiana's favorite activity and is led by the staff person with whom she has the closest relationship. At the same time, Tommiana is moody, and in the middle of the year begins to withdraw from the dance program. Furthermore, Tommiana stops coming to the center for a few weeks in March, after losing to a peer in a center-wide competition. No one appears to follow-up on her absence, suggesting that she may have been somewhat lost in the shuffle. In this chapter, we will see how West River provided important support for Tommiana, but also had some costs. Her case illustrates one of the strengths of a comprehensive youth center, wherein relationships with staff can spread across activities and different PARCs can complement each other. Yet it also reminds us of the importance of the fit between individual youth and a program's culture, particularly around issues of competition. Finally, Tommiana's story provides a look at the missed opportunities for support when staff fail to capitalize on potential linkages beyond the walls of the center.

IN THE BEGINNING

Tommiana is a petite girl who prides herself on being well dressed. She has been coming to West River since she was in the first grade and most of her friends also attend the center. Tommiana tells us that she used to attend the club every day. In third grade, she stopped coming as regularly because she lived further away from

259

West River. She reports this period of lesser attendance as a "bad" event in her history at the center. At the time of our study, she reported coming almost every day but was observed at the center less frequently as the year progressed – something we discuss further throughout the chapter.

Tommiana's social network map includes fourteen people, equally split between adults and kids. She gives all the peers on her map except one the highest closeness rating, a five. The exception is Midnight, a seventeen-year-old male who is the focus of our other youth case study at this center (see Chapter 11). She calls Midnight a friend, rating her closeness to him a three. Despite her overall positive peer profile, she shares in an interview that the thing she likes least about herself is "that people think that I think of myself as Miss Perfect and rich cause I get clothes everyday and get good grades on my report card." This suggests she may have had some tension with peers that was not visible to us.

Of the seven adults on Tommiana's map, all but one is a relative. Victoria is the only non-familial adult listed. Tommiana indicates that Victoria knows an auntie who is also included on her map.[1] Just as she does with respect to her peers, Tommiana gives the highest possible closeness rating to most of her relationships with adults. In other interviews, she mentions close relationships with several adults in her extended family as well as a couple of West River staff members, including one who is also a relative.[2] Interestingly, although she lives with her mother, Tommiana names her father as the person who has the most influence on her life. She says that he "gives [her] tips like don't give up no matter what people say."

Overall, Tommiana reports that she does reasonably well in school. She tells us that she had been getting all A's and B's up until the prior year, when her math grades began to slip. Despite this, she says she likes her current school and gets decent grades in most subjects. She likes history and wants to improve her math grades.

Generally good natured and often seen at the center dancing, talking, or playing around with friends, Tommiana is also prone to

---

[1] "Auntie" is a term that is typically used in the African-American community to refer to an older female who has a close relationship with the family but is not a blood relative.

[2] This staff person is not identified in order to ensure Tommiana's anonymity.

some moodiness. Over the course of the year, she becomes some-what more temperamental, She appears to grow irritable and react more negatively to small frustrations with staff and friends. For example, one October afternoon in the game room, Tommiana is playing ping-pong with a group of youth and staff when her frustration gets the better of her:

> *Tommiana did not know how to play at all but was willing to learn. When she got up to play [against another girl] she could not even hit the ball because her hand-eye coordination was not honed for the game. After completely missing three in a row, she hit her paddle on the table and stormed off. Ben jumped down from the desk where he had been sitting and hurried over to the main door where she was sulking.... [Ben said] "Whoa, whoa, what's wrong, why are you so upset ... its OK, we will work on it together and you can learn this."*

Similarly, in February, when kids are required to bring their report cards to the club, Tommiana misplaces hers. Rather than approach-ing one of the staff members to whom she is close, or even just ask-ing other kids if they saw it, Tommiana withdraws and begins to sulk in the corner:

> *Tommiana came in the back door and sat down on a chair about ten feet from us. She had her sweatshirt hood up over her head and she sat with her head bowed forward, so that it was almost impossible to see her face. Nelson saw her sit down and he looked at her for a couple minutes. She was alone and did not change her posture. Eventually, he got up and walked over to where she was sitting. He put his hand on top of her head and said, "Tommiana, what's wrong?" She did not respond so he bent at the waist and leaned closer and said, "Tommiana, tell me what's wrong." She did not seem to want to speak and only mumbled "my report card." Nelson pushed her to say more, "What about your report card?" Tommiana elaborated, "I left it in the auditorium and now it's gone." He replied, "Oh, did you look for it?" She nodded her head and he continued "it will turn up, nobody wants your report card; it prob-ably just got picked up by accident. Did you ask Miss Victoria if she has seen it?" Tommiana shook her head no and Nelson continued "OK, well go ask Miss Victoria and if she don't have it ask [the front desk staff] to make an announcement about it. OK?" Tommiana nodded her head yes, got up, and left the way she came.*

Despite Tommiana's generally engaged personality, these types of emotional reactions are fairly common for her during the year.

Puberty may have played some role in her behavior.[3] Indeed, the
portrait above likely sounds typical for anyone who spends time
with twelve-year-olds. Yet Tommiana's home life also presents a
number of risk factors that may be influencing her emotional well-
being and moods.

Tommiana lives with her mother and a few siblings. Her mother
is a single mom who had Tommiana as a teenager. Tommiana sometimes feels that her mother favors her other siblings over her and there
appears to be some amount of tension between her and her mother
throughout the year.[4] In addition, Tommiana reports that one of her
close relatives is an alcoholic and that one of her older siblings recently
has gotten in serious trouble at school. Furthermore, she shares that a
number of significant events have taken place in her immediate and
extended family over the past year, including people moving, dying,
and losing their jobs. Tommiana herself has moved a number of times
in the past three years and as a result attended multiple schools. In
our initial survey, she reports feeling "somewhat safe" in her neighborhood, but also tells us later that drug dealers frequent the corner
by her home, at times resulting in shootings on the street.

Tommiana looks fairly average on our measures of overall and
domain-specific self-esteem.[5] Yet she is lower than average on
measures of adult relatedness, indicating some level of discomfort with and distrust of adults.[6] This is surprising given that she

---

[3] Given Tommiana's age, it is likely that she was experiencing puberty. Some
of her moodiness may have been a result of the accompanying hormonal and
physical changes combined with stressors in her environment. Although there
is increasing consensus that puberty per se does not increase moodiness for all
adolescents, there is evidence that, for girls in particular, some of the physical
changes associated with puberty can lead to changes in mood, body image, and
depression (Petersen, 1988; Petersen, Compas, Brooks-Gunn, Stemmler, Ey, &
Grant, 1993, Steinberg & Morris, 2001).

[4] A meta-analysis of the literature on parent-child conflict (Laursen, Coy, &
Collins, 1998) found that levels of conflict were highest at early adolescence and
decreased with age. Conflicts were most negatively charged in mid-adolescence.
Although this review did not address whether parent-child conflict is greater
in early adolescence than in childhood, previous researchers have reported
such findings (Smetana, 1989, as cited in Laursen, Coy, & Collins, 1998). Some
research suggests that mother-daughter conflict in particular increases at puberty
(e.g., Holmbeck & Hill, 1991).

[5] T-scores were as follows: global self-esteem – 54.9, peer self-esteem – 56.9, academic self-esteem – 57.0.

[6] Tommiana's T-scores were 34.5 for our measure of trust toward adults and 62.1
for our measure of interpersonal sensitivity in relationships with adults, which

reports having close relationships with a number of adults, including Victoria, whom she feels she can talk to about private things. Their relationship is discussed in depth later in the chapter. Given Tommiana's age and environmental risk factors, she is at risk for decline in her self-esteem over the coming years. Decreased feelings of self-worth may not seem like a big deal on the surface. Yet, for youth in Tommiana's age group, such declines can bring with them increased susceptibility to symptoms of depression as well as a host of other interpersonal, behavioral, and academic difficulties.[7] For Tommiana, a twelve-year-old girl with a somewhat difficult home life, West River provides a developmentally supportive context, a place where she can fit in, have fun, and find role models. At the same time, not all is rosy, and there are some bumps in the road along the way.

TOMMIANA'S YEAR AT THE AFTER-SCHOOL CENTER

We first meet Tommiana in a venue that is her regular stomping ground: dance practice. In addition to dance, Tommiana participates in Smart Girls, a psychosocial program for adolescent girls. Both programs are led by Victoria, the staff person with whom Tommiana reports having the closest relationship at the center. Both programs provide fairly strong PARCs (see Table 12.1), although the culture of the dance team may also have some negative implications, as will be discussed. The two PARCs appear to balance each other, as they are quite different in terms of both how they engage girls and their overall cultures, one centering on competition and dedication and the other on trust and validation. In addition, both programs support Tommiana's relationship with Victoria as well as her peer relationships.

indicate lower level of trust and a heightened level of sensitivity in relationships with adults compared to other youth in our sample.

[7] It is unfortunately normative for girls, especially, to experience decreases in self-esteem in early adolescence. During this age period, girls' self-esteem tends to drop more than boys, and on average remains lower (Kling, Hyde, Showers, & Buswell, 1999). Of particular note, some research has found girls similar in age to Tommiana to be more susceptible than boys to a steady and marked drop in feelings of worth (Zimmerman, Copeland, Shope, & Dielman, 1997). Such drops in self-esteem have been linked to outcomes such as increased symptoms of depression, poorer academic performance, and substance use (Hirsch & DuBois, 1991; Zimmerman et al., 1997).

TABLE 12.1. *Tommiana's PARC profile*

Starts at beginning of year

P dance
A rehearsals, auditions for performances, competitions
R Victoria, peer dancers
C engagement, discipline, motivation, some validation for talents, competitiveness

P Smart Girls
A discussions about developmental issues facing girls
R Victoria, girls in the group
C trust, accountability

P –
A game room
R peers, Victoria, Ben
C fun, hanging out with staff and peers

Starts in middle of the year

P Miss West River
A center-wide pageant
R unclear
C competition, rejection

Starts at end of the year

None

Tommiana reports feeling fairly close to all three of the major staff people at the center. The fact that she is related to one staff member may have made her more visible to other staff than she would have been otherwise. Tommiana also has several friends at the center. We often observe her in a group of three to five girls, talking or dancing. She seems to care for other kids, as in the interaction in the following field note excerpt, in which she tries to comfort a younger girl who is icing an injury after being hurt by another youth.

> *Jasmine was still crying rather forcefully and one of her braids was against the wound and therefore under the ice. Tommiana said to her in a nurturing tone, "You don't want that there, let me move it." Jasmine lifted the ice and allowed Tommiana to push the hair back.*

Although Tommiana is engaged in a variety of activities and relationships over the course of the year, her negative experience with the Miss West River pageant, which will be described later, appears to put a pall over the rest of her year at the center. She stops coming for a few weeks following the pageant, and although she eventually returns, she does not appear to come as often. The situation as a whole serves as a missed opportunity for more proactive intervention by the staff. This is surprising. The staff at West River are fairly proactive and, as can be seen in the earlier field notes that capture some of Tommiana's interactions with Ben and Nelson, usually are not shy about following up with youth who appear to be upset.

Overall, Tommiana's year at West River is characterized by some close relationships, which, given the risks in her home and neighborhood environments, likely serve as a protective factor for her. At the same time, as will be discussed, it is not clear that she makes any specific developmental gains or that she fully bounces back from the disappointment she encounters at the center during the year.

Closest Staff Relationship

As noted, Tommiana's closest staff relationship at West River is with Victoria, who is the leader of both dance and Smart Girls. Tommiana refers to Victoria as being like a "big sister" to her. This is despite the fact that an actual family member works at West River. In fact, whereas Tommiana puts Victoria on her social network map, she does not list the staff person to whom she is related. When comparing Tommiana's ratings of her interactions with the three major staff members at the center, what stands out is the much higher rating she gives Victoria on the item asking whether she talks with the staff person about things that are very private. This is reinforced in our interviews with Tommiana:

> If I am mad [Victoria] will take me in the office and ask me what the problem is. If for example my mom was making me mad, [Victoria] will listen to me and give me advice like stop having an attitude ... it seems like I can talk to her about anything and she wouldn't tell anyone, it would just stay between me and her.

Her relationship with Victoria also allows Tommiana to take her mind off things in her life that may be troubling her.

> If I have something that I have been holdin' onto for a couple of years I can let it out to her and put it off my mind so that I can concentrate on other things. I feel like it is off my mind and don't have to think about it anymore.

As with Bill and Pocahontas, from the Midwest Center, there are a number of things in Tommiana's environment that create stress. She, too, finds some solace from these stressors in a relationship with a staff person and in working with that person in engaging activities.

Given that Tommiana by her own report appears to be somewhat distrustful and prone to emotional sensitivity in her relationships with adults, her feelings of trust and rapport toward Victoria are particularly notable. Of significance, too, is that there is a clear care-taking dimension to their relationship:

> *When my mom is not at home, [Victoria] will take me home, drive me home. We live near each other.*

Thus, similar to what we saw with Pocahontas and Manuel, Victoria plays a familial role, ensuring Tommiana gets home safely in a neighborhood that poses real risks.

Despite the one-on-one interactions that Tommiana talks about when describing why her relationship with Victoria is important, most of the mentoring that we observe between them comes in the group contexts of dance and Smart Girls. This has some benefits. For example, Victoria sometimes praises Tommiana, providing her with public validation. This is illustrated in the field note excerpt which follows, taken during a Smart Girls session when the girls were reporting on what they did to complete their "homework":

> *Victoria nodded encouragingly. "Anyone else?" Tommiana raised her hand and said that one time it was the day they were supposed to take school pictures and one of the girls in her class had forgotten and so had worn some clothes that didn't look very nice so Tommiana let the girl borrow her shirt so that she could look nice in her pictures. Victoria told everyone that they all should have done nice things like this during the week.*

Later in the same session, she again validates Tommiana's contributions to the group.

> *After we all clapped for them, Victoria asked the group what could have been different so that everyone would have been happy and had high self-esteem at the end. Tommiana raised her hand and said that Patience should have told Haley and Sally that they could all be friends and hang out with one another instead of just being two versus one all of the time. Victoria agreed and said that Patience did the right thing*

by Haley not to be mean to the others but that Patience should have been more positive towards Haley and built a "bridge" between all three of the girls.

Yet, perhaps as a result of their relationship taking place primarily within group contexts, Victoria does not report feeling as close to Tommiana as Tommiana does to her. Whereas Tommiana rates their closeness a 4 on a 5-point scale, Victoria provides a rating of 2.5 to 3. Victoria also has a difficult time talking about and describing Tommiana, often saying "I don't know" as an initial response to questions and only elaborating on follow-up from the interviewer.[8] Victoria does cite many of the same topics of conversation that Tommiana mentions, including an almost verbatim report of their conversation about how Tommiana feels that her mom pays more attention to her sibling than to her. This suggests that, rather than actually remembering different experiences, Victoria and Tommiana may perceive the meaning and significance of their interactions differently. Despite this, Victoria believes that she has significant influence on Tommiana "in every area, school, Smart Girls, dance."[9]

Activities and Program Participation

Dance
As noted earlier, the dance program is a major PARC for Tommiana throughout the year. It has several positive components, most notably an activity in which she is highly engaged and a relationship with an important adult mentor. At times, Tommiana receives reinforcement for her talents within dance. Thus, this PARC offers a culture of validation and support for her self-esteem. In the following excerpt, another staff person praises Tommiana's skills in front of the group.

[8] This was also true for at least one of Victoria's interviews about other youth, however, so it is unclear whether such responses were specific to her feelings about her relationship with Tommiana or were more generalized.

[9] Evidence of the benefits of mentoring provided by after-school staff in group contexts has been reported previously (see Hirsch, 2005). In Tommiana's case, the discrepancy in closeness reported by youth versus staff is likely a result of the group context, wherein Victoria has relationships with multiple youth, possibly diluting the strength of her feelings toward any single youth. Research on group mentoring is still in its infancy and, thus, the significance, if any, of this discrepancy is unclear.

One junior girl ... asked Natasha why Tommiana gets to be in the front row. Natasha replied "cause her beat is always right on and steady, she's never speeding up or slowing down."

Yet within that culture of validation, Victoria holds the girls to high standards. Team members must still audition to compete in local and regional competitions. She makes clear that she expects girls to try their hardest and to be dedicated to the team. For example, when Tommiana mentions in a Smart Girls session that one of her goals is to be a good dancer, Victoria emphasizes the discipline that takes:

Tommiana talked about wanting to be a good dancer and Victoria elaborated this with the things you need to do or not do to accomplish that goal. Victoria wrote the word "Disciplined" on the poster to describe the general things to accomplish Tommiana's ideal self.

This interaction highlights a positive aspect of the Smart Girls and dance PARCs for Tommiana – the presence of Victoria in both and the transference of the supportive and motivating aspects of that relationship between these contexts.

Interestingly, though, five days later, Tommiana is dragging her feet on auditioning for dance.

Tommiana [and two other girls who were also in Smart Girls with her] were standing [at the end of the basketball court in the gym]. Tommiana asked if [the dance team] was still having auditions. When I said yes she said "we better get back up there," but made no move to leave. [One of the other girls] chimed in "she been acting weird lately, I don't like it." Tommiana added, "Yeah, I don't feel good. I don't."

It is not clear, given Tommiana's reported love of dance and desire to be a good dancer, what causes this lack of interest in the auditions. Three months later, during another round of dance team auditions, she displays the same lack of focus, this time in front of Victoria, who calls her out on it.

Victoria emerged out of her office at this point and said "Okay, y'all we are going to be practicing for a while here tonight cause we just have three more days before this competition on Friday ... they respect us but the only way they gonna keep respectin' us is if we keep performing at a top level. So, I can only have ten of you guys on stage at a time so today we are going to start figuring out who those ten people are gonna be. So what I want to happen is to go through each song and have two people go up and perform for me at a time so I can see who knows which dance the best and I can put you in." ... The only two that were left were Tommiana and Shelby. When they were about to start Tommiana still had not gotten up from her chair where she was sitting. "What is it girl – you tired? What's goin' on?" Victoria asked her. Tommiana just shook her head. "Are you sick?" "No," Tommiana responded. Victoria said "Well then you better get up there and show me what you got so I can put you in this show." While this was going on Shelby was explaining in a loud voice that she had just learned this yesterday and if she messed up that was why. When the music started they got through about two minutes before Tommiana got fed up and just walked off and went and sat down in her chair. Shelby continued to try to keep dancing but she really didn't know much of it so she kept improvising. When it was done Victoria looked at Tommiana and said "Look, Shelby didn't know it and she kept going. What's wrong with you? Why are you so down? You gotta keep going Tommiana, I know you know this and if you don't you better start practicing!" She then at that point asked [another girl] to come in and dance with Shelby so Shelby could watch her. Just as the music started again Tommiana jumped up and joined in doing the entire dance perfectly. When it was done everyone was clapping and when Tommiana sat down Victoria looked at her straight in the eye and said "you see, I know you could do it. You just gotta self motivate, right?" Tommiana just nodded back.

Tommiana appears to resent the audition process. In an earlier field note segment we saw that other staff view Tommiana as talented. And at end of the incident in the previous field note, she receives applause from her peers. Yet despite such positive support she resists engaging in the competition. Tommiana even walks off the stage in front of Victoria, an adult whose opinion of her we know that she values and who she generally sees as a positive source of motivation:

If I am down on myself she [Victoria] always says to keep trying and she motivates me.... She tells you I can do it. Like with the dances, she says just try one more time and you can get it.

In fact, Victoria's encouraging attitude is evident in the interaction presented in the previous field notes. Yet not until Tommiana's position is threatened, by Victoria calling up another girl to take her place, does she give in and perform at the level that Victoria expects of her.

It is unclear whether Tommiana's ambivalence is related to her overall tendency toward moodiness or is more specific to dance. It is possible, particularly given what comes later in the context of the Miss West River pageant, that the competitive nature of the dance program is a negative for her even given Victoria's support.

Smart Girls

Smart Girls is a national-level program that features a curriculum focused on topics such as body image, self-esteem, and other issues of concern to early adolescent girls. In our prior research, we saw this program implemented with various levels of success at different Boys & Girls Clubs.[10] The success of the program often appeared to rest on the talents of the staff leader. At West River, Victoria is in charge of Smart Girls, which is a boon to Tommiana. Not only is Victoria a gifted group facilitator, but Tommiana already has a close relationship with her, increasing the odds of her engaging in the program at a level that could yield benefits.[11] In fact, Tommiana sometimes says things that could be straight out of the Smart Girls curriculum, such as to respect yourself and that you do not have to be skinny and perfect like girls on television. In the hands of less capable facilitators, a manualized program such as Smart Girls can become routinized and not very engaging.[12] Yet Victoria seems more than up for the challenge. She often expresses her own excitement about topics, for example, by jumping up and down or reacting emotionally to a comment within the group:

> [One of the girls] brought up something she had heard on television, that women have babies and use them to trap men. This set Victoria off. She told [the girl] that she was wrong and she made up a new Smart Girls rule – do not quote things from television. She talked at length about how hurtful it is to claim that women trap men with babies because it takes two to make them.

As noted earlier, Tommiana also receives positive validation from Victoria for her contributions to Smart Girls. Not only is she primed to receive the lessons of the curriculum due to her close relationship with Victoria, but Tommiana also is able to build trust with Victoria through the program and gain tools with which to navigate adolescence.

---

[10] Hirsch (2005).

[11] See Jones & Deutsch (in press) for discussion of how staff members utilize their relationships with youth strategically to engage them in psychosocial programs.

[12] Hirsch (2005).

Miss West River Pageant

The Miss West River pageant is a single event, but it deals a large blow to Tommiana. We do not witness the pageant, in which youth compete with each other in areas such as talents, career goals, and fashion. We hear about it from Victoria, however, and know that Tommiana uses dance as her talent in the contest. In mid-March, our researchers notice that they have not seen Tommiana at the club for a week or two. Victoria explains that Tommiana competed in the Miss West River pageant. When she got home the night before the results of the competition were announced, she was locked out of her house. When her mother came home and could not find Tommiana, she became very angry and called the police. When Tommiana then hears that she has not won the competition, she is extremely upset and does not come back to West River for two or three weeks. Even after she returns, we see her less frequently.

The emotional fallout of not winning is clearly made worse for Tommiana by the concurrent incident with her mother at home, which comes on top of an already tense relationship. Yet, her specifically staying away from West River, where she usually finds solace from her family issues, suggests that she is hurt by the results of the competition and that she is not bouncing back quickly from the disappointment. The staff's inability to predict that losing the competition would upset her and their neglecting to address it with her is a shortcoming that is discussed later in the chapter.

DEVELOPMENTAL GAINS OVER THE YEAR

Tommiana did not make any obvious developmental gains over the course of the year. There were few observations of her in the spring, however, so we are limited in our conclusions by what data were available on Tommiana from the end of the year (primarily these come from interviews and surveys). It seems that her grades may have improved slightly, after a drop the previous year, but she appears to have had consistently pretty good grades, so even that is unclear. Instead of gains, there may have been more preventative benefits associated with Tommiana's participation in the center. Although we can only speculate in this regard, it is noteworthy that Tommiana lived in a neighborhood that posed significant risk due to its level of violence and drugs and that the presence of youth-serving organizations in such neighborhoods appears helpful in preventing aggression and delinquency.[13] In our prior research, we similarly found that positive relationships with after-school center staff, such as Tommiana's with Victoria, appeared to have the greatest influence on youth from high-risk neighborhoods.[14] Furthermore, as noted earlier, Tommiana reported average self-esteem. Because girls this age are susceptible to declines in self-esteem, which are associated with depression and other negative outcomes, West River may have served as a context that buffered her from such problematic outcomes.[15]

At the same time, in light of Tommiana's struggles with dance and the Miss West River pageant, we should not overlook the possibility that the center could have inadvertently provoked some negative emotions about herself. By the end of the year, she was coming to the center less often. It is thus not clear to us where her trajectory would lead after we left.

TOMMIANA IN THE WEST RIVER CENTER: STRENGTHS, SHORTCOMINGS, AND SYNERGIES

Strengths

When considering Tommiana's year at West River, her relationship with Victoria, opportunity for involvement in developmentally enriching programs (Smart Girls and dance), and access to a positive and safe environment in the after-school hours all stand out as significant strengths of the center. As a girl struggling to navigate entry into adolescence and all that this entails, Tommiana is a prime candidate to benefit from a relationship with a strong female role model. Her relationship with Victoria addresses this need. As a successful African-American young woman, Victoria offers Tommiana an identification figure to whom she can relate and aspire to emulate. Available research suggests that such similarities by themselves do not necessarily tip the scales heavily in favor of greater benefits for youth.[16] As we have discussed, however, Victoria consciously

---

[13] Molnar, Cerda, Roberts, & Buka (2008).

[14] Hirsch (2005).

[15] In a study of more than 500 14-year-olds, Mahoney, Schweder, and Stattin (2002) found that adolescents who both participated in an after-school activity and perceived high support from their activity leader were especially likely to report low levels of depressed mood. Support from after-school activity leaders was particularly important for a sub-group of youth characterized by highly detached relations to their parents – a descriptor that could well apply to Tommiana.

[16] Sanchez & Colon (2005).

conducts herself in a manner that is intended to leverage her potential to function as a visible and positive role model for Tommiana and other girls at the center.[17] Aided by the forum of Smart Girls, she also is clearly comfortable dispensing advice on topics that are highly salient concerns for Tommiana and other girls in her age group, ranging from boys to body image. That Tommiana can recite verbatim so many of Victoria's messages and has begun to embrace them as her own is a testament to their value and effectiveness. In view of this impact, and the added breadth to the relationship that comes from frequent discussions about Tommiana's academics and home life, it is not surprising that she equates Victoria's role in her life to that of a "big sister."[18]

In many respects, Tommiana's relationship with Victoria can be seen as a natural outgrowth of the West River staff's commitment to fostering positive youth development. The center's emphasis on hiring staff from the surrounding area likely deserves credit as well. Victoria's rootedness in the community enhances her credibility and effectiveness as a role model for Tommiana. It also facilitates her being in a position to ensure Tommiana's safe passage home on occasion.

Smart Girls and dance, the programs that Victoria led at West River, are noteworthy too in considering Tommiana's year at the center. Smart Girls is tailor-made for youth such as Tommiana who are beginning to face the myriad challenges that can come with being a female adolescent. The program's skill-based orientation, coupled with a gender-specific format and curriculum, is closely aligned with the characteristics of programs that research suggests are most likely to be effective in promoting positive outcomes for girls in after-school settings.[19] Based on what we know about Tommiana, the Smart Girls program seems an especially good fit for her. As a youth who does well in school, those aspects of the program

---

[17] The importance of role model behaviors is supported by research in which the degree to which adolescents reported that the very important adults in their lives engaged in problem behaviors (e.g., theft) was predictive of the adolescent's own tendency to engage in similar behavior (Greenberger, Chen, & Beam, 1998).

[18] Relationships that serve a variety of functions have been described as being high in complexity (Heaney & Israel, 2008) or multiplex. In our earlier research (Hirsch, 2005), we found that it was not unusual for after-school staff to provide this type of relatively comprehensive mentoring to youth, devoting attention to both academic and non-academic concerns to a greater extent than either kin or school adults.

[19] LeCroy & Mann (2008).

(e.g., homework assignments) that come with its relatively more structured orientation are less likely to be an issue or "turn-off" in the same way that they could be for some other youth.[20] She also is already beginning to struggle with many of the topics and concerns that are addressed in the program, thus ensuring that they resonate with her personally and have immediate relevance.[21] Ideally, we would like to see all youth attending comprehensive after-school centers have the opportunity to benefit from programs that are this well matched to their individual profiles.

Several aspects of dance make it similarly well tailored to Tommiana's developmental needs. This activity provides her the experience of working cooperatively with others her age in the context of meaningful and engaging project-based learning, with capable adult oversight. Dance offers support for Tommiana's budding interest in a career in entertainment and for her development of important work readiness skills including discipline, persistence, and practice. As noted earlier, it is also an activity in which others viewed her as talented, thus providing her validation in an area that is important to her emerging identity and plans for her future.

A further, overarching strength of the programs at West River is the opportunity they offer Tommiana to receive mentoring from staff within group settings.[22] Given what we know of her somewhat sensitive nature, especially when dealing with adults, these small-group contexts may have been valuable as indirect conduits for connecting her with adult guidance, thus circumventing the feelings of insecurity that more confrontational, one-to-one encounters might have engendered. We see, too, that when staff did direct their attention to Tommiana in such programs, they drew on the group's activities (e.g., preparation for a dance performance) in ways that likely enhanced the salience of their messages.

---

[20] When seeking youth input in the development of a gender-specific program for young adolescent ethnic minority girls, a recurring concern was that the program should not be too much "like school" (DuBois et al., 2008).

[21] When asked about her future goals and expectations for herself, for example, Tommiana cites being "more sure and confident in myself" and "to not care what other people say," reflecting the salience of the prototypically adolescent concerns of self-esteem and peer pressure.

[22] In our earlier research (Hirsch, 2005), we similarly observed that after-school center staff predominantly interacted with youth in group settings and that such interactions offered rich contexts for mentoring.

The broader value of the West River center for Tommiana deserves note as well. The setting's sustained availability to her throughout her elementary school years stands in contrast to the relative instability of her school life. As such, her enduring connection to the center may have helped buffer the impact of the stress associated with her multiple school transitions and the required adjustment to several new settings and peer groups. We see, too, how toxic elements of her neighborhood create a profound need for her to have a safe and reliable outlet for fun and recreation in the after-school hours. It is hardly surprising, in view of these considerations, that Tommiana reports experiencing the West River as a "second home."

Shortcomings

When we consider shortcomings of West River for Tommiana, our attention is drawn primarily to the Miss West River competition and her reaction to not being selected for this honor. At an organizational level, questions can be raised regarding the wisdom of holding this type of competition in the first place. Youth are not necessarily equipped to respond well when activities are structured so that there are many more losers than winners. In this case, of course, there was only one winner.[23] Research suggests, too, that girls in particular are more likely than boys to prefer cooperative approaches to learning[24] and to favor forms of competition that are focused on achieving personal goals rather than besting others.[25] This is not to say that a competition such as Miss West River is without potential value. Among other things, participating in this sort of activity could serve to reinforce the value of hard work and preparation, be a source of useful feedback on personal strengths and limitations, and, for non-winners, foster resiliency to similar disappointments or setbacks in the future. Such benefits, however, are likely to depend on competitive activities being structured with these ends in mind.

---

[23] In game theory (e.g., Buchanan, 2001), situations in which winners must be coupled with losers are referred to as zero-sum games. In contrast, positive-sum games are "win-win" as they are designed in such a way that all participants can profit in one way or the other. The Miss West River pageant most resembles a zero-sum game, although, as we discuss, it might have been possible to structure it so that was more akin to one that was positive-sum.

[24] Johnson & Engelhard (1992).

[25] Smith & Collins (1988).

The Miss West River pageant, for example, could have been set up so that all the girls involved were recognized for their participation, received constructive feedback on their applications, and had the opportunity to "de-brief" with staff following the announcement of the winner. To our knowledge, no provisions like these were in place. Had they been, the outcome of Tommiana's participation in the competition could have been much less problematic and perhaps even beneficial.

The reactions that Tommiana has to not winning – emotional upset and temporary withdrawal from the center – also point to significant organizational issues. During the time that Tommiana stops coming to West River, as best we can tell, staff make no effort to reach out to her or her family. Nor, for that matter, is it clear to what extent staff, other than Victoria, even take note of the development. This is not surprising given that the center lacks a formal system or set of procedures for ensuring that a youth such as Tommiana does not become "lost in the shuffle" when there is a need for outreach or additional support. What we can imagine being helpful here, in part, is careful monitoring of youth attendance patterns and staff who specialize in providing outreach when there are unexpected interruptions to a given youth's attendance. The success of such efforts ultimately is likely to hinge on effective communication and coordination with those staff who have the greatest day-to-day interactions and strongest relationships with the youth involved. In the case of Tommiana, this would certainly include Victoria; more fully apprised of the situation, Victoria could have been more proactive in helping Tommiana cope with her disappointment and in so doing facilitated her reengagement with the center. The shortcomings of West River that are suggested by this part of Tommiana's year at the center, therefore, are multifaceted and go beyond simple tracking of youth attendance.

Synergies

When viewed collectively, positive, negative, and missed synergies are all apparent in Tommiana's experiences at West River. Several facets of her joint involvement in Smart Girls and dance are reflective of positive synergy. We see, for example, how dance provides rich opportunities for Tommiana to apply the messages she is exposed to through Smart Girls, such as believing in yourself and the importance of hard work and setting goals. This process of transfer across activities facilitates the internalization of key themes from Smart Girls and also helps fuel the motivation that Tommiana needs for successful engagement in dance. It is readily apparent as well that Tommiana's relationship with Victoria would be robbed of much of its value had they not been involved together in these activities.[26] We expect, too, that these types of synergy are amplified by the combination of curriculum- and activity-based programs. Neither instruction in the abstract nor hands-on experience without opportunity for reflection and generalized learning is ideal. Together, the limitations of each may be offset. Ideas and actions can be connected and staff can be more effective and credible as mentors and role models.

In terms of potential for negative synergy, it is noteworthy that Miss West River is not the only dimension of Tommiana's experiences at the center that has a competitive or evaluative element. Within dance, it is clear that the strongest performers receive special distinction and opportunities. We see, furthermore, that Tommiana is clearly not comfortable with some of the more competitive aspects of this activity (e.g., auditions). Such reactions may be accentuated by Victoria's role in leading dance. As Victoria is a mentor figure to her, Tommiana is likely concerned with not wanting to feel that she has disappointed Victoria or fallen short of her expectations. These considerations suggest that Tommiana's participation in dance may have "primed" her for the emotional fallout she experiences as a result of not winning the Miss West River pageant. The potential for negative synergy is accentuated by the fact that she used dance as her talent in the competition.

Also of concern is the absence of systematic attention to either forging or capitalizing on connections between center staff and important persons in Tommiana's life outside of the club. Tommiana, for example, shares during one of our interviews with her that she is pleased when Victoria and her mother run into each other in the community and have a friendly conversation: "We seen her in the store – it's good … they be talkin' like they best friends." She also includes a connection between Victoria and her mother in her social network map. There is, however, no arrangement to facilitate regular communication between them. Had there been, the information shared could have facilitated more coordinated and

---

[26] As we have noted previously, research suggests that mentoring relationships for youth are enhanced when there is involvement in instrumental activity (Hamilton & Hamilton, 1990), such as is the case for Tommiana and Victoria in Smart Girls and dance.

effective support for Tommiana. This type of center-home linkage might have proved especially valuable at critical junctures, such as when Tommiana learns she has not been selected Miss West River, a stressor which is then compounded by an incident at home.[27] It will be recalled too that Tommiana reports Victoria is friends with one of her "aunties." In view of the significance Tommiana attaches to her relationships with both women, opportunities for them to be more collaborative could have enhanced the support they each provided to her. Keeping in mind that she regards West River as a second home, stronger linkages between the center and Tommiana's family could also have resulted in a more integrated and reinforcing sense of connectedness across the two settings.[28]

CONCLUSION

This case study raises several important issues for consideration. Some of these involve elaboration of themes introduced in earlier chapters, whereas others are newer concerns introduced by our analysis of this particular youth's year in a comprehensive after-school center. As with other youth, such as Pocahontas and Midnight, we see that Tommiana benefited from a PARC profile that includes an intersection between a developmentally enriching activity or program and a strong mentoring relationship with a staff person. For her, what is most striking is that this is characteristic of two distinct components of her PARC profile (those involving her participation in Smart Girls and dance, respectively). It is tempting to conclude that multiple positive PARCs are likely to be better than one when it comes to promoting positive outcomes for youth in after-school centers. If so, this could constitute a distinctive advantage for centers that are comprehensive in orientation relative to those that are more program-specific and limited in scope. We suspect, however,

[27] Accumulations of stressful events are more common among youth from low-income backgrounds and are related to poorer emotional and behavioral adjustment (Grant, Compas, Stuhlmacher, Thurm, McMahon, & Halpert, 2003).

[28] Research has found greater feelings of connectedness among adolescents to be associated with better psychological and behavioral adjustment (see, e.g., Detrie & Lease, 2008; Karcher & Finn, 2005). There is also support for distinguishing between adolescents' experiences of connectedness across different parts of their lives (Karcher & Sass, 2010). Our suggestion is that when these types of experiences align, such as across the youth's home and after-school center, there may be added value.

that the reality is more complex and dependent on other additional considerations. In the case of Tommiana, for example, there appears to be significant added value associated with the same staff person leading both of the activities involved. And, as we have noted, their complementary curricular- and activity-based orientations may be a further benefit. Such possibilities suggest the usefulness of after-school centers helping youth strategically chart out participation in specific combinations of activities that seem most likely to promote their overall development. Likewise, when circumstances do not permit involvement in multiple activities with the same staff person, as was the case for Tommiana, collective mentoring across different staff may be essential in order to tap fully into potential synergies. These are ideas to which we will return in the final chapter when making recommendations for practice.

We also see in the case of Tommiana missed opportunities for after-school centers and their staff to systematically forge connections with outside persons and institutions that are important in the lives of participating youth. For Tommiana, the lost potential benefits seem especially noteworthy given that her most salient sources of adult support include some that are concentrated inside the center (Victoria) and others that are situated almost exclusively outside of it (her mother and auntie). And, with credit due to West River's practice of hiring staff from the local community, it appears that Victoria already shared some level of familiarity with these members of Tommiana's family. This is something that could have been capitalized on in the interests of providing more coordinated support for Tommiana. Such potential, although unrealized for her (and likely most other youth at West River), raises the idea of extending the concept of collective mentoring to encompass collaboration among the full spectrum of adults who are important sources of support in a young person's life. In other words, there may be significant value associated with communication and coordination not only among the staff who work with a particular youth, but also between those staff and the youth's overall network of adult support figures.[29]

---

[29] A 2010 report from *Child Trends* pointed to family involvement as an important component of successful after-school programs, one that may be related to both youth attendance and the overall quality of programs (Moore, Bronte-Tinkew, & Collins, 2010a).

The dynamics of competition and evaluation that factor into Tommiana's year at West River are a more unique feature of this case, but no less noteworthy. In charting their approach, all after-school centers must in one way or another make decisions about such issues. In doing so, they are likely to be influenced to some extent by the inherent value that tends to be attached to competition and individual achievement within our society. A further consideration may be the conclusion of some that the current generation of youth has been poorly served by an overemphasis on promoting their self-esteem, independent of actual accomplishment.[30] Such views, in our estimation, do not take adequate account of the well-established importance that a sense of positive self-regard has throughout young people's development.[31] Nor do they give due attention to evidence that youth programs and activities can be structured to simultaneously foster gains in both skills and feelings of self-worth.[32] When such balance and integration is not present, after-school centers run the risk of inadvertently exacerbating areas of vulnerability among the youth they serve. For Tommiana, a primary concern would be the potential for unhealthy forms of competition to tip the scales toward low self-esteem and associated difficulties as she transitions into adolescence. Clearly, too, as is also illustrated by our study of Tommiana's year at West River, under such circumstances centers also may be less successful in sustaining desired levels of youth attendance and engagement.

Although Tommiana does return to the center following the Miss West River pageant, it is not clear if she has rebounded completely emotionally or whether she will fully reengage with the center. Regardless, as we have discussed, there is much potentially to be gleaned from West River's lack of an effective response to this situation. These considerations point to a broader tension between comprehensive after-school centers as enterprises in which there is a

---

[30] A recent book, *Generation Me*, by psychologist Jean Twenge (2006) has been particularly influential in fueling concerns about the so-called self-esteem movement. On the basis of her analysis, Twenge concludes that levels of both self-esteem and narcissism – a trait that involves tendencies toward excessive self-admiration and self-centeredness – have increased among young people in the United States, and that the absence of a more realistically anchored sense of self-worth has contributed to a rise in problems such as depression, anxiety, cynicism, and loneliness during the same time period.

[31] Harter (1999).

[32] DuBois, Flay, & Fagen (2009).

pressing need for attention to organizational concerns, such as program delivery and activity supervision, but in which more nuanced forms of support and monitoring also may be essential in order to achieve optimal benefits for individual youth. As we will argue in our concluding recommendations, this dilemma is not without possible solutions. Tommiana's year at West River is illustrative of both the potential benefits and inherent challenges that may be associated with mounting such efforts.

13

Putting It All Together: What Have We Learned?

We now need to take stock of what broader insights can be gleaned from our studies of the West River center. As it is the last center we will be examining, we use this chapter as an opportunity to integrate our findings across our studies of all three centers. Our aim in doing so is to arrive at a set of conclusions regarding the conditions under which comprehensive after-school centers are most likely to realize their potential for promoting positive youth development. Our conclusions provide the foundation for the practice recommendations that we present in the next and final chapter.

West River is the strongest of the after-school centers we examined on most dimensions. So it is natural to use this center, and our studies of youth there (Midnight and Tomianna), as a counterpoint to many of the weaknesses and limitations that are apparent for the Midwest and North River centers. Our intention is not to suggest either that the latter centers are entirely lacking in positive features or that West River is without areas in need of improvement. Neither of these, of course, is the case. Indeed, as we will discuss, there are some concerns that stand out as in need of attention at all three centers and, we suspect, to a large degree among comprehensive after-school centers more generally. As researchers, this process of comparing and contrasting is one of our major analytic tools.[1]

Our conclusions are organized around five sets of concerns, each of which can be reflected in a question that might be posed when

---

[1] The approach we use in analyzing and drawing inferences from our case studies of the different centers and youth is closely akin to the "constant comparison method," which is widely used in qualitative research (Patton, 1990).

taking stock of a given after-school center and its potential for facilitating positive youth outcomes:

1. To what degree does the center prioritize youth development not only in words, but in actions?
2. Do youth attending the center have adequate opportunity to connect to a positive niche within the larger setting?
3. To what extent is there likely to be synergy across the different experiences that a youth has within the center, such that the whole is greater than the sum of the parts?
4. What does the center do to ensure that it is hiring quality staff and providing them with optimal levels of training and supervision?
5. What processes are in place within the center for continuous organizational learning and improvement?

PUTTING YOUTH DEVELOPMENT FIRST

A common refrain among those working in youth programs is that "it's all about the kids." It is not surprising, then, that all three centers we studied subscribed in one way or other to the goal of promoting the positive development of the youth who were under their care, which is also the stated objective of the larger, national organization (Boys & Girls Clubs of America). Practices reflecting this goal also are evident to some degree at each center. Recall, for example, the opportunities that older youth such as Pocahontas and Bill have to demonstrate leadership and responsibility at the Midwest center and the mentoring that Beyonce and Tweetie receive at the North River center.

It is only at West River, however, that positive youth development is a consistent priority and focus. West River's strong orientation toward promoting youth development is reflected in its relatively rich array of program and activity offerings and the quality with which they are implemented, the active mentoring of youth by staff, and the center's overall culture of appreciating youth strengths and encouraging youth voice to a greater extent than is the case at either Midwest or North River. We find no evidence that West River's emphasis on youth development comes at the expense of addressing other key organizational goals for the clubs, namely fun and safety. If anything, putting youth development first and foremost may enhance achievement of these other aims. Consider, for example, that youth are likely to find activities ultimately most rewarding when they are not just fun "in the moment," but also provide opportunities for meaningful accomplishment and growth.[2] Similarly, with respect to safety, which has a significant emotional component, we expect that youth attending centers such as West River benefit from the comfort of knowing that they can express their opinions to staff without fear of negative repercussions.

These findings and considerations lead us to conclude that a strong and consistent emphasis on positive development within comprehensive after-school centers is likely to be of fundamental importance for facilitating desired youth outcomes. This type of commitment is apt to be multifaceted and difficult to measure precisely. As we see with West River, much of it comes through "on the ground" in the day-to-day practices and operations of a center.

Our findings underscore the importance of center leadership as an influence on the level of commitment that the organization demonstrates to promoting youth development. Administrators have considerable leeway to embrace an orientation toward strengthening youth development that reflects their personal values and priorities. Although leadership at each center endorses the general principle of positive youth development, there is marked variability in what this means at a more specific level of understanding. At Midwest, leadership puts special emphasis on community outreach and attending to youth deemed most at-risk; at North River, a premium is placed on ensuring an orderly and well-controlled environment; and at West River, a guiding concern is how well programs and staff are actively engaging youth in personal growth and the development of new skills.

There is nothing intrinsically wrong with leaders putting their personal stamp on what positive youth development will mean at their site. Indeed, this may be inevitable to some extent. The problem that arose at Midwest and North River is that the resulting vision was not sufficiently comprehensive. There are many admirable features to the emphasis that Bob, the Midwest director, puts on community outreach and the most at-risk youth, but it left out most of the young people who actually came to the center. And

[2] Larson (2000).

certainly Mr. Jones, the North River director, should be alert to the potential for violence and mayhem given the community context, but his was a tunnel-vision that ventured no further.

Leaders' interpretations of positive youth development will also influence their response to possible new program initiatives. It is worth noting that at Midwest and North River, several of the thwarted initiatives focus on the needs and interests of girls. These gender-specific efforts are in accord with perspectives on youth development that emphasize the importance of equity, inclusiveness, and counteracting negative effects of broader societal forces (e.g., sexism).[3] We can only assume, from the responses that gender-related initiatives elicited from leadership, however, that such principles were not central to their understanding of what it meant for their centers to be aligned with the goal of promoting positive youth development. And this is despite the fact that both club directors had been in place during a major, region-wide gender equity initiative only a few years earlier.

At both Midwest and North River, administrators watered down considerably what positive youth development meant in practice, as compared to West River. At both of these sites, the vision was much more limited and the bar was set considerably lower than at West River. Leaders will always be able to shape a vision to their liking, but we need to make sure that the bar is never set too low. It is important for the after-school field to articulate more effectively what positive youth development entails and to do so in a manner that enables centers, as well as stand-alone programs, to be held accountable.

POSITIVE NICHES FOR YOUTH

Our earlier comparison of the youth we studied at the Midwest and North River centers highlighted the importance of whether each young person attending a comprehensive after-school center is involved in a more circumscribed, positive niche within the larger setting. We called attention, in particular, to whether each youth had been able to find a complete, positive PARC, comprised of a rewarding program or activity, a strong relationship, and a supportive cultural dimension. For Bill and Pocahontas

---

[3] Kenny, Horne, Orpinas, & Reese (2009).

at Midwest, who each enjoyed such a PARC, it anchored their participation in the center. Moreover, it seemed to offer added benefit beyond that which would be expected had the same elements been spread across multiple different PARCs. Our studies of Midnight and Tomianna at West River offer further support for this idea. It is difficult to imagine, for example, that Midnight would derive the same benefits from his involvement in dance (which served as a complete, positive PARC for him) if it did not also include his close relationship with Victoria and, culturally, strong threads of collaboration and mutual support. By the same token, when it comes to Midnight's mentoring of younger charges at the center, the lack of a clearly defined role (a cultural element) or program to support this activity seems to diminish what he is able to take away from this PARC. Likewise, for Tomianna, we have abundant evidence that her relationship with Victoria is integral to the benefits she derives from Smart Girls (her strongest and most complete PARC). Conversely, the absence of a supportive relationship or cultural dimension for the PARC that revolves around her participation in the Miss West River competition appears to be problematic. Thus, our findings suggest there is "value added" in having more complete, positive PARCs, such that a youth's PARC profile provides information beyond that which is available by merely counting the youth's programs and activities, positive relationships with staff and peers, and exposure to different cultures within the center.

What types of centers are most likely to achieve a high percentage of youth with at least one niche of this type (i.e., a complete, positive PARC)? It will likely be important for there to be diverse programs and activity offerings that are both well-aligned with the needs and interests of the youth being served by the center and well-implemented by motivated staff. Clearly, too, the types of human resource and organizational learning practices we discuss later in this chapter may be important considerations. And, as suggested by our earlier discussion, success in realizing any such objectives may be influenced both for the better and for the worse by club leadership. For example, is there a rational and transparent process in place for responding to staff initiatives for new programs or activities? Are staff interests taken into account in deciding which programs and activities will be implemented and who will be assigned to implement which ones?

THE WHOLE IS GREATER THAN THE SUM OF THE PARTS

At the outset of this book, we suggested that one of the most distinctive features of comprehensive after-school centers is the potential for different facets of a youth's experience within such settings to combine synergistically, so that the whole of their impact ends up being greater than the sum of the parts. In our findings, the strongest evidence in support of this possibility involves collective mentoring. We first observed and highlighted this process, in which multiple staff collaborate and assume shared responsibility for a youth's development, in our case study of Pocahontas. It will be recalled how staff at Midwest worked in concert to foster a familial-like environment that made the site a "second home" for her. Now in West River, we see how Midnight similarly receives reinforcing messages and guidance from multiple staff there. In his case, the benefits of collective mentoring seem to fall in the areas of prevention (avoiding risk behaviors), support for involvement with younger club members, and messages of concern for his welfare. Pocahontas and Midnight provide our best exemplars of collective mentoring.

We should note, however, that even in these instances there is a general absence of overt coordination or planning among the staff involved. Rather, the reinforcing and complementary nature of their actions seems to be primarily a by-product of more indirect processes. For Pocahontas, these include the opportunities for reinforcing validation and support from different staff that arise in response to the many instances in which she helps out around the club. For Midnight, the emphasis on active promotion of youth development that infuses the broader staff culture at West River appears to be similarly influential. We suspect that more intentional and direct efforts at collective mentoring by after-school center staff also can have significant value and, in some circumstances, will be a necessity for fully addressing a youth's needs. Yet, in view of our current findings, we would caution against discounting those situations in which such mentoring develops more organically within the activities and culture of an after-school center.

In other instances, we were forced to speculate as to what might have been possible had greater collective mentoring occurred. In our chapters focused on North River, for example, we noted ways in which greater dialogue and sharing of information among staff at the center could have proved beneficial for both Beyonce and Tweetie. Our studies of Midnight and Tomianna at West River elaborate on this theme by highlighting the potential value of unrealized linkages between staff and those adults who have important roles in the lives of these youth outside of the club. A more encompassing perspective on collective mentoring would include ties that exist outside of the center and broaden the scope of potential practices to support them. Most prior research has been limited to consideration of the effects of mentoring that a youth receives from a single adult.[4] When ties with multiple staff in after-school centers have been examined, measures have not addressed the extent to which these are likely to fit with our concept of collective mentoring.[5] Accordingly, a prime topic for future research is to assess the mentoring that youth who attend comprehensive after-school centers receive in a more coordinated and holistic sense and the conditions under which such mentoring offers unique value.

A second type of synergy that is suggested by our findings involves the potentially interdependent and cumulative effects of a youth's involvements in multiple positive (or negative) PARCs at an after-school center. This possibility was first touched on when considering the experiences of Pocahontas and Bill at the Midwest club. We noted how each youth experiences both a core PARC and a range of other opportunities to demonstrate responsibility and make a meaningful contribution at the center and that it seems unlikely the benefits associated with either would be as great in the absence of the other. At West River, Tomianna has PARCs revolving around her participation in dance and Smart Girls. In this instance, the benefits we see may be dependent on the same staff person (Victoria) leading the activities that define each of the PARCs as well as their complementary features.

Although the prior examples all focus on positive synergies, we have seen also the potential for multiple, negative facets of a youth's experiences within a center to compound one another in ways that seem likely to heighten their overall impact. The manner in which the effects of Beyonce's negative relationship with Scottie are exacerbated by the limited opportunities for youth to choose their own

---

[4] Keller & Blakeslee (in press).
[5] See, for example, Arbreton (2009).

activities at Midwest comes to mind as one salient example of this phenomenon. It would be a mistake, we think, to not give balanced attention to both the good and the bad when it comes to synergistic processes in comprehensive after-school settings.[6]

Potential synergies are by no means definitively addressed within our findings. The phenomena of interest here tend to operate at a relatively complex, systems level of analysis. Because of this, they are inherently more difficult to pin down. And, as we have noted, such processes have received very limited attention in prior research on after-school centers or, for that matter, on youth programs more generally. We thus acknowledge that our conclusions in this area are especially tentative and preliminary. Taken in their entirety, however, they suggest the value of taking a holistic approach when seeking to engineer positive and beneficial experiences for youth within comprehensive after-school centers. At a practical level, this might include a focus on supporting a youth's overall PARC profile to include multiple PARCs (either at the same time or in a sequence) that would be expected to be growth-inducing for that young person.

FINDING AND DEVELOPING STRONG STAFF

Like many, if not most, enterprises, our findings underscore the reality that comprehensive after-school centers are "operator dependent." That is, the extent to which centers achieve desired outcomes with youth appears likely to be a function in significant part of their ability to both find and develop strong staff. The centers involved in our research are consistent in their emphasis on hiring staff from the surrounding community. As in our prior research,[7] we find that such staff tend to relate well to youth and are able to mentor them in ways that convey a first-hand appreciation for the circumstances that they face in their lives outside of the center. Our consideration of Tomianna's relationship with Victoria at West River suggests, too, that staff who have strong ties to the youth's community may be especially well-positioned to serve as potent role models.

---

[6] A recurring finding throughout many different areas of research, in fact, is that negative aspects of human experience carry more influence than those that are positive (Baumeister, Bratslavsky, Finkenauer, & Vohs, 2001).

[7] Hirsch (2005).

There are two weaknesses that stand out in what we observe in terms of staff hiring at the centers. The first is that they do little to intentionally leverage, to strategic advantage, the connections that their staff have to the surrounding community. The social ties that many staff already have with the families of youth attending the center, as seen with both Midnight and Tomianna at West River, seem especially ripe for greater utilization. The second is that the centers pay little attention to the interests and hobbies of potential hires that could be drawn on as the foundation for new activities. One of the most successful activities or programs we found, for example, was the chess club at Midwest, which was based on the love of chess that Manuel brought with him to the club. There likely are any number of staff interests that could correspondingly be drawn on to enrich center offerings.[8] Hiring staff who bring such interests with them to the site could be a priority; this strategy can be especially valuable when opportunities for training are limited, as the adults would already know the activity well and have enthusiasm for it.

Indeed, we see only limited attention to staff training and development across the three centers. West River does the most in this regard. In this club, job shadowing is a component of the initial training of all staff. The director and second-in-command devote considerable time and energy to the ongoing supervision and evaluation of staff. They are not reluctant, moreover, to dismiss those who they find to not be measuring up. Even here, though, we see a number of significant limitations. Training is limited in scope and restricted to "on boarding" new staff.[9] Supervision of staff, furthermore, lacks a clearly defined structure (e.g., regularly scheduled meetings), and staff evaluations seem largely impressionistic and based predominantly, if not exclusively, on the observations of club administrators.

---

[8] This is similar to the approach of After School Matters, a prominent after-school program for high school students in Chicago (http://www.afterschoolmatters. org; Hirsch, Hedges, Stawicki, & Mekinda, 2011). After School Matters hires those who have high-level skills in a certain activity or profession and trains them how to work with youth. They do not need to train them in the activity – potential staff members bring that with them. This reduces training costs and increases the breadth of activities that can be offered. Also see the case study of Region 7 middle school for a very interesting use of this approach in a school setting, where teachers frequently taught mini-courses reflecting their own personal interests and hobbies (Lipsitz, 1984).

[9] For research supporting the value of ongoing training for staff and volunteers within youth programs, see DuBois, Holloway, Valentine, & Cooper (2002).

It is striking, in fact, how little attention is paid in any of these centers to staff development. By and large, it appears that administrators, such as Joe Bryant at West River, believe that you either have a talent for working with youth or you do not. Supervision, in this model, is primarily to make sure that you do what you are capable of doing. There is little thought or action directed to raising staff capabilities. One cannot help but wonder if the modest attention to staff development suggests real limits to the extent to which centers such as these can focus on promoting youth development. Should not these processes go in parallel? Can one really push the limits of youth development while giving so little priority to the potential for staff to develop – and the need for staff development in order to enhance the quality of programs and activities?

It is not as if there is no knowledge to access. There are human resource practices that are relatively commonplace in fields such as business and education that could serve as a model. Corporations, for example, have found it useful to make arrangements for newer, less experienced employees to be mentored by those who are more experienced, but not in a supervisory role.[10] When the performance of an employee is found to be lacking in one or more areas in a business setting, it is also typical for a "performance improvement plan" to be developed as a first course of action prior to contemplating dismissal of the employee. In schools, it is standard practice for teachers to be coached and evaluated based on formal observations of their instructional practices. And, in many more innovative educational settings, teachers are asked to prepare portfolios that include statements of their instructional philosophy and samples of key work products. Had some of these practices been in place at the centers we studied, we might have seen less unevenness in key barometers of quality such as program implementation and mentoring, not to mention less staff turnover, all of which would be expected to ultimately strengthen youth outcomes.

We do not intend to suggest that after-school centers will be best served by mimicking the human resource practices of business or education. But there is no compelling rationale to put on blinders either. Practices in widespread use in other settings, when adapted

---

[10] A meta-analysis found that career-related mentoring was associated with both subjective (e.g., job satisfaction) and objective (e.g., promotions) benefits for protégés (Allen, Eby, Poteet, Lentz, & Lima, 2004).

appropriately, could be of significant value. There is room and need for much more reflection on how to develop after-school staff as resources. Directions for after-school centers to improve in this area are explored further in the next chapter.

LEARNING AND GROWING AS AN ORGANIZATION

As with other centers, we see that organizational learning is generally not in evidence at West River. Job shadowing is the most noteworthy exception. This practice, however, as noted earlier, serves primarily a training function. As a one-shot activity that occurs only during the staff on-boarding process, we doubt that it goes very far in fostering critical reflection and dialogue among staff. The absence of sharp points of contrast across the clubs in this area again somewhat limits the strength of the conclusions we are able to draw from our data. Nonetheless, our findings do highlight multiple instances in which a lack of structure or practices to support organizational learning seems to limit the capacity of centers to be responsive to factors that are hindering their effectiveness.

It will be recalled, for example, that at both the Midwest and North River centers there seem to be "blind spots" regarding some issues that are clearly having a negative impact on the broader cultures of these clubs. At Midwest, the director seems not to appreciate the damage to staff morale that is engendered by either his focus on outreach or his dismissive response to many of the staff's programming initiatives. At North River, neither leadership nor staff seem to have a good handle on the culture of the negativity that permeates the setting or the pernicious effects it has on areas such as staff collaboration and support for youth initiatives. At West River, too, we see that some staff feel the center as a whole is not sufficiently responsive to youth agency and voice. From an organizational learning perspective, the "truth" of such perceptions is not necessarily a primary concern. Rather, what would be most important is the institutionalization of processes that allow the varying perspectives and experiences of leadership, staff, and youth to come to light and then be used as a basis for exploring potential courses of action.

We see considerable evidence, too, to suggest the value of organizational learning for strengthening programming within after-school centers. There are clearly significant shortcomings in program offerings and implementation at both the Midwest and North River clubs. West River is not immune from these either. Even though Torch Club and Keystone are designed with a focus on promoting youth leadership and initiative, their implementation at West River falls short of this ideal (as it does at the other clubs as well). There is little, if any, effort to systematically collect data that might bring such concerns to the attention of leadership at any of the centers. Nor do staff meetings (or any other venue) provide a viable forum for critical dialogue or reflection in this area. If such avenues for organizational learning had been available, they could have served as a catalyst for strengthening programs to support academic achievement – an area of weakness within all of the centers. They also could have facilitated reflection on relatively more nuanced issues, such as the dynamics that account for differences in the success of programs and activities that on the surface may have similar characteristics. Why is it, for example, that dance is one of the most popular and well-respected programs at West River, whereas another activity with a strong competitive dimension, the Miss West River contest, proves highly problematic for at least some youth (Tomianna)? Keeping in mind that chess is a similarly successful, but also competitive activity at the Midwest center, we see value in reflective discussions about this complex topic.

In the context of discussing collective mentoring earlier in this chapter, we noted the potential value of more deliberate and intentional collaboration among after-school center staff in their work with particular youth. One way to do this would be to develop a stronger shared understanding among staff of how to support youth with similar needs or interests. At North River, for example, had other youth such as Beyonce with social skills concerns been identified, staff might have profited from sharing their observations of these youth and their ideas for how to offer them effective mentoring. At West River, the same potential for staff collaboration exists in relation to understanding and addressing the needs of older youth such as Midnight.

As noted, considering the relative absence of organizational learning activity within the clubs we studied, our findings can offer only indirect support for its capacity to bolster the quality and effectiveness of comprehensive after-school centers. In keeping with the conceptual framework presented in Chapter 1, however, we are confident in asserting that cultural, programmatic, and relational features of after-school centers are all likely to be important areas of focus when mounting improvement efforts under the auspices of organizational learning. As our discussion now moves to consideration of recommendations for practice, these intersecting influences will continue to be salient points of reference.

CONCLUSION

14

Recommendations for Improving Practice

In this book we have seen wonderful after-school staff such as Manuel and Victoria who mentored young people and established high-quality programs in chess and dance. We also became acquainted with Mateo, to whom youth were attracted but who spent too much time taking it easy rather than capitalizing on his popularity to actively mentor or develop new programs. As we slide further and further away from excellence, we come to North River, where the director's obsession with order and authority thwarted youth development and led to a revolt by the basketball team and cheer-leaders. In thinking about how to improve after-school centers, we need to consider how to push and coach staff like Mateo so that they become more like Manuel and Victoria. We also need to set up mechanisms to ensure that fundamental changes are made at centers like North River and that even good centers like West River can achieve a higher order of excellence.

In the remainder of this chapter we outline a strategy for continuous quality improvement for after-school centers that grows out of our research and reflects the broad conclusions presented in the last chapter. Given the nature of our approach, it should come as no surprise that we emphasize organizational-level initiatives for staff development and program improvement. An organizational response has the potential to benefit the most staff and youth and thus gives the biggest possible bang for the buck. This approach creates structures and processes that make strategic use of staff strengths that we have seen in these centers, rather than relying on pricey consultants. It is based on organizational learning strategies that have been successfully employed in other social service, educational, and health settings, and tailors them to the after-school world.

TABLE 14.1. *Recommendations for improving practice*

1. Have a strong, explicit focus on promoting positive youth development
2. Conduct regular reviews of youth progress, including intensive case conferences
3. Encourage collective mentoring
4. Use training sessions as a means of promoting reflective dialogue among staff
5. Have staff observe other good after-school programs to learn more about best practices
6. Form youth councils to make sure youth voice is heard
7. Schedule regular external reviews and site visits
8. Require leadership to engage in regular supervision and coaching

We put our recommendations together as an integrative strategy designed around the goal of promoting positive youth development. Together, the recommendations guide organizations toward powerful collaborations among staff through regular communication about youth progress, the practice of collective mentoring, and thoughtful discussion of approaches to working with youth. The recommendations should also inspire the ongoing reflection on and improvement of practice through solicitation of youth perspectives, observation of other quality programs, and regular site visits and feedback from external reviewers. Of course, to be successful, the strategy depends on the leadership and guidance of program administrators and supervisors.

The strategy will work well if staff have good training opportunities, but is also well suited for centers that lack such opportunities, where training is infrequent or not all that good. Frankly, the latter is what we found at these three sites and we suspect that it is much more common than suggested in public relations reports from segments of the after-school community. So either way, if training is good or bad, frequent or rare, we think these recommendations can improve the quality of practice.

We have sought to keep this concluding chapter brief and focused to maximize its potential impact on after-school program practices. Our specific recommendations are summarized in Table 14.1.

HAVE A STRONG, EXPLICIT FOCUS ON PROMOTING POSITIVE YOUTH DEVELOPMENT

In the business world or in education, benchmark goals can be more easily specified, such as increasing profits or market share, or improving graduation rates, attendance, or test scores. There is nothing so clear-cut in the after-school world. Yes, these centers, and many others across the country and the rest of the world, say they subscribe to a positive youth development model. But too often, as we have seen in this book, in practice this has translated into keeping kids under control or – a bit of an improvement – enabling them to have fun. And if attendance stays at acceptable levels, doesn't that mean that we're doing a good job?

By contrast, several staff at West River engaged young people in activities that challenged them to improve their skills and confidence. Staff like Manuel mentored them so that they set goals and made important strides in their life. What we have seen in these instances should be the standard across the board. The driving force for each program and center, the beacon for staff efforts, should be to promote development.

You do not need to hire a developmental psychologist as a consultant to determine what constitutes development. Reading what has been written, such as in any decent college textbook, is not a bad idea, but need not be the first step. Center leaders and staff already know a lot about young people. They should just ask some simple questions: Is this young person getting better at something? Growing more psychologically resilient? Getting along with peers and adults? Learning new skills and exploring potential new interests? Doing well in school? Becoming more responsible and mature?

In short, the focus should be on whether a young person is maturing and growing, becoming more competent and prepared for the future as time goes by. We have great confidence that the staff at these centers, and others like them, are quite capable of making these judgments. But they need to become focused on the objective of promoting positive youth development and think about it constantly. If they do so, that focus will inevitably lead to a concern for action. To promote positive youth development, staff need to be proactive. This will mean a change in the culture of centers such as Midwest and North River. Being proactive means not waiting until there is a problem to take action. Being proactive means anticipating what will be helpful and taking action accordingly. It means taking this approach with individual youth, programs, and the center as a whole.

Staff need to regularly assess youth progress. They need to offer programs and activities that are both challenging and supportive.

They need to seek out and cultivate mentoring relationships. They need to assess the availability of complete, positive PARCs. Thus, centers need to focus on the overarching goal of promoting positive youth development and work proactively to achieve it. Our remaining recommendations focus on how centers can best achieve these goals.

CONDUCT REGULAR REVIEWS OF YOUTH PROGRESS, INCLUDING INTENSIVE CASE CONFERENCES

From what we heard from staff at all three of these centers, staff meetings focused almost exclusively on operational details. Meetings with such an agenda are necessary. But if centers are to commit to a focus on positive youth development, they need to create a culture of staff learning and continuous improvement. If staff are focused on promoting positive youth development, they will need – and want – to keep getting better at what they do, so that they can better help young people. For that, new types of meetings will be crucial. These meetings should focus on reviewing the progress of a select group of youth on important indices of youth development (such as those specified in the prior section). This review should include an action plan to move each young person forward, to help the youth make important gains over the next specified time period. The role of various staff members in helping implement the action plan for each young person should be considered (more on this shortly when we discuss collective mentoring). As these meeting are conducted on a regular basis, part of the review will naturally focus on the success of the plans formulated at the last meeting. Staff need to focus not merely on what they can learn from this review to help a particular young person, but also on what those reviews tell them about how well they are doing more generally in assessing youth, developing strong action plans, and implementing these plans effectively.

In many settings, there will be too many youth to review all of them, even over several meetings. In such instances, staff can select representatives of certain types of youth along dimensions such as gender and age, personality and interests (e.g., the quiet ones, the best athletes or artists), and areas of need (e.g., those who are not doing well academically) and review them with the aim of generalizing from those examples to the broader group of young people to whom they are similar.

It is important to review a good number of youth so that the center actively promotes positive development on a broad front. At the same time, we believe that it will be important to use some of these reviews as opportunities for intensive staff learning and development, so on some occasions the meetings should focus on just one or two young people. These latter meetings are generally referred to as case conferences. They are used extensively in graduate health and counseling training programs (among others). Rather than operations, the focus is on brainstorming how to understand particular young people, the effectiveness of their PARCs and PARC profile, and planning for their development. Staff in a real sense become researchers, striving to improve their understanding of young people and of what it takes to design and implement effective action plans.

Caution: It will be easy to fall into a trap of looking at things in the same old way rather than considering fresh perspectives and new approaches. Every group develops a certain way of thinking about things, and it can be hard to break out of that mold. This was true at the Midwest center where they had difficulty appreciating some of Bill's concerns that fell outside of their stereotypical way of viewing strong young guys.

We ourselves experienced some of this groupthink when we conducted case conferences on the youth who we ultimately presented in this book. We decided that the best way to avoid this trap was to designate one of us as a sort of "devil's advocate" who would purposefully challenge assumptions, demand supporting evidence, question the benefit of proposed action plans, and so on. It may be helpful to the group if different staff play the role of devil's advocate during different sessions. This minimizes the psychological burden of playing this role repeatedly and gets all staff used to encouraging out-of-the-box thinking. As the group realizes its blind spots in how it thinks about youth, programming, or mentoring, it can develop a checklist of these that it could routinely go over at subsequent meetings to make sure that it is not falling into the same old traps once again.

ENCOURAGE COLLECTIVE MENTORING

Staff need to learn together, plan together, and act together on behalf of youth. We have identified collective mentoring as an important process by which this can occur. Collective mentoring was most evident for Pocahontas and appeared to play a major role in her growth over the year. At the opposite end, at North River, had Sharon and Scottie talked over their experiences and responses to Beyonce, Scottie might have found the impetus and insight needed to change his behavior, and Beyonce might have had a much more positive experience at the center and made more developmental gains.

The potential for collective mentoring should routinely be explored. Certainly this should be a regular feature of youth review and planning sessions. But staff should not wait for formal meetings, especially when they are frustrated with a particular young person. Identify who has the best relationship with that youth and problem-solve together on best approaches. Collective mentoring is likely to work best when staff members approach discussions with an open mind and a readiness to question their assumptions and behavior in working with a particular young person. It is an axiom of human services work that no helper can be fully objective in understanding a client or evaluating their work with that person. Youth workers are not immune to this principle and should engage with others accordingly. It may be useful, too, when disagreements are salient, to adopt an "experimenting" mindset and agree to try out approaches that reflect one or the other person's perspective.

USE TRAINING SESSIONS AS A MEANS OF PROMOTING REFLECTIVE DIALOGUE AMONG STAFF

Reflective dialogue among teachers has been found to be a key element of ambitious school reform efforts[1] and it should be an important part of the youth review sessions and case conferences just discussed. Reflective dialogue among staff about how to best promote positive youth development should be encouraged and any number of occasions should be examined for their potential to further this organizational objective.

Discussing training sessions after participation provides an important opportunity for reflective dialogue. At the Midwest club, we saw that Juan and Manuel had very different reactions

---

[1] Elmore, Peterson, & McCarthey (1996); Gamoran, Anderson, Quiroz, Secada, Williams, & Ashman (2003); McLaughlin & Talbert (2001); Newman & Associates (1996).

to a training session on counseling skills. Juan did not see himself as a counselor or recognize the value of those skills, whereas Manuel was intrigued by their potential value (see Chapter 2). Rather than just conveying a thumbs-up or thumbs-down, they could have talked about and fleshed out their different perspectives in ways that might increase their mutual understanding of youth and, if they remain at odds (which is not necessarily a bad thing), how they might still complement each other's approach in working with specific youth. In some instances, the post-session reflective dialogue may be more important than anything presented during the session. This may especially be true when the available training leaves much to be desired, which was certainly true for staff at these centers.

Although there was little reflective dialogue at any of the centers we studied, we believe that it is crucial to a staff culture that focuses on constantly improving its ability to promote positive youth development. Even at West River, the best of these three centers, there was room for improving staff practice and for improving organizational practice beyond firing weak staff.

HAVE STAFF OBSERVE OTHER GOOD AFTER-SCHOOL PROGRAMS TO LEARN MORE ABOUT BEST PRACTICES

There is nothing like seeing with your own eyes how someone good in your field goes about doing his or her work to give you ideas about how to improve your own practice. It is one thing to read about what someone does, and another to hear that person talk about it, but nothing compares to seeing it live. Sometimes what someone actually does is different than what the person says they do. And when you see it live you can be attentive to all of the subtle cues to which people might be responding and using in their communication. Actually seeing something in action may also convince you that this approach is worth trying out and that you, too, are capable of doing something similar. Thus, observation has motivational as well as informational value.

This kind of observational learning is fundamental in medicine and similar fields, where doctors will observe a surgical procedure or an experienced physician interviewing a patient, or even, as some of this book's authors have done, watch a skilled psychotherapist behind a one-way mirror. A picture can well be worth a thousand words, and after-school centers should seek out such rich learning and motivational opportunities.

Once again, to draw optimal benefit from such experiences, upon returning to home base, the staff should meet to reflect on the value of what they observed and how it might be applied at their center.

FORM YOUTH COUNCILS TO MAKE SURE YOUTH VOICE IS HEARD

High-quality programs, activities, and relationships need to be fostered if after-school centers are to effectively promote positive youth development. Having access to the perspectives of youth – in terms of their personal goals and for how life should be at the center – is essential for evaluation and planning.[2] Youth perspectives can also act as a check and balance on staff blind spots and biases. As just noted with regard to the importance of dialogue among staff, it is human nature that these blind spots and biases will exist, and it is to be expected that some will be shared across staff.

Once again, staff will need to engage in reflective dialogue, both with youth and among themselves, in response to input from youth councils. This will not always be easy. As much as adult staff in youth programs may subscribe to (or acquiesce in) rhetoric about youth voice or empowerment, the reality of having young people advocate for something you don't want can pose a difficult challenge to staff and leadership. Centers will need to work on developing their capacity to respond effectively to the councils and make them a productive part of a continuous improvement process.

SCHEDULE REGULAR EXTERNAL REVIEWS AND SITE VISITS

Even for a well-functioning center such as West River, regular (every few years external reviews of the site) can lead to important gains. The process of preparing for the review and site visit can focus administrators and staff like nothing else on strengths and weaknesses. The site visit team should have access to center leadership,

---

[2] Zeldin (2004), Zeldin, Camino, & Mook (2005), and Kirshner (2008) have done interesting researching on youth participation in decision making in different types of organizations.

staff, and youth, as well as to parents and important external players. For these three centers, that would have involved the regional Boys & Girls Club headquarters. Major funders should also be interviewed. The review team should prepare a written report, with recommendations, to the center. As the center reflects on and responds in writing to the report, there is a great opportunity for learning and organizational development. Each year the center should evaluate its progress to meet the goals and implementation standards identified in its response to the outside review.

Of course, for a center such as North River, an outside review and site visit can be the last resort to protect the interests of young people. The youth there desperately needed outside intervention to halt and reverse the culture of negativity that worked against positive youth development.

REQUIRE LEADERSHIP TO ENGAGE IN REGULAR SUPERVISION AND COACHING

Successful implementation in after-school centers involves making sure that programs, activities, and mentoring work as intended. This means that leadership will need to actively supervise staff, assessing the quality of their work with youth and coaching them on how to improve their skills.[3] In schools, this has been referred to as instructional leadership and has been thought to be of fundamental importance to improving student outcomes.[4] We have known many after-school administrators who have the knowledge and experience to do this kind of supervision, and it needs to be made a standard part of their job.

Of course, staff can and should learn from each other as well; the role of the supervisor in this instance is making sure this happens and, when appropriate, arranging for one staff member to seek out another who has the needed expertise. For example, a good supervisor at North River would have made sure that Scottie talked with Sharon about how to understand and work with Beyonce.

---

[3] Supervision is receiving increased attention in the after-school world (e.g., Wilson-Ahlstrom & Yohalem, 2010; Burkhauser & Metz, 2009; Collins & Metz, 2009; Garza, Borden, & Astroth, 2004). For similar ideas of supervision within a learning organization context, see Austin & Hopkins (2004).

[4] Blase & Blase (1998).

For those centers seeking to implement our recommendations, supervisors will play a critical role in making sure that action plans that grow out of youth review sessions, case conferences, or external reviews are implemented well and sustained over time. In this instance, they would manage the process and emphasize the importance of follow-through.

It will be important to hire or promote individuals to supervisory positions who have – or can be expected to acquire – the requisite skills.

CONCLUSION

Comprehensive after-school centers can provide multiple opportunities for learning and development. In the field's initial phase of research on these sites, the focus has largely been on exemplary programs and, more recently, on overall evaluations of effectiveness. It is now time to take a more in-depth approach, to take a sympathetic yet critical view, to examine not only successes but also failures and the many instances in between, where some good has been done but outcomes fell short of their potential. In this final chapter, we have recommended a coordinated series of steps that after-school centers can take to do a better job of promoting positive youth development. We have emphasized focusing more sharply on youth development and using their own staff as resources to learn how to more effectively design and implement high-quality programs, activities, and mentoring relationships.

In looking at these three centers overall, we find the glass to be both half-full and half-empty. We need to appreciate that much good work is being done. At the same time, there is much room for improvement. Both of these are important to remember.

APPENDIX

Data Sources

OVERVIEW

Site Visits

- *Ethnographic Observations*: Trained members of the research team visited each club to conduct ethnographic observations, typically two times a week, beginning in September and continuing through the end of the school year in June. Observers recorded detailed field notes after each visit (see Field Note Template later in this appendix). Each field note included the team member's observations and reflections as well as an account of any conversations with youth or staff. The principal investigator (Hirsch) reviewed the field notes on an ongoing basis. Developments or issues that might benefit from additional investigation were highlighted for follow-up during subsequent visits to the club.
- *Social Climate Ratings*: Following each visit to a club, the research team member involved completed ratings of the social climate of the club on several different dimensions, such as cooperation and conflict among staff and youth enjoyment and participation in decision making (see Field Note Template later in this appendix).

All Youth Attending Each Center

- *Youth Background Questionnaire*: This questionnaire was completed at the start of the year by all youth at each of the clubs who were ten years of age or older. The survey included questions

307

that asked youth for basic demographic information, their levels and history of participation in the club, how safe they felt in their neighborhoods, and whether they experienced the club setting as a "second home." Each youth also was asked on the survey to identify the staff person at the center with whom he or she had the closest relationship.

Sample of Thirty Youth Selected for Intensive Study*

- *Youth Interview #1*: Youth were asked questions about their background and life outside of the after-school center.
- *Photography Project*: Youth took pictures to show what was important to them in different part of their lives both inside and outside of the club; youth then were interviewed about the photographs they had taken.
- *Social Network Map*: Youth drew a map of their social networks and were asked several questions about each network member, such as the person's age and gender and whether they saw the person at the after-school center.
- *Time Lines*: Youth created visual timelines of significant events in their lives both inside and outside of the after-school center.
- *Structured Observations*: As part of their visits to the after-school centers, research team members conducted structured observations of interactions that youth in the intensive study sample had with staff at the centers.
- *Youth Interview #2*: Youth were asked about their relationships with different staff members at the club, with a particular focus on each youth's tie with the staff person to whom he or she felt the closest at the center.
- *Youth Interview #3*: Youth were administered standardized scales to assess their attitudes and experiences in a variety of areas, such as self-esteem, relationships with peers and adults, and aspirations for the future.
- *Youth Interview #4*: Completed at the end of the school year. Youth were asked about benefits they had derived from attending the after-school center, current grades in school, and an assortment of other topics that had not been addressed in prior interviews.

---

* This sample includes the six youth who were subsequently selected to be the focus of the in-depth case studies that are included in this book.

Primary Staff Members

- *Staff Interview #1*: Staff were asked about their personal backgrounds, including whether they grew up in a neighborhood similar to the ones served by the center, as well as their education and history of employment at the club and other youth organizations.
- *Staff Interview #2*: Staff were asked for their perspectives on different aspects of the club's organizational characteristics, such as administrative leadership and levels of staff cooperation and conflict.
- *Staff Interview #3*: Staff were asked about their relationships with each youth from the intensive study sample who had identified him/her as the staff person to whom they felt closest at the after-school center.

FIELD NOTE TEMPLATE

Researcher:
Time (beginning and ending):
Club:
Date:

Executive Summary:

Social Climate Codes:
Research team members coded the presence or absence of each of the facets of social climate listed below.

1a___ / b___. INTERSTAFF support/cooperation VS conflict/lack of cooperation

2a___/ b ___. STAFF positive remarks VS complaints (club/youth related)

3a___ / b___. STAFF engagement/enthusiasm VS low involvement or negativity

4a___/ b___. YOUTH enjoyment VS boredom, going through the motions

5a___/ b___. YOUTH participation in decision making VS staff autocratic

6a ___/ b___. STAFF OR YOUTH (attempted) enforcement of club rules

7a___/b ___ .YOUTH positive remarks VS complaints (re: club, staff, club youth)

8a___/b ___ .STAFF discuss youth's parent(s) w/youth OR parents at club

General Field Notes:

YOUTH BACKGROUND QUESTIONNAIRE

1. Age: _____ Date of Birth [month/day/year]: _____
2. Gender: Male; Female
3. Please check the box of the ethnic group(s) you belong to (check all that apply): Black/African American; White; Hispanic; Asian American
4. Do you get free or reduced lunches at school? Yes; No
5. Is this the first year that you have attended this Club? Yes; No
   (a) If No, how old were you when first came to the Club?
6. How many days a week do you usually come to the Club? 1–2; 2–3; 3–4; 4–5
7. How long do you usually stay each day at the Club? Less than 1 hour; 1–2 hours; 2–4 hours; more than 4 hours
8. Please check how safe you feel in your neighborhood. Very safe; Somewhat safe; Not very safe; Not safe at all.
9. Please check how your last report card was. Mostly A's & B's; Mostly B's & C's; Mostly C's & D's; Mostly D's & F's
10. What are some of your favorite activities at the Club?
11. Of all the staff in the Boys and Girls Club, circle the name of the staff who is the closest to you. (By "closest" we mean the staff who you can count on the most, who cares the most about you and how you are doing, who inspires you to do your best, and who has the most influence on the choices you make.)
12. Some kids have described the Club as a "second home" to them. Other kids do not seem to think of the Club as a home. Would you describe the Club as a "home" to you? Yes; No.

YOUTH INTERVIEW #1

1. Which school do you go to?
2. How far away is that from your home (e.g., in minutes & blocks)? How long does it take for you to get there? How do you get there?

3. What grade are you in?
4. What grades are in your school (e.g., K–8, 6–8, 9–12, etc.)?
5. How many teachers do you have for your main academic subjects (i.e., not counting gym, art, etc.)?
6. What are your favorite subjects (e.g., academic subjects such as math, science, English, etc.)? How come?
7. Which subjects do you like the least? How come?
8. Starting with when you began first grade, how many schools have you attended? [If more than two schools, ask: Have you moved around a lot?]
9. What kinds of things do you like to do outside of school? What kinds of hobbies, favorite activities, or pastimes do you have? What kinds of things do you do on the weekends?
10. What do you like to do with your friends?
11. Do most of your friends come to the club or are most of your friends from outside the club? [If friends are from outside of the club, then ask: do you have a different set of friends at the club? If so, how are your friends at the club and your friends from outside of the club different? Are there reasons why your friends from outside of the club do not come to the club?]
12. Are gangs or violence a problem in your neighborhood? How?
13. Have any of the following happened to you (or someone in your family) in the last year? [For events that have happened ask, as appropriate, who, what, when, where, and/or why.] Events: Death of a close friend or relative; Serious illness; Problems with money or losing a job; Separation or divorce in family; Victim of crime; Moving to another city or country; Change in school; New family member of someone getting pregnant; Suspended/dropped out/expelled from school; Problems with the law.
14. Who lives at home with you? [Ask for approximate ages.]
15. Who usually takes care of you? [Is that person usually home when you get home from school or the club? Is that person generally home when you are or usually gone (i.e., at work)?]
16. If the youth has siblings, then ask: Do any of your siblings come to the club or did they used to come to the club? [If yes, what are or were the siblings' experiences of coming to the club? If the siblings stopped coming to the club, why did they stop?]

17. If the youth has siblings, then ask: Do you have to take care of any of them? Do you have to take care of anyone else? [How often? Do you enjoy taking care of them?]
18. Which adult in your life, other than your parents or guardian, are you closest to? [Why is this person important to you? How do you know this person? How long have you known this person? What kinds of things do you do with this person? What kinds of things do you talk about with this person? What do you like about this person?]
19. Can you think of a time when you tried to talk to someone and that person really listened or helped you out? [Can you tell me about that or give me an example? How did that make you feel? Did that situation affect your relationship with that person?]
20. Can you think of a time when you tried to talk to someone and that person did not really listen? [Can you tell me about that or give me an example? How did that make you feel? Did that situation affect your relationship with that person?]
21. Who do you think has the greatest influence on your life? Why? How?
22. What is something that has happened in your life that makes you really proud?
23. What is the most upsetting thing that has happened in your life?
24. What do you like the most about yourself?
25. What do you like the least about yourself?
26. What is your favorite or best memory?

PHOTOGRAPHY PROJECT

Youth were provided a disposable camera and given a sheet of instructions that asked them to take photographs relating to different areas of their life and interests both inside and outside of the after-school center. The specific guidelines given to youth were as follows:

Inside the After-School Center

Take four pictures. The pictures can be kids or staff who you like, your favorite places in the club, activities that you enjoy or that are important to you.

Outside of the After-School Center

Take one picture each of:

- an adult who you are close to
- a friend who you are close to
- something you enjoy doing
- a group of people who are important to you
- somewhere you like to spend time alone
- the building where you live
- a place that you like in your neighborhood
- a place that you don't like in your neighborhood

Youth were encouraged to use the remaining pictures to show people, places, activities, and so forth that would help further share who they were and the story of their lives.

Two sets of each youth's pictures were developed, one for the youth to keep (and an album in which the pictures could be placed) and the second for use in the research. Each youth then completed a semi-structured interview in which they were asked to describe each photo, their motivation for taking it, and how it was related to things that were important to them inside or outside of the after-school center. The complete interview protocol is available upon request.

SOCIAL NETWORK MAP

Youth were asked to draw a "map" of their social network (a procedure adapted from Hirsch, 1980). They were instructed to draw maps of youth and adults who were significant parts of their lives both inside and outside of the after-school center. Youth were asked to identify how close they were to different network members visually by placing the initials of persons to whom they were closer near their own initials and those of more casual acquaintances farther away. They were also asked to identify the following characteristics for each network member (recorded on a separate page by the interviewer):

- Name
- Age (if younger than 25)
- Gender

- Age when person was first met
- Closeness to the person (on a scale of 1–5: 1 = not at all, 5 = extremely)
- How the youth knows the person (family, friend, club, church, etc.) and, if family, what relation.
- If from the club, whether the person is a club member, staff, volunteer, or mentor.

TIME LINES

With facilitation of a research team member, each youth made time lines to represent major experiences and relationships over the course of his or her attendance at the center and during his or her life overall. Each time line was constructed on a large sheet of paper, with grades in school written on the bottom starting with kindergarten and going up through the youth's current grade. Running down the left-hand side of the sheet were five categories. For the club time line, the categories were attendance, good, bad, activities, and staff. For the life time line, the categories were events, good, bad, activities, and friends. Youth were given different colored slips of papers to write on (representing the different categories on the left-hand side of the page), which they then pasted onto the sheet according to category and time period in which they happened. Probes were used to help elicit information within each category of the time lines.

STRUCTURED OBSERVATIONS

Research team members conducted up to two structured observations of interactions between staff and youth in the study sample during each of their visits to the clubs. The observation periods were selected purposefully to capture episodes of interaction that were judged to be noteworthy and that, whenever possible, involved interactions between one or more study youth and the staff person(s) with whom they reported being closest to at the after-school center. During each observation period, youth-staff interactions were coded for the presence of thirty-eight different characteristics within the broader domains of Content (e.g., school, peer relationships), Process (e.g., instruction, behavior management), Setting (e.g., informal, psycho-educational program), and Relationship Development (e.g., shared past experiences, current relationship). These characteristics were coded separately for the interactions of staff with each study youth who was present during an observation period. In doing so, interactions were differentiated according to whether they were directed toward an entire group, the target youth, or other youth. The full coding guidelines are available upon request.

Youth's Closest Relationship with Staff Member

1. I'd like to begin by asking you for a general description of [primary staff at club]. I'm going to ask what you like and dislike about each of them. [Ask what youth likes and dislikes about each staff]
2. On the questionnaire you filled out, we asked you which staff person here at the club you were closest to. You wrote down [name of staff]. What kinds of things has [closest staff person] said or done that make you feel close to him/her?
3. So could you try to tell me why you are closer to [closest] than, say [names of other staff]?
4. How did you first meet [closest]? When was that?
5. What do you [and closest] usually do together or talk about?
6. Do you learn stuff from what [closest] says or does? What kinds of stuff? Is this important? Why?
7. How much stuff would you say you have learned from [closest]? Would you say a lot, a moderate amount, a bit, or not all that much?
8. Does [closest] ever help you with your homework? How often?[1]
9. What does s/he do? Did you get a better grade on the assignment/test? Better grade in the course? [probe: class and grade]
10. Does being with [closest] make you feel better about yourself? How? In what ways?
11. Now you remember how we said that we would be asking everyone about personal stuff they might talk about with staff. And how because this can be important to some kids, we need to understand it better to help staff do a better job at it. So please take a moment and think about whether you ever talk about personal stuff with [closest].

a. What kinds of things do you or have you talked about? How does [closest] respond?

b. Do you wind up feeling better? If so, how? Do you ever end up feeling worse? If so, how?

c. About how often do you share personal stuff with [closest]?[1]

12. Does [closest] ever give you advice? About how often?[1]
What kind of advice has he or she given you? Anything else? Did this have any effect on you [probe: advice taken and not taken]?

13. Does [closest] do things so that you *know* that s/he respects you? What kinds of things? Do other staff do this, too? Which ones?

14. Does [closest] ever give you any special responsibilities? If so, what kinds of responsibilities? How does that make you feel?

15. Does [closest] ever give you any special privileges? If so, what kinds of privileges? How does that make you feel?

16. When you are older, are you more likely to do certain things or be a certain kind of person because of [closest]? Tell me about that.

17. Has your relationship with [closest] changed at all from what it was like last year to what it's like now? In what ways? How do you feel about that? If not, would you have liked it to have changed – in what ways?

18. Was there ever a time when you were not close to [closest]? How did you get closer to [closest]?

19. Ever times when you [and closest] were not getting along? How did you get over that?

20. Do you ever talk to your parent(s) about [closest]?

a. About what kinds of stuff?

b. About how often do you talk about [closest]?[1]

c. How does your parent respond?

21. We know at other clubs that some parents really like the staff person that their child is closest to, others do not seem too interested, and some parents do not seem to like the person or may even be a little jealous of the relationship their child has with that staff. What about your parent?

21. Do your parents' views have anything to do with how [closest] gets along with any of your siblings or relatives here – or who used to come to the club? How?
22. Has [parent] actually met [closest] or talked on the phone with him/her? About how often? How did that go?

[1] Responses coded as every week, every two weeks, every month, every two or three months, or once or twice a year.

Youth's Relationships with Primary Club Staff

[For each item, youth are asked to provide a rating for each primary club staff on a scale from 1 = never/almost never to 5 = always/almost always.]

1. I talk to [name of staff] about problems I'm having with my friends.[a]
2. I talk to [name of staff] about problems with my parent(s) or family.[a]
3. Sometimes I think that [name of staff] does not like me.[c]
4. I feel safe when I am with [name of staff].[a]
5. [name of staff] gives me useful advice in dealing with my problems.[b]
6. I do not like things [name of staff] says or does.[c]
7. [name of staff] cares about how I'm doing in school.[a]
8. [name of staff] is very sure that I can do well in school and in the future.[a]
9. [name of staff] cares about me even when I make mistakes.[a]
10. [name of staff] has qualities or skills that I would like to have when I'm older.[b]
11. I tell [name of staff] about things that are very private.[a]
12. I learn how to do things from watching and listening to [name of staff].[b]
13. [name of staff] introduces me to new ideas, interests, and experiences.[b]
14. [name of staff] is too busy to pay attention to me.[c]
15. [name of staff] and I get angry at each other.[c]
16. [name of staff] pushes me to succeed at the things I want to do.[b]
17. I talk to [name of staff] when something makes me angry or afraid.[a]

18. [name of staff] really listens and understands me when I talk to him/her.[a]

19. [name of staff] looks out for me and helps me.[a]

20. I feel [name of staff] will let me down.[c]

21. If I tell [name of staff] what I'm thinking, he/she will laugh at me.[c]

22. [name of staff] and I both have fun when we are together.[a]

Source: Pagano (2001).

[a] Item for Trusts/Feels Valued scale. Coefficient alphas for this scale for the study sample were .90 for the staff person with whom youth had their closest tie and .85 for other staff persons.

[b] Item for Mentoring scale. Coefficient alphas were .64 for closest staff person and .60 for other staff persons.

[c] Item for Negativity scale. Coefficient alphas were .63 for closest staff person and .69 for other staff persons.

YOUTH INTERVIEW #3

Global Self-Efficacy

1. I can do just about anything I really set my mind to.
2. I have control over the things that happen to me.
3. There is no way I can solve some of my problems.[a]
4. I am confident about my ability to do new things.
5. When I set goals, I know I can reach them.
6. If I fail at something, I keep trying until I am successful.
7. What happens to me in the future mostly depends on me.
8. There is a lot I can do to deal with the problems in my life.
9. Sometimes I feel that I'm being pushed around in life.[a]
10. I have the ability to do whatever is needed to make improvements in my life.

Response Scale: Strongly Disagree, Disagree, Agree, Strongly Agree. Coefficient alpha for the study sample was .73.

Source: Items adapted from Mastery Scale (Pearlin & Schooler, 1978) and Sherer, Maddox, Mercandante, Prentice-Dunn, Jacobs, and Rogers (1982).

[a] Item is reverse scored.

Does [closest staff person] ever do or say things that help you feel good about how well you can do things?[1]

Global Self-Esteem

1. I am happy with myself as a person.
2. I am the kind of person I want to be.
3. I like being just the way I am.
4. I am happy with the way I can do most things.
5. I often feel ashamed of myself.[a]
6. I wish I had more to be proud of.[a]
7. I am as good a person as I want to be.
8. I sometimes think I am a failure (a "loser").[a]

Response Scale: Strongly Disagree, Disagree, Agree, Strongly Agree.
Coefficient alpha for the study sample was .71.

Source: Global scale of Self-Esteem Questionnaire (DuBois, Felner, Brand, Phillips, & Lease, 1996).

[a] Item is reverse scored.

Does [closest staff person] ever do or say things that help you feel good about how well you can do things?[1]

Academic Self-Efficacy

1. You are assigned a long chapter in a tough subject for a quiz tomorrow. Finishing and understanding the chapter is ...
2. You are reading a book for school. Writing a report about the book is ...
3. You are taking a test to get into a school you really want to go to. Passing the test is ...
4. You do not understand what your teacher is talking about in class. Figuring it out on your own is ...
5. You have a homework assignment to complete in a tough subject. Finishing the assignment is ...[a]
6. Your teacher is explaining something important in class. Paying attention and listening carefully is ...[a]
7. You have a project to complete for school. Doing a good job on the project is ...[a]
8. You get a failing grade on a test. Doing better on the next test is ...[a]

Response Scale: Really Easy, Sort of Easy, Sort of Hard, Really Hard.
Coefficient alpha for the study sample was .64.

Source: Academic Self-Efficacy Scale (Seidman et al., 1994)

[a] Additional item not included on the source scale.

Academic Self-Esteem

1. I am as good a student as I would like to be.
2. I am doing as well on school work as I would like to.
3. I get grades that are good enough for me.
4. I feel OK about how good of a student I am.

Response Scale: Strongly Disagree, Disagree, Agree, Strongly Agree. Coefficient alpha for the study sample was .91.

Source: School scale of the short form of the Self-Esteem Questionnaire (DuBois, 2009).

Peer Relations Self-Efficacy

1. A group of people wants to play a CD that you do not like. Asking them to play a CD you like is ...
2. There is a new kid who you would like to get to know better. Starting a conversation with this person is ...[a]
3. A group of kids are saying some things you disagree with. Telling them your opinion is ...[a]
4. Someone needs more people to be on a team. Asking to be on the team is ...
5. Someone always wants to be first when you play a video game. Telling the person you are going first is ...

Response Scale: Really Easy, Sort of Easy, Sort of Hard, Really Hard. Coefficient alpha for the study sample was .72.

Source: Selected items from Social Self-Efficacy Scale (Seidman et al., 1994)
[a] Additional item not included on the source scale.

Peer Relations Self-Esteem

1. I have as many close friends as I would like to have.
2. I am as well liked by other kids as I want to be.
3. I feel good about how well I get along with other kids.
4. I feel OK about how much other kids like doing things with me.

Response Scale: Strongly Disagree, Disagree, Agree, Strongly Agree. Coefficient alpha for the study sample was .80.

Source: Peers scale of the short form of the Self-Esteem Questionnaire (DuBois, 2009).

Trust: Adults

1. Feeling that most adults can be trusted.
2. Feeling that adults are interested in helping you out.
3. Feeling that adults try to take advantage of you.[b]
4. Feeling that adults care about what happens to you.
5. Feeling that adults are worth getting to know better.[a]

Response Scale: Not at All, A Little Bit, Moderately, Quite a Bit, Extremely. Coefficient alpha for the study sample was .67.

Source: Items adapted from Faith in People Scale (Rosenberg, 1957).
[a] Additional item not included on the source scale.
[b] Item is reverse scored.

Does [closest staff person] ever do or say things that make you feel you can be more trusting of other adults in your life?[1]

Interpersonal Sensitivity: Adults

1. Your feelings being easily hurt by adults.
2. Feeling critical of adults.
3. Feeling adults do not understand you or are unsympathetic.
4. Feeling that adults are unfriendly or dislike you.
5. Feeling uneasy when adults are watching or talking about you.

Response Scale: Not at All, A Little Bit, Moderately, Quite a Bit, Extremely. Coefficient alpha for the study sample was .77.

Source: Items adapted from the Interpersonal Sensitivity scale of the SCL-90 (Derogatis, Lipman, & Covi, 1973).

Does [closest staff person] ever do or say things that make you feel less bothered by what other adults in your life do or say?[1]

Trust: Peers

Same items as listed under "Trust: Adults" with "adults" changed to "other kids." Coefficient alpha for the study sample was .55.

Interpersonal Sensitivity: Peers

Same items as listed under "Interpersonal Sensitivity: Adults" with "adults" changed to "other kids." Coefficient alpha for the study sample was .64.

Possible Selves

This part of the interview takes a look at who you want to be and who you do not want to be. Each of us has an idea of what we will be like and what we want to avoid being like in the future.

Think about next year – imagine what you will be like, and what you will be doing next year. Tell me what you expect you will be like and what you expect to be doing next year. [List expectations/goals individually on chart]

[Next ask for each expectation/goal]: *Are you doing something to be that way? (i.e., Are you currently doing something to get to that expectation or goal?)* [If yes, ask]: *What are you doing now to be that way next year?* [List responses on chart]

[Repeat above process for things that youth wants to avoid being like or doing next year.]

Source: Possible Selves Questionnaire (Oyserman, 2004).

Does [closest] ever do or say things that make you think about what you want to be like or accomplish in the future?[1]

Now let us talk about the opposite. Does [closest] ever do or say things that make you think about what you want to *avoid* for yourself in the future?[1]

Does [closest] ever do or say things that help you get closer to reaching your future goals for yourself?[1]

Academic Expectations

1. As things stand now, how far in school do you think you will get? (Choose one: Will not finish high school, Will graduate from high school, but will not go any further, Will go to vocational, trade, or business school after high school, Will attend college, Will graduate from college, Will attend a higher level of school after graduating college)
2. How sure are you that you will graduate from high school? (Choose one: Very sure I will graduate, I will probably graduate, I probably will not graduate, Very sure I will not graduate)
3. How sure are you that you will go on for further education after you leave high school? (Choose one: Very sure I will

go, I will probably go, I probably will not go, Very sure I will not go)

Source: Items are from National Educational Longitudinal Study (National Center for Education Statistics, 1996).

Global Identity

1. Some kids know who they are inside as a person BUT Other kids sometimes have trouble knowing who they really are as a person.
2. Some kids often feel like they do not know who the "real me" is BUT Other kids do feel like they know who the "real me" is.
3. Some kids have a good sense of what their "true self" is like BUT Other kids often are not sure what their "true self" is like.

Response Scale: Choose the statement that is most like you. Then tell me if it is Really True of You or Sort of True of You. Coefficient alpha for the study sample was .59.

Source: Self-Knowledge scale of True Self Questionnaire (Harter et al., 1996).

Does [closest staff person] ever do or say things that help you become more sure about who you are or want to be as a person? This might be about your values or beliefs, your interests and talents, how you act, or plans for the future.[1]

Does [other positive staff] ever do or say things that help you become more sure about who you are or want to be as a person? This might be about your values or beliefs, your interests and talents, how you act, or plans for the future.[1]

[1] Follow-up questions for this item: [If yes:] Tell me about what [closest] does? About how often does [closest] do any of these things? Would you say every week, every two weeks, once a month, every two or three months, or once or twice a year?

YOUTH INTERVIEW #4

1. Does your parent or guardian work? What does s/he do? What kind of shifts or hours does s/he usually work? [*Be sure to ask for both parents if not a single parent household.*]
2. We would like to know how far your [parent(s)] went in school? Responses coded as: High school but did not graduate;

High school graduate; Some college or associate or vocational degree; College (4 year) graduate; or Master's degree or higher.

3. How close are you to your parents or guardian on a scale of 1 to 5? 1 = Not at all and 5 = Extremely. [*Obtain a rating for each parent/guardian.*]
4. Would you say things have changed in your relationship with your [parent] now that you are older? How?
5. What grades did you get for your last marking period? [*Record letter grade, including +/-, for each subject.*]
   Did your grades change at all from last fall? From a year ago, last spring? How?
6. What is school like for you? How do you feel about it?
7. How do you feel about your teachers?
8. Do you have any friends or associates who ...

   a. Have dropped out of school? If yes, how many?
   b. Have gotten into trouble with the law? If yes, how many?
   c. Belong to a gang? If yes, how many?
   d. Do or sell drugs? If yes, how many?

6. We would like to know what you feel you have gotten out of coming to the club *over the whole time you have been coming.* Do you feel like you would be the same person if you had never come to the club? Go ahead and take a minute to think about this seriously before answering.

STAFF INTERVIEW #1

1. How long have you been working at the club?

   a. How did you come to this job?
   b. Were you specifically seeking out opportunities to work with youth?
   c. Were you specifically seeking out opportunities to work in this community?
   d. What interested you about the job?
   e. What were the most appealing aspects of considering working at the club?
   f. How does the job match the expectations you had?

2. What did you do before you started working here?

3. Have you worked or volunteered at other Boys & Girls Clubs or youth organizations? [If no, had you worked or volunteered with youth in any capacity before coming here? Did that shape your interest in working here? If yes, what about those experiences made you want to continue your involvement with the clubs?]
4. Did you attend a Boys & Girls Club or other youth organization as a kid?

   If yes:

   a. Did that influence your decision to work here in any way?
   b. How is this club similar and/or different from the one you went to as a kid?
   c. Do you think about your own experiences of club staff from childhood in approaching your job now?

   If no:

   a. Do you think your experience as a staff member has been different in any way from staff who did attend a club as a kid? How/why?
5. What about your family members? [If yes, do any attend now? This club? If so, how does that change your job, if at all?]
6. Do you live in the neighborhood of the club?

   a. Did you grow up in the neighborhood of the club?
   b. Where did you grow up (get neighborhood if in Chicago)?
   c. What was growing up in your neighborhood like compared to what growing up in this neighborhood is like for club youth?
   d. Does this influence your ability to relate to the kids in any way?
7. What is your educational background? Are you taking any courses now? [If yes, what is the nature of the courses? How many courses? Where?]
8. What are your future job plans or goals?
9. Have they changed since you have worked here? [If yes, how?]
10. Would you want to move up within the Boys & Girls Club (either within this club or on an organizational level)? [If yes, do you see opportunity for yourself to do so? Why would you/would you not want to move up with the Boys & Girls Club organization?]

There is a little bit of personal information we would like to ask you in order to get to know you better.

11. Are you married or involved with someone? [If yes, what does he or she think of your job?]
12. What do you like to do when you are not at work? Any particular hobbies or interests?
13. How old are you/what year were you born?

STAFF INTERVIEW #2

1. How would you describe your job to someone not familiar with the Boys & Girls Club?
2. a. What would you say are the most important aspects of your job?
   b. How much of your time do you feel that you spend managing youth's behavior or disciplining youth?
   c. How much of your time do you feel that you spend hanging out with the kids and participating in activities with them?
3. What do you think are the skills or traits that make someone an effective staff member at the club?
4. a. How do you see your relationship to the kids at the club?
   b. Do you consider yourself as a friend, mentor, or a counselor to kids?
   c. Does this vary by the kid's age or gender (race if applicable) of the youth?
   d. What does being a mentor mean to you? If a mentor, how much of your time do you feel that you spend mentoring kids? If not a mentor, why not?
   e. What does being a counselor mean to you? If not counselor, do you think that staff should counsel kids?
   f. What determines what role you play with different kids?
   g. What is your relationship with the kids' families?

5. a. One thing that some kids have told us that they appreciate about staff is that they see them as friend-like adults, adults who understand what they are going through more so than other adults in their lives. How do you feel about that?
   b. Do you ever feel a tension between being a friend and being an adult to the kids? How do you switch between the two?

6. What do you see as your strengths in this job? Weaknesses?
7. a. What are the things that you like most about your job?
   b. Are there things that the club could do or ways the club could be structured that would make those things more prominent in your daily life here?
8. a. What are your favorite things to do with the kids?
   b. Do you prefer structured activities or unstructured time with kids? Does this vary by age group?
9. What do you contribute to these kids' lives?
10. What is your motivation for working with them?
11. a. What are your greatest frustrations with your job?
    b. Are there things that the club could do or ways the club could be structured to make this less prominent in your daily life at the club?
    c. Do you feel that other staff share your frustrations?
12. What are the biggest challenges you have faced as a staff member?
13. Are there things that the club or the organization as a whole could do to make your job easier for you?
14. If you could change one thing about the club, what would it be?
15. Do you feel supported by other staff and club leadership? If yes, how so? If no, why not?

STAFF INTERVIEW #3

1. What is the best thing about working with kids?
2. What is the most challenging thing about working with kids?
3. What would you say is your approach to working with kids?

   Staff were asked the remaining questions in the interview about each of the youth from the intensive study sample who had identified him/her as the staff person to whom they felt closest at the after-school center.

4. How long have you known [name of youth]?
5. On a scale of 1–5, how close do you feel to [youth]? (1=not at all, 5=extremely)
6. What is [youth] like? How would you describe her/his personality? How easy is she/he to get to know?

7. How does [youth] interact with her/his peers? (i.e., does she/he get along with them, does she/he get into conflicts or arguments with them?)

8. How does [youth] interact with the staff? (i.e., does she/he get along with them, does she/he get into conflicts or arguments with them?)

9. Does [youth] participate in club activities? Which ones? Does she/he seem to be engaged in the activities? Does she/he enjoy them?

10. What is the best thing about [youth]?

11. What is the most difficult or challenging thing about [youth]?

12. What do you know about [youth]'s home life? How about her/his school life?

13. Do you know [youth]'s family? What kinds of interactions do you have with her/his parent(s)? How often?

14. Has your relationship changed with [youth] at all? In what ways? Why? How do you feel about that?

15. Were there any times you and [youth] were not getting along? How did you get over that?

16. What do you usually do or talk about with [youth]?

17. Do you ever have one-on-one conversations with [youth]? What kinds of things do you talk about?

18. Do you generally talk about behavior and discipline or more about personal stuff with [youth]? How much personal stuff does she/he talk about? [or how much personal stuff is she/he willing to talk about?]

   a. About how often does [youth] share personal stuff with you?[1]

19. Do you ever give advice to [youth]? What kind of advice? How does she/he respond? (i.e., Does this seem to have any effect on her? Does she/he seem to take the advice?)

   a. About how often do you give advice to [youth]?[1]

20. How much influence would you say you have on [youth]? How or in what context?

   a. Do you purposely try to have an influence on her/him or would you say you have influence on her/him by just being a role model?

   b. How do you go about doing this? What kind of methods do you use?

   c. What do you find works? What do you find doesn't work?

---

[1] Response scale: every week, every two weeks, once a month, every two or three months, or once or twice a year.

REFERENCES

Abel, M. H. (2002). Humor, stress, and coping strategies. *Humor: International Journal of Humor Research, 15,* 365–381.

Alexander, K. L., Entwisle, D. R., & Kabbani, N. S. (2001). The dropout process in life course perspective: Early risk factors at home and school. *Teachers College Record, 103,* 760–822.

Alexander, W. M. & George, P. S. (1981). *The exemplary middle school.* New York: Holt, Rinehart, and Winston.

Allen, T. D., Eby, L. T., Poteet, M. L., Lentz, E., & Lima, L. (2004). Career benefits associated with mentoring for proteges: A meta-analysis. *Journal of Applied Psychology, 89,* 127–136.

Ames, J. (2007, June). *California's afterschool expansion: The planning for implementation of Proposition 49 and considerations for planners in other states.* New York: William T. Grant Foundation.

Arbreton, A. (2009). *Making every day count: Boys & Girls Clubs' role in promoting positive outcomes for teens.* Philadelphia: Public/Private Ventures.

Arbreton, A., Bradshaw, M., Metz, R., & Sheldon, J. (2008). *More time for teens: Understanding teen participation – frequency, intensity and duration – in Boys & Girls Clubs.* Philadelphia: Public/Private Ventures.

Arbreton, A., Sheldon, J., & Herrera, C. (2005). *Beyond safe havens: A synthesis of 20 years of research on the Boys & Girls Clubs.* Philadelphia: Public/Private Ventures.

Argyris, C., & Schon, D. (1978). *Organizational learning: A theory of action perspective.* Reading, MA: Addison-Wesley.

Arnett, J. (1999). Adolescent storm and stress, reconsidered. *American Psychologist, 54,* 317–326.

Arthur, W. B. (1994). *Increasing returns and path dependence in the economy.* Ann Arbor: University of Michigan Press.

Arthur, W. B., Durlauf, S., & Lane, D. (Eds.). (1997). *The economy as an evolving complex system II.* Reading, MA: Addison-Wesley.

Asher, S. R., Parker, J. G., & Walker, D. L. (1996). Distinguishing friendship from acceptance: Implications for intervention and assessment. In W. M. Bukowski, A. F. Newcomb, & W. W. Hartup (Eds.), *The company they keep: Friendship in childhood and adolescence* (pp. 366–405). New York: Cambridge University Press.

Austin, M., & Hopkins, K. (Eds.). (2004). *Supervision as collaboration in the human services: Building a learning culture*. Thousand Oaks, CA: Sage.

Bagwell, C. L., Newcomb, A. F., & Bukowski, W. M. (1998). Preadolescent friendship and peer rejection as predictors of adult adjustment. *Child Development, 69*, 140–153.

Balsano, A., Phelps, E., & Theokas, C. (2009). Patterns of early adolescents' participation in youth development programs having positive youth development goals. *Journal of Research on Adolescence, 19*, 249–259.

Bandura, A. (1986). *Social foundations of thought and action: A social cognitive theory*. Englewood Cliffs, NJ: Prentice-Hall.

Barker, G. (1998). Non-violent males in violent settings: An exploratory qualitative study of prosocial low-income adolescent males in two Chicago (USA) neighborhoods. *Childhood, 5*, 437–460.

Baumeister, R. F., Bratslavsky, E., Finkenauer, C., & Vohs, K. D. (2001). Bad is stronger than good. *Review of General Psychology, 5*, 323–370.

Baumrind, D. (1991). Parenting styles and adolescent development. In R. Lerner, A. Petersen, & J. Brooks-Gunn (Eds.), *Encyclopedia of adolescence* (pp. 746–757). New York: Garland.

Benson, P. L., & Scales, P. C. (2009). The definition and preliminary measurement of thriving in adolescence. *The Journal of Positive Psychology, 4*, 85–104.

Berman, P., & McLaughlin, M. (1978). *Federal programs supporting educational change: Vol. 8. Implementing and sustaining innovations*. Washington, DC: U.S. Office of Education.

Birmingham, J., Pechman, E. M., Russell, C. A., & Meilke, M. (2005). *Shared features of high-performance after-school programs: A follow-up to the TASC evaluation*. New York: The After-School Corporation. Retrieved from http://www.tascorp.org/content/document/detail/1353/

Blase, J., & Blase, J. (1998). *Handbook of instructional leadership: How really good principals promote teaching and learning*. Thousand Oaks, CA: Corwin.

Bogat, G. A., & Liang. B. (2005). Gender in mentoring relationships. In D. L. DuBois & M. J. Karcher (Eds.), *Handbook of youth mentoring* (pp. 205–217). Thousand Oaks, CA: Sage.

Boys & Girls Clubs of America (2009). *2008 Annual Report*. Atlanta: Author.

Branch, C. W. (1999). Pathologizing normality or normalizing pathology? In C. W. Branch (Ed.), *Adolescent gangs: Old issues, new approaches* (pp. 197–211). Philadelphia, PA: Brunner/Mazel.

Bronfenbrenner, U. (1979). *The ecology of human development*. Cambridge, MA: Harvard University Press.

Brown, B. (2004). Adolescents' relationships with peers. In R. Lerner & L. Steinberg (Eds.), *Handbook of adolescent psychology* (2nd ed., pp. 363–394). New York: Wiley.

Brown, L., & Gilligan, C. (1992). *Meeting at the crossroads: Women's psychology and girls' development*. New York: Random House.

Bryk, A., & Schneider, B. (2002). *Trust in schools: A core resource for improvement.* New York: Russell Sage.

Buchanan, J. M. (2001). Game theory, mathematics, and economics. *Journal of Economic Methodology, 8,* 27–32

Burkhauser, M. & Metz, A. (2009). Using coaching to provide ongoing support and supervision to out-of-school time staff. *Research-to-Results Brief.* Publication #2009–06. Washington, DC: Child Trends.

Camazine, S., Deneubourg, J.-L., Franks, N., Sneyd, J., Theraulaz, G., & Bonabeau, E. (2001). *Self-organization in biological systems.* Princeton, NJ: Princeton University Press.

Cartwright, D. S., Howard, K. I., & Reuterman, N. A. (1980). Multivariate analysis of gang delinquency: IV. Personality factors in gangs and clubs. *Multivariate Behavioral Research, 15,* 3–22.

Cassidy, J., & Shaver, P. (Eds.). (1999). *Handbook of attachment: Theory, research, and clinical applications.* New York: Guilford.

Clark, C. M. (1992). Deviant adolescent subcultures: Assessment strategies and clinical interventions. *Adolescence, 27,* 283–293.

Coleman, J. S. (1961). *The adolescent society.* New York: Free Press.

(1990). *Foundations of social theory.* Cambridge, MA: Harvard University Press.

(1974). Youth: Transition to adulthood. *Report of the Panel on Youth of the President's Science Advisory Committee.* Chicago: University of Chicago Press.

Collins, A., & Metz, A. (2009). How program administrators can support out-of-school time staff. *Research-to-Results Brief.* Publication # 2009–32. Washington, DC: Child Trends.

Conway, J. M., Amel, E. L., & Gerwien, D. P. (2009). Teaching and learning in the social context: A meta-analysis of service learning's effects on academic, personal, social, and citizenship outcomes. *Teaching of Psychology, 36,* 233–245.

Costello, E., Mustillo, S., Erkanli, A., Keeler, G., & Angold, A. (2003). Prevalence and development of psychiatric disorders in childhood and adolescence. *Archives of General Psychiatry, 60,* 837–844.

Cotterell, J. L. (1996). *Social networks and social influences in adolescence.* New York: Routledge.

Crick, N. R., Casas, J. F., & Nelson, D. A. (2002). Toward a more comprehensive understanding of peer maltreatment: Studies of relational victimization. *Current Directions in Psychological Science, 11,* 98–101.

Croninger, R. G., & Lee, V. E. (2001). Social capital and dropping out of high school: Benefits to at-risk students of teachers' support and guidance. *Teachers College Record, 103,* 548–581.

Cross, A., Gottfredson, D., Wilson, D., Rorie, M., & Connell, N. (2010). Implementation quality and positive experiences in after-school programs. *American Journal of Community Psychology, 45,* 370–380.

Cyert, R., & March J. (1963). *A behavioral theory of the firm.* Englewood Cliffs, NJ: Prentice-Hall.

Damon, W. (1990). *The moral child: Nurturing children's natural moral growth.* New York: The Free Press.

Dane, A., & Schneider, B. (1998). Program integrity in primary and early secondary prevention: Are implementation effects out of control? *Clinical Psychology Review, 18,* 23–45.

Darling, N. (2005). Mentoring adolescents. In D. L. DuBois & M. J. Karcher (Eds.), *Handbook of youth mentoring* (pp. 177–190). Thousand Oaks, CA: Sage.

Darling, N., Hamilton, S. F., & Niego, S. (1994). Adolescents' relations with adults outside the family. In R. Montemeyor & G. R. Adams (Eds.), *Personal relationships during adolescence* (pp. 216–235). Thousand Oaks, CA: Sage.

Davies, S. L., Dix, E. S., Rhodes, S. D., Harrington, K. F., Frison, S., & Willis, L. (2004). Attitudes of young African American fathers toward early childbearing. *American Journal of Health Behavior, 28,* 418–425.

Day, J., & Newburger, E. (2002). The big payoff: Educational attainment and synthetic estimates of work-life earnings. *Current Population Reports,* Series P23–210. Washington, DC: U.S. Government Printing Office.

Derogatis, L. R., Lipman, R. S., & Covi, L. (1973). SCL-90: An outpatient psychiatric rating scale – preliminary report. *Psychopharmacology Bulletin, 9,* 13–28.

Deschenes, S. N., Arbreton, A., Little, P. M., Herrera, C., Grossman, J. B., & Weiss, H. B. (2010). *Engaging older youth: Program and city-level strategies to support sustained participation in out-of-school time.* Philadelphia: Public/Private Ventures.

Detrie, P. M., & Lease, S. H. (2008). The relation of social support, connectedness, and collective self-esteem to the psychological well-being of lesbian, gay, and bisexual youth. *Journal of Homosexuality, 53,* 173–199.

Deutsch, N. (2004). *There are birds in the projects: The construction of self in an urban youth organization.* Unpublished doctoral dissertation, Northwestern University, Evanston, IL.

(2008). *Pride in the projects: Teens building identities in urban contexts.* New York: New York University Press.

Deutsch, N., & Hirsch, B. J. (2002). A place to call home: Youth organizations in the lives of inner city adolescents. In T. Brinthaupt & R. Lipka (Eds.), *Understanding early adolescent self and identity: Applications and interventions* (pp. 292–320). Albany: State University of New York Press.

Deutsch, N., & Jones, J. (2008). "Show me an ounce of respect": Respect and authority in adult-youth relationships in after-school programs. *Journal of Adolescent Research, 23,* 667–688.

Dierkes, M., Antal, A. B., Child, J., & Nonaka, I. (Eds.). (2001). *Handbook of organizational learning and knowledge.* New York: Oxford University Press.

Dimitriadis, G. (2001). Border identities, transformed lives, and danger zones: The mediation of validated selves, friendship networks, and successful paths in community-based organizations. *Discourse: Studies in the Cultural Politics of Education, 22,* 361–374.

Douvan, E., & Adelson, J. (1966). *The adolescent experience*. New York: Wiley.

Downey, D. B., & Condron, D. J. (2004). Playing well with others in kindergarten: The benefit of siblings at home. *Journal of Marriage and Family*, 66, 333–350.

DuBois, D. L. (2009). *Short form of the Self-Esteem Questionnaire*. Unpublished instrument, University of Illinois at Chicago, Chicago, IL.

DuBois, D. L., & Felner, R. D. (1996). The quadripartite model of social competence: Theory and applications to clinical intervention. In M. Reinecke, F. M. Dattilio, & A. Freeman (Eds.), *Cognitive therapy: A casebook for clinical practice* (pp. 124–152). New York: Guilford.

DuBois, D. L., Felner, R. D., Brand, S., Phillips, R. S. C., & Lease, A. M. (1996). Early adolescent self-esteem: A developmental-ecological framework and assessment strategy. *Journal of Research on Adolescence*, 6, 543–579.

DuBois, D. L., Flay, B. R., & Fagen, M. C. (2009). Self-esteem Enhancement Theory: Promoting health across the life span. In R. J. DiClemente, R. A. Crosby, & M. C. Kegler (Eds.), *Emerging theories in health promotion practice and research* (2nd ed., pp. 97–130). San Francisco: Jossey-Bass.

DuBois, D. L., Holloway, B. E., Valentine, J. C., & Cooper, H. (2002). Effectiveness of mentoring programs for youth: A meta-analytic review. *American Journal of Community Psychology*, 30, 157–197.

DuBois, D. L., Neville, H. A., Parra, G. R., & Pugh-Lilly, A. O. (2002). Testing a new model of mentoring. In J. E. Rhodes & G. A. Bogat (Eds.), *A critical view of youth mentoring* (New Directions for Youth Development: Theory, Research, and Practice, No. 93, G. Noam Series Ed., pp. 21–57). San Francisco: Jossey-Bass.

DuBois, D. L., & Silverthorn, N. (2005a). Characteristics of natural mentoring relationships and adolescent adjustment: Evidence from a national study. *Journal of Primary Prevention*, 26, 69–92.

DuBois, D. L., & Silverthorn, N. (2005b). Natural mentoring relationships and adolescent health: Evidence from a national study. *American Journal of Public Health*, 95, 518–524.

DuBois, D. L., Silverthorn, N., Pryce, J., Reeves, E., Sanchez, B., Silva, A., Ansu, A. A., Haqq, S., & Takehara, J. (2008). Mentorship: The GirlPOWER! program. In C. W. LeCroy & J. E. Mann (Eds.), *Handbook of prevention and intervention programs for adolescent girls* (pp. 325–365). Hoboken, NJ: Wiley.

Durlak, J. A., & DuPre, E. P. (2008). Implementation matters: A review of research on the influence of implementation on program outcomes and the factors affecting implementation. *American Journal of Community Psychology*, 41, 327–350.

Durlak, J., Mahoney, J., Bohnert, A., & Parente, M. (2010). Developing and improving after-school programs to enhance youth's personal growth and adjustment: A special issue of AJCP. *American Journal of Community Psychology*, 45, 285–293.

Durlak, J., Weissberg, R., & Pachan, M. (2010). A meta-analysis of after-school programs that seek to promote personal and social skills in children and adolescents. *American Journal of Community Psychology*, 45, 294–309.

Dynarski, M., & Gleason, P. (2002). How can we help? What we have learned from recent federal dropout prevention evaluations. *Journal of Education for Students Placed at Risk, 7*, 43–69.

Dynarski, M., Pistorino, C., Moore, M., Silva, T., Mullens, J., Deke, J., Gleason, P., Mansfield, W., James-Burdumy, S., Heaviside, S., Rosenberg, L., & Levy, D. (2003). *When schools stay open late: The national evaluation of the 21st-century community learning centers program*. Washington, DC: U.S. Department of Education.

Easterby-Smith, M., & Lyles, M. (Eds.). (2003). *The Blackwell handbook of organizational learning and knowledge*. Malden, MA: Blackwell.

Elbaum, B., Vaughn, S., Tejero Hughes, M., & Watson Moody, S. (2000). How effective are one-to-one tutoring programs in reading for elementary students at risk for reading failure? A meta-analysis of the intervention research. *Journal of Educational Psychology, 92*, 605–619.

Elmore, R., Peterson, P., & McCarthey, S. (1996). *Restructuring in the classroom: Teaching, learning, and school organization*. San Francisco: Jossey-Bass.

Erikson, E. (1963). *Childhood and society* (2nd ed.). New York: Norton.

(1968). *Identity: Youth and crisis*. New York: Norton.

Fergusson, D. M., Woodward, L. J., & Horwood, L. J. (1999). Childhood peer relationship problems and young people's involvement with deviant peers in adolescence. *Journal of Abnormal Child Psychology, 27*, 357–369.

Finn, J. D. (1989). Withdrawing from school. *Review of Educational Research, 59*, 117–142.

Flannery, D. J., Huff, C. R., & Manos, M. (1998). Youth gangs: A developmental prospective. In T. P. Gullotta & G. R. Adams (Eds.), *Delinquent violent youth: Theory and interventions* (Vol. 9, pp. 175–204). Thousand Oaks, CA: Sage Publications, Inc.

Fredricks, J., Hackett, K., & Bergman, A. (2010). Participation in Boys and Girls Clubs: Motivation and stage environment fit. *Journal of Community Psychology, 38*, 369–385.

Fuehr, M. (2002). Coping humor in early adolescence. *Humor: International Journal of Humor Research, 15*, 283–304.

Fullan, M. (1991). *The new meaning of educational change* (2nd ed.). New York: Teacher's College Press.

Gambone, M. A., & Arbreton, A. J. A. (1997). *Safe havens: The contributions of youth organizations to healthy adolescent development*. Philadelphia: Public/Private Ventures.

Gamoran, A., Anderson, C., Quiroz, P., Secada, W., Williams, T., & Ashman, S. (2003). *Transforming teaching in math and science: How schools and districts can support change*. New York: Teachers College Press.

Gardner, H. (1993). *Multiple intelligences: The theory in practice*. New York: Basic Books.

Garza, P., Borden, L. M., & Astroth, K. A. (Eds.). (2004). *Professional development for youth workers* (New Directions for Youth Development: Theory, Research, and Practice, No. 104, G. Noam Series Ed). San Francisco: Jossey-Bass.

Geiger, T. C., & Crick, N. R. (2001). A developmental psychopathology perspective on vulnerability to personality disorders. In R. E. Ingram & J. M. Price (Eds.), *Vulnerability to psychopathology: Risk across the lifespan* (pp. 57–102). New York: Guilford Press.

Gleason, P., & Dynarski, M. (2002). Do we know whom to serve? Issues in using risk factors to identify dropouts. *Journal of Education for Students Placed at Risk, 7*, 25–41.

Goddard, Y. L., Goddard, R. D., & Tschannen-Moran, M. (2007). A theoretical and empirical investigation of teacher collaboration for school improvement and student achievement in public elementary schools. *Teachers College Record, 109*, 877–896.

Goleman, D. (1997). *Emotional intelligence: Why it can matter more than IQ.* New York: Bantam Books.

Goodey, J. (1998). Understanding racism and masculinity: Drawing on research with boys aged eight to sixteen. *International Journal of the Sociology of Law, 26*, 393–418.

Gordon, R. A., Lahey, B. B. K., & Rolf, E. L. (2004). Antisocial behavior and youth gang membership: Selection and socialization. *Criminology, 42*, 55–87.

Gottfredson, D. (2001). *Schools and delinquency.* New York: Cambridge University Press.

Gottfredson, D., Cross, A., Wilson, D., Rorie, M., & Connell, N. (2010). Effects of participation in after-school programs for middle school students: A randomized trial. *Journal of Research on Educational Effectiveness, 3*, 282–313.

Gottfredson, D. C., Gerstenblith, S. A., Soulé, D. A., Womer, S. C., & Lu, S. (2004). Do after school programs reduce delinquency? *Prevention Science, 5*, 253–266.

Granger, R. (2010). Understanding and improving the effectiveness of after-school practice. *American Journal of Community Psychology, 45*, 441–446.

Granger, R., Durlak, J. A., Yohalem, N., & Reisner, E. (2007). *Improving after-school program quality.* New York: William T. Grant Foundation.

Grant, K. E., Compas, B. E., Stuhlmacher, A. F., Thurm, A. E., McMahon, S. D., & Halpert, J. A. (2003). Stressors and child and adolescent psychopathology: Moving from markers to mechanisms of risk. *Psychological Bulletin, 129*, 447–466.

Greenberger, E., Chen, C., & Beam, M. R. (1998). The role of "very important" nonparental adults in adolescent development. *Journal of Youth and Adolescence, 27*, 321–343.

Gronn, P. (2000). Distributed properties: A new architecture for leadership. *Educational Management and Administration, 28*, 317–338.

Grossman, J., Campbell, M., & Raley, B. (2007). *Quality time after school in brief.* Philadelphia: Public/Private Ventures.

Grossman, J., Price, M., Fellerath, V., Juvocy, L., Kutloff, L., Raley, R., & Walker, K. (2002). *Multiple choices of after school: Findings from the extended-service initiative.* Philadelphia: Public/Private Ventures.

Grossman, J., & Rhodes, J. E. (2002). The test of time: Predictors and effects of duration in youth mentoring relationships. *American Journal of Community Psychology, 30,* 199–219.

Grotevant, H., & Cooper, C. (1998). Individuality and connectedness in adolescent development: Review and prospects for research on identity, relationships, and context. In E. Skoe & A. von der Lippe (Eds.), *Personality development in adolescence: A cross national and life span perspective* (pp. 3–37). London: Routledge.

Hall, J. (2001). *Canal town youth: Community organization and the development of adolescent identity.* Albany: SUNY Press.

Halpern, R. (1992). The role of after-school programs in the lives of inner-city children: A study of the "Urban Youth Network". *Child Welfare, 71,* 215–230.

(2009). *The means to grow up: Reinventing apprenticeship as a developmental support in adolescence.* New York: Routledge.

Halpern, R., Barker, G., & Mollard, W. (2000). Youth programs as alternative spaces to be: A study of neighborhood youth programs in Chicago's West Town. *Youth & Society, 31,* 469–506.

Hamilton, M. A., & Hamilton, S. F. (1990). *Linking Up: Final report of a mentoring program for youth.* Ithaca, NY: Cornell University, College of Human Ecology, Department of Human Development and Family Studies.

Hamilton, S. F. (1990). *Apprenticeship for adulthood: Preparing youth for the future.* New York: Free Press.

Hamilton, S. F., & Hamilton, M. A. (2004a). Contexts for mentoring: Adolescent-adult relationships in workplaces and communities. In R. Lerner & L. Steinberg (Eds.), *Handbook of adolescent psychology* (2nd ed., pp. 395–428). New York: Wiley.

Hamilton, S. F., & Hamilton, M. A. (Eds.). (2004b). *The youth development handbook: Coming of age in American communities.* Thousand Oaks, CA: Sage.

Hamilton, S. F., Hamilton, M. A., & Pittman, K. (2004). Principles for youth development. In S. F. Hamilton & M. A. Hamilton (Eds.), *The youth development handbook: Coming of age in American Communities* (2nd ed., pp. 3–22). Thousand Oaks, CA: Sage.

Harris, J. R. (1998). *The nurture assumption: Why children turn out the way they do.* New York: The Free Press.

Hart, A. W. (1998). Marshaling forces: Collaboration across educator roles. In D. Pounder (Ed.), *Restructuring schools for collaboration: Promises and pitfalls* (pp. 89–120). Albany: SUNY Press.

Harter, S. (1999). *The construction of the self: A developmental perspective.* New York: Guilford.

Harter, S., Marold, D. B., Whitesell, N. R., & Cobbs, G. (1996). A model of the effects of perceived parent and peer support on adolescent false self behavior. *Child Development, 67,* 360–374.

Heaney, C. A., & Israel, B. A. (2008). Social networks and social support. In K. Glanz, B. Rimer, & K. Viswanath (Eds.), *Health behavior and health education: Theory, research, and practice* (4th ed., pp. 189–210). San Francisco: Jossey-Bass.

Heller, M., & Firestone, W. (1995). Who's in charge here? Sources of leadership for change in eight schools. *Elementary School Journal, 95,* 65–86.

Hess, R. S. (2000). Dropping out among Mexican American youth: Reviewing the literature through an ecological perspective. *Journal of Education for Students Placed at Risk, 5,* 267–289.

Hirsch, B. J. (1980). Natural support systems and coping with major life changes. *American Journal of Community Psychology, 8,* 159–172.

(2005). *A place to call home: After-school programs for urban youth.* Washington, DC, and New York: American Psychological Association and Teachers College Press.

(2006). *Making the most of Proposition 49 after-school funds.* Paper presented at the Conference on Poverty in California, Los Angeles.

Hirsch, B. J., & DuBois, D. L. (1991). Self-esteem in early adolescence: The identification and prediction of contrasting longitudinal trajectories. *Journal of Youth and Adolescence, 20,* 53–72.

Hirsch, B. J., Hedges, L. H., Stawicki, J., & Mekinda, M. (2011). *After-school programs for high school students: An evaluation of After School Matters. Technical report.* Evanston, IL: Northwestern University.

Hirsch, B. J., Mekinda, M., & Stawicki, J. (2010). More than attendance: The importance of after-school program quality. *American Journal of Community Psychology, 45,* 447–452.

Holleman, M., Sundius, M., & Bruns, E. (2010). Building opportunity: Developing city systems to expand and improve after school programs. *American Journal of Community Psychology, 45,* 405–416.

Holmbeck, G. N., & Hill, J. P. (1991). Conflictive engagement, positive affect, and menarche in families with seventh-grade girls. *Child Development, 62,* 1030–1048.

Hufferd-Ackles, K., Fuson, K., & Sherin, M. G. (2004). Describing levels and components of a math-talk community. *Journal for Research in Mathematics Education, 3,* 81–116.

Ingersoll, G. M., Scamman, J. P., & Eckerling, W. D. (1989). Geographic mobility and student achievement in an urban setting. *Educational Evaluation and Policy Analysis, 11,* 143–149.

Jackson, C. K., & Bruegmann, E. (2009). Teaching students and teaching each other: The importance of peer learning for teachers. *American Economic Journal: Applied Economics, 1*(4), 85–108.

James-Burdumy, S., Dynarski, M., & Deke, J. (2007). When elementary schools stay open late: Results from the national evaluation of the 21st century community learning centers program. *Educational Evaluation and Policy Analysis, 29,* 296–318.

James-Burdumy, S., Dynarski, M., & Deke, J. (2008). After-school program effects on behavior: Results from the 21st century community learning centers program national evaluation. *Economic Inquiry, 46,* 13–18.

Johnson, S. M., Berg, J. H., & Donaldson, M. L. (2005). *Who stays in teaching and why: A review of the literature on teacher retention.* Cambridge, MA: Harvard Graduate School of Education.

Johnson, C., & Engelhard, G. (1992). Gender, academic achievement, and preferences for cooperative, competitive, and individualistic learning among African-American adolescents. *Journal of Psychology: Interdisciplinary and Applied, 126,* 385–392.

Johnstone, J. (1983). Recruitment to a youth gang. *Youth & Society, 14,* 281–300.

Jones, J. N., & Deutsch, N. L. (in press). Relational strategies in after-school settings: How staff-youth relationships support youth development. *Youth & Society.*

Karcher, M. J. (2007). Cross-age peer mentoring. In J. E. Rhodes (Ed.), *Research in Action Series* (Issue 7, pp. 3–17). Alexandria, VA: MENTOR/ National Mentoring Partnership.

(2005). Cross-age peer mentoring. In D. L. DuBois & M. J. Karcher (Eds.), *Handbook of youth mentoring* (pp. 266–285). Thousand Oaks, CA: Sage.

Karcher, M. J., & Finn, L. (2005). How connectedness contributes to experimental smoking among rural youth: Developmental and ecological analyses. *The Journal of Primary Prevention, 26,* 25–36.

Karcher, M. J., & Sass, D. (2010). A multicultural assessment of adolescent connectedness: Testing measurement invariance across gender and ethnicity. *Journal of Counseling Psychology, 57,* 274–289.

Kauffman, S. A. (1995). *At home in the universe: The search for laws of self-organization and complexity.* New York: Oxford University Press.

Kauh, T. (2010). *Recruiting and retaining older African American and Hispanic boys in after-school programs: What we know and what we still need to learn.* Philadelphia: Public/Private Ventures.

Keller, T. E. (2005). The stages and development of mentoring relationships. In D. L. DuBois & M. J. Karcher (Eds.), *Handbook of youth mentoring* (pp. 82–99). Thousand Oaks, CA: Sage.

Keller, T. E., & Blakeslee, J. (in press). Social networks and mentoring. To appear in D. L. DuBois & M. J. Karcher (Eds.), *Handbook of youth mentoring* (2nd ed.). Thousand Oaks, CA: Sage.

Kelly, J. G. (2006). *Becoming ecological: An expedition into community psychology.* New York: Oxford University Press.

Kenny, M., Horne, A. M., Orpinas, P., & Reese, L. (Eds.). (2009). *Realizing social justice: The challenge of preventive interventions.* Washington, DC: American Psychological Association.

Kirshner, B. (2008). Guided participation in three youth activism organizations: Facilitation, apprenticeship and joint work. *Journal of the Learning Sciences, 17,* 60–101.

Kling, K. C., Hyde, J. S., Showers, C. J., & Buswell, B. N. (1999). Gender differences in self-esteem: A meta-analysis. *Psychological Bulletin, 125,* 470–500.

Knox, M., Funk, J., Elliott, R., & Bush, E. G. (1998). Adolescents' possible selves and their relationship to global self-esteem. *Sex Roles, 39,* 61–80.

Krohne, H. W. (2003). Individual differences in emotional reactions and coping. In R. Davidson, K. Scherer & H. Goldsmith (Eds.), *Handbook of affective sciences* (pp. 698–725). New York: Oxford University Press.

Kupersmidt, J. B., Coie, J. D., & Dodge, K. A. (1990). The role of poor peer relationships in the development of disorder. In S. R. Asher & J. D. Coie (Eds.), *Peer rejection in childhood* (pp. 274–305). New York: Cambridge University Press.

Laird, J., DeBell, M., Kienzl, G., & Chapman, C. (2007). *Dropout rates in the United States: 2005*. Washington, DC: U.S. Department of Education, National Center for Educational Statistics.

Larson, R. (1993). Youth organizations, hobbies, and sports as developmental contexts. In R. K. Silbereisen & E. Todt (Eds.), *Adolescence in context: The interplay of family, school, peers, and work in adjustment* (pp. 46–65). New York: Springer-Verlag.

(2000). Toward a psychology of positive youth development. *American Psychologist, 55*, 170–183.

(2006). Positive youth development, willful adolescents, and mentoring. *Journal of Community Psychology, 34*, 677–689.

Larson, R., & Walker, K. (2010). Dilemmas of practice: Challenges to program quality encountered by youth program leaders. *American Journal of Community Psychology, 45*, 338–349.

Larson, R., Walker, L. & Pearce, N. (2005). A comparison of youth-driven and adult-driven youth programs: Balancing inputs from youth and adults. *Journal of Community Psychology, 33*, 57–74.

Laursen, B., Coy, K. C., & Collins, W. A. (1998). Reconsidering changes in parent-child conflict across adolescence: A meta-analysis. *Child Development, 69*, 817–832.

Lefcourt, H. M., Martin, R. A., & Ebers, K. (1981). Coping with stress: A model for clinical psychology. *Academic Psychology Bulletin, 3*, 355–364.

Leithwood, K., & Duke, D. (1999). A century's quest to understand school leadership. In J. Murphy & K. Louis (Eds.), *Handbook of research on educational administration* (2nd ed., pp. 45–72). San Francisco: Jossey-Bass.

Leithwood, K., & Jantzi, D. (2000). The effects of different sources of leadership on student engagement in school. In J. Murphy & K. Louis (Eds.), *Leadership for change and school reform: International perspectives* (pp. 50–66). London: Routledge/Falmer.

Leondari, A., Syngollitou, E., & Kiosseoglou, G. (1998). Academic achievement, motivation and future selves. *Educational Studies, 24*, 153–163.

Lerner, R. M. (2004). *Liberty: Thriving and civic engagement among America's youth*. Thousand Oaks, CA: Sage.

LeCroy, C. W., & Mann, J. E. (Eds.). (2008). *Handbook of prevention and intervention programs for adolescent girls*. Hoboken, NJ: Wiley.

Levine, D.U., & Lezotte, L.W. (1995). Effective schools research. In J.A. Banks & C.A. Mcgee Banks (Eds.), *Handbook of research on multicultural education* (pp. 525–547). New York: Macmillan.

Li, X., Stanton, B., Pack, R., Harris, C., Cottrell, L., & Burns, J. (2002). Risk and protective factors associated with gang involvement among urban African American adolescents. *Youth & Society, 34*, 172–194.

Little, P. M. D., Wimer, C., & Weiss, H. B. (2008). After-school programs in the 21st century: Their potential and what it takes to achieve it. *Issues and Opportunities in Out-of-School Time Evaluation, 10.* Cambridge, MA: Harvard Family Research Project, Harvard School of Education.

Lipsitz, J. (1984). *Successful schools for young adolescents.* New Brunswick, NJ: Transaction.

Loder, T., & Hirsch, B. (2003). Inner city youth development organizations: The salience of peer ties among early adolescent girls. *Applied Developmental Science, 7,* 2–12.

Louis, K., Kruse, S., & Marks, H. (1996). Schoolwide professional development. In F. Newman & Associates (Eds.), *Authentic achievement: Restructuring schools for intellectual quality* (pp. 170–203). San Francisco: Jossey-Bass.

Louis, K., Toole, J., & Hargreaves, A. (1999). Rethinking school improvement. In J. Murphy & K. Louis (Eds.), *Handbook of research on educational administration* (2nd ed., pp. 251–276). San Francisco: Jossey-Bass.

Luthar, S. S., Cicchetti, D., & Becker, B. (2000). The construct of resilience: A critical evaluation and guidelines for future work. *Child Development, 71,* 543–562.

Lutkus, A., Weiner, A, Daane, M., & Jin, J. (2003). *The nation's report card: Reading 2002, trial urban district assessment.* Washington, DC: U.S. Department of Education, National Center for Education Statistics.

Lutzke, J. R., Ayers, T. S., Sandler, I. N., & Barr, A. (1997). Risks and interventions for the parentally bereaved child. In S. A. Wolchik & I. N. Sandler (Eds.), *Handbook of children's coping: Linking theory and intervention* (pp. 215–243). New York: Plenum.

Maccoby, E., & Martin, J. (1983). Socialization in the context of the family: Parent-child interaction. In P. Mussen (Ed,), *Handbook of child psychology* (Vol. 4, 4th ed., pp. 1–101). New York: Wiley.

Mahoney, J. L., & Cairns, R. B. (1997). Do extracurricular activities protect against early school dropout? *Developmental Psychology, 33,* 241–253.

Mahoney, J. L., Larson, R. W., Eccles, J. S., & Lord, H. (2005). Organized activities as developmental contexts for children and adolescents. In J. L. Mahoney, R. W. Larson & J. W. Eccles (Eds.), *Organized activities as developmental contexts: Extracurricular activities, after-school and community programs* (pp. 3–22). Mahwah, NJ: Lawrence Erlbaum Associates.

Mahoney, J. L., Parente, M., & Zigler, E. (2009). Afterschool programs in America: Origins, growth, popularity, and politics. *Journal of Youth Development, 4,* 25–44.

Mahoney, J. L., Schweder, A. E., & Stattin, H. (2002). Structured after-school activities as a moderator of depressed mood for adolescents with detached relations to their parents. *Journal of Community Psychology, 30,* 69–86.

Mahoney, J. L. Vandell, D., Simpkins, S., & Zarrett, N. (2009). Adolescent out-of-school activities. In R. Lerner & L. Steinberg (Eds.), *Handbook of adolescent psychology: Contextual influences on adolescent development* (Vol. 2, 3rd ed., pp. 228–269). New York: Wiley.

Mandara, J. (2006). How family functioning influences African American males' academic achievement: A review and clarification of the empirical literature. *Teachers College Record, 10,* 205–222.

Marcia, J. E. (1966). Development and validation of ego-identity status. *Journal of Personality & Social Psychology, 3,* 551–558.

(1980). Identity in adolescence. In J. Adelson (Ed.), *Handbook of adolescent psychology* (pp. 159–187). New York: John Wiley & Sons.

(1987). The identity status approach to the study of ego identity development. In T. Honess & K. Yardley (Eds.), *Self and identity: Perspectives across the lifespan* (pp. 161–171). New York: Routledge.

(1994). The empirical study of ego identity. In Bosma, H. , Graafsma, T. , Grotevant, H., & de Levita, D. (Eds.), *Identity and development: An interdisciplinary approach* (pp. 67–80). Thousand Oaks, CA: Sage.

Martin, J. (1992). *Cultures in organizations.* New York: Oxford University Press.

(2002). *Organizational culture: Mapping the terrain.* Thousand Oaks, CA: Sage.

Martin, R. A. (1996). The situational humor response questionnaire (SHRQ) and coping humor scale (CHS): A decade of research findings. *Humor: International Journal of Humor Research, 9,* 251–272.

Maslow, A. (1968). *Toward a psychology of being* (2nd ed.). New York: Van Nostrand.

McLaughlin, M., Irby, M., & Langman, J. (1994). *Urban sanctuaries: Neighborhood organizations in the lives and futures of inner city youth.* San Francisco: Jossey-Bass.

McLaughlin, M., & Tablert, J. (2001). *Professional communities and the work of high school teaching.* Chicago: University of Chicago Press.

Mishkinsky, M. (1977). Humour as a "courage mechanism." *Israel Annals of Psychiatry & Related Disciplines, 15,* 352–363.

Molnar, B. E., Cerda, M., Roberts, A. L., & Buka, S. L. (2008). Effects of neighborhood resources on aggressive and delinquent behaviors among urban youths. *American Journal of Public Health, 98,* 1086–1093.

Moore, K. A. (2006). Cumulative risks among American children. *Research-to-Results Brief.* Publication #2006–13, October, 2006. Washington, DC: Child Trends.

Moore, K. A., Bronte-Tinkew, J., & Collins, A. (2010a). Practices to foster in out-of-school time programs. *Research-to-Results Brief.* Publication #2010–02. Washington, DC: Child Trends.

Moore, K. A., Bronte-Tinkew, J., & Collins, A. (2010b). Practices to avoid in out-of-school time programs. *Research-to-Results Brief.* Publication #2010–03. Washington, DC: Child Trends.

Morrow, K. V., & Styles, M. B. (1995). *Building relationships with youth in program settings: A study of Big Brothers/Big Sisters.* Philadelphia: Public/Private Ventures.

Murnane, R., & Levy, F. (1996). *Teaching the new basic skills: Principles for educating children to thrive in a changing economy.* New York: Free Press.

Musick, J. (1993). *Young, poor, and pregnant: The psychology of teenage motherhood.* New Haven, CT: Yale University Press.

Nakkula, M. J., & Harris, J. T. (2005). Assessment of mentoring relationships. In D. L. DuBois & M. J. Karcher (Eds.), *Handbook of youth mentoring* (pp. 100–117). Thousand Oaks, CA: Sage.

Nakkula, M. J., & Harris, J. T. (2010). Beyond the dichotomy of work and fun: Measuring the thorough interrelatedness of structure and quality in youth mentoring relationships. *New Directions for Youth Development, 2010*(126), 71–87.

National Center for Education Statistics. (1996). *National Educational Longitudinal Study: 1988–1994, Data files and electronic codebook system. Public use.* Washington, DC: Office of Educational Research and Improvement, U.S. Department of Education.

National Council of Teachers of Mathematics. (2000). *Principles and standards for school mathematics*. Reston, VA.

National Middle School Association (2004). *NMSA Research Summary: Interdisciplinary Teaming (May 2004)*. Retrieved from http://www.nmsa.org/ResearchSummaries/Summary21/tabid/250/Default.aspx

National Research Council and Institute of Medicine (NRC/IOM) Committee on Community-Level Programs for Youth. (2002). *Community programs to promote youth development* (J. Eccles & J. Gootman, Eds.). Washington, DC: National Academy Press.

Nelson, R., & Winer, S. (1982). *An evolutionary theory of economic change*. Cambridge, MA: Harvard University Press.

New York City, Department of Youth & Community Development (2010). *Middle school initiative within Beacon Community Centers: DYCD's response to PSA's evaluation report on year 2*. New York: Author.

Newman, F. M., & Associates (1996). *Authentic achievement: Restructuring schools for intellectual quality*. San Francisco: Jossey-Bass.

Noam, G., Biancarosa, G., & Dechausay, N. (2003). *Afterschool education: Approaches to an emerging field*. Cambridge, MA: Harvard Education Press.

Noam, G., & Miller, B. (Eds.). (2002). *Youth development and after-school time: A tale of many cities*. San Francisco: Jossey-Bass.

Nonaka, I., & Takeuchi, H. (1995). *The knowledge-creating company: How Japanese companies create the dynamics of innovation*. New York: Oxford University Press.

Nower, L., Derevensky, J. L., & Gupta, R. (2004). The relationship of impulsivity, sensation seeking, coping, and substance use in youth gamblers. *Psychology of Addictive Behaviors, 18*, 49–55.

Ogawa, R., & Bossert, S. (1995). Leadership as an organizational quality. *Educational Administration Quarterly, 31*, 224–243.

Oyserman, D. (2004). *Possible selves citations, measure, and coding instructions*. Unpublished document, Department of Psychology, School of Social Work, University of Michigan.

Oyserman, D., & Markus, H. R. (1990). Possible selves and delinquency. *Journal of Personality and Social Psychology, 59*, 112–125.

Pagano, M. E. (2001). *Non-parental social support and the well-being of low-income, minority youth*. Unpublished doctoral dissertation, Northwestern University, Evanston, IL.

Patton, M. (1990). *Qualitative evaluation and research methods*. Thousand Oaks, CA: Sage.

Pearlin, L. I., & Schooler, C. (1978). The structure of coping. *Journal of Health and Social Behavior, 19*, 2–21.

Pedersen, S., & Seidman, E. (2005). Contexts and correlates of out-of-school activity participation among low-income urban adolescents. In J. Mahoney, R. Larson, & J. Eccles (Eds.), *Organized activities as contexts of development: Extracurricular activities, after-school and community programs* (pp. 85–109). Mahwah, NJ: Lawrence Erlbaum Associates.

Pederson, J., de Kanter, A., Bobo, L. M., Weinig, K., & Noeth, K. (1999). *Safe and smart: Making the after-school hours work for kids*. Washington, DC: U.S. Department of Education.

Perie, M., Grigg, W. S., & Dion, G. S. (2005). *The nation's report card: Mathematics 2005 (NCES 2006–453)*. U.S. Department of Education, National Center for Education Statistics. Washington, DC: U.S. Government Printing Office.

Perie, M., Grigg, W., & Donahue, P. (2005). *The nation's report card: Reading 2005 (NCES 2006–451)*. U.S. Department of Education, National Center for Education Statistics. Washington, DC: U.S. Government Printing Office.

Peters, T., & Waterman, R. (1982). *In search of excellence: Lessons from America's best-run companies*. New York: Warner.

Petersen, A. (1988). Adolescent development. *Annual Review of Psychology, 39*, 583–607.

Petersen, A. C., Compas, B. E., Brooks-Gunn, J., Stemmler, M., Ey, S., & Grant, K. E. (1993). Depression in adolescence. *American Psychologist, 48*, 155–168.

Pierce, K., Bolt, D., & Vandell, D. (2010). Specific features of after-school program quality: Associations with children's functioning in middle childhood. *American Journal of Community Psychology, 45*, 381–393.

Pittman, K., Tolman, J., & Yohalem, N. (2005). Developing a comprehensive agenda for the out-of-school hours: Lessons and challenges across cities. In J. Mahoney, R. Larson, & J. Eccles (Eds.), *Organized activities as contexts of development: Extracurricular activities, after-school and community programs* (pp. 375–398). Mahwah, NJ: Lawrence Erlbaum.

Putnam, R. (2000). *Bowling alone: The collapse and revival of American community*. New York: Simon & Schuster.

Quinn, J. (2005). Building effective practices and politics for out-of-school time. In J. Mahoney, R. Larson, & J. Eccles (Eds.), *Organized activities as contexts of development: Extracurricular activities, after-school and community programs* (pp. 479–495). Mahwah, NJ: Lawrence Erlbaum.

Reisner, E. R., Vandell, D. L., Pechman, E. M., Pierce, K. M., Brown, B. B., & Bolt, D. (2007). *Charting the benefits of high-quality after-school program experiences: Evidence from new research on improving after-school opportunities for disadvantaged youth*. Washington, DC: Policy Studies Associates.

Rhodes, J. E. (2002). *Stand by me: The risks and rewards of mentoring today's youth*. Cambridge, MA: Harvard University Press.

(2004). The critical ingredient: Caring youth-staff relationships in after-school settings. In G. G. Noam (Ed.), *After-school worlds: Creating a new social space for development and learning* (pp. 145–161). San Francisco: Jossey Bass.

(2005). A model of youth mentoring. In D. L. DuBois & M. J. Karcher (Eds.), *Handbook of youth mentoring* (pp. 30–43). Thousand Oaks, CA: Sage.

Rizzo, M. (2003). Why do children join gangs? *Journal of Gang Research, 11,* 65–75.

Robertson, R. (1997). Walking the talk: Organizational modeling and commitment to youth and staff development. *Child Welfare, 76,* 577–589.

Rogoff, B. (2003). *The cultural nature of human development.* New York: Oxford University Press.

Rosenberg, M. (1957). *Occupations and values.* Glencoe, IL: The Free Press.

Roy, A. (1985). Early parental separation and adult depression. *Archives of General Psychiatry, 42,* 987–991.

Rumberger, R. W. (1987). High school dropouts: A review of issues and evidence. *Review of Educational Research, 57,* 101–121.

Russell, C., LaFleur, J., Scott, T., Low, M., Palmiter, A., & Reisner, E. (2010). *The Beacon Community Centers middle school initiative: Report on implementation and youth experience in the initiative's second year.* Washington DC: Policy Studies Associates.

Rutten, E. A., Stams, G. J. J. M., Biesta, G. J. J., Schuengel, C., Dirks, E., & Hoeksma, J. B. (2007). The contribution of organized youth sport to antisocial and prosocial behavior in adolescent athletes. *Journal of Youth and Adolescence, 36,* 255–264.

Rutter, M. (1979). Protective factors in children's responses to stress and disadvantage. In M. W. Kent & J. E. Rolf (Eds.), *Primary prevention of psychopathology: III. Promoting social competence and coping in children* (pp. 49–74). Hanover, NH: University Press of New England.

Sameroff, A. J. (2000). Dialectical processes in developmental psychopathology. In A. Sameroff, M. Lewis, & S. Miller (Eds.), *Handbook of developmental psychopathology* (2nd ed., pp. 23–40). New York: Kluwer Academic/Plenum Publishers.

Sanchez, B., & Colon, Y. (2005). Race, ethnicity, and culture in mentoring relationships. In D. L. DuBois & M. J. Karcher (Eds.), *Handbook of youth mentoring* (pp. 191–204). Thousand Oaks, CA: Sage.

Sanchez, B., Esparza, P., & Colon, Y. (2008). Natural mentoring under the microscope: An investigation of mentoring relationships and Latino adolescents' academic performance. *Journal of Community Psychology, 36,* 468–482.

Schoenfeld, A. (2002). Making mathematics work for all children: Issues of standards, testing and equity. *Educational Researcher, 31,* 13–25.

Seaton, G. (2007). Toward a theoretical understanding of hypermasculine coping among urban black adolescent males. *Journal of Human Behavior in the Social Environment, 15,* 367–390.

Seidman, E., Allen, L., Aber, J. L., Mitchell, C., & Feinman, J. (1994). The impact of school transitions in early adolescence on the self-system and social context of poor urban youth. *Child Development, 65,* 507–522.

Seligman, M. E. P., & Csikszentmihalyi, M. (2000). Positive psychology: An introduction. *American Psychologist, 55,* 5–14.

Senge, P. (1990). *The fifth discipline: The art and practice of the learning organization.* New York: Currency Doubleday.

Sheldon, J., Arbreton, A., Hopkins, L., & Grossman, J. (2010). Investing in success: Key strategies for building quality in after-school programs. *American Journal of Community Psychology, 45,* 394–404.

Sherer, M., Maddox, J. E., Mercandante, B., Prentice-Dunn, S., Jacobs, B., & Rogers, R. W. (1982). The self-efficacy scale: Construction and validation. *Psychological Reports, 51,* 663–671.

Shernoff, D. (2010). Engagement in after-school programs as a predictor of social competence and academic performance. *American Journal of Community Psychology, 45,* 325–337.

Sipe, C. (1996). *Mentoring: A synthesis of P/PV's research: 1988–1995.* Philadelphia: Public/Private Ventures.

Smetana, J. G. (1989). Adolescents and parents reasoning about actual family conflict. *Child Development, 60,* 1052–1067.

Smith, C., Peck, S., Denault, A.-S., Blazevski, J., & Akiva, T. (2010). Quality at the point of service: Profiles of practice in after-school settings. *American Journal of Community Psychology, 45,* 358–369.

Smith, J., & Cage, B. (2000). The effects of chess instruction on the mathematics achievement of southern, rural, Black secondary students. *Research in the Schools, 7,* 19–26.

Smith, K. L., & Collins, C. (1988). Attitudes toward competition in a youth organization. *The Journal of the AATEA, 29*(2), 40–48.

Snyder, H., & Sickmund, M. (1999). *Juvenile offenders and victims: 1999 National Report.* Washington, DC: Office of Juvenile Justice and Delinquency Prevention.

Spencer, R. (2006). Understanding the mentoring process between adolescents and adults. *Youth & Society, 37,* 287–315.

(2007a). "I just feel safe with him": Emotional closeness in male youth mentoring relationships. *Psychology of Men & Masculinity, 8,* 185–198.

(2007b). Naturally occurring mentoring relationships involving youth. In T. D. Allen & L. T. Eby (Eds.). *The Blackwell handbook of mentoring: A multiple perspectives approach* (pp. 99–118). Malden, MA: Blackwell Publishing.

Spergel, I. A. (1992). Youth gangs: An essay review. *Social Service Review, 66,* 121–140.

Spillane, J., Halverson, R., & Diamond, J. (2001). Investigating school leadership practice: A distributed perspective. *Educational Researcher, 30,* 23–28.

Steinberg, A., Johnson, C., & Pennington, H. (2006). *Addressing America's dropout challenge: State efforts to boost graduation rates require federal support.* Washington, DC: Center for American Progress. Retrieved from http://www.all4ed.org/publication_material/straight_as/6/23/#2

Steinberg, L. (1990). Autonomy, conflict, and harmony in the family relationship. In S. Feldman & G. Elliott (Eds.), *At the threshold: The developing adolescent* (pp. 255–76). Cambridge, MA: Harvard University Press.

Steinberg, L., & Morris, A. S. (2001). Adolescent development. *Annual Review of Psychology, 52,* 83–110.

Stoiber, K. C., & Good, B. (1998). Risk and resilience factors linked to problem behavior among urban, culturally diverse adolescents. *The School Psychology Review, 27,* 380–397.

Swigert, T., & Boyd, B. L. (2010). The impact of Boys & Girls Club/Keystone Club participation on alumni. *Journal of Leadership Education, 9,* 69–86.

Temple, J. A., & Reynolds, A. J. (1999). School mobility and achievement: Longitudinal findings from an urban cohort. *Journal of School Psychology, 37,* 355–377.

Tesser, A. (1988). Toward a self-evaluation maintenance model of social behavior. In L. Berkowitz (Ed.), *Advances in experimental social psychology* (Vol. 21, pp. 181–227). San Diego, CA: Academic Press.

The Partnership for 21st Century Skills (2009). *Framework for 21st Century Learning.* Retrieved from http://www.p21.org/index.php?option=com_content&task=view&id=254&Itemid=120

Thoits, P. A. (1990). Emotional deviance: Research agendas. In T. Kemper (Ed.), *Research agendas in the sociology of emotions* (pp. 180–203). Albany: SUNY Press.

Thornberry, T. P. (1998). Membership in youth gangs and involvement in serious and violent offending. In R. Loeber & D. P. Farrington (Eds.), *Serious & violent juvenile offenders: Risk factors and successful interventions* (pp. 147–166). Thousand Oaks, CA: Sage.

Tierney, J. P., & Grossman, J. B. (1995). *Making a difference: An impact study of Big Brothers/Big Sisters.* Philadelphia: Public/Private Ventures.

Tolan, P. H., Gorman-Smith, D., & Henry, D. B. (2003). The developmental ecology of urban males' youth violence. *Developmental Psychology, 39,* 274–291.

Tseng, V., & Seidman, E. (2007). A systems framework for understanding social settings. *American Journal of Community Psychology, 39,* 217–228.

Twenge, J. M. (2006). *Generation Me: Why today's young Americans are more confident, assertive, entitled – and more miserable than ever before.* New York: Free Press.

University of Wisconsin-Extension (2009). *Wisconsin 4-H youth development policies.* Madison, WI: Author.

Vaillant, G. (1977). *Adaptation to life.* Boston: Little, Brown.

Vandell, D., Reisner, E., Pierce, K., Brown, B., Lee, D., Bolt, D., & Pechman, E. (2006). *The study of promising after-school programs: Examination of longer term outcomes after two years of program experiences.* Unpublished manuscipt, University of Wisconsin.

Vigil, J. D. (1988). Group processes and street identity: Adolescent Chicano gang members. *Ethos, 16,* 421–445.

(2003). Urban violence and street gangs. *Annual Review of Anthropology*, *32*, 225–242.

Vilaythong, A. P., Arnau, R. C., Rosen, D. H., & Mascaro, N. (2003). Humor and hope: Can humor increase hope? *Humor: International Journal of Humor Research*, *16*, 79–89.

Villarruel, F., Perkins, D., Borden, L., & Keith J. (Eds.). (2003). *Community youth development: Programs, policies, and practices*. Thousand Oaks, CA: Sage.

Vygotsky, L. S. (1978). *Mind in society: The development of higher psychological processes*. Cambridge, MA: Harvard University Press.

Wagner, B. M. (1997). Family risk factors for child and adolescent suicidal behavior. *Psychological Bulletin*, *121*, 246–298.

Waldrop, M. M. (1992). *Complexity: The emerging science at the edge of order and chaos*. New York: Simon & Schuster.

Walker, K., & Arbreton, A. (2001). *Working together to build Beacon Centers in San Francisco: Evaluation findings from 1998–2000*. Philadelphia: Public/ Private Ventures.

Wallace, M. (2002). Modeling distributed leadership and management effectiveness: Primary school senior management teams in England and Wales. *School Effectiveness and School Improvement*, *13*, 163–186.

Warren, C., Brown, P., & Freudenberg, N. (1999). *Evaluation of the New York City Beacons: Phase 1 findings*. New York: Academy for Educational Development.

Way, N. (1998). *Everyday courage: The lives and stories of urban teenagers*. New York: New York University.

Wentzel, K. (2002). Are effective teachers like good parents? Teaching styles and student adjustment in early adolescence. *Child Development*, *73*, 287–301.

Werner, E. E. (1995). Resilience in development. *Current Directions in Psychological Science*, *4*, 81–85.

Wilson-Ahlstrom, A. (2007). *Building quality improvement systems: Lessons from three emerging efforts in the youth-serving sector*. Washington, DC: Forum for Youth Investment.

Wimer, C., Bouffard, S., Caronongan, P., Dearing, E., Simpkins, S., Little, P. M. D., & Weiss, H. (2006). *What are kids getting into these days? Demographic differences in youth out-of-school time participation*. Cambridge, MA: Harvard Family Research Project.

Wilson-Ahlstrom, A., & Yohalem, N. (2010). *Out-of-School-Time Policy Commentary #16: Shining a light on supervision: Lessons from the Beacons*. Washington, DC: Forum for Youth Investment.

Wood, M., Furlong, M. J., Rosenblatt, J. A., Robertson, L. M., Scozzari, F., & Sosna, T. (1997). Understanding the psychosocial characteristics of gang-involved youths in a system of care: Individual, family, and system correlates. *Education & Treatment of Children*, *20*, 281–295.

Yohalem, N., & Wilson-Ahlstrom, A. (2010). Inside the black box: Assessing and improving quality in youth programs. *American Journal of Community Psychology*, *45*, 350–357.

Zeldin, S. (2004). Youth as agents of adult and community development: Mapping the processes and outcomes of youth engaged in organizational governance. *Applied Developmental Science, 8,* 75–90.

Zeldin, S., Camino, L., & Mook, C. (2005). The adoption of innovation in youth organizations: Creating the conditions for youth-adult partnerships. *Journal of Community Psychology, 33,* 121–135.

Zimmerman, M. A., Bingenheimer, J. B., & Behrendt, D. E. (2005). Natural mentoring relationships. In D. L. DuBois & M. J. Karcher (Eds.), *Handbook of youth mentoring* (pp. 143–157). Thousand Oaks, CA: Sage.

Zimmerman, M. A., Copeland, L. A., Shope, J. T., & Dielman, T. E. (1997). A longitudinal study of self-esteem: Implications for adolescent development. *Journal of Youth and Adolescence, 26,* 117–141.

INDEX